# SLAVERY BY ANY OTHER NAME

Reconsiderations in Southern African History
*Richard Elphick*, Editor

# SLAVERY BY ANY OTHER NAME

## African Life under Company Rule in Colonial Mozambique

### Eric Allina

UNIVERSITY OF VIRGINIA PRESS

*Charlottesville and London*

University of Virginia Press
© 2012 by Eric Allina
All rights reserved
Printed in the United States of America on acid-free paper

*First published 2012*
*First paperback edition published 2021*
ISBN 978-0-8139-4727-3 (paperback)

1 3 5 7 9 8 6 4 2

The Library of Congress has cataloged the hardcover as follows:
Allina-Pisano, Eric.
Slavery by any other name : African life under company rule in colonial Mozambique /
Eric Allina.
p. cm. — (Reconsiderations in southern African history)
Includes bibliographical references and index.
ISBN 978-0-8139-3272-9 (cloth : alk. paper) — ISBN 978-0-8139-3275-0 (e-book)
1. Forced labor—Mozambique—History. 2. Mozambique—History—1891–1975.
3. Mozambique—Economic conditions—To 1975. 4. Portugal—Colonies—Africa—
Administration. 5. Labor policy—Mozambique—History. 6. Companhia de Moçambique—
History. I. Title. II. Series: Reconsiderations in southern African history.
HD4875.M85A45 2012
331.117309679—dc23
2011032979

Illustration Credits: *Maps 1 and 2,* Michael Southern; *illustration gallery pp. 1–9,* Arquivo Histórico de Moçambique; *illustration gallery p. 10,* Biblioteca Nacional, Portugal.

# Contents

*Illustrations follow page 104*

# Preface

Teaching English in western Kenya more than twenty years ago, I encountered for the first time a hundred-year old belief about race and work in Africa. Michael Lubale, a seventeen-year-old Kenyan, showing me the building site for his future house, explained that he would soon reach the age to move out of the dwelling he shared with his younger brothers and into his own on the family compound. I offered to lend a hand in construction, and with a mischievous smile, Michael looked at me and asked, "Can *mzungu* dig?" I soon learned that, notwithstanding the smile he flashed, his question was a sober one, for I lacked the knowledge and ability to engage competently in many tasks that might be called "unskilled" labor, including the vital matter of hauling water. I still like to think Michael's question reflected his general beliefs of *wazungu* (Kiswahili for non-Africans or, sometimes, whites in particular), rather than a specific assessment of my capabilities.

Since then, as the focus of my scholarly work shifted from the present to the past, I have come to understand how attitude as much as ability figures in the history of work in twentieth-century colonial Africa. Europeans believed, or at least claimed to believe, that physical labor in tropical climes was beyond their capacity, one justification for having Africans take on, almost in its entirety, the physical task of transforming the continent into an outpost of empire. Over the past twenty years I have continued to observe Africans' skepticism, sometimes well founded, about whites' capacity for manual labor. I hope the story told here goes a little way toward answering Michael's question.

I could not have learned this story or written this book without the extensive documentation from the Mozambique Company's long-lost archives, held in Maputo at the Arquivo Histórico de Moçambique. The company archives—generated by the private chartered company that governed the central Mozambican provinces of Manica and Sofala with near sovereign authority from 1892 to 1942—countless stacks of files with millions of pages, documenting Portugal's initial conquest, its policies, and its mundane daily operations, spent the decades after 1942 in a mysterious limbo. When the company's charter ended that year, the archives were packed into zinc-lined wooden crates and stored in a warehouse at the Indian Ocean port of Beira to await the sea voyage to Portugal. For reasons unknown, the crates remained in that port warehouse for the next thirty-five years, lost and, mostly, forgotten.[1] Mostly forgotten, but not entirely. In 1969, Alexandre Lobato, a historian of the colonial period and director of the Arquivo Histórico de Moçambique, journeyed to Beira from the colony's southern capital in search of information on the missing archives' passage to Portugal. The company's Lisbon administration claimed never to have received the wooden crates. When Lobato searched the old customs registers for the name of the ship on which the crates were to have sailed, he discovered that some company crates, contents unspecified, had remained in a Beira warehouse for a number of years before removal to another location. The site was unspecified.[2] Not until a 1974 coup in Lisbon ended Portugal's dictatorship and brought independence to Mozambique was the mystery solved. As the director of the archives, Maria Inês Nogueira da Costa, later described it, archival staff dispatched on a hunt in 1977 had "ransacked older buildings and warehouses in Beira, without uncovering any leads," then returned, in search of new clues, to the headquarter buildings of Beira's Civil Administration, which the Mozambique Company had built and transferred to the colonial state.[3] There they found several locked outbuildings locals said had been shut up for years, their contents and the whereabouts of the keys unknown. They forced open the locked doors, and there were the long-lost archives.

The director of the archives, faced with the formidable task of tabulating, logging, and organizing the contents of several thousand boxes to create an inventory, placed the material under embargo until that work could be accomplished. A foreign scholar in Mozambique at the time, hoping to conduct research on the company, was denied access and could report only on "reputedly extensive" holdings.[4] A Mozambican student who wrote an unpublished master's thesis on the company in the 1980s had only partial scattershot access to the archives.[5] Not until the mid-1990s, when my own research for *Slavery by Any Other Name* began, did the entire contents of the crates become accessible for scholarly use.

This book is the first to make use of that long-lost trove, a singular lode documenting the Mozambique Company's comprehensive, and often brutal, system of forced labor, more extensive and longer-lasting than nearly any other in colonial Africa.

Although the noncorrosive zinc lining of the crates in which the documents rested for decades before relocation to the more controlled archival environment had protected them from moisture and pests, some reports, maps, correspondence, and memos showed the ravages of time. In the 1890s and early 1900s, some company officials wrote with quill or nibbed pens on tissuelike paper; a century later, the centers of their pen strokes had fallen out of the paper. Working in sometimes dimly lit reading rooms, I deciphered these documents best by holding them up to let the light stream through to illuminate the now hollowed-out letters. Perusal was easier for later papers since, by 1910, most officials, except in outlying backwater districts, had typewriters. On some reports that had made their way up the administrative hierarchy, successive readers had scrawled comments directly on the text, hard to read but providing useful information on the response of readers on the documents' journey. In these vast holdings I uncovered records of work gangs and "wizards" (colonial officials' sometime name for indigenous healers), of river dredging and rumors of rebellion, and other extensive documentations of the regime of colonialism in central Mozambique.

There are some figures whose ongoing and important presence in the narrative told here begs for biographical treatment, but details on individuals are often hard to uncover. This is true almost as much for some Europeans as for Africans; while the backgrounds of personalities well known in other contexts, such as Gungunhana, Edward Ross, or Joaquím Carlos Paiva de Andrada, can be easily fleshed out, such information for others is more elusive. The difficulty is most acute for many Africans, who, in documentary sources, are usually identified only by a first name and perhaps by district of origin, but the same is the case for the company's minor employees. One of the company's more intriguing personalities was José Luiz Ferreira, who served as district administrator in Moribane for the better part of two decades and was a persistent critic of company labor policy, presenting trenchant and principled critiques of forced labor, a self-confessed "negrophile" and proud of it. Unfortunately, however, I know only his name, which, while not quite as common as John Smith (Andrew Jones might be closer), does not help in tracing origins, which might explain his critiques.

The biographies of some company officials, such as João Pery de Lind, are more easily explored. Educated at the prestigious *Colégio Militar*, Pery de Lind was a senior official in Portugal's customs service when the company tapped him in 1900 to develop its customs regime. Six years later he became district administrator in Manica and, amid conflict between white settlers and the company governor in 1910, assumed the governorship when the sitting governor fled the territory. His eleven-year mandate as governor was the longest of any, and the hallmark of his administration was a near unflagging support for the largely Portuguese white farming community, centered in Manica and Chimoio. The sentiment was mutual, for the farmers have been said to have demanded that the district center be named for him, as it was, going by Vila Pery de Lind from the mid-1920s until independence in 1975. As much as Pery de Lind's origins explain his role, it is more or less what one might expect, because Portugal's aristocratic elite were almost invariably fervent supporters of its empire. On the other hand, the actions of a figure such as Ferreira are less easily explained and would make for a more unusual and engaging story that unfortunately cannot be told.[6]

Nor could I have written this book—or understood the history of the company or colonial rule in Mozambique more generally—without the interviews I conducted in 1997 and 1998 with more than a hundred individuals, mostly in Manica District. Some interviews were one on one; others occurred in small groups of from two to six people and with the assistance of a translator. The importance of what these interlocutors told me became clear during my first series of interviews in May and June 1997. Having passed most of the previous four months spending forty hours or more a week in Maputo's archives, I found that the language and mind-set of company officials had suffused my thinking. Their relentless use of the term "recruitment" to describe the often violent seizure of Africans for contract labor affected how I first heard people's descriptions of company rule. I remember how, when I asked if those who were taken for contract work had any choice in the matter, the response was dismissively descriptive: "He who wants, he who doesn't want—let's go."[7] That answer, repeated by many, usually accompanied by a facial expression suggesting that my question was naive, at best, made clear to me what appeared only rarely in the company's written records: the question of consent was entirely beside the point. The company's contract labor was a modern slavery in which choice played no meaningful part.

In conducting these interviews, I gave my assurance that each individual's identity would be kept confidential; thus I do not include interviewees' names or ages or birthdates. For most individuals, in fact, I do not possess birthdates, because, though I started out asking interviewees when they were born, I found that many elderly residents did not readily remember their birthdates, and others did not know them. A small minority responded by producing their identity card (*bilhete de identidade*); several possessed only an identity card issued during the colonial period. Others would apologize, saying that they had not brought their "pass" with them. As an outsider, often taken for a *branco* (white) of Portuguese origin or nationality, I quickly became uneasy with the exchange I had unwittingly reproduced, uncomfortably reminiscent of the colonial past, when a white official would compel Africans to produce their pass to be inspected to see if they had paid their tax or fulfilled the "obligation to work." In one other mortifying instance, all too similar to my mind of colonial *machila* travel, a farmer easily twice my age picked me up and carried me across a small stream—so that I might not have to remove my shoes, roll up my pants, and wade across—after which I decided to avoid, in any way I could foresee, following in pathways established in the colonial era. In many cases, dates on identity cards are only approximate; I interviewed a number of persons several times, and tried to discern their ages by different means, referring to events such as the world wars (for example, "Hitler's war"), the 1917 Makombe uprising, and the Spanish influenza epidemic, which proved to be a reliable point of reference.

The research for this book has its roots in my 2002 Ph.D. thesis, and while this book bears little resemblance to that work, the people and institutions who supported me have grown in number as the years passed.

Financial assistance came from the Foreign Languages and Area Studies fellowship program (under Title VI of the U.S. Higher Education Act), the Yale University Program in Agrarian Studies, the Yale University Department of History, a William Clarence and Ruth Anna Gaines Dissertation Fellowship from the Yale Graduate School, the Yale University Center for International and Area Studies, and the Fulbright-Hays doctoral dissertation fellowship program. Funds from the Colgate University Division of Social Sciences supported a return visit to Maputo in 2004. The American Political Science Association gave me a marvelous place to work as a Centennial Center visiting fellow in 2005. As a research fellow in 2006 at Yale's Gilder Lehrman Center for the Study of Slavery, Abolition, and Resistance, I had ready access to the Yale University libraries, allowing me to accomplish a great deal in a brief time. The University of Ottawa provided financial support for some late stages of research and, of outstanding importance, a leave from teaching in 2008; my thanks to François Houle for making that possible. I undertook my final pre-production review of the manuscript in the comfortable setting and with the kind support of re:work, the International Research Center on Work and Lifecycle in Global History, at Humboldt University in Berlin. The Biblioteca Nacional de Portugal granted permission to reproduce illustration 19, "Portugal is not a small country."

My affiliation as a research associate at the Boston University African Studies Center gave me among the most valuable of all scholarly resources: good ideas. Students in two courses here in Ottawa, "Modern Slavery" and "Esclavage Comparée," gave me the chance to work through some of those ideas out loud and asked useful questions about how to think about slavery.

A great number of people in Maputo helped me over the years, and while I cannot list them all, I would like to express my thanks in no particular order to Marielle Rowan, Michael MacDonald, Emmanuel Kreike, Carol Martin, Catherine Jazynka, Dona Rebecca and Sr. Solomão and the Bila family, Joel das Neves Tembe, Yussuf Adam, the Chernysh family, Custódio and Fernanda Langa, Vanessa Coelho, Júlio Ribeiro, Ilídio Matusse, David Hedges, Gerhard Liesegang, Rodrigues Sainote, Gerónimo Simões, Sra. Annabella, and Solange Macamo. Jeanne Marie Penvenne provided helpful introductions at an early stage of my research. The local staff at the U.S. Information Service in Maputo were an endless source of crucial information about how to get things done, and they helped me with countless tasks that I might never have been able to tackle on my own.

Special thanks go to Teresa Cruz e Silva, then director of the African Studies Center at Eduardo Mondlane University, and Luís António Covane, at the Ministry of Culture, two institutions that gave me key logistical support.

Thanks are also due to Maria Inês Nogueira da Costa, director of the Arquivo Histórico de Moçambique (AHM) at the time I conducted much of my research, who greatly facilitated my work. I would like to express boundless gratitude to the staff of the AHM, who tolerated my initially atrocious language skills and general ignorance in the early days of my research and gradually helped me work more effectively.

I join a long list of scholars who pay homage to the exhaustive knowledge of António Sopa at the AHM. His guidance and suggestions were tremendously helpful, as were his quiet encouragement and interest.

In Manica, I received assistance from a number of people, including Henrique Querol, Abdurramane Machon, Samuel Ganhão, José Gumbo, and Sr. Corrence. Special thanks go to Guilherme Chazuca, who shared his warm hospitality and knowledge of his father's chiefdom. Nicholas Chazuca provided some timely help with translations. Domingos Artur do Rosário, then head of the Arquivo Património Cultural office in Chimoio, offered generous support on a number of occasions.

I owe an enormous debt to Sr. Davide Franque of the Manica District office for Education, Culture, and Youth. Sr. Davide was of immense help in contacting potential interviewees and organizing interviews. His contacts in Manica proved invaluable in collecting oral testimony, and he was exceptionally generous with his time.

As a graduate student at Yale I received tremendous support from Bob Harms, who guided my research with a steady hand. Jim Scott taught me the value of reading omnivorously, and Geoffrey Parker drilled me in important research skills, while Paul Landau shared his careful, nuanced reading of southern African history. Sandra Sanneh and Ann Biersteker helped me learn Shona. From the Agrarian Studies Program I learned how to engage across disciplines and world regions. While I was an undergraduate at Harvard, Leroy Vail was a great influence on my early and continuing interest in African history, and I have deep regret that he did not live long enough to read and improve this work.

Elsewhere, I was supported by many friends and colleagues, including some who, happily enough, fall into both categories. They include Eric Morier-Genoud, M. Anne Pitcher, Martin Murray, Sue Cook, Charles Mironko, Bruce McKim, Didier Péclard, Sarah and Laina Bay-Cheng, Jarrett Barrios, Douglas Hattaway, Robert Bowers, Susan O'Donovan, Heidi Gengenbach, Jessica Schafer, Jolie Olcott, Andrew Jones, Fred Cooper, Jane Burbank, and Thomas McDow. Special thanks go to Benedict Carton, whose interest in my work was essential to its progress.

Jessica Allina-Pisano was a constant sounding board during much of the time I worked on this book, and she contributed to my thinking in important ways.

Dick Holway, at the University of Virginia Press, and Richard Elphick, editor of the Reconsiderations in Southern African History series, gave their consistent support and helped bring the book through a prolonged journey toward publication. Raennah Mitchell, also at the Press, made sure I kept to schedule and answered many of my questions. Robert Burchfield did a marvelous job copyediting the manuscript, using his fine eye for detail to ensure an even style, making certain that I closed any remaining gaps that might otherwise plague a reader. Mark Mones carefully saw the manuscript through to bound books. Michael Southern drew the maps.

With my editor, the late Jeannette Hopkins, I was able to write a book I could never have imagined at the outset. I am glad to have benefited from her fierce resolution and indeed refusal to let the book be anything short of the best it could be.

My family provided more indirect but no less vital support. Amy Allina invested unshakeable confidence in me, important from anyone but all the more so from a wise big sister. To my parents, I owe a good part of my love for ideas and care for learning, as well as gratitude for their unfailing interest in and encouragement for my work, even when it took me far away for long periods of time.

Allison Hewlitt has given me more than I imagined possible, showing a bedrock faith that exceeds any other. Most recently, she and our daughter, Zoe Hanna Hewlitt Allina, have offered irresistible motivation to spend time away from this endeavor. If I stay lucky, it will always be so.

All translations here are my own, unless otherwise indicated.

# SLAVERY BY ANY OTHER NAME

# Introduction

SLAVERY HAS DEEP HISTORICAL ROOTS IN AFRICAN societies. Long before the seventeenth century, when Europeans began to buy vast numbers of slaves for their New World colonies, many Africans had been held as slaves, and countless others were sent in servitude across the Red Sea and the Indian Ocean.[1] Enslavement of Africans by Africans was diverse, unlike the more uniform chattel bondage of the Caribbean and the Americas; some African-owned slaves were held as chattel, but many, possibly most, had meaningful, if limited, rights as members of their masters' communities.[2] Slaveholding by European settlers in Africa began in the mid-seventeenth century in the hinterland of the Cape of Good Hope, where the Dutch East India Company established a settlement at the continent's southernmost point, and in the Zambezi Valley, where Portugal founded large landed estates.[3] Still, such slaveholding was relatively small scale compared to the later export of millions of Africans into the Atlantic world, a forced migration that, for centuries, made blackness virtually synonymous with bondage. By the nineteenth century, when Europeans ended their slave trading and freed their slaves, large-scale chattel slaveholdings had existed in New World outposts of colonial empire for hundreds of years. But the equation of slavery with chattel status did not end with abolition; it would continue to dominate twentieth-century colonial administrations across nearly all of Sub-Saharan Africa.[4]

For Portugal itself, slavery was part of a pioneering past in Africa that began in 1415 with the sacking and occupation of the North African city of Ceuta, known at the time as the "flower of all other cities of Africa."[5] First among the European empires to expand to Africa, Portugal led the way in slave trading from the mid-fifteenth century until midway through the seventeenth, when its empire's influence began to wane worldwide. For another two centuries, it continued to occupy a series of entrepôts along the west, west-central, and east African coasts, and by the later nineteenth century's "Scramble" for Africa, memories of past dominance led Portugal to assume an outsized role compared to its lesser status in the broad imperial pantheon. In that era of "high imperialism," without the political, financial, and human capital to compete with powers like Britain, France, and Germany, Portugal decided to outsource parts of its African empire, especially in the southeast region known as Mozambique, long reputed to have been a land of biblical wealth.[6] Europe's other imperial powers had depended on chartered companies three centuries earlier in their seaborne scrum in south and southeast Asia, and now, as they vied for African territory, nearly all once again established private companies to reinforce their presence in Africa.

In the crucial early phase of outsourcing empire in Africa, European colonizers chartered private companies to undertake the strategically vital but costly and bloody tasks of conquest and of colonial occupation. Cecil Rhodes's British South Africa Company governed the territory later known as Southern Rhodesia until 1923. British entrepreneurs also created companies in Kenya (the Imperial British East Africa Company) and in Nigeria (the Royal Niger Company). Germans did so in Tanganyika (the German East Africa Company). The French government rented out more than 270,000 square miles of France's claim in central Africa to concessionary companies, and the Belgian king, Leopold II, on his own, since his government had no interest in an African empire, pursued a vast private fiefdom in the present-day Democratic Republic of the Congo, leasing parts to private companies in return for a share of the profits. In the face of international protest over abuses, the Belgian state was persuaded in 1908 to take over the territory from Leopold. Most outsourcing companies held statelike powers for a decade or so and then were replaced by formal colonial administrations around the turn of the twentieth century. Only the companies Portugal established in Mozambique outlived Rhodes's own.

Under a fifty-year charter granted by the Portuguese Crown in 1892, the Mozambique Company ruled much of central Mozambique (the state ruling the rest), and it ruled longer and with more autonomy from the state than any other chartered company in Africa. The company's founder, Joaquím Carlos Paiva de Andrada, a staunch supporter of Portuguese imperial ambitions, had launched several expeditions in Mozambique's Zambezi Valley and neighboring regions in the 1870s, a decade before many other adventurous European explorers ventured

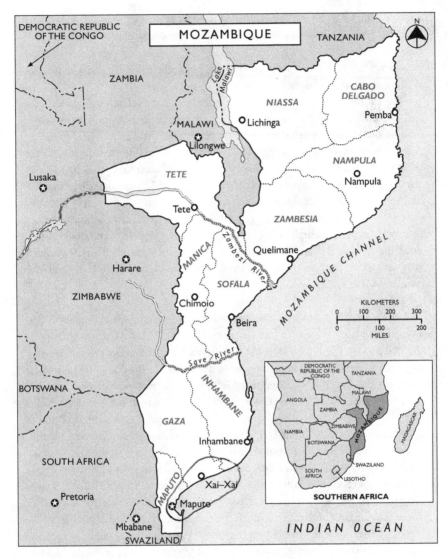

Map 1. Mozambique in southern Africa

into the "Dark Continent." His efforts to harness private capital to state authority achieved little until, in 1888, he established the Mozambique Company and
received a royal charter, its final terms fixed four years later. In return, the Portuguese Crown was to receive 7.5 percent of all net declared profits and a 10 percent
holding of company shares.[7]

The Mozambique Company, fusing state and commercial enterprise, built
and operated the colonial apparatus with an economic monopoly in its more
than 60,000-square-mile concession. Its rule rested on a foundation of forced
African labor that differed from, and in some respects surpassed, past forms of
bondage. When the company's charter expired half a century later, in 1942, its
territory, comprising the provinces of Manica and Sofala, passed to direct control
of the Portuguese colonial state, which had continued to rule the rest of Mozambique. The colonial state bureaucracy absorbed the company's administration,
with most company employees continuing in their posts in a colonial government that was to last another thirty-two years, until a revolt in 1974 by junior
army officers in Lisbon overthrew the Portuguese dictatorship. Independence
came to Mozambique a year later.[8]

*Slavery by Any Other Name* is the story of how the Portuguese empire ushered in
a vast forced labor system, of its ideological posture toward Africans, of its policies and practices and their impact on Africans' lives, and of how Africans with-
stood oppression, employing strategies to outmaneuver the company's schemes.
Many African forced laborers perished in the process, but some prospered.

The freeing of chattel slaves worldwide had begun with the Haitian Revolution of 1791, and the era of abolition continued, propelled especially by Britain's
prohibition of the slave trade in 1807 and by British abolition of slavery in 1838.
The era ended with Brazil's outlawing of slavery in 1888.[9] But in the last weeks of
the century, Portugal passed a new colonial labor law that led to a system of subcontracted slave labor within its now shrunken empire of Angola, Guinea-Bissau,
Mozambique, and São Tomé e Principe (two islands off the West African coast).[10]
The Mozambique Company's royal charter to administer part of central Mozambique had been awarded in 1892, and Lisbon's 1899 labor law applied to "natives"
only, not settlers—therefore, to blacks and not to whites. By its mandate, "All natives of Portuguese overseas provinces are subject to the moral and legal obligation to seek to acquire through work the means they lack for subsistence and to
improve their own social condition." The law exempted, or purported to exempt,
certain classes of people: chiefs, women, men over sixty, boys under fourteen, the
sick and invalid, and those serving in police forces. Thus, youth fifteen and older
and men up to sixty who were judged "fit" were compelled to work: "They have

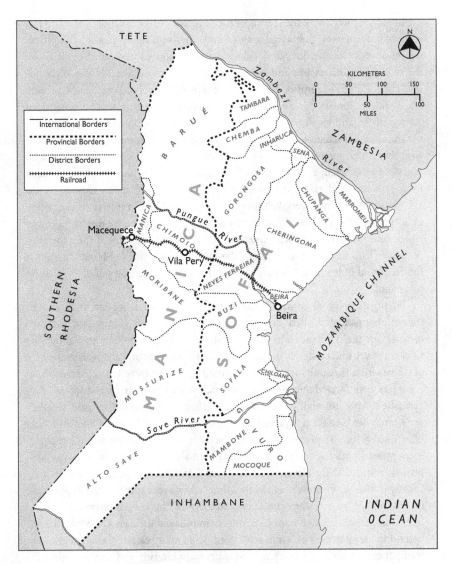

Map 2. The Mozambique Company territory in central Mozambique

the full liberty to choose the means of meeting this obligation, but, if they do not comply in some way, public authorities may impose it upon them."[11] The phrasing "choose the means" implied a choice, and for some there was; but for most, the reality was otherwise, and hence the law introduced a new form of bondage. The statutory exemptions of certain groups were honored only in the breach: when white colonists' demands for workers exceeded the number of those judged "fit for labor" and legally liable for seizure, colonial officials took not only them but those by law exempted: elderly men, young boys, women, and even chiefs as well. Even Africans with wealth or those who found work on their own, or who practiced an officially recognized profession (such as tailoring), or who cultivated fields of a specified extent (the precise size determined by local officials), could also be swept up in helter-skelter operations that one administrator described as "a type of 'steeple chase.'"[12] At such times, the colonial police might "take any which one."[13] Elderly men who spoke with me in 1997 and 1998 of their own experiences with forced labor recalled "the time of *pata pata*" (a Shona ideophone for the sound of feet striking hard surfaces) to express the noise of an onrushing press gang.[14]

Portugal's colonial administrators enforced the new labor law by a system they euphemistically called "contract labor." The "contract" committed Africans to work for the colonial state administration or for private employers, but the workers never saw, or signed, a copy of an actual written contract. Nor, in the face of threats from the state's armed police, could they have given true consent. Sham contracts were carried out with sham wages, workers paid rarely, and wages often garnished. And although the contracts specified a fixed period of time, workers were often held longer if replacements were late or hard to find. Official reports often used, without self-consciousness, the term *"rendição"* to refer to the replacement group; it may be translated as "relief" but also, more accurately in this context, as "ransom."[15] The slaveholders of South Carolina's rice plantations or Jamaica's sugar plantations never denied that they held slaves captive through purchase or inheritance, in a system endorsed and enforced by law. In colonial Mozambique, on the other hand, administrators camouflaged their coercion of Africans behind the legal fiction of "contracts." And while many earlier slave owners were frank about considering black people inherently inferior and hence justly subjugated, the Portuguese administrators who oversaw subcontracted slave labor claimed that compelling Africans to work, "by force if necessary," would improve the Africans' "moral and material well-being." They justified their modern labor slavery as Europe's moral duty to civilize the "Dark Continent" and "transform beasts into men."[16] Thus, António Enes, who led the commission that prepared Portugal's colonial labor code, wrote in 1893: "Work is the most moralizing of missions, the most instructive of schools . . . the education that will manage to transform beasts into men. . . . I don't know if Africa will some day have a Messiah; if it might, the good news of its Gospel will be a commandment to work, and its radiant heavens will be opened only for the happy workers!"[17] The success of the abolition movement, Enes argued, had granted Africans the "liberty not to work" and thus the freedom to remain in a "savage state."[18] Colonizers bore a responsibility to correct this excess; compulsory labor would civilize the savage.

Imposing such burdens on Africans as part of the colonizing project alarmed some observers, especially missionaries and others who saw through the faux contracts. Critics, perhaps inspired by the victories of the early 1900s campaign by English and American activists against the rubber atrocities in Belgian king Leopold's Congo Free State, pressed colonial powers to bring their governing practices in line with the rhetoric of the civilizing mission.[19] Some singled out the contract labor system in São Tomé, where African slaves (mostly from Portugal's west-central African colony, Angola) toiled to produce cocoa for the British chocolate manufacturer Cadbury.[20] One, Henry Nevinson, published an article in *Harper's* in 1906 lambasting what he called Portugal's "modern slavery," which he claimed was no different from "the old-fashioned slavery of our grandfather's time."[21] Others, through the second decade of the twentieth century, targeted Portugal's reliance on servile labor in Angola and Mozambique, where forced labor was the backbone of the colonial economy to a far greater extent than in other regions in Africa.

In 1924, the League of Nations formed the Temporary Slavery Commission to investigate "the question of slavery" worldwide, and in 1926 the league passed the Convention on Slavery, its aim to eliminate "slavery in all its forms," but, in fact, reflecting the era's orthodox definition of slavery, defined it as "the status or condition of a person over whom any or all of the powers attaching to the right of ownership are attached."[22] The convention did note that forced labor could develop into "conditions analogous to slavery," but left to local authorities the power to decide how and whether to change forced labor practices. Even the league's 1930 Convention on Forced Labor left a number of loopholes and lacked enforcement mechanisms.[23]

None of the other colonizing powers relied on forced labor to the great extent Portugal did, nor had any granted private companies the nearly complete autonomy the Mozambique Company enjoyed, though they, too, were unwilling to yield forced labor. France objected to proposed League of Nations' limitations, such as limits to length of enforced service and a ban on the use of military conscripts for nonmilitary labor, and continued to recruit forced labor widely throughout its African colonies. Forced labor similarly underpinned Britain's

African empire from the Cape to Cairo, and forms of unfree labor some considered "analogous to slavery" existed elsewhere in British-ruled territories in Asia.[24]

The open criticisms of colonial labor practices and ensuing debate in closed League of Nations commission hearings reflected an uneven transition from an older imperial politics to an incipient international order guided partly by new humanitarian principles. Part of what made it uneven was the inchoate discussion of those principles, evident in disagreement over what forms of labor were consistent with postabolition ethics. The fiercest opponents of coerced colonial labor, some nearly direct descendants of abolitionists, seized on the political language they knew best and condemned colonial practices as "a modern slavery," but, blinded by their faith in the civilizing mission and too attached to the idea of their "grandfathers'" slavery, they were unable to develop a critique of new forms of coercion. Neither the missionary critics who asked, "Africa: Slave or Free?" nor League of Nations investigators questioned the premise of colonial rule itself, and so the resulting debate sought only to draw distinctions among policies considered acceptable and not acceptable in a European-dominated Africa.[25] But even consensus colonial policies were ambiguous in their impact. No one was more aware of such ambiguity than those charged with putting policy in to practice; but the resulting ambivalence and occasional dissent voiced by the Mozambique Company's local officials were typically lost on the higher-ups.

At the most senior levels of Portugal's colonial administration, government officials resisted criticism, whether from within or without, of its colonial rule, and, with the rise of António Salazar in 1928 (a supporter of Franco's dictatorial rule in Spain and an admirer of the era's fascist movements of Italy and Germany), the hostility to outside interference grew. Nor did the Salazar dictatorship tolerate internal dissent; officials in the colonies went to great lengths to impede the efforts of inquisitive visitors who sought to investigate its policies there.[26] In the Depression years, international concern over abuses in the colonies diminished. In the aftermath, fascism in Europe championed the subordination of citizen to nation and individual to society, viewing the labor of colonized and otherwise subjugated peoples, in Africa and in Europe, as a contribution to the collective good, an injunction most cynically and chillingly expressed in the concentration camp injunction *"Arbeit macht frei."* Ironically, with World War II came a remarkable expansion of forced labor in Africa as the Allies mobilized resources to clothe, feed, and equip the world's fighting forces.[27] The end of the Mozambique Company's charter in 1942 did not end its practice of forced labor.

With the war's end, Britain and France banned legalized forced labor in their African colonies. Britain, if reluctantly, granted independence to India under the sustained civil disobedience of Gandhi's nationalist movement. The "wind of change" began to blow through Africa, but Portugal only stepped up white settlement and investment in its African colonies; with its control of the Azores, a refueling point for transatlantic flights vital to Cold War strategists, it escaped the international impetus for change.[28] Salazar's rigid mercantilism demanded that Portugal's colonies support the home country with raw materials for industrial production. Protestant missionaries, who had earlier kept track of labor abuses, had been weakened by Portugal's 1940 agreement with the Vatican to grant the Catholic church special status in its colonies in return for a measure of control over mission personnel posted to Portuguese Africa. It became more difficult for troublesome Protestant groups to operate there.[29]

In 1961, Ghana, newly independent and led by pan-Africanist Kwame Nkrumah, filed a complaint with the International Labor Organization about Portugal's colonial labor practices, claiming a violation of the Forced Labor Convention of 1957, to which Portugal was a signatory. Although the resulting investigation did not reach such a finding, the international attention led Lisbon to abolish its system of legalized forced labor in 1961, a century and more after its abolition of chattel slavery. Empire was ending in Africa, and most colonies were emerging as independent sovereign states.[30] Yet Portugal's African colonies were not yet free; like South Africa, which was effectively independent from Britain since 1934 under the Statute of Westminster, and like Southern Rhodesia, whose white minority regime unilaterally declared its independence from Britain in 1965, they were no longer outposts of empire but independent islands of white domination.[31] Independence for Portugal's colonies did not come until 1975, after a dozen years of guerrilla warfare against white rule by African nationalist groups, most with Chinese or Soviet backing, and after the 1974 coup against the dictatorship in Lisbon by Portugal's junior army officers—most of modest social origins, without the nostalgic attachment to empire of the aristocratic top brass, and weary of colonial wars. Five and a half centuries after Prince Henry the Navigator led Portugal's first African conquest in 1415, of Ceuta in North Africa, the Portuguese empire had come to an end.[32]

In the precolonial era, in most parts of Africa lasting until the last quarter of the nineteenth century, African slaves were rarely treated as chattel, but as socially marginal individuals with fewer rights than others. Various studies have explored the processes through which diverse categories of people lost rights and tumbled into subordinate status; a number explain how internal political and social hierarchy shaped Africans' participation in international trade networks, most especially in the Atlantic slave trade, and some of these studies acknowledged, ambivalently, that certain of the related practices constituted slavery.[33]

Frederick Cooper has noted that many who wrote of African slavery, especially during the 1970s, partially disavowed the word by putting it within quotation marks ("slavery") or employed euphemisms such as "adopted dependent," "captive," or "serf," "for fear of conjuring up the entire bundle of traits commonly associated" with slavery itself.[34] Since such past practices of compulsory labor had something in common with certain continuing forms of social and political inequality in contemporary African societies of the postcolonial era, scholars sympathetic to African governments in power, or aware of the sensitivity of the subject, were reluctant to illuminate the similarity.[35]

The era of colonial rule, a decade longer for Portugal's colonies than for others, brought new forms of servitude. It restricted Africans' rights, enacted new laws authorizing lengthy enforced labor, and imposed new systems of labor exploitation, with little public recognition from contemporary observers or scholars that in some cases these practices had more than a passing resemblance to the exploitation of the now disavowed chattel slavery. The imperial powers' claim to have eliminated legalized slavery in Africa was, partly, justification for their empires' expansion to the continent; they acknowledged slavery's continued existence only in areas beyond their own control, as in independent Ethiopia or the remote reaches of the Sahara or in practices largely excluded from colonialism's formal institutions, as within private spheres governed by religion (especially Islam) or gender (especially marriage). Colonial rulers, too, were reluctant to acknowledge such ongoing slavery in the African societies under their rule since doing so would have exposed their acceptance of it. Reluctant to involve themselves in spheres of life they considered to be governed by tradition or custom, colonial governments preferred to allow indigenous types of slavery, seen as embedded in private cultural life and considered more benign than chattel bondage, to die a "slow death" rather than be burdened with responsibility for and consequence of their abolition.[36] When colonial rule introduced new mechanisms to acquire African labor power cheaply or for nothing, colonizers' enslavement of Africans went by the label administrators gave it, most often, "contract labor," even though none other than Frederick Lugard, a leading figure in the British colonial establishment, suggested Africans themselves would call such unpaid forced labor "a white man's slavery."[37] Scholars who studied this history nourished the idea that "real" slavery, or "slavery proper," as Lugard put it, meant only chattel bondage, total ownership of the body and the laborer.[38]

Even critics who attacked colonial labor policy in Mozambique and elsewhere in Africa failed to expose the creation, and maintenance, of a new form of enslaved labor. Early and midcentury missionary activists largely shared colonizers' rationale for enforced work: that it was justified by African inferiority and on the grounds that many would not work in the absence of constraint. Nor were such attitudes exclusive to Europeans: Blaise Diagne, a Senegalese representative to the French National Assembly, claimed, in 1930, that Africans "are by nature indolent and so incapable that we really require force and compulsion; that even under stress and famine we are not capable of finding food in the forest unless someone compels us to do it."[39] The "question of slavery," as the League of Nations called its investigations into the matter in 1924, arose at a time, and in a political arena, in which slavery was still legally defined as chattel slavery, that is, as the exercise of the right of property by one person over another, reflecting the overpowering legacy of centuries of Atlantic world slavery. Scholars did not view colonial innovations in servitude as a form of slavery because such servitude did not resemble the "ideal type" so commonly associated with slaveholding in the U.S. South. Yet even in the antebellum southern United States, the iconic opposition of master and servant that prevailed in the decades leading up to the Civil War represented but a particular moment; the nature, conditions, and impact of slavery had varied over circumstance and time and place. Ira Berlin captures this idea in the title of his magisterial *Generations of Captivity,* a study of how the institution of slavery evolved over time in North America, changing with successive generations of human beings, slave and free, who struggled to maintain, modify, or end it.[40]

Colonial forced labor avoided designation as a form of slavery in part also because of the disjuncture between law and practice. Laws such as Portugal's that authorized forced labor carefully specified who might be seized, for what type of work, and for how long—all such limitations designed to justify the practice—although administrators across colonial Africa routinely ignored or departed from those limits in implementing such laws. These "men on the spot," as local-level administrators in Africa have sometimes been called, had great latitude in transforming law and policy into daily practice, and the resulting improvisations on the legal order led to many practices that were, in a formal sense, illegal.[41] As one British official in Kenya described it, success in supplying laborers to white settlers "depended on how far [a chief] could be induced to exceed his instructions."[42]

Those responsible for creating and managing colonial labor regimes were often loathe to acknowledge what they had done. Thus, when death rates for forced laborers on public works scandalized even British administrators, the chief secretary for Kenya's governor noted, in 1912, "His Excellency cannot agree to the proposal to pay a bonus to the families of those who have died as such payment would argue the admission by the Government of negligence."[43] And because this bondage fell outside the law, with much of its violent, indiscriminate, abusive, and exploitative nature neither legally authorized nor acknowledged, it was far less vulnerable to abolition or formal regulatory limit; it is difficult to push for elimination of practices whose existence is not recognized. Under colonial rule in Mozambique and in much of the rest of Africa, Africans were subject to the law but rarely protected by it, leaving them intensely vulnerable. Evidence of colonial enslavement remained shielded by repressive governance and by administrators' aversion to outside investigation and reluctance to reveal abuse. The evidentiary trail rarely entered the record, and, as Frederick Cooper has noted, the "historian can obtain little more than glimpses into the sordid world of labor recruitment."[44]

The Mozambique Company's own records, for so many years hidden and sealed in wooden crates in an outbuilding at a seaside port, awaiting a voyage to Lisbon that never came, reflect the bureaucratic organization of the modern colonial state and lay bare the intricate behavior of a colonial compulsory labor regime. *Slavery by Any Other Name* examines this new evidence on how colonial rule transformed and sustained servile labor in Africa. A common refrain among Mozambicans I interviewed in research for this book was, "We were sold" (*"fomos vendidos"*). Historians of colonial Africa have often noted that Africans themselves spoke of colonialism as slavery, and, indeed, Carolyn Brown's 2003 study of Nigerian coal miners, *"We Were All Slaves,"* takes their words for its title.[45] Evidence I discovered in long-lost records of Portugal's rule in central Mozambique confirms Africans' claims that colonial forced labor was, in fact, virtual slavery. Their experience of inequality and exploitation transcends the history of Mozambique and of Africa and resonates with the wider history of slavery.

The argument of *Slavery by Any Other Name* differs from previous studies of Portuguese Africa in certain important ways. Unlike Nevinson, Anderson, and others, I argue that the African experience of forced labor in Mozambique was not fundamentally different from that which had prevailed elsewhere in colonial Africa, despite a forced labor system in central Mozambique that lasted much longer than others and despite having been privatized under Mozambique Company rule, under the euphemism of legal "contracts." Portugal's practice of forced labor had its analogs in Belgian, British, and French colonies (and German as well up through World War I, after which Germany's African colonies were divided among Belgium, France, and Britain), and such practices continued until after World War II. Portugal did distinguish itself by its system's longevity, lasting until 1961.[46]

France, throughout its vast West African territory, conducted widespread conscription, ostensibly for military service, reserving the so-called second portion (that is, 50 percent) of those rounded up for forced labor for public works and, at times, for private endeavors as well, a practice not abolished until 1946.[47]

In France's equatorial African territory, an area larger than France itself was turned over to private concessionaires; with thin administrative staffing and scant public oversight, the concession holders operated freely into the 1930s, impressing Africans into service far beyond what French law allowed.[48] Britain, notwithstanding its crusade against slavery "in all its forms," depended heavily on forced labor in its African colonies, often for public works, and coerced Africans into service for private interests in Ghana, Malawi, Zambia, Zimbabwe, and South Africa, and for overlooked and illegal private actions, which lasted through World War II, when hundreds of thousands of Africans served as forced laborers in the British war effort.[49] What distinguished forced labor in Portugal's colonies was its longevity and its dominance of the colonial economy.

Portugal has long been considered to have imposed a more brutal form of colonialism in Africa, especially as compared with British or French versions, its brutality explained, both by humanitarian critics and by contemporary scholars, as a function of weakness: Portugal, the poorest of the colonial powers, was considered to lack the resources to "develop" its colonies or the political sophistication to promote an ideology that might induce Africans' cooperation.[50] But this focus on weakness betrays a scholars' preoccupation with European history; in colonial Africa itself, it makes little sense to speak of the weakness (or strength) of the imperial powers based on their metropolitan standing. The capacities of European colonizers in Africa depended far more on the local resources and on the nature of the colonial administrations. If Portugal's modernity was short of Britain's, the distance narrowed as one traveled from London to Lourenço Marques or from Lisbon to Lagos. Africans who lived under colonial rule, whether in Mozambique, Malawi, or Mali, were unlikely to view the brutality of their colonial masters as an expression of weakness.

In central Mozambique, the Mozambique Company elevated such excesses to a form of governance. Shielded from the public oversight that sometimes limited violent and exploitative practices in other colonial territories, the company developed a system of forced labor more efficient and extensive than any in Africa. Company officials wrote openly of their reliance on coercion, and the evidence contained in their long-lost letters, reports, and memos reveals the full impact on Africans' lives. The story told here is of greatest significance and interest not only for the unvarnished view this evidence provides into the company's world of forced labor recruitment but also for what it suggests for other areas of colonial Africa.

Though annual labor levies in Mozambique superficially resembled a medieval serf's obligation, forced labor regimes created by colonial rule were modern, both in the justifications offered for their existence and in the mechanisms that organized and supported them. The colonial state's bureaucratic administration, with its capacity for rapid communication, decentralized decision making, and easily dispersed resources—revealed here in the Mozambique Company's long-lost records—put the untrammeled power of the modern state behind the imperial project. Such a system approximated an industrial process, even when the work itself was nearly premodern: like mass-produced parts of factory floor machinery, African workers were replaceable. Labor departments easily resupplied new workers, and, in a system driven by ambition and greed, death seldom slowed the work down. In the popular image of slavery, above all in the history of the United States, masters at times treated slaves with great brutality but regarded them as valuable property. Those who exploited modern slaves in colonial Africa had no such investment and paid virtually nothing for their labor. To have been the object of ownership claims might have protected African workers, but, bound by contract to servitude, law left them vulnerable. The Mozambique Company governor noted in 1910: "As a general rule the farmers in Manica and Chimoio treat the blacks supplied by the Company much worse than any ass or ox they possess, for the simple reason that if the black falls ill and even ends up dying, their only task is to send him to the hospital or home, whereas with the death of an ox or an ass they are out the money it cost them."[51] An Angolan remarked, in 1924, that "the slaves were better fed then we forced laborers are for we are not property."[52] As those condemned to penal labor a world away on Mississippi's Parchman Farm could testify, forced labor could be "worse than slavery."[53] In parts of colonial Africa, employers who used forced labor were only loosely constrained by the legal provisions that put African workers at their disposal; unbound by law, they gave little thought to workers' well-being or survival.

*Slavery by Any Other Name* understands unfree labor, both chattel and forced labor, as a denial and loss of personal sovereignty, with loss of control over the physical self. But no one—not even the most absolute of monarchs or the most powerful of slaveholders—can be wholly sovereign; all individuals possess layers of sovereignty. The more layers, the more sovereignty a person possesses and the more control one can exercise over the self. Enslavement strips layers away, exposing an individual to violation. The violations of subcontracted slave labor under colonial rule in Mozambique involved the use of violence or the threat thereof; the appropriation of labor; and a lack of remuneration beyond the basic needs of physical survival.[54]

The attention to personal sovereignty shares Orlando Patterson's interpretation of slaves as individuals who are socially dead—people who, by their highly circumscribed social status, can neither make claims on others nor defend themselves against demands made upon them. Patterson emphasizes the importance of violence—proximate or otherwise—in severing ordinary social ties and rendering people vulnerable to enslavement, and points to the accompanying debasement that brings dishonor and further social isolation and vulnerability.[55] Yet social death characterizes few individuals' circumstances; slaves retain the impulse and capacity to forge or alter some measure of social connections.[56] Patterson's model implicitly acknowledges this, in his explanation of how, over time, slaves may reestablish social relationships, reacquiring the obligations and rights that may ameliorate, to some degree, slave status, and achieve social resurrection.

Forced labor did not shear the web of social relations that sustains individual identity and personal sovereignty as thoroughly and completely as did chattel slavery. Still, it became difficult or impossible for Africans subject to forced labor to exercise rights or call on those relations for support. While at work, they were isolated and faced peril that, for some, knew no bounds. Once returned home, where they regained their place in their natal community, forced laborers could mobilize some support; the result, at times, was trouble for local administrators, who could not avoid facing the practical limitations to otherwise nearly limitless coercion. For some administrators, dealing with the consequences thereof triggered doubts about their role in the system, and they made plain their resentment at shouldering the bulk of the dirty work of what senior officials blandly defended as "recruitment."

*Slavery by Any Other Name* documents, so far as is possible, the history of people who, for the most part, left no written record of their experiences, but whose enslavers' records reveal more than the authors recognized, describing, through official records and correspondence, how people who toiled in bondage in central Mozambique responded to subordination and why they acted as they did, with a repertoire of tactics in strategic pursuit of goals of their own choosing. Thus, African forced laborers employed diverse strategies to counter the demands of the colonial administration: personal mobility and flight; entry into wage labor markets; adaptation to markets for agricultural goods; and selective cultural assimilation. Flight could offer immediate relief, although the modern bureaucratic colonial state made independent maroon communities, such as existed in the Atlantic world, nearly impossible.[57] Some laborers pursued strategies of more durable relief, farming a surplus they sold at market, like their New World counterparts earning independent income, some even gaining an exemption from compulsory labor.[58] And, like American slaves with artisanal skills who were hired out and who saved some of their earnings, so some Africans in Mozambique found skilled work that freed them from forced labor and made possible a modest prosperity.[59] Individuals resorted to different strategies according to location, with those in border regions more easily able to flee, and according to social position, with higher-status individuals better able to escape conscription.

Although histories of slavery show rare instances of open rebellion, and although the vast majority of slaves did not attempt to run away, narratives of New World slavery reveal countless slaves engaged in hidden resistance, through sabotage or subterfuge at work; in satirical songs, jokes, or nicknaming; and, in the life of the mind, entering a sometimes forbidden world of religious belief for spiritual, or even material, relief.[60] The rigidity of the now orthodox domination-resistance dyad does not do justice to the complex and multiple struggles of Africans in Mozambique and elsewhere.[61] Africans in Mozambique moved beyond thralldom or open resistance to a realm in-between, where many were able to modify, or partially eclipse, their subservient status, compelling colonial rulers, in turn, to respond. By creating or reestablishing connections, social and economic, with others, Africans recovered degrees of sovereignty, although such actions frequently involved a measure of exploitation and encroachment on the freedom of others: fathers of sons, men of women, chiefs of followers.[62] In making their own world bigger, even as it became smaller for others, they gained in sovereignty.[63]

*Slavery by Any Other Name* explores this fluid dynamic of response and counterresponse to illuminate the reach and the limits of colonial power in Mozambique and to underscore how Africans' engagement with that power affected relations within African societies as much it did without. Africans' undertakings belied their formal submission and resulted in outcomes colonial masters had not imagined.

# Ending Slavery and
# Creating Empire in Africa

### From the "Indelible Stain" to the
### "Light of Civilization"

PORTUGAL'S PRESENCE IN SOUTHEAST AFRICA BE-gan with Vasco da Gama's arrival on the east African coast in 1498, but conquest did not come until four centuries later, in the age of "high impe-rialism." East Africa had not been da Gama's destination; from the earliest voy-ages of the 1440s, Portugal's goal was India and its access to great Asian wealth, above all, in the spice trade. Instead of India, da Gama sailed into a global net-work little known to Europe that linked the east African coast to the Middle East and, across the Indian Ocean, to South and Southeast Asia. Swahili merchants had been plying the east African coast, others riding the monsoon winds to take gold and slaves north to the Arabian peninsula and eastward to Asia, returning westward with textiles and porcelain. For da Gama and those who followed him, east Africa, and what would become known to Europeans as Mozambique, be-came a way station on the route to Asia.[1] Not until travelers learned of the gold mines in the remote south-central African hinterland did the Portuguese seek out the ore in what they imagined to be the fabled biblical land of Ophir. Their initial efforts, of the 1560s and 1570s, to capture Manica, the gold-bearing region, were a spectacular failure, Portuguese forces defeated by stout opponents and by malaria.[2]

The Portuguese remained nonetheless, founding settlements on the coast and along southeast Africa's Zambezi River, whose navigability reached deep into the interior. It was from Sena, one of those fortified river settlements, that a Portu-guese Dominican priest, João dos Santos, wrote with horror, and, perhaps, some hyperbole, of the Zimba, "a warlike people who not only eat all the men they kill in war, but also eat their captives when they have grown old and are not up to working. Nor are they content to eat what they need for sustenance, but sell the surplus in the market as if it were beef or mutton."[3] In his *Ethiopia Oriental* of 1609, the priest dos Santos recounted several clashes with the Zimba, who defeated Portuguese forces and butchered them nearly to a man. Yet the Portuguese presence survived, clinging to often precarious toeholds in southeast Africa for another 300 years before they and other European powers set about colonizing the region in earnest.[4] Though they failed to capture Manica's gold mines, they sought to control the gold trade and maintained their settlement stopovers for the route east.

## Imperial Expansion and "Suppressing Slavery"

Despite its ineffective and halting beginning, Portugal had a pioneering role in the Indian Ocean world. The Portuguese presence stretched from Mozambique in the west to Goa, a South Asian trading port, in the east, though before long, they would lose their leading position to competing European powers, chiefly, the Dutch, English, and French. The first two, creating powerful chartered companies (the Dutch East India Company and the English East India Company, respectively) that married investors' private wealth to publicly authorized armed force, soon displaced the Portuguese as the dominant European powers of imperial expansion. The European trading companies were drawn deep into the spice and textile trades, generating great wealth, but production remained in indigenous hands. In the emerging Atlantic world colonies, in contrast, Europeans took direct control, seizing gold and silver mines and planting endless fields of sugarcane, possible only with the purchase and export of millions of African slaves to the Americas and the Caribbean. Slave labor produced the Atlantic world's wealth. In the "new world," the Portuguese profited immensely from Brazil; it fueled Portugal's golden age up until the colony's independence in 1822.

Especially in comparison to Brazil, Portugal's east African entrepôts were more of strategic than economic value. Despite episodic skirmishes with more powerful European rivals along Mozambique's coast and northward, the Portuguese proved difficult to dislodge. In the Zambezi Valley, Portuguese settlers held seemingly boundless estates, or *prazos;* these transfrontiersmen married into local African ruling lineages, establishing an enduring hybrid form of rule (much as some Dutch East India Company colonists, leaving the formal settlement at the Cape of Good Hope, developed close ties with African societies in the colony's hinterland, emerging later as South Africa's Afrikaners).[5] Portugal's more formal settlements in Mozambique were mostly sleepy backwaters of little significance until well into the nineteenth century, when a new imperial politics of a changing Europe revived interest in Mozambique and the south-central African interior. As well, the effort at abolition of the slave trade attracted more European attention to southeast Africa, where a clandestine trade flourished in unpoliced waters.

Bowing to British pressure, Portugal had, in 1836, banned its citizens from engaging in the slave trade, which the decree's preamble condemned as an "indelible stain on the history of modern nations." Two decades later, French authorities were still seeking to recruit "free workers" from Portuguese Mozambique for sugar planters on the Indian Ocean island of Reunion.[6] Ministers in Lisbon refused; recruitment "could never be done with free inhabitants, not only because of the aversion felt by the black population all along the coast to board a ship, but also because agricultural endeavors in the Province need the people who are sought from there."[7] Anyone taken would have come from the interior, "bought from tribal chiefs. And when those chiefs do not have enough, they naturally make war upon one another to acquire prisoners they sell as slaves."[8] With this clever argument, an antislavery position was employed to fend off competition for African labor.

Any stoking of the slave trade would hardly be in keeping with a royal decree, soon to be issued in 1858, committing Portugal to speed emancipation and complete abolition twenty years hence. All concerned, in Mozambique, Lisbon, and Paris, assumed that the *émigrés*—as the French called the "free workers"—were nothing but slaves under another name. Ministers in Lisbon referred obliquely to "many difficulties" in their relations with Britain, where abolitionists were in full cry.[9] But to the frustration of Portugal's Colonial Ministry, some officials in Mozambique defied Lisbon's orders banning "recruitment" for the French, possibly in expectation of payoffs from French buyers.

Soon after appointment as governor of Mozambique in 1857, General João Tavares de Almeida seized the French vessel *Charles et Georges*, its crew, and its cargo of 110 Africans. Its captain was sentenced at trial to two years of "community service."[10] When France objected strenuously, Portugal stood firm, until France sent warships within range of Lisbon. Portugal looked in vain for international support, but London abandoned its longtime ally, despite its otherwise staunch opposition to clandestine slaving. Portugal released the ship and its captain.[11]

The incident, with nearly open slave trading taking place under Portugal's nose, underscored the tenuousness of Portugal's hold on southeast Africa. Portugal claimed sovereignty over this vast region but in reality controlled no more than a scattering of isolated settlements along the coast and the Zambezi River. Even there, its sway was uneven, its local officials often governing more with an

eye toward their own interests than those of the government. Now Portugal renewed its southeast African claims, under pressure from abolitionists at home
and especially abroad to interdict the covert trade in African slaves, all the stronger in Indian Ocean waters, with aggressive British naval patrols off the coast
of West Africa.[12] British missionaries, too, moving north from South Africa,
founded missions in the African interior; their presence, at a time of quickening
imperial tensions in Europe, stimulated renewed Portuguese activity. Portugal
sponsored, in 1877, a coast-to-coast expedition to explore the interior, in hopes of
asserting a claim to the lands that lay between Mozambique and its sister colony
of Angola in west-central Africa.[13] Claims to, and control of, the hinterland remained contested, with Britain, in particular, resisting Portugal's pretensions to
a southern African colony that would reach across the continent's breadth.[14] The
surging power of a unified German state soon increased pressure on all the European powers to maneuver for favorable position.

With the southern African mineral discoveries (of diamonds at Kimberly in
1867 and gold on the Witwatersrand in 1886) still decades off, Portugal and investors dreamed of great agricultural wealth. The Portuguese faced the same balancing act as Britain and France, who strove to keep their island sugar industries (in
the Caribbean and Indian Ocean) strong, while seeking sufficient servile labor to
replace slaves (freed in the 1830s and 1840s) while paying, at minimum, lip service to the principle of abolition and the practice of free labor. Britain could draw
on its South Asian colony for labor, and it did, sending millions of indentured
laborers to its African and Caribbean colonies.[15] Tiny Portugal, by comparison,
could look only to the African territories it claimed.

By the time Lisbon took steps to occupy Mozambique a quarter century
later, Portugal faced challenges far more serious than disobedient governors or
inconstant allies. The Gaza state, one of the nineteenth century's most powerful
African empires, had long controlled much of Mozambique south of the Zambezi River, its armies inspiring such terror that one Portuguese observer called
them "modern Zimbos."[16] Armed groups of African soldiers once again roamed
the region, but those they captured were shipped to sugar plantations on Indian
Ocean islands.[17] In a terrible irony, abolitionists' earlier nineteenth-century success in suppressing the export of slaves from west African shores had pushed
slaving into new and less well patrolled areas, among them the southeast African
interior. The British missionary and explorer David Livingstone, who had visited
the Zambezi Valley in the late 1850s, noted that the Gaza were so secure in their
supremacy that they "consider[ed] the Portuguese a conquered tribe."[18] Pointing to Portugal's scattered and insecure settlements, Livingstone had argued that
southeast Africa was no more a Portuguese possession than was the whole of
China for the tiny Portuguese settlement at Macao.[19] As European powers po-

sitioned themselves for a land grab of staggering proportions, southeast Africa became a tangle of open rivalries, shifting alliances, and duplicitous agreements among Africans and Europeans. Various maps depicted a territory called Mozambique, but no borders were internationally recognized or fixed until the last decade of the nineteenth century.

By the mid-1880s, Europe's imperial powers moved to fix their claims to African territory. Latecomer Germany was especially aggressive, as was Belgian king Leopold, aware of his country's limited stature in Europe, yet hoping to aggrandize it via an immense African empire. In response, German chancellor Otto von Bismarck convened the Berlin Conference of 1884–1885, without a single African representative attending. There, the Great Powers (chief among them Belgium, Britain, France, Germany, and Portugal) agreed to ground rules for eventual partition and conquest of Africa. The 1885 Berlin Act sought to ensure that the colonizing powers did not export to Africa the quarrels and internecine warfare that had ravaged the Old Continent for much of the century. The act's preamble expressed the signatories' wishes "to regulate the conditions most favorable to the development of trade and civilization," and to further "the moral and material well-being of the native peoples."[20] To develop "civilization," the treaty committed the powers to "protect and favour all religions, scientific, or charitable institutions . . . which aim at instructing the natives and bringing home to them the blessings of civilization," to "watch over the preservation of the native tribes," and "to help in suppressing slavery, and especially the slave trade."[21]

Missionaries, especially Scottish Presbyterians and the French cardinal Lavigerie, dismayed by the persistence of slaving in Africa, called for imperial action against it.[22] The Brussels Conference of 1890 was the result; the Brussels Act pointed to colonizers' "firm intention of putting an end to the crimes and devastations engendered by the traffic in African slaves."[23] Overlooking European nations' past role in promoting, protecting, and profiting from that traffic, the act laid out suppression of the slave trade in the "African territories placed under the sovereignty or protectorate of civilized nations."[24] Special emphasis was put on regulating trade in arms and liquor (both frequently exchanged for slaves), and on road and rail construction that could spread means of rapid transport (to replace human portage, mostly undertaken by slaves, especially for east African ivory caravans).[25]

## Outsourcing Conquest and the Southern African "Scramble"

In the decade following the Berlin Conference, what the British colonial secretary had then called the "sudden Scramble for colonies" in Africa accelerated, as European rivals sped to demonstrate "effective occupation" to legitimize their claims.[26] After the 1886 discovery of seemingly bottomless gold mines in South Africa, the scramble became a headlong rush. South of the Zambezi River the British, Germans, and Portuguese hoped to strike it rich with a "second Rand" as glittering as the just-found gold of the Witwatersrand. The Afrikaner rulers of the independent Transvaal Republic (descendants of the Dutch East India Company employees who settled at the Cape of Good Hope in the seventeenth century) sought access to the sea through Delagoa Bay in southern Mozambique, while the British—hoping to bring the upstart republic and its gold deposits under the Union Jack—aimed to contain them. The competition was especially fierce between the British, driven in part by the ambition of the British adventurer and financier Cecil Rhodes, and the Portuguese, whose nationalist boosters were re-luctant to abandon the dream born of their golden age. The eventual winners of the scramble, Britain and Portugal, would soon learn that, as important as con-trolling African territory, would be controlling African laborers, in abundance and at minimal cost.

The British and Portuguese coveted central Mozambique, whose mountain-ous region of Manica was the source of the gold trade that attracted Portugal to the interior almost 400 years earlier, a prize now just out of reach of European adventurers. Manica was situated in a littoral zone on the eastern edge of the Great Zimbabwe plateau, within a mountain range declining eastward toward the Indian Ocean, lying in a political littoral as well, between the Gaza empire to the east and the Ndebele kingdom to the west. Both African states arose after the 1820s great upheaval in southern Africa, when powerful centrifugal forces of "crushing" or "shattering" (*mfecane* or *difaqane*) spun off militarized groups fleeing violence and in search of areas to colonize.[27] The Gaza state, established in the 1830s, held territory from the Delagoa Bay hinterland in the south to the lower Zambezi Valley in the north, and westward into the foothills of Manica's highlands along the Zimbabwe plateau. The Ndebele state, southwest of Manica, extended over the central Great Zimbabwe plateau. Independent, though subject to Gaza raids for tribute, Manica was sandwiched between the two. No scram-bling European power could reach it except through Ndebele- or Gaza-controlled territory.

In the mid-1880s, Portugal signed a treaty with the Gaza ruler Gungunhana, and Britain with the Ndebele ruler Lobenguela, both nations hoping to establish control of Manica's mineral wealth through their African allies.[28] Neither African potentate had firm control over Manica, but Gungunhana's dominance in Mo-zambique served Portugal's interests, since any fragmentation of the Gaza state would have produced a political vacuum filled by numerous weaker local chiefs less able to stand up to encroaching European powers. Portuguese scramblers realized the Gaza ruler's strength was useful in the short term. One supporter of empire wrote to a Portuguese government official, "Our interest is in maintaining Gungunhana as a powerful ruler."[29] Britain, with far greater human and financial resources, was better positioned to exploit the opportunity for control.

In Britain's and Portugal's efforts to strike alliances with local African rulers, two men played a central role in each: Cecil Rhodes, the notorious British politician and businessman, and his less notorious Portuguese counterpart, Joaquím Carlos Paiva de Andrada. Rhodes had already made one fortune in South Africa's diamond fields, but now seeking more gold and more glory, he set up the British South Africa Company in 1889 as a vehicle for his hopes to seize a large chunk of south-central and southeast Africa.[30] Andrada, like Rhodes a champion of imperial ambitions and leader of a consortium of investors, founded the Mozambique Company in 1888, in a similar effort to further his country's commercial and political interests.[31]

Portugal's imperial boosters imagined a colony stretching from Angola's Atlantic shores to Mozambique's Indian Ocean beaches, spanning the whole of south-central Africa. One map, drawn in Lisbon, which depicted a rose-colored band of territory across the width of south-central Africa, provoked British ire, in view of London's own pretensions to much of the same area.[32] The Portuguese government, burdened with crushing external debt and riven by domestic political factions, could not, or would not, undertake in its entirety the project of conquest and occupation but instead outsourced exploration (and eventual governance) of central Mozambique to Andrada's company, under the Portuguese flag.[33] The company, it hoped, "would disprove the allegation that Portugal was too effete and decadent to rule her empire effectively."[34] A compatriot of Andrada, sent in 1889 to explore deep into the interior, was instructed to "widen our influence in that region, taking advantage not only of the good will and respect that the Portuguese name enjoys among the natives of those parts but also the ill will and repugnance with which some of them receive the English."[35]

Andrada secured a royal charter for his Mozambique Company, authorized to act in the name of the Portuguese Crown; the concession was half again as large as Portugal itself. It was to be autonomous, though within Portugal's empire and subject to it, but with its own laws, state administration, and fiscal authority. Along with such powers came obligations: to maintain a police force to enforce its own and Portugal's laws; to settle 1,000 colonists within five years; to establish schools and missions; and to construct a port, dock works, a railway, roads, and a telegraph system. The Crown placed few limits on the company's sovereignty: it could not negotiate treaties with foreign governments, and it must honor Portugal's treaties and agreements. The company pledged to pay to the Portuguese government 7½ percent of all net declared profits.[36] Its backers and directors expected that its economic monopoly would generate enormous profits.

Portugal and its commercial proxies, chief among them Andrada's Mozambique Company, were under great pressure to occupy the territory to which it laid claim and to prove a capacity for "effective occupation," for despite the ground rules set at the Berlin Conference, European rivalries continued to drive policy in Africa. German and, to a lesser extent, British interests harbored hopes of dismembering and dividing the Portuguese colonies between them. Portuguese anxiety was all the more intense because Lisbon was deeply in debt to both London and Berlin.[37] In outsourcing parts of Mozambique to be governed by private companies, Portugal was attempting to square its political and economic goals with practical realities. Domestic nationalist sentiment pushed strongly for the Portuguese state itself to occupy and administer Mozambique and the other colonies in Africa. International political considerations, too, militated toward direct state administration to demonstrate Portugal's sovereign power in its colonies. Yet the Crown's resources were already thinly stretched, and capital for colonial investment was limited, further constraining the state's capacity. In creating private companies for colonial governance, Portugal charted a middle course, issuing a charter to a second company, the Niassa Company, and shedding responsibility for the remote far north of Mozambique and allowing eager private investors to take control of much of the center. The state maintained a presence in the historic outposts in the upper Zambezi Valley and the south for direct rule, the better to make a strong showing for Portuguese sovereignty, since the south bordered South Africa, home to foreign interests that might challenge Portuguese claims to Mozambique.

This strategy was itself the product of intense struggle within Lisbon's governing circles, with a history that reached back decades earlier. Portugal hoped that Mozambique might fulfill its dreams for a reinvigorated African empire and help Portugal recapture the wealth and glory it lost in 1822 with Brazil's declaration of independence. From the middle decades of the century, powerful men both in and out of government looked for ways to create "another Brazil in Africa," whose natural resources could bolster Portugal's place, and put it once again at the forefront of European imperial ventures.[38] For some, it was a matter of pride and what one observer saw as a commitment to "national triumph," especially to relieve Portugal of its inferior status as a very junior partner to Britain.[39] Others saw, in a Portuguese African empire, the opportunity for personal wealth and renown. In the 1880s, influential men of finance and fiercely patriotic military men pressed the government to act on its African claims, lest more powerful imperial rivals shoulder Portugal out of the way. (The Mozambique Company's founder, Andrada, sought both status and wealth, but active in Mozambique, he spent little time lobbying in Lisbon.[40]) Men of finance and men of the military elite held ambition for an African empire reborn but clashed over how it might be achieved.[41]

For captains of finance and industry seeking markets and materials to rescue Portugal from economic woes, the solution was clear: the government should outsource the process by establishing chartered companies, ideally with Portuguese investors, but if with foreign capital, British or Belgian, so be it, as long as the colonial territories themselves remained Portuguese. Business elites in the Lisbon Commercial Association, stung by Britain's dismissal of Portugal's "historic" claims to much of south-central Africa, saw a resurgent imperial economy as salve for the "righteous pain and resentment of the nation at the unheard of violence which has just been inflicted upon it," but the ultimate prize was to support the metropolitan economy.[42]

Imperial boosters among Lisbon's military elite, painfully aware of Portugal's status as a minor European power, were determined that their African territories remain Portuguese in all respects: politically, culturally, and economically. The military men and their allies were loathe to see any part of the empire "denationalized." They pointed to the dangers of privatizing imperial governance, with one leading member of the Lisbon Geographic Society (a forum for many imperial matters) arguing it would be impossible to "organize a powerful company with Portuguese capital, and that inevitably, it would have a Portuguese mask with an English head, which will rise up at the right moment for imposing itself."[43]

At a time when 45 percent of government revenue went toward debt service, the challenge of government underwriting of the occupation of African territory made ministers blanch.[44] Chartered companies' appeal lay in their hybrid nature, joining private capital with coercive military force that was essential in subjugating sovereign African authorities. The companies supplied investment vital to infrastructure development that proponents of empire saw as necessary. They promised to make as yet unconquered territory safe for capital. The tilt toward outsourcing increased in 1890, when Portugal's fragile economy went into freefall, undermined by a plague that devastated Portuguese wine production and by political upheaval in Brazil that choked off remittances from Portuguese immigrants.[45] Early in 1891, the government declared bankruptcy, and the Ministry of Naval and Overseas Affairs authorized one land concession after another in a bid to attract investment and to accelerate "effective occupation" of Portugal's African claims. In addition to the Mozambique and Niassa companies' concessions already in place, others followed for large areas of southern Mozambique and north of the Zambezi, and also in Angola and Guinea, though most of these new concessions failed to attract investors and saw little or no follow-through. The zenith (or, for opponents of the policy, the nadir) came with one member of Parliament's proposal to sell Mozambique outright and use the proceeds to pay down Portugal's foreign debt.[46]

Opponents of outsourcing pushed back in 1894 when, under the leadership of the conservative *Partido Regenerador,* the Crown issued a "break decree," which took concession-granting powers out of ministerial hands and put them under parliamentary control.[47] The ban had no impact on concessions already granted, including the Mozambique Company's charter, but exposure to parliamentary politics effectively halted the trend toward concession. Even after 1901, when the ban was reversed in an effort to draw more overseas investment, the momentum for subcontracting had eased. The Mozambique Company remained, among the companies in Portugal's African colonies, the largest and the most independent.

A map of Mozambique at large had become much like a patchwork quilt, with no overarching administration to unify the disparate pieces of what some maps of the day called "Portuguese East Africa."[48] The very southern region of Mozambique, immediately south of the company's concession, was under direct administration of the Portuguese colonial state, as were parts of the extensive Zambezi Valley region. Other parts of the Zambezi region were run by sprawling plantation companies (without government charters), operating largely independently. The far north was controlled by the Niassa Company, which held its territory under terms similar to the Mozambique Company's. Between the Niassa Company's far northern concession and the plantation companies of the lower Zambezi lay Mozambique District, governed directly by the Portugal Crown.

Both Portuguese-chartered companies in Mozambique—the Mozambique Company and the Niassa Company—held what were ordinarily powers of state: the right to make their own laws, to hire their own officials, and to control movement in and out of their territory. (The plantation companies in the Zambezi Valley, though much less independent, held taxing authority and could issue their own currency.[49]) The Niassa Company, hundreds of miles distant, remote from any existing European settlements, with a wholly separate administration and ownership, had no known commercially viable resources. Unlike the storied Manica, it attracted little investment and fewer colonists, its activity limited effectively to hut tax collection (an annual levy on each African resident's dwelling) and leasing labor migrants to South African mines. Many fled its rule northward to German-ruled Tanganyika (inherited by Britain after World War I).[50] In a bygone era, Portugal had projected its power worldwide; now, Portugal's influence had shrunk to match its perch on Europe's westernmost edge. In the strategically vital and contested hinterland of central Mozambique, Portugal relied on the Mozambique Company to defend its claims, advance its interests, and exploit Manica's wealth in the name of empire.

Manica was considered the true prize, though its real potential for generating wealth was unknown. One adventurer wrote, in the *Beira Post,* that Manica was, "undoubtedly, [the area] from whence the Queen of Sheba got the large quantities of gold with which she made her presents to King Solomon."[51] Others cited more recent tales of treasure, of "mines equal in value to anything on the Rand which if judiciously managed will make it an important factor in the world's production of gold."[52] But the company's first challenge in Africa was to occupy its vast concession, like most of the rest of Mozambique entirely unconquered by Portugal; as one observer remarked, Portugal's claims to sovereignty over the company's concession were "little more than a question of words and traditions."[53] The bulk of the provinces of Manica and Sofala fell under the dominion of the Gaza state, and that part which did not, primarily in the Zambezi Valley, was controlled by *prazeros,* local rulers who claimed descent from seventeenth-century Portuguese settlers who had married into African ruling lineages and South Asian merchant communities, vital linchpins in the Indian Ocean network that linked Asia and Africa. Except for Beira, the site of the company's capital, only the fortified outposts of Sena and Tete along the Zambezi River were under firm Portuguese control. The path to colonial power would begin with negotiation and diplomacy and only later proceed to battle and force.

Gungunhana's Gaza state was the immediate concern, for it controlled access to Manica's goldfields, vital both to generate income and to attract settlers and investment. The Gaza ruler was a shrewd negotiator, managing to hold off Portuguese, British, Afrikaner, and German designs on his empire through the 1880s by taking careful measure of the scramblers' strengths, both relative to his own and to one another. He may have perceived, correctly, that between the British and the Portuguese, Portugal was the less threatening of the two, and an easier ally to control. Gungunhana placed little importance on the treaty he had signed with Lisbon, telling Portugal's representative in Gazaland, "the paper is good only for fishing for lands."[54]

The company's moving force, Andrada, had, over the past decade, become such a well-traveled visitor in the interior of southeast Africa, largely unknown to Europeans, that some Africans bestowed on him the nickname *Mafambisi,* "the hurrier."[55] But he lacked a steady supply of African labor power to transport him and his equipment and supplies. He encountered special trouble hiring porters between coastal Beira and Manica's highlands, where the company oversaw pioneering mine works from as early as 1888. The company's steam launches could manage along the lower, navigable reaches of the Pungué and Buzi rivers closer

to the coast, but from the midlands halfway from the coast to Manica's mountainous heights, transport proved difficult. Tsetse fly and the deadly sleeping sickness
it spread precluded the use of draft animals, and rail line construction was still a
decade off.[56]

Although Andrada was willing to pay carriers for their services, Africans were
reluctant to leave their fortified settlements to join his employ, with Gaza raiding parties levying tribute and occasionally killing adult men and taking women
and children prisoner, "reigning as absolute lords," as Andrada's lieutenant put
it.[57] Andrada turned to local chiefs for political support and for his requests for
porters, and when chiefs wavered, fearful they might run afoul of the Gaza leader,
Andrada reassured them that Gungunhana had authorized the company's operations. Andrada often traveled with a Gaza representative who spoke "in the name
of the chief [Gungunhana] that [local authorities] should supply the necessary
hands for the Company's work."[58] One local chief, Ganda, balked at a meeting to
hear Andrada's requests, whereupon Andrada hinted that he would send word
to Gungunhana of Ganda's refusal. Ganda met with Andrada before the day was
out.[59] When João Rezende, an Andrada associate, was confronted by Gaza bel-
ligerents who menaced the company's fully loaded steam launch, he threatened
to inform Gungunhana, and they backed off.[60] Some chiefs would do nothing
without Gungunhana's express order; others went to ground and hid. Still others
came seeking protection from Andrada, but he could do little more than bluster.[61]

Gaza overrule and menace, together with the rising tensions stirred by European probing, put many local leaders on edge unless they could receive weapons
or protection. The Portuguese had brought valuable and useful trading goods:
glass beads, iron hoes, and breech-loading rifles.[62] Beads were of little practical
use, but were sought after as an item of exotic prestige that might strengthen the
bonds of fealty between lord and vassal. Iron hoes were of great value to farming communities and were sometimes exchanged as bride wealth in matrimonial
transactions. The breech-loading, rapid-fire rifles could upgrade chiefs' arsenals
and preserve their independence.[63] With such goods Andrada and his collaborators reached agreements with many chiefs, who accordingly flew the Portuguese
flag as a sign of their allegiance. Andrada's British counterparts chose instead to
target select rulers whose lands lay in strategically vital areas. The difference in
strategy proved decisive, for the Portuguese alliance, which by 1890 reached deep
into the Zimbabwe plateau, never enlisted the chief Mutasa, ruler of Manica's
richest gold-bearing lands. He saw the Portuguese as untrustworthy collaborators
with the Gaza menace. Andrada sought his support to supply men to open a road
between the company's mine diggings and its outpost in Macequece (its inland
headquarters). In their negotiations, Mutasa concentrated on Gungunhana, but

when João Rezende asked when Mutasa might fulfill a pledge to send workers, Mutasa only ignored the question and "returned to speak of Gungunhana and Gaza soldiers, who were his principal preoccupation."[64] He expected the company to supply the same advanced firearms Andrada had traded to Manguende, Macone, and other neighboring rival chiefs. When Rezende rejected the request, Mutasa "could not hide his anger."[65] Portuguese activities had put him at a tactical military disadvantage, surrounded on all sides by hostile forces. Mutasa sought alliances with his better-armed neighbors but was rebuffed at every turn. Rumors of an impending Gaza reoccupation increased his sense of isolation.[66]

In September 1890, Mutasa granted to Rhodes's British company a concession in Manica in exchange for a cash payment, trade goods, and guns. Soon thereafter, Andrada—unaware of the agreement—came to meet with Mutasa in his mountaintop stronghold and walked into a trap. British South Africa Company forces captured Andrada and shipped him by oxcart to Cape Town; Rhodes's company occupied Manica and pushed toward the sea, threatening to split Portugal's claims to southeast Africa in two. Throughout the first half of 1891, the two imperial proxies vied for control of the region, but neither Lisbon nor the company could match London's or Rhodes's power and influence, and Britain and Portugal soon settled the conflict, largely in Britain's favor. To Portuguese nationalists, Portugal's capitulation recalled the "immense disaster" of 1578 (the military defeat in Morocco that triggered sixty years of Spanish overrule) and the "pungent shame" of 1808 (Napoleon's invasion that forced the Royal Family into Brazilian exile).[67] In gambling aggressively to claim most of what would become Mozambique and Zimbabwe, Andrada came close to losing all of the fabled land of Ophir. After the debacle of what became known as Britain's Ultimatum of 1891, Andrada left active service in Portugal's African empire to others. Despite losing his bid for a greater Manica, he did maintain, for his company and for Portugal, a grip on what would become Mozambique's narrow midlands.[68]

By the mid-1890s, the Portuguese had greatly increased their military capacity with more advanced weaponry and more troops and could now dare to challenge the Gaza state. António Enes, the royal commissioner stationed in the Mozambican capital, Lourenço Marques, striking an aggressive stance, attacked Gaza in late 1895, routing the bulk of its army, burning Gungunhana's capital, and forcing him to flee.[69] Gungunhana was captured, taken to Portugal, and paraded through the streets of Lisbon, before being exiled to the Açores, where he died in 1906.[70] With the routing of Gaza, the Mozambique Company was now free to impose its rule throughout its territory. At 62,000 square miles, it was, as some of its backers liked to point out, larger than England and Wales.[71] No less formidable was the company's charter, granting it a "complete monopoly to all the territory's economic resources." But force of arms had granted exclusive rights to "build and use any form of communication"; to levy and collect taxes, duties, and fees; and to issue licenses, giving it statutory control over "every form of trade, industry, and profession."[72]

Once mining began in earnest, the authors of the company *Handbook* (which combined a pitch to potential investors with various company regulations on, among others, mining, land, and timber concessions) wrote, the "hosts of game now enjoying the solitudes of Manica and Sofala will have their quiet disturbed by the thud of heavy stamps and the explosions of dynamite, while the financier and the statistician will alike be interested in watching and recording the important additions to the world's gold supply coming from the district which, by many competent authorities, may have in long-past centuries provided the riches of Solomon and the Queen of Sheba, and which in our day will prove to be such an important factor."[73] Reminding readers that before the discovery of gold in 1848, California had been "almost an unknown country, inhabited by a few savages," the *Handbook*'s authors asked, "why should not Manica and Sofala follow in the steps of and rival California, for it possesses as great riches in gold and soil even more fertile?"[74]

The Mozambique Company hoped that Manica, like South Africa's Witwatersrand, would attract large-scale capital investment and draw a large white settler population. The company considered the development of Beira's port crucial, not just for the territory, but for the whole landlocked hinterland claimed by the British as well—what would become the Rhodesias and Nyasaland. (Portuguese nationalists were gratified that neighboring British colonies must depend on a Portuguese port.) Once rail lines linked the interior to Beira, a virtual sea of commerce and people would flow through the company's port. But the company's initial capitalization, 250,000 *milreis,* or about £55,000, was embarrassingly modest, especially in comparison to the £700,000 raised for the British South African Company.[75] Rather than investing directly in opportunities the Mozambique Company hawked to investors, risking its capital, the company emulated the Portuguese government itself, conferring countless private concessions for mining, agriculture, wild rubber collection, and port and railway construction, taking a minority shareholding in these subsidiary firms and reserving for itself the task of public administration. It derived its principal revenue from taxes, fees, and duties on people and services, and on the goods that moved into and out of the territory. The rationale was that without thriving plantations, farms, mines, and commerce, there would be no taxes to collect, no fees to charge, and no import or export duties to levy.

Such impeccable logic aside, the success of the Portuguese empire, the company, and any European settlers would, in fact, depend—as throughout British,

French, Belgian, and German colonies in Africa—on the breadth of Africans' backs. In the words of António Enes, who had commanded the forces that defeated the Gaza and who would become one of Portugal's leading imperial proponents, "whoever imagines, that the white could settle along the banks of the Zambezi or the Incomati [River] to work with a hoe has never broiled in the rays of the African sun." Enes—who would write Portugal's colonial labor code—held that the "tough work" of developing Mozambique "must be done by blacks."[76] Company governors and local officials alike spoke of Africans as the "indispensable element of work in tropical climates," without whom "there could be neither agriculture nor industry."[77] White settlers who came "striving to earn that 'almighty dollar' that all men are so fond of," as one writer in the *Beira Post* put it, could neither develop the territory's wealth nor "firmly establish the sovereignty of Portugal."[78] The African population of Manica and Sofala was, as one company director eventually admitted, the company's "most valuable asset."[79]

## Company Rule: "Establish Our Sovereignty and Civilize the Black"

The Mozambique Company's 1893 *Handbook* described its territory as "a country rapidly passing from an undeveloped and savage condition to a state of civilization."[80] It predicted the company's activities would do much in "spreading the light of civilization throughout the dark portions of Africa." The *Handbook's* authors skirted the question of just who would undertake the labor these activities would require.[81]

In 1897, two years before a commission led by António Enes, the royal commissioner who had led the Portuguese forces that conquered the Gaza empire, issued the labor code that established the legal basis for forced labor in Portugal's colonies, a Mozambique Company administrator in Manica argued that "it is indispensable that [the company's labor law] provide the necessary force so that an ill-conceived leniency does not come to destroy completely the work begun which should establish our sovereignty and civilize the black."[82] This district-level official shared the worry of higher-ranking officials, like Enes, that the abolitionist impulse, in banishing slavery, might leave Africans with too much freedom to choose how they disposed of their labor. The official proposed a labor law to compel Africans to engage in "healthy labor that would reform them and bring them out of the state of brutality and inferiority in which they are presently found."[83] A "good and fair" law would compel all adult men to work for six months out of each year, and though "this might seem a bit severe the truth is if we want the ends we must use the means and right now we don't have a choice: either we must dominate the black or he us."[84]

Enes believed that abolitionists' "dread for slavery" had led them to "abandon law and morals, common sense and economic necessity, in teaching the negro that he has the liberty to continue to live in a state of savagery, since that is the inevitable consequence of the freedom *not to work.*" That freedom, Enes believed, had been "carefully protected by regulations which imposed severe restrictions on the right to persuade the negros to work, and to contract them for work."[85] For one who believed in the "moralizing mission" of labor, this was entirely misguided, because, as Enes put it, the "savage who takes up work becomes captive to civilization; it is that which might discipline him."[86] "The holiest of principles" had now become "pernicious social doctrine," and abolitionist ideals had been taken too far.[87] The ban on slavery had made it too difficult to impose the labor obligations Enes and others believed were necessary. The labor code justified forced labor with the injunction, in Enes's words, that Africans "obtain through labor the means they lacked to live as civilized men."[88]

In a report on Mozambique written several years earlier for the Portuguese government, Enes wrote, "I even feel an inner fondness for the Negro, this big child, instinctively bad like all children. . . . I do not consider him to be destined to extermination for the necessity of the white race, although I may believe in his natural inferiority. Still I neither understand nor know of any moral or legal doctrine by which our metropolitan legislators can justify their scruples in not obliging the half-savage African, innocent or criminal, free or captive, to work for himself and society, to be forced to work when he refuses to do so voluntarily."[89] Enes suggested, in 1899, that Portugal would civilize "those backward negroes of Africa, those ignorant outcasts of Asia, those half-savages of Oceana, on which the same state also imposes, up to the point of extermination, as many other obligations as might benefit them."[90]

Whether Enes and his coauthors had it in mind or not, the Portuguese labor code of 1899 closely echoed the language of the Berlin Act of just fourteen years earlier, which bound the European colonizing powers to "care for the improvement of the conditions of [Africans'] moral and material well-being."[91] It could appeal to secular and evangelical modernists alike, with its social Darwinian suggestion that Africans were a lower class of beings, "lazy by nature," and in need of improvement, and its humanitarian impulse to "watch over the native tribes" and suppress slavery.[92] It was an article of faith among colonial planners that the African population of colonial territories would not work unless compelled. One French official in West Africa maintained that "the black not under supervision works little or not at all." A British officer in Zanzibar, overseeing an African population recently freed from enslavement at the hands of Arab masters on the island's clove plantations, remarked that "steady, regular work is just what your slave or free slave dislikes very much."[93] Enes's commission had expressed the same concern in its report to the Portuguese government: "The state, not only as a sovereign of semibarbaric populations, but also as a trustee of social authority, should have no scruples in *obliging* and, if necessary, *forcing* them to work, that is, to better themselves through work, to acquire through work means for a more prosperous existence, to civilize themselves through work."[94]

In the labor law, Portugal expressed an urgency to act, stating, "Portugal must, absolutely must, without delay make her African inheritance prosper."[95] The 1899 labor code remained largely the same until 1930. Africans in Mozambique—and, indeed, all "natives" throughout the Portuguese empire—were required to work for a period of time determined by local authorities. Exempt were indigenous chiefs or other authorities, women, children under fourteen, men over sixty, those with disabilities, and those serving in the police or armed forces. The obligation was considered met if men already had sufficient capital to support themselves, or if employed in a profession or in commerce, or if they cultivated a defined area of land, or if they were engaged in wage labor for a specified period of time each year (both the extent of cultivation and period of wage work were to be specified by local administrators). Otherwise, "public authorities would compel [others to work] by whatever means they had at their disposal."[96]

The Mozambique Company, no doubt, regarded with envy the large plantation companies to the north of its concession, established on the remaining vast estates (*prazos*) Portugal had created in the seventeenth century. The African population there had come to recognize the rights of *prazo*-holders to claim taxes and labor from those living within the borders of the estate, a system that combined elements of both European and African practices of exploitation. After several decades of predatory slaving, followed by a dozen years of conquest and revolt, by the end of the nineteenth century some Zambezi Valley Africans were willing to surrender their labor for work on European-run sugar, sisal, and coconut palm plantations for some months of the year in exchange for being otherwise left alone.[97]

In the company's territory and farther south, gold fever had gripped the imagination of white settlers, who flowed into the region in the thousands. The largest gold deposits in South Africa, exceedingly deep and composed of relatively low-grade ore, created a voracious demand for labor power to drill deep and process large quantities of gold ore. Realizing the threat posed by a freely bargaining African working class, the South African Chamber of Mines pushed for restrictive labor laws and in 1900 created the Witwatersrand Native Labor Association to channel and control the labor supply for the mines. The association had free rein in Mozambique's southern provinces, directly administered by the Portuguese colonial state rather than by the company, to recruit Mozambican men to work in South Africa's gold mines. The association deployed an army of recruiters, touts, and runners, reaching down to the village level into Mozambique and throughout the wider region. As a result, just a decade after the first gold strikes on the Witwatersrand, tens of thousands of Mozambicans were at work in South Africa.[98] Southern Rhodesian employers, especially the colony's white miners, learned the lesson quickly and imitated South African mine operators, forming an analogous Rhodesian Native Labor Bureau in 1903. Aided by the British South Africa Company's tax and land policies designed to drive Africans off their land, the bureau soon ensured the profitability of Rhodesian mines with the mobilization of thousands of forced African laborers.[99]

Both neighboring colonies were trying, openly and under the table, to import African workers from the Mozambique Company's territory.[100] Freelancing Rhodesian labor agents were sneaking into company territory to recruit workers for mine labor in the British colony, and even stealing Africans at work in Manica. The South African Witwatersrand Native Labor Association requested recruiting privileges in Mozambique Company territory, offering to reserve 20 percent of recruits for mine operations in Manica; the Mozambique Company governor rejected this offer.[101] The British South Africa Company, in turn, asked the Mozambique Company's permission to recruit within its territory; hoping to curry favor, it assured the company governor that its agents "would receive explicit instructions not to interfere in any way with natives who are already in employment."[102] The company governor, in response, fended off all such efforts to poach, gently pointing out to his English counterpart the illegality of freelance recruiting, and asking him to "be so kind as to make this known so that people from Rhodesia will not come over the boundary to engage natives, which is a punishable offense."[103] Company officials reported that "the labour question" was "at the moment seriously occupying our attention, and, we are now endeavouring to organize the supply which exists in these Territories in such a manner as we trust will not only enable us to supply adequately all employers within our own boundaries but will also permit the exportation of a certain amount of labour annually."[104] Mozambique Company administrators, considering imitating their neighbors' systems of labor mobilization, inquired about the labor regulations and laws in Southern Rhodesia and South Africa.

By 1900, the Mozambique Company's labor regulations required all Africans to meet a six-month labor obligation, "a beneficial guardianship." Officials and colonists were to "use all possible methods to reform and educate, punishing them in moderation, as if they were children."[105] One company governor, reporting on his administration's efforts, wrote, "I consider the undertaking of civilizing action a moral duty."[106] The company concentrated most of its own resources in

Manica, which it hoped would prove the territory's riches: the labor compound there was built with South African mining compounds in mind.[107] Company law permitted private employers to "recruit" workers on their own, but most preferred to rely on the company to supply this African labor.

As the company put into place its native labor department, João Pery de Lind, the governor who oversaw its formation, explained that it arose out of "the need to govern the native properly."[108] Pery de Lind, previously Manica's district administrator, had written earlier of Africans' "well-known repugnance for work," and of his mobilizing African workers as "bringing about the conquest of native labor."[109] When Africans taken for forced labor fled their assigned workplace in Manica or other locations, the administrator in a neighboring district assumed it was solely "to devote themselves to their innate laziness."[110] Or, as another district administrator put it, "the black's dream is not to work."[111] António Cardoso de Serpa, who, like Pery de Lind, rose in company ranks from a district-level position in Manica to become the company's director of native affairs and secretary general, held a similar view, that wherever "the native does not work, administrative authorities must bring him to do so, by education, by example, and by advice; and, in the last instance, by applying the laws which punish laziness."[112] Early in his tenure in Manica, Cardoso de Serpa dourly noted the tenacity with which Africans foiled his efforts to compel contract work; he blamed African "laziness" and desire "to work freely only for employers chosen of their own free will."[113]

A decade later, in the mid-1920s, when the League of Nations undertook to investigate slavery's persistence under colonial rule in Africa, Portugal would suggest, in correspondence to the league, that the "negro has to be civilised by his labour and must be made to co-operate by this labour in the process of civilising himself and developing tropical Africa."[114] Any African who did not work "must be induced to work by persuasion and kindly and gentle methods." It was, after all, "not reasonable that the colonisation and development of uncivilised countries, with the advantages which accrue to the natives therefrom, should be the result of colonists' work and organization alone, without any assistance on the part of the native."[115] Only thus, said Portugal, could African life be improved and Africans be "educated, instructed and made moral."[116] Such attitudes were to persist over the course of empire; in 1939, after forty-seven years of company rule in Mozambique, one official quoted António Enes word for word: "after drunkenness, Africans consider idleness to be the most perfect state of blessedness."[117] Colonial administrators' conviction that Africans embodied a natural savagery conflicted with empire's self-apparent civilizing mission to bring progress and illumination to the "Dark Continent."

## White Settlers: "Insatiable" for African Laborers

Much of Lisbon's rationale for its scheme of forced labor under the guise of "contracts" was clearly in its own self-interest, whatever role it might have claimed to be playing for the "benefit" of Africans. One early visitor to the Mozambique Company territory, concerned about how exactly Africans might be made "moral," urged the company to support Africans' own interests, in particular, agricultural production, in part, by convincing its European settlers that "they have an educational duty to fulfill towards the natives."[118] Yet most of the territory's first white colonists, according to the company's own administrators, could teach no one; they were so ignorant of how to wrest a living from the soil that they "would have died from hunger" had it not been for charity received from the company, and, as it turned out, for the forced labor of African agricultural workers.[119] The emigrants from Portugal had been settled in the Meyrelles Colony, founded in 1897 and named after an early company governor, Francisco de Menezes Meyrelles do Canto e Castro, located by the company in what it considered healthy highlands, expected to provide the white settler community with ideal resources. The colony became, instead, a total failure.

It had been difficult to find Europeans to serve (let alone settle in Mozambique), as the company's first governor, Joaquím José Machado, admitted in an early report. Fearing an early death, from disease or otherwise, potential settlers and employees demanded either government-guaranteed indemnities or insurance policies to provide for their families in case of need, but insurers themselves, learning that applicants would serve or settle in Africa, refused to provide policies "at any price," so Machado said.[120] Of the thousand or so early colonists the company brought to the territory, few had much interest in settling in the interior, some admitting they knew nothing of agricultural work. Among those who did try their luck at the Meyrelles Colony, some fell ill, some returned to Portugal, and others fled to avoid repaying loans they had received from the company.[121] In 1899, to provide Europeans for Meyrelles, the company removed a number of unemployed white men from Beira, dumping them unceremoniously at the colony.[122] And despite its charter-stipulated requirement to settle 1,000 colonists in its territory in its first five years of operation, the company became reluctant to finance the costs of settlement, especially, as the managing director explained to the government's representative on the board, "in light of the poor results obtained so far."[123]

In a postmortem assessment of Meyrelles's failure, Manica's district administrator attributed the failure to the colonists' lack of farming skills, but not that alone; he cited their origins in the southern Portuguese regions of Alentejo and

Extremadura, which meant that they were not "real men . . . hard working, sober, patient, and less contaminated by vice," not like men from the northern regions of Beira and Minho.[124] There was an ironic parallel in company officials' views of the Portuguese settlers and of the African population of the territory. Africans lived in a "state of brutality," and settlers suffered from a "brutal and violent despotism."[125] However, the corrective treatment diverged sharply; Africans were supposed to "civilize themselves through work," by force if necessary, while white settler farmers, as one administrator put it, were to be "supported with understanding, care, and patience."[126] Even once the white farmers in Manica found their footing, a district administrator there remarked on the settlers' dependence, describing them as "insatiable for laborers" supplied by the company.[127]

Though most company officials were reluctant to underwrite the costs of white settlement, one administrator made a case for ever greater levels of colonization, lest a moribund economy be taken as evidence that "the Portuguese do not know how to colonize."[128] The territory's *Beira Post* editorialized that the "chartered Company . . . has a very large commercial interest at stake and the individual interest of the trader *or* settler and that of the company are idendical [*sic*]; as the prosperity of the people is the strength of a nation, so should the success of the trader or settler, be the success of a chartered Company."[129]

The company's grudging support to settlers gradually grew more generous, and out of the ruins of the Meyrelles Colony emerged a largely Portuguese farming community, no longer threatened by starvation, but far from the yeoman class desired. Their faltering first years had earned them the pity of the *Revista de Manica e Sofala* (*Manica and Sofala Review*), whose editors wrote of "the poor colonists of Manica, who vegetated there for years, using up their dwindling resources with little to show for it."[130] The farmers, as noted, had the benefit of Manica's rich farmland, some of it abandoned by the local African population in retreat from the company to the district's less accessible areas. The company supplied the settlers with key material assistance; maize seed at cost; free seeds for experimental crops, such as wheat, tobacco, and cotton; and subsidized use of company-owned cattle, tractors, threshing equipment, and maize drying facilities. Those who used mechanized equipment had access to subsidized fuel. But despite this largess, none would have been productive without a new resource— conscripted African workers.[131]

The farmers' dependence on the company's coerced labor soon overwhelmed the company's ability to meet their demands. In 1910, Governor Alberto Celestino Ferreira Pinto Basto decided the company should shed its role as supplier of forced labor: "The problem of native labor . . . caused me so many reversals, hardships, and annoyances." Pinto Basto would let subcontracted private interests struggle with the task—either by coercion or incentive—of enticing Africans to work for the territory's colonists.[132] He would "liberate our administration from the moral obligation (which in customary use is little by little becoming a required task) of supplying labor, relieving our district administrators from that harrowing work which up to now has weighed upon them with such anguish." His assessment suggested he was truly at his wits' end, for he described this work as this "heavy cross borne on the road to Calvary."[133] The company offered a contract to supply African labor throughout the territory to its longtime employee Carlos Picardo, who had served in district-level administration for more than a decade. Picardo, in turn, set up his own private labor agency, but it offered incentives no better than the company's own, and his agents—unlike company administrators—lacked a credible threat of violence to compel Africans to accept a labor contract. Pinto Basto himself blamed Picardo's difficulty in supplying workers on the white settlers, "above all" on "the horrid reputation that Manica's miners and farmers have for ill-treating and poorly feeding their native workers, especially when they are tied to a contract or when supplied by the Mozambique Company. The ill-treatment and bad food are, unfortunately, a reality."[134]

The settlers who employed forced workers charged that Picardo's laborers were insufficient and unsuitable: many fled; some were "true skeletons"; others lacked the necessary skills, particularly for mining.[135] Since Manica's maize farmers, especially, considered access to low-cost African labor a part of Portugal's "African inheritance" to which they were entitled, by November 1910 the territory's white population took a threatening stand. The *Beira Post* reported: "The farmers have mealies [maize plants] in the ground or were waiting to plant them. They must have labour and they were not going to wait six months for boys [African workers]. The farmers and miners and commercial men had made the country . . . it was time that the men who made the country ruled it."[136] For the company, whose rights to the territory were chartered by the monarchy, such populist demands were worrisome, particularly arising only a month after the overthrow of the Portuguese Crown and the declaration of a republic.

White employers in Manica, after a series of secret meetings, descended on Beira by train to register their displeasure. João Pery de Lind, the employer-friendly administrator of Manica District who, as tensions escalated, had been named interim secretary general, intervened, "using [his] personal influence over those from Manica to deal with their complaint."[137] Amid the unrest—and alarming rumors of a possible attack on the governor's residence—the governor, Pinto Basto, fled on the next boat to Lisbon, his last official act to name Pery de Lind as his replacement. Among Pery de Lind's first acts as governor was a meeting with the protesting delegation and cancellation of the subcontract to Picardo.[138]

Mollified, the white settlers returned to Manica, and, so the district administrator there observed, "behaved in a most orderly manner."[139] Pery de Lind ordered all district administrators to resume conscripting workers for Manica "with greatest urgency,"[140] and with the company's coercive machinery now back in operation, within a month more than 1,000 conscripts arrived to work for the settlers.[141]

The farmers' resistance to any reduction in company-supplied labor continued to feed hostility with administrators, especially in Manica, where João Mascarenhas Manuel de Mendonça Gaivão, district administrator for much of the 1910s, wrote reports that bristle with the resulting tension. Gaivão, frustrated by what he saw as some farmers' aversion to labor-saving mechanization, wrote, in 1911, of "vast lands in which cultivation is conducted in between limbless tree trunks," and of other farmers who, while having cleared their land of trees, "are so wedded to rudimentary methods that they use blacks in field preparation, seeding, and weeding."[142] Manica's maize farmers, in "monomaniacal" greed, so it seemed to Gaivão, were unwilling to invest in "more modern and economic" methods if they required capital investment, however modest. He derided the settlers' farming techniques as a "kaffir-like system."[143] One governor, who came close to suggesting that Manica's white farmers were too stupid to know better, seconded Gaivão's assessment. "The poorest colonists," he said, "prefer to work alone, using the primitive means at their disposal, due to their ignorance of [agricultural] methods."[144] More than a decade later, the company inspector of finances and exploration dismissed the white farmers as "savage beasts" and lambasted their "brutality of behavior and stupidity of technique."[145] Another governor who had especially difficult relations with the territory's employers wrote in bitter sarcasm to his immediate superior, the managing director, that the territory's "farmers and miners forget that, except in special circumstances, the Mozambique Company cannot force all the natives to go to work in Manica and Chimoio."[146]

Gaivão at times mocked what he saw as white farmers' erratic and uninformed demands for workers. "The work of the RTI [native labor department]," he wrote, "cannot be dependent on the adjustments that the farmers decide to make in their planting schedules, nor on the need for labor that might arise from a change in the weather. Such a system would require district personnel to do nothing but go around the villages recruiting people because Farmer So-and-So decided at the last minute to clear an additional 20 hectares, because Cicrano thought to plant more potatoes, because Beltrano—seeing that the rains started suddenly—had to proceed with the weeding of maize seedlings." They wanted, in the rustic image Gaivão used, "sun on the threshing floor and rain on the garden."[147] "Our farmers, who, as in general with all uneducated Portuguese . . . [are] almost entirely ignorant, indolent by temperament, negligent by nature, end up neglecting their own interests, undermining those of collective concern, and harming those of the Company completely."[148] Three years later, thoroughly frustrated with what he called the farmers' "special nature," Gaivão sputtered: they "start out with nothing and in the Metropole [Lisbon] would be no more than a simple day laborer or factory worker. They are blinded by the first fistful of gold they acquire, and seized by an obsession with wealth, embark upon all sorts of speculations . . . instead of limiting themselves to cultivating the earth which so generously rewards work well done."[149]

The inspector general wrote, in 1914, "Unfortunately, I must admit that . . . without assistance from the Company [our farmers] would never have succeeded as they have done."[150] The governor had urged that Manica's farmers receive preferential access to company-supplied labor, over other European employers who sought company conscripts, but the priority provoked a dissent from the managing director. He thought preferential treatment should follow performance. Able farmers could be singled out, as long as they "were good. Those that we have are not, for the most part."[151] Still, the preferences continued out of company and Lisbon self-interest. The white maize farmers served their economic (and political) goals, by providing a low-cost local alternative to the costly imported rice previously supplied to feed African workers. The result was that Manica's mining industry slashed its operating costs.[152] The company continued to provide white farmers with forced African labor and other extensive logistical and financial support until the Great Depression forced most of the settlers out of business.

## Maintaining an Illusory Abolition: *"Só Para o Inglês Ver"* (Just for the English to See)

Beyond so-called recruitment and the ersatz "education" white settlers were to provide, the company's labor law and practices, together with fictional devices, camouflaged the coercion that underlay its labor regime. In the last decades of the slave trade, slavers who hoped to circumvent abolitionist enforcement (and armed naval patrols) had referred to the African slaves they shipped from the continent as *engagés* or *émigrés,* as the French operators of the *Charles et Georges* had done, as though the passengers had come voluntarily; but captives were typically brought to the coast by force. They came from an interior region where antislaving oversight was lax to nonexistent. Once at the coast in Mozambique they were asked—perhaps in coastal Swahili, a language foreign to people of the distant hinterland—whether they objected to serving a five-year stint of plantation labor. When captives—euphemistically referred to as "free workers"—could not understand the question, their consent was assumed, and they were shipped off to become work slaves.[153] The linguistic circumlocutions used by slavers in the past had provided protective cover for slave ship captains and conniving customs officials. Company officials, too, now sought to avoid criticism from missionaries and others by casting modern labor slavery as a moral, even spiritual endeavor, the fulfillment of a civilizing mission.

The company's system of governance was *"só para o inglês ver"* (just for the English to see), a reference to the, mainly, English critics of Portuguese labor practices.[154] They cloaked a set of strictly formal instructions with language that concealed the actual purpose and practices in an aura of enlightened modernity. The activity by which the company enslaved tens of thousands of Africans annually, cynically, and falsely was called "recruitment," though it amounted to nothing more than mass seizure, either at the hands of armed police or the threat of their deployment. All those the company conscripted were said to have been "contracted" for work. That the workers never saw, much less signed, a written contract made no difference, nor did the fact that only a tiny fraction of those seized for work would have been able to read a contractual document had one been given to them to read and sign.

The linguistic misdirection was important, because a contract is an agreement, freely entered into, between two willing parties. The company's African workers were referred to, in consequence, as *"recrutados"* (recruits) or *"contratados,"* (contracted). Only when Africans were held to have broken a law (for example, for drunkenness, gambling, or theft), and openly sentenced to unpaid labor as punishment, was there any direct reference to coercion in public statements, with such workers labeled *"compelidos"* (from *compelir*, to compel). Two decades into company rule, one local official wrote with rare openness, "Naturally, in all the Territory the recruitments are composed of *servicaes compelidos*."[155] Even seventy years later, elderly African women and men in central Mozambique recalled to me the days of forced labor—"Forced, let's get going. He who wants, he who doesn't. Let's go."—speaking of it not with the term *"chibaro,"* commonly used throughout other parts of Mozambique and Zimbabwe to mean forced labor, a referent to earlier local forms of unfree labor, but rather as *"mtrato,"* a borrowing of *"contrato"* (contract) into the local Shona language.[156]

Only when company officials were compelled to discriminate between ordinary force used to recruit workers and extraordinary force used at times of especially difficult "recruitment" did they lay bare the prevailing standard. The company briefly experimented, in 1910, with Carlos Picardo, the private labor recruiter, under the subcontracting arrangement by which the company governor had hoped to recruit workers without force or threat of violence. In Picardo's contract, a clause carried on the pretense, threatening the subcontracted recruitment agency with sanctions "if at any time it is found that the natives of the Territory are recruited and not presented voluntarily."[157] The opposition of recruited versus voluntary workers made clear what the euphemisms of "contract" and "recruitment" tried to conceal. Nearly two decades later, in the late 1920s, when the company again partially subcontracted the work of "recruitment" to a private association, administrators' language again revealed the true nature of the contract system. The association foundered, unable to find willing workers, whereupon a district administrator, aware of the negative associations of the concept of a contract, offered some advice. Labor agents were to avoid saying to potential workers "that they are making contracts but rather arrangements."[158] Concealment piled on concealment.

The same company legislation that authorized the "recruitment" of workers for "contract" labor regulated the wage regime. Among the tens of thousands of laborers the company seized every year, some did receive payment, but almost never the amount specified under law, and the company and the employers so successfully used a variety of tactics to defraud Africans of their earnings that some ended their periods of toil in debt. So, too, the company's regulations established that half of the contracted wage be paid while the worker was at work, the balance due only on the worker's return to his home district.[159] A worker might be granted an advance lump sum, calculated as a fraction of the wages to be paid over the life of the contract period, with half of that lump sum deducted on a prorated basis each month from any payments at work, the other half to be deducted from the balance due upon return to his home district. Under the system, a typical *contratado* on a six-month contract in 1913, with a monthly wage of 3$375 *reis*, could receive 6$000 *reis* upon being taken for work. While there, he would be slated to receive half the month's wages, or 1$687.5 *reis*, less $500 *reis* deducted each month to pay down the lump sum advance, for a total of 1$187.5 *reis* each month. Once home, at the end of the contract, he was to receive the balance of accrued wages, or 7$125 *reis*.

Any payment due to a worker was subject to multiple separate transactions, each with the potential for wage theft. All contract workers received an iron serving bowl for their rations, the cost deducted from their wages, as was the cost of a blanket, if they chose to request one.[160] Any advance payment against a recruit's future wages could be claimed by the home district administrator, who oversaw all such recruitment, in an amount equal to the worker's hut tax liability, which might be from 75 to 100 percent of the advance. Further, such payments were made only in the presence of a household head or a chief, who might extract an additional, informal, levy on the basis of seniority or as compensation for serving as guarantor.[161] Any other payments due to a worker on return home might be confiscated under similar conditions.

The territory's financial balkanization—with multiple currencies in use—provided more opportunities to reduce payments due to workers. The company issued its own currency, a right it held by its charter, which, as a gold-backed currency, maintained a premium over the silver-backed Portuguese currency that circulated in neighboring territories to the north and south under the direct control of the Portuguese colonial state.[162] The company required Africans to pay their hut tax in gold currency, but typically paid its forced laborers in Portuguese silver, as did the great majority of employers in the territory.[163] Thereby, Africans lost even more of their earnings, since the company forced them to pay an additional levy for paying their tax in the silver currency in which they were paid. They similarly lost out when, to acquire the required gold currency, they exchanged their silver for gold with Asian merchants who operated rural stores and trading posts, offering poor rates of exchange, aware that Africans had little choice but to accept.[164] Even after the company changed its regulations and required employers to pay Africans in gold currency, employers continued to use Portuguese silver; workers' wages declined even further through the 1920s and 1930s, as Portuguese silver lost value steeply.[165]

The portion of the contracted wage due to a worker while at work might be slated for payment directly from the employer or from a company official, creating additional ambiguity about who bore responsibility for those payments and further opportunities not to make them. The territory's numerous small-scale businesses, most of which suffered from poor cash flow and many operating on credit, rarely passed on an opening to reduce their wage bill. So rife was the tendency that each of the company's successive labor regulations—beginning in 1900 and continuing through three subsequent iterations to 1930—specifically prohibited employers from imposing fines on workers or from making any unauthorized deductions from their wages.[166] The legal prohibitions establish suggestive evidence of actual practice. Letters, reports, and investigations written by company employees and housed in the company's archives provide corroboration.

Manica's district administrator, writing in 1904, urged that workers who committed minor offenses should receive corporal punishment by company police, "either on their own initiative or at the request of employers." "This punishment," the administrator advised, "was much more effective than that which is practiced all over, officially or not, of imposing deductions on their partial payments."[167] His argument ignored cases in which employers invented other pretexts for cutting wages, as when forty workers from Sena requested the relish (typically a stew, supposed to contain meat, fish, or other protein) required by law to be served with their maize meal (in this instance, they received only half of the mandated amount of maize meal). The farmer for whom they worked provided the stew but reduced their wages accordingly, paying only 1$500 *reis* the first month, 1$000 *reis* the second, $500 *reis* the third, and nothing at all in their fourth month of work.[168]

Even more common than cutting wages in return for the basic food ration was a "miscounting" of the number of days worked. Or setting impossible daily tasks and refusing to count the day's labor if a task was not completed. Or negating an entire day's labor when a worker paused to urinate or quench his thirst. For some types of work, these tactics were especially perverse, as when workers had been set to crushing rock (for ballast) along the rail line. Two men from a group of fifty-two who fell ill early in one contract period were repatriated to their home district, the employer deducting the equivalent of three days' wages from each of the remaining fifty workers "as compensation for the expenses he had incurred acquiring them."[169] Employers' abusive physical treatment of contract workers— denying food, rest, and proper lodging—undermined workers' health, and many fell ill. If ill and unable to work, they were not paid, and $100 *reis* was deducted for each day's work they missed.[170] With some workers suffering from extended bouts of respiratory or intestinal ailments, the deductions could erode their contracted wage, with some workers ending up in debt, not having worked enough days to generate the necessary fees to pay off the advance they been granted (and likely forced to relinquish) when originally put under "contract."[171]

If such practices lacked a certain logic—employers reduced their labor costs but also reduced their available labor—company officials understood, and clearly described, the rationale underlying the pattern of psychological abuse against *contratados* and *voluntários* alike (the company's terminology for Africans who sought out work on their own). The director of the native labor department did not take long to notice how, "when it suits them to reduce the number of natives they have in service and cannot return them [midcontract] . . . they provoke their flight and thus are freed of them and the costs they came with."[172] Other employers, the administrator in Manica noted, "resort to extraordinary measures on pay days, so as to drive off the *voluntários* whose labor they have in this manner freely exploited during the month."[173] He later told the governor that the company should oversee the payment of *voluntários* as well as *contratados* because the former are "not rarely, dismissed at the end of the month on some pointless pretext that poorly hides the aim of not paying them."[174] He may have been earnest in the impulse to protect the workers or looking for the opportunity to help himself to the wages of *voluntários* as well. Some of the district's employers—miners and farmers alike, he reported—took on *voluntários* for short-term work, but only with the premeditated intention of later "dismissing them under some futile and unfounded allegation or making arbitrary and unjustified deductions from their salaries."[175]

If employers' behavior was not far from that of the thoughtless "brutes" some company officials considered them to be, it was effective as a tactical maneuver, for it eliminated both an obligation to pay their workers—however meagerly—as well as any future obligation. By transforming *recrutados* into *evadidos,* an employer created the very real likelihood that one-time employees would become *compelidos,* sentenced to correctional labor with no wage at all. In the assumption of the right to command African labor and the violence employed to do so, colonists' actions recapitulated the practices that underwrote empire more broadly.

Three centuries after Father João dos Santos had written of Portugal's early struggles in Mozambique, Manica and its mythic wealth lay within Portugal's grasp. With borders drawn and African rulers formally subjugated, the company occupied the territory Portugal claimed in southeast Africa. The company's forced labor regime was a product of its easy recourse to coercion and its bureaucratic organization; the first made terrible the consequences of falling prey to the labor regime, and the second made evasion difficult. For those drawn into the system, options for exit were few and opportunities for protest mostly nonexistent.

# From Law to Practice

## "Certain Excesses of Severity"

TOWARD THE END OF MAY 1929, A MOZAMBICAN
named Massungue advised seven African contract laborers, most likely
destined for assignment to Portuguese-run maize farms along the rail
line through central Mozambique westward from the coast to then British-ruled
Southern Rhodesia. Massungue told the men they could expect the "worst possible treatment" from the labor agent who had sought them out: he would "punish them violently with his own hands," and the rations they would receive would
be insufficient for nourishment. The agent, Massungue warned, "sold blacks as if
they were chickens and goats."[1]

The agent in question disputed these accusations, complaining bitterly of
Massungue's "propaganda," charging it had led many laborers to flee, including
those he had just rounded up after hunting for twenty-one days in a vast region.[2]
Yet only months earlier he had acknowledged bad treatment; he had written to
an employer, "I hope also that on your part you might stop beating our workers
which, as you know, is expressly prohibited, leaving you subject to a fine, which
could become disagreeable."[3] Although Portugal's colonial labor law prohibited
employers from administering corporal punishment and prescribed, in minute
detail, the amount and variety of food that must be provided, colonial administrators rarely enforced these rules. Vulnerable Africans workers were left with no
forum for appeal or protest.[4]

To suffer beatings without recourse and to be forced to forage for sustenance,
as were many contract workers, were acutely humiliating, reflecting another di-

mension, dishonor, of Massungue's warning. Though his words may have been well meant, they were also insulting. When Massungue spoke of chicken and goats, small stock, rather than cattle, which represented true wealth, his warning was doubly demeaning. Chicken and goats were not valuable; they were eaten, rather than used to reproduce wealth. Consumed and used up, they are expendable.

As sweeping as Portugal's legal framework for forced labor was, the gap between law and forced labor practices in Mozambique was vast. One settler had commented, earlier in the nineteenth century, on the persistence of slave trading in Mozambique, after Portugal's prohibition of the trade in 1836: "These Lisbon-born laws are very stringent, but somehow, possibly from the heat of the climate, here they lose all their force."[5] At the local level, however, the effect was frequently reversed; the Mozambique Company's administrators established some labor practices that went far beyond what the law permitted. The territory's enormous demand for African labor, employers' unwillingness to pay wages sufficient to draw voluntary workers, the company's political and financial investment in concession-holders' success, and the near-total autonomy of local administrators all meant that there was little to stand in the way of pervasive enslavement of the African population. Many of the company labor law's legal provisions—among them, proscribing corporal punishment, limiting the workday from "sun to sun," or requiring employers to supply meals containing meat or fish, and mandating exclusion of women, young boys (under fifteen), and elderly men (over sixty) from compulsory labor—were honored mainly in the breach.

## Company "Recruitment": An "Unjust and Degrading System"

With a conscription monopoly in central Mozambique through the first three decades of the Mozambique Company's rule from 1892 until 1926, its officials continually refined their efforts to deploy the power of the bureaucratically organized state administration to reduce Africans' autonomy. The period of labor enslavement slowly increased over the years. The Mozambique Company's 1900 labor regulations, developed specifically for Manica, where demand for African laborers was highest, defined as a vagrant any African who "did not have an employer or who did not want to sign up for work," a definition that called in question how faithfully the law's exemptions were respected.[6] Those selected were taken under guard, sometimes tied together by the neck in groups of four in a practice reminiscent of slaving days past.[7] They trudged perhaps many miles from their homes to a compound to wait assignment, either for service to the company itself or frequently for service with the settler maize farmers and miners in Manica.

The district administrator there, commenting, in 1911, on what Africans faced as company conscripts, most especially those who toiled for Manica's white settler farmers, referred to "this unjust and degrading system of cheating the black."[8]

In conducting the annual census, district administrators recorded not only a hut count for tax purposes and overall population figures but also careful tallies (updated each year) of the number of male residents in each chiefdom deemed "fit for labor," but the selection often fell to each chief to identify just who would shoulder the burden.[9] When company staff or police arrived at the chief's premises, bearing orders to produce laborers, chiefs were required to muster the number of men demanded. Those unfortunate enough to be designated were compelled to comply. The chief, or an individual he appointed (at times a son), would identify to company police the homes of men to be taken for labor service, sometimes accompanying the police to locate them.[10] In some instances, the chiefs would "choose among those who have not yet worked, the number previously assigned to them, which is in proportion to their male population."[11] But as one administrator reported, many persons sent for forced labor "were those abandoned by fortune," left "unprotected by chiefs and village heads."[12] Gustavo de Bivar Pinto Lopes, chair of the company commission that designed its native labor department, tried for greater equity when recruiting in Gorongosa District: he sent an assistant and a literate *cipai* (an African policeman) out with a list specifying how many workers each village head must supply. This method had "the advantage of avoiding the inequalities that could have come from leaving the choice to the whim of the *cipais* and chiefs, and still more of avoiding the bribing that used to occur."[13] Another district administrator described what could only have been a best-case scenario, whereby company staff, together with police and the district's chiefs, conducted "recruitment . . . taking every care to maintain the greatest equity in the number of natives recruited in each chiefdom."[14]

Far more often the company's district-level personnel used enormous influence to direct recruitment operations in pursuit of their personal interest, whatever the law provided. One of the company's early mines directors, observing how some administrators used their free hand, remarked caustically, "how they might use their influence in their private interest, perhaps guarding their influence jealously and avoiding however possible that the cafres [Africans] under their administration might be disturbed, such is their fear [of] losing their so-called friendship."[15] The mines director's reference was to an almost certainly fictional friendship, but the private interest he mentioned was completely real. In recognition of the great work involved in traveling throughout a district to conduct the annual census, and in pursuing reluctant taxpayers, the company paid out 10 percent of a district's tax receipts to the district personnel who undertook these activities (typically the district administrator and his secretary).[16] An administrator, with an eye toward the annual tax receipts—and his cut thereof—might consider more than his standing orders when deciding just how vigorously to carry out "recruitment" for the native labor department, particularly in border districts where residents might easily flee. One district administrator claimed in a letter to the governor that there were others who "can't find the necessary patience to supply people, only to manage to increase the hut tax receipts from one year to the next, become popular and also, your Excellency might permit me to say, with an eye to the respective percentage."[17]

Moreover, it was a semiregular occurrence for administrators in Manica to report, as one did with some annoyance, that a group of mine workers sent from the southern district of Govuro consisted "mostly of children and old men generally so weak and puny that no one would take them into service."[18] Neither the law that prohibited their seizure nor the illogic of their seizure had spared them. The 1911 regulations establishing the company's department of native labor specified that "for light cleaning work and watching cattle or fields, young boys between 12 and 14 may be supplied, if they voluntarily present themselves seeking work, and as long as the employers who request them clearly specify the type of work to which they will be set, guaranteeing that they will not reassign them to other work."[19] There was little oversight on just how "voluntarily" such youngsters presented themselves, and perhaps even less of the work they were assigned. On white farmers' remote maize fields, such preteens were hidden from supervision. The loophole provision itself was buried in sixty-one articles—it was forty-seventh.

During the expansion of white settler farming in Manica prior to World War I, demands for the company's modern slaves drove what the company called "recruitment" to such a frenzied pace that the district secretary for native affairs complained he could not keep up. "This Section was given six police," he noted, "but the demands of its operation are so great that many days I don't have a single one available. It is necessary to send some of them into the bush on a daily basis because of the great activity this Section currently has."[20] The numbers bore him out: from a monthly average of 205 forced laborers in Manica in 1905, the number grew to 353 in 1906, 545 in 1907, and 904 in 1908.[21] The district administrator called for an extension of Manica's labor catchment area, arguing that the local population was "insufficient to reach the ongoing and growing demand for workers," and that if the company were to try to raise additional levies from Manica or the immediate surroundings, it ran the risk of entire villages "fleeing to Rhodesia, where no work is required of them." He warned that the labor supply was "tightening, threatening to undermine . . . the region's economic growth."[22]

The company adjusted its grip accordingly, and district administrators throughout the territory described the pressure tactics they used; according to the administrator in Chiloane, it was standard practice "for the chiefs to be called to the district office and notified that on such and such a date they had to supply a certain number of men to go work; generally, as they never bring [them] because they cannot manage to organize the number of workers requested, one or more police go to help the chiefs who fell short."[23] In Tambara, the process was much the same; even when given a minimum of eight days to come up with the number of men demanded, the chiefs "never bring the men requested, it being necessary to search for them in the villages . . . to force them to go to Manica to work."[24] Gustavo de Bivar Pinto Lopes, the administrator in Gorongosa, from where hundreds of men trudged annually to work on Manica's maize farms, wrote: "The natives' reluctance to be recruited for work in Manica is not something new, but it has worsened so much that I find here old requests for natives yet to be met. The *inhacuacuas* [chiefs] declare themselves impotent and the police charged with mustering the labor brigades find only women in the villages, with all the men having hidden themselves in the bush."[25] Luciano Lanne, who undertook similar efforts as district administrator in Mossurize, concurred: "To satisfy the requests for workers in Macequece I found myself forced to tighten up a bit more on recruitment in this region, which resulted in the withdrawal [to Southern Rhodesia] of a good number of huts. . . . Putting aside the chiefs' exaggerations and the natives' natural inclination for laziness, I think it might be time to listen a little to their constant protests."[26]

These seasoned operatives were pointing out to their superiors, in a typically understated fashion, the limits of coercion, but their measured words did not conceal that its effectiveness was limited. As Pinto Lopes put it in 1909, "There is a certain reluctance on the part of the chiefs, who are constantly sending men to Manica," a reluctance surmountable only at the cost of "greater difficulty in recruiting them." The administrator in Mocoque sounded a similar note, "I acknowledge that there is no bad faith on the part of the chiefs, with Chibumo giving orders to his headmen to recruit people and these going about this work."[27] Despite the chief's orders and the accompanying district police, a twelve-day sweep produced just forty-one men and fourteen boys for Manica.

Irregularities between law and practice extended beyond the rounding up of workers into the workplace itself, where African conscripts labored in conditions banned by law, to the workday itself. Company labor legislation permitted a workday that ran from "sun to sun"—in theory, a twelve-hour workday—but many of the district's farmers, flouting the law, kept company-supplied conscripts at work in the fields deep into the night.[28] The law also mandated a two-hour break from 11 a.m. to 1 p.m., yet employers regularly denied workers this rest, leaving them to work in the fields exposed to the fierce midday sun at Manica's high altitude.[29] Workers ordinarily did receive a midday meal, but rations were meager. Had they had their two-hour break, they could have foraged for more, as one farmer gave them permission to do, gathering wild tomatoes to supplement their scant repast.[30]

One of the district's farmers who forced her field hands to exceed the legal workday and gave them poor and insufficient food also, as one official remarked with disgust, "forced them to drink stagnant water even while there was no shortage of clean water for the livestock and garden."[31] The company's regulations stipulated that employers provide meals containing meat or fish—typically in the form of a stew referred to as "relish"—but of those vital sources of protein some workers received "not even a whiff."[32] The curiously precise wording of company regulations that specified that employers must provide food "in a perfect state of conservation" hinted at cost-cutting efforts by employers who distributed rations of moldy maize meal, saving money on grain that could not be sold.[33] The language of the company's regulations provided indirect and passive proof of conscripts' complaints.

On the eve of the Great Depression, more than thirty years after the first European colonists arrived in the territory, a labor agent visited the farm of Conde Von Sparr to investigate worker complaints of insufficient food. Observing for himself the distribution of the workers' supper, the agent saw that each man had received only 266 grams of maize flour (not the required 500), and that there may as well have been no accompanying relish, "because they could not eat the bones they received [in place of relish]."[34] He asked the workers what they had eaten at midday, thinking they had perhaps received the bulk of their daily rations at that meal, but "they all declared as one that they received a little flour and the relish was not enough, such that they could not perform the work assigned." The agent asked to see the measure used to allot the workers' daily rations and found that it held only 700 grams, 300 grams short of the required kilogram. He requested that workers receive additional rations, but Von Sparr "not only refused to comply with this request, with strong words and gesticulations, but also said that he would give not one more gram of flour or relish."[35]

Nor were such practices confined to the small-scale settler farmers who had long balanced their books on the backs of African conscripts. On one of the properties of the Bank of Beira, which operated a number of farms throughout the territory, workers reported that the bank's representative had not paid them and had confiscated the "tickets" that recorded their time of service, leaving them nine days without food. Waiting for their payment, the workers approached neighboring Asian merchants "begging for food, which they were obliged to give." All this was reported to the district administrator, who was instructed to take action against the bank's representative, "a man of bad character."[36]

Conscripts found little comfort in the short hours of rest employers grudgingly allowed, for, far from the "hygienic lodging" mandated by law, some employers provided no shelter at all.[37] On Sunday, the one mandated (but not always observed) day of rest, workers could construct their own shelters, but time was brief and building material only grass and reeds, and some employers denied even this respite. A company commission investigating living conditions found flimsy structures in which servile laborers slept for months on end, even during the wettest months of the year, and declared conscript housing "the worst, of huts worse than one might find in the bush."[38] Africans from warmer, low-lying districts shivered during the cooler months through Manica's near-freezing nighttime temperatures. Nor were these conditions limited to the growing pains of the fledgling maize farming industry. As late as 1919, the district administrator reported that farm encampments for forced laborers were "miserable, unsuitable even for housing animals," located in manifestly unhealthy locations, sometimes next to pigsties or in marshy areas prone to flooding.[39]

Higher-ups defended the system and dissimulated in the face of criticism, but on the front lines of the forced labor system, some of the company's "men in the middle" raised objections even as they carried out the day-to-day operation of conscription. Some decried the manifold abuses. For others, their disgust seemed also a matter of self-concern, ashamed of being implicated in a "degrading" system that stole Africans' labor and ignored their humanity. Despite, or because of, their frontline position, local administrators often had a grasp not only on how best to meet their "recruitment" quotas but also on the broader consequences. They warned their superiors of worker flight and uncooperative chiefs, and of negative repercussions that might follow from company policy—falling tax revenue, breakdown in chiefly authority, and widespread social disruption. Men such as Pinto Lopes, in Gorongosa, and Lanne, in Mossurize, who complied with orders to oversee conscription in districts at opposite ends of the company's territory, both understood the weaknesses of the colonial system and urged caution and moderation.

## African Workers Treated No Better Than "Donkeys and Dogs"

If the road most forced laborers traveled did not end at one of the company's hastily dug graves, as it did for many, the violence of the system went beyond the theft of labor, the abuse that stood in for discipline, the near starvation-level meals, and the wretched structures that sheltered them. The labor regime was more than an exceptionally harsh system of control; it undertook to punish, beyond any requirement for restraint, and sought to eliminate even the smallest space for individual action. Physical assaults by employers, their supervisors, and company police, combined with a near unending work regime, left laborers with little sense that even control of their own bodies was allowed or possible. The district administrator in Manica, the destination for many thousands of the company's "recruits," suggested one year that the territory's colonists "needed to be convinced that the native, indispensable element of work in tropical climes, deserves better treatment and care than the donkeys and dogs that many farmers mind with more diligence."[40]

Many men's first encounter with the company's demands for forced labor, in fact and as metaphor, embodied colonial servitude—hauling company officials overland in canopy-covered litters, or *machilas*.[41] *Machilas* were borne by four carriers, or *machileiros*: two in front, two behind, the total number required for *machila* travel many times that, depending on the length of the trip. As one of the company's founders put it in 1891, "Hammocks require the service of many men." His own party, of at most four people, was accompanied by 120 carriers.[42] Viewed from above from the territory's mountainous heights, such long processions may have looked like dark serpents slowly encircling the area and winding upward, trailing a plume of dust raised by scores of feet trodding the dry-season soil.

To be a *machileiro* was, in the most fundamental sense, to serve as a beast of burden. The work went best when all four carriers were close in height and strength and learned to match their strides to maintain balance and steady motion. A misstep might skew the load radically and force a fellow carrier to his knees. It was a constant struggle on the narrow, winding paths to keep one's balance, especially when a passenger shifted his weight. Crossing rivers and streams or ascending and descending steep slopes forced the carriers to contort themselves to keep their privileged passenger level and aloft. For those unlucky enough to be conscripted in the hotter months of October through February, the earth itself could burn the soles of their bare feet.[43]

Of all the work in the territory, mine wages (when they were paid), especially for underground work, were better than most, as throughout southern Africa; other wage rates varied greatly from one part of the region to another, but mining salaries held that premium across the board.[44] Still, working in a mine was difficult, disagreeable, and dangerous, all the more so in mines that skimped on operating expenses, run by the cash-poor or speculative firms that abounded in Manica. Mines without sufficient capital were more likely to shortchange their workers and less likely to invest time and funds in safer and more modern equipment.

So, too, underground mine work required great physical strength and stamina in shafts that were dark and poorly ventilated or unventilated. The high water table in Manica left those who worked underground sometimes standing in water, conditions that, according to the director of mines, led some to "abandon work immediately."[45] He noted that workers had special "repugnance" for the "Bragança" mine, where upon leaving the shaft elevator at one level, workers would find themselves "completely soaked . . . entering water which covers them up to the waist." Not even an offer of "incomparably superior" rations and scrupulous commitment to salary payment schedules could entice Africans to work there willingly.[46]

Some work, such as hand hammering a drill into a granite rock face while stooped in a space perhaps four feet high, was excruciating no matter what the shaft or gallery conditions. Even less-specialized tasks, such as loading ore onto trucks and "tramming" them to the shaft for removal to the surface above, were arduous. The air, stagnant at best, was often choked with dust from explosive charges set in the drill holes to free the ore. Working in a crouch or on their knees, men on the usual twelve-hour shift followed a dreary and predictable rhythm: drilling, followed by charge setting, blasting, and then shoveling the blasted ore into containers to be hauled to the surface.

Underground work was a psychological assault as well, as the men descended into the shaft, most likely by wooden ladder, by a mechanical pulley system, or, in the largest mines, in a cagelike elevator. To breathe was to choke on the damp, dark, suffocating air, to remain cut off from sun, sky, wind, or any sign of life from the outside world. Waiting in the dim, cramped space for the blasts to clear, men often found danger lurking: a slip in the shaft, falling rock, or a blasting accident.[47] No wonder that many preferred, as some miners put it, to remain "on the earth and not in it."[48]

For people from Manica, with its 900-year history as a mining center, the risks of flooding, cave-ins, and suffocation made work in the new European-run mines entirely unwelcome. Such risks were not unknown to locals with their own mining tradition, but the idea of working with dynamite 300 feet and more below the earth's surface would probably have seemed sheer lunacy.[49] Thus, men from Manica who were willing to transport and crush ore, cut and haul fuel wood, or carry out other tasks on the surface, refused almost categorically to work underground. The director of mines reported, "they were afraid to descend the shafts or enter in the galleries."[50] Either through such grudging reluctance or poor job performance, the "Manicas," as they were sometimes called, convinced mine managers that, when it came to mine work, they were a "very inferior native race . . . [whose] poor physical condition" made them "unsuited" for mine work.[51]

Manica's mine operators often clamored for workers from Mossurize, where, closer to South Africa, many had prior experience with mine work. But the dangerous work imperiled even skilled miners, and when, in August 1910, two of the district's men were killed when a gallery collapsed in the "Mozambique Mines," the administrator in Mossurize reported difficulties in recruiting men for Manica. His troubles "reached such a point that, in the beginning of the year, [for] each recruitment operation . . . it was necessary to seize natives under cover of the night." In a later letter he wrote, "there is no other means of capturing them save encircling their villages at night."[52]

Bad as litter bearing and mine work were, both paled in comparison to the demands of field work for Manica's maize farmers under more mundane but often far riskier conditions. During the first decade of maize farming in Manica, when most white farmers were engaged in opening the "closed bush" to start or expand their fields, forced labor required felling trees, clearing brush, and removing rocks from the soil. Even after Manica's white farmers had become better established, the labor lightened little.[53] Early forced laborers in Manica's maize fields bore the cost of white farmers' poverty, for few colonists from Portugal were willing or able to devote the time and capital required to clear their fields completely. Many had come to Mozambique nearly penniless and saw, in the forced laborers the company readily supplied, an opportunity to make Portugal's "African inheritance" pay for them.[54] They deployed African conscripts to remove brush and undergrowth but only to lop off tree branches, leaving standing the limbless trunks around which the farmers planted their crops, saving some labor in the initial stages of field clearance by avoiding de-stumping.[55] The scheme was, in the end, far more labor intensive: on land littered with stumps, farmers could not employ plows, seeders, or harrows pulled by livestock, which many farmers, in any case, lacked the means to purchase.[56] As a result, Africans performed by hand all the heavy field work—from clearance to tilling, planting, weeding, and harvesting. Forced laborers strove to complete their duties "curved over their hoes," as their employer and tormentor bellowed, "Two strokes deeper!"[57] For workers who were contracted for the September through March growing season, any field work would have been enervating, but it especially drained the spirit of those who knew their absence from home meant that family members were struggling to complete similar work on their own fields. The settlers' theft of the African workers' labor power impoverished not only them but also those who would have shared in the fruit of the work on their own land for their own well-being.

Some farm workers reported that the midday meal break, set by law, never came, and the farmer had their meals brought to them in the fields, left at their feet so that they might "eat and work as one continuous act."[58] Other farmers forbade field workers to pause for the moment it took to light a cigarette, quench their thirst, or even find seclusion to urinate or defecate in private.[59] Underground mine workers faced similar constraints, as the following description of one mine manager's "success" makes clear: "All latrines are on the surface. The Manager of the mine informs me that every effort is made to prevent nuisances from being committed in the mine by the natives. Should a nuisance occur the tickets of all the boys on the nearest face are not marked for the day. The result is satisfactory."[60] This "satisfactory" arrangement meant that the miners had to hold their bowels for twelve consecutive hours; the day's work was not counted for those charged with a "nuisance" and whose tickets went unmarked. A regime of total control denied rest to the mind and relaxation to the body.

It was thus hardly surprising that the district administrator in Sena, an annual supplier of thousands of forced laborers, reported, "it was rare for a group of workers to return from Manica expressing satisfaction." Their experience at work suggested white employers refused to recognize African workers' "need for healthy conditions . . . food, and a regular work schedule."[61] When farmers drove their workers into the fields before dawn and kept them "bent over their hoes" into the dark of night, the long hours were not just an effort to "take all [the workers] could give," but an implicit denial that the workers' strength and endurance had human limits.[62] When conscripts received rotting maize meal or were forced to scrounge for wild-growing tomatoes for sustenance, they were seen as akin to livestock left to find fodder.[63] And when employers delivered work instructions with clouts upside the head or worse, it conveyed an unspoken idea that these laborers could not recognize human speech. Those within the system saw forced labor for what it was: neither Africans' "self improvement through labor" trumpeted by Portuguese colonial labor legislation nor, as a French counterpart put it, the protection of "the native against his own nature," but rather the dehumanization of individuals made vulnerable by force of conquest.[64]

Many forced laborers lost their health, their limbs, and even their lives to the long days of hard work, physical abuse, insufficient food, and poor shelter. Those whose stamina would not withstand the workload but were conscripted nonetheless faced a peril poignantly captured in the refrain of a work song they sang to coordinate their movements as they struggled to clear the maize fields of large boulders or massive tree trunks:

| | |
|---|---|
| *Mangenda pinduka* | The Portuguese has changed his mind, |
| *Tapera.* | We're finished. |
| *Wo-ho.* | Wo-ho. |
| | |
| *Mangenda pinduka,* | The Portuguese has changed his mind, |
| *Tapera.* | We're finished. |
| *Wo-ho.*[65] | Wo-ho. |

"*Tapera*"—"we're finished," meaning "we're done for"—was a true cry of distress in the face of employers' capricious demands.

Especially at risk were young boys, elderly men, and famine-stricken conscripts; even though all lacked what company administrators called the "necessary robustness" for work in Manica, the insatiable and unyielding regime sent them onward nonetheless. "All too frequently," the district administrator noted, labor contingents contained children "whose bodies atrophied under the heavy burden of field work."[66] Elderly men past their prime working years could not keep pace with the demands of Manica's white farmers. And the famine-stricken, perhaps hoping to escape starvation in drought-stricken areas, stood little chance of surviving the forced labor gauntlet in Manica.

Many had arrived in Manica already weakened from a long journey.[67] Not until the later 1920s was motor or rail transport commonly used to transport workers, and forced laborers had to walk hundreds of miles, with meager rations and makeshift shelters on the way. One employer, aghast at the condition of workers who arrived for work on maize farms, described them as "true human rags," their bodies unable to endure manual labor.[68] Conscripted as "fit for labor," by the time they reached Manica some were fit for little more than a stay in what the company called its "hospital," though the facility did not deserve that name.[69] The ever-stingy company invested little in the limited medical facilities for Africans, and, even in the late 1920s, the hospital in Manica was described as a "frigid cement space," more a holding pen than an infirmary.[70]

Some recruits had to enter the hospital "even before beginning work," due to the weakened state in which they arrived in Manica.[71] Meticulous data on hospitalization recorded by the company itself during the height of the regime confirms the workers' own assessment of their predicament. During the hottest and wettest months of the year, hundreds of conscripts flooded the hospital. Between 1911 and 1926, the years during which the company kept the best records, an average of 17 percent of the workforce required hospitalization between October and April, the period of peak agricultural labor demand.[72] When hospitalizations spiked in early 1913—with one-third of the workforce hospitalized—even the company's own inspector general was compelled to note that treatment of conscripts in Manica "has left very much to be desired. Our natives have in some cases been shockingly treated."[73]

Most forced laborers were reluctant to go to the hospital in Manica, understaffed and at times overwhelmed by the number of people in need of care, since for a decade or more it was the only one serving the entire maize-growing region that straddled the rail line.[74] Many patients were discharged "incompletely cured," only to relapse and to return within a few days.[75] Those released prematurely to free up space for those even sicker, at times too weak for the trek—sometimes fifteen miles or farther—back to the farm on which they were employed, perished on the way.[76] The company's response was to build a second infirmary in neighboring Chimoio District, also a maize-growing center, from which conscripts who fell ill had previously had to travel more than fifty miles round-trip to seek treatment in Manica.

Employers probably kept ill conscripts at work as long as possible; those they left to die on the farm may have been reported as having fled, with employers seeking to hide their deaths. Countless others who were ill stayed on, hoping to regain their health, fearful of the fate that awaited them in the hospital; still others fled homeward in search of treatment from an indigenous healer. The director of the native labor department himself acknowledged that "the native has great repugnance for being treated by whites and much more so for entering the hospital, because they think that once they enter that place they'll never leave." "Perhaps," he admitted, "there is some logic in their actions, because if sometimes they receive good care, at others it leaves a little to be desired."[77] At best, the hospital was a respite (from forced labor), at worst, a place to die alone, far from home and family. People greatly feared the latter prospect, for beyond death itself, dying in the hospital meant hasty burial in a shallow grave, from which their corpse might be dug up some night by roaming hyenas.[78] At home, their relatives would bury them deep and watch over the grave.

After harvests failed in 1912 and conscripts arrived in Manica in a famine-weakened state, the maize farms became killing fields, with scores of workers dying that agricultural season. When Spanish influenza, in the worldwide pandemic of 1918, struck the region, nearly 12 percent of the workforce in Manica died, with terrified conscripts, hoping to outrun the disease, striking out for their home districts, many dying on the way, their bodies extended with their hands reaching out toward home.[79] Nor were such horrors confined to the pandemic period; they were among the ordinary atrocities the company's modern slaves faced. One man appeared at the hospital in Manica in mid-June 1927 semicomatose and nearly nude, clad in only a ragged bit of sacking against the chilly winter temperatures. Unaccompanied, unable to speak, and without identification, he died alone and unknown.[80]

Even minor ailments turned into serious threats to workers' well-being; incidental cuts and scrapes became infected in the unhygienic housing on the maize farms and festered into painful, debilitating ulcers.[81] Dysentery was a major problem, and the dehydrating effect of heavy physical labor combined with inedible food provided only prolonged and intensified their distress.[82] As striking as the data on injury, illness, and death is the company's indifference toward that evidence. In the "Extraordinary Occurrences" section of monthly labor reports, administrators seldom remarked on worker deaths. When they did, the notation read death "due to natural causes," an astonishing claim for men judged "fit for labor" only months earlier.[83] When 117 workers died in Manica between 1 October 1912 and 31 March 1913—a fivefold rise in the mortality rate over the previous year—the local administrator, still apparently unconcerned, offered no explanation.[84] Even this number may well have been an undercount, since it would not have accounted for deaths among the part of the workforce not conscripted by the company, nor would it have recorded the deaths of those who fled for home (a total of 272 *evadidos* [from *evadir,* to flee]) and died on the way or after reaching their destination.[85] The administrator in Manica, where more than one in four conscripts entered the hospital, did, however, try to explain the rising hospitalizations, attributing them to a workforce drawn from a famine-stricken African population.[86] The simple calculus behind this lack of response was that dead conscripts cost the company nothing; those in the hospital incurred additional costs.

The company seldom compensated conscripts for injuries suffered at work and almost never compensated family members for conscripts' deaths. The payments it did make were scant: when an adult man died at work, his family was to receive a one-time payment of just 50$000 *reis,* a miserly sum considering that his yearly salary would have been 36$000 *reis.* (Few conscripts ever received this much. Employers followed the practice of imposing fines and making deductions for often imagined infractions or costs.) Company legislation determined the compensation levels; an adult woman's death would merit a payment of 35$000 *reis* and an adolescent's brought just 20$000 *reis.*[87] If the generally abusive system of forced labor was not enough of an insult to those who slaved away within it, the amount paid further denigrated African labor, falling far short of their earning potential over their working years. The same regulations that authorized compensation payments made the district administrator where the death occurred responsible for making the payment, leaving family members who might be hundreds of miles distant dependent on his sense of duty.[88]

Few families who lost a relative in Manica ever received even those modest payments. Of the reported 274 recruits who died in Manica from 1911 through 1914, only one death qualified for compensation, based on the company's legislation that provided for compensation only in "work-related accidents," often recognized only in the mining industry.[89] Mining accidents accounted for the majority of the deaths judged eligible for compensation, though only a minority of actual deaths. In 1915, for example, 4 of the 5 worker deaths eligible for compensation in Manica were in mining, and overall, 8 of the 13 compensation payments that year were to mine workers. The native labor department provided no details in such cases, noting only, for example, in 1915, that a payment of 50$00 *escudos* was made to the "family of the native no. 74 Mansa of contingent no. 3/1914 from Mossurize who was victim of an accident from which he died in the Bragança

Mine."[90] That same year a total of 55 deaths were reported (of a total of just under 20,000 forced laborers), but the circumstances surrounding the 51 noncompensated deaths went without comment. That only 13 people received any compensation for injuries they suffered at work—out of the total of 20,000 forced laborers, 3,000 of whom were hospitalized—points to the company's reluctance to acknowledge the danger its modern slaves faced.[91] It was difficult to deny the risks to which the company exposed Africans when a worker was run over by a rail car, blown up by dynamite, or killed in a fall down a mine shaft, but being worked to death in the maize fields seldom if ever qualified for compensation.

The company and employers alike never granted workers the care or attention bestowed on valuable resources. Instead, as an administrator in Sena District, who oversaw the conscription of thousands of workers annually, suggested, they were not treated as "living beings . . . but as men-machines."[92] Even the director of the company labor department echoed this view, remarking that many employers "regard the black a perfect machine, that they suppose they can employ as they see fit, without taking into consideration that it is a human being they are dealing with."[93] Systematic coercion secured a steady supply of forced laborers, replaceable parts for those workers worn out through abuse and neglect. The men the company seized were reduced from human beings to factors of production to be expended, consumed, and used up.

## Compelling Consent: The Company's "Methods of Persuasion"

From its inception, the company operated on the unstated principle that the labor law established only the starting point for Africans' servitude; in proceeding from law to practice, company officials opened a yawning and, for Africans, perilous gap. The company's first labor code compelled all men to work for six months annually—half again as long as the period established by Portugal's labor code— and though the company suspended the law almost as soon as it was published, pending Portugal's resolution of its own labor legislation, the company made its own labor regime using its sovereign authority. Wholesale press ganging went forward as local administrators met demands for Africans to work for the company and the settlers.[94] The absence of a formal legal foundation stopped nothing, and it was only in 1907, when the Portuguese Parliament finalized the imperial labor code, that the company had to bring its own law into line with Portugal's. As company "recruitment" operations evolved, it gradually developed administrative measures that, while still backstopped by menace, couched its pressures in indirect and concealed ways to produce a coerced consent.

For the first eighteen years of company operation, from 1892 to 1910, labor recruitment and supply was piecemeal and reactive: when the demand for labor exceeded the number of workers that could be taken locally, an administrator would simply write to the governor, who would, in turn, forward the request to another district administrator with an order to send the workers demanded. This ad hoc process intensified after 1905, when the white settler community in Manica began to expand; new to farming and unfamiliar with the environment, the settlers constantly revised upward their requests for African labor. With no central administration or planning, their requests wound a circuitous route from employer and through district-level employees to the governor's office and back down to another district administrator. Delays were endemic, settlers were impatient, and those charged with rounding up African workers had difficulty keeping pace with the farmers' demands. Gustavo de Bivar Pinto Lopes, the company's administrator in Gorongosa, wrote in polite frustration to the governor in 1910, "It is rare the mail arrives without a note requesting now 36 workers, now 106, now 25. This system is inconvenient.... [It] tires the chiefs and so occupies the police that there is hardly ever one available for other types of work."[95]

The governor at the time, Alberto Celestino Ferreira Pinto Basto, reported in 1909 that "until recently the labor supply in our Territory met the ongoing needs of industry, commerce, and agriculture—all day-to-day blessedly growing new initiatives and activities which, requiring labor, don't permit our natives the indispensable free time to busy themselves with their plantings and rest from their toils." "Nevertheless," the company faced "the moral duty to assist those who might come to its Territory to slave away, enriching it and increasing its value, with the means to do so."[96] White colonists, many dreaming of riches like those discovered in South Africa, had not come to "slave away"; it was Africans who were expected to do so. Pinto Basto offered this assessment to his superiors in Lisbon: "I see in the Territory clear tendencies for enormous development which will soon exhaust our labor, and, at the same time, I notice that the strategy of the '[Witwatersrand] Native Labour Association' will surround the Province of Mozambique on all sides, enveloping us in its powerful tentacles. In another year, no one will be able to scare up, save at its weight in gold, a single negro."[97] Regional competition might bid up the price of labor. To mimic the success of South African mine operators with the Witwatersrand Native Labour Association, the company's managing director had replied to Pinto Basto: "It is in [the company's] interest to facilitate however possible the hiring of natives for work."[98] Yet the Lisbon-based managing director, far removed from day-to-day company operations, had little sense of how policy emerged as practice. His use of the word "hiring," for example, no more described what the company did in procuring African workers than had "pacification" accurately described the company's violent conquest and occupation of the territory.

In 1910, six months after the company's brief and unsuccessful experiment with a private labor agency, the governor, João Pery de Lind, convened a commission to overhaul the company's labor regime. Under the direction of Gustavo de Bivar Pinto Lopes, administrator of Gorongosa District, the commission replaced the haphazard operation of the past decade and a half with a new native labor department whose director would report directly to the governor. Pery de Lind's order establishing the new department left no doubt about its purpose; "It had become indispensable and of the greatest urgency to meet the growing needs of agricultural and mining activities for native labor so as to avoid however possible difficulties which might hinder those activities."[99] Private efforts to "recruit" African workers "had produced meager results." Although the company had "no obligation to recruit and supply labor to private employers, there was no doubt" that it would continue in that role, "with the sole intention of helping, insofar as it is reasonable and possible, those who put their energy and capital to work in this territory."[100]

The company's native labor department now created the administrative infrastructure to identify, locate, conscript, transport, and oversee tens of thousands of African laborers every year. District administrators became, in law as they had been in fact, at once government representatives and overseers of labor conscription. State power and labor control were merged. Local administrators drew up maps noting the location of each chiefdom and village, and indicating in each the number and age of the men, women, and children, and the number of boys and men "fit for work." Twice yearly, district administrators sent police out on fixed dates that replaced the surprise labor raids of the past. As each forced laborer entered the system, the company recorded a wealth of data: name, village, and chiefdom; length of contract, advance payment if any, and wage rate; dates of departure from and arrival to the sites of conscription and of work; name of employers, type of work, and location; salary paid at work, illnesses, injuries (including compensation for work-related injuries or death), sick days, and salary due upon return home; and instances of flight, death, or "re-enlistment." Labor department workers were required to carry a pass bearing fingerprints and an identification number, name, chiefdom, date and district of conscription, name of employer, length of contract, pay rate, sick days, and employers' comments on their abilities and conduct.[101]

The department's rationalized procedures notwithstanding, one administrator wrote, of its operations, "All recruitment has always been done, and is done, by force."[102] The regulations that established the company labor department left unchanged Africans' original statutory vulnerability to temporary enslavement (the "legal and moral obligation to work"), fixed by the company's 1907 labor law at four months, but the department's regulations extended the term, first, in 1911, to six months and then, in 1920, to a full year.[103] Company personnel embraced the "duty" of supplying coerced labor in the territory with something of a martyr's fervor. The director of the native labor department reported that "if a private company, even should it be formed by the farmers and miners themselves, were to take charge of supplying labor, it would soon be forced to declare itself impotent to carry out its thorny mission." The director's 1920 report included what had become an almost ritual refrain: "So thankless and thorny is the work which is our burden, it is well-known to all and without exaggeration we can assert that it is also one of the Company's most tiresome.... One must, moreover, equip oneself with an evangelical patience."[104]

But even after a full decade's operation (and nearly thirty years after the company's charter had been granted), the director of native labor saw the need for a "rural police force" to be attached to the department to conduct inspections to ensure that workers did in fact receive their wages, and "to verify, from time to time, that the blacks are given the weekly rest [Sunday] established under regulations."[105] The proposed force never amounted to any more than a few sentences in his annual report.

After labor practices in Portugal's African empire came under scrutiny in the League of Nations in 1925, the company considered changing its role as conscripter-in-chief of the territory, although the previous year the governor had ruled out employer-directed recruitment as impossible. In 1926, the company abolished the native labor department, declaring it absolutely necessary for "its authorities to cease labor recruitment for private employers."[106] Retaining its right to conscript workers for its own purposes, the company helped set up, as a substitute, a privately run native labor association to service private employers' demands.[107] Much of the association's financial support came from the territory's larger businesses, including the Bank of Beira, Beira's shipping and loading firms, and the Buzi Company, which operated a large sugar plantation and factory. Still, of the labor association's initial capital of £10,000, the company contributed 38.5 percent. The association's director, Armindo Gonçalves Forte, one of seven individual founding investors, made a small but symbolically important investment of his own.[108]

Bolstered by the law that required Africans to work, the association planned to post recruiting agents throughout the territory. Its structure mimicked the extinct department it was to replace: a headquarters in Beira and agents dispatched to areas that had become informal labor reserves.[109] Agents were to receive a fee for each worker "contracted"—the amount scaled to the term of the contract, a strong incentive since agents' income would grow with the number and the length of service of the contracts they made. It was, in effect, a doubling of colonial outsourcing: from the Portuguese state to the Mozambique Company and from the Mozambique Company to the association, thus, a privatization of the company's own native labor department. The association differed from the company labor department in one crucial respect: it was intended to operate without what its director, Forte, called the "direct and violent coercion which disgusts us, but with tenacious and corrective action that might reinforce the native's moral obligation to work."[110] Its agents, at least at first, were not to count on open cooperation from district administrators (or their police); after the dismantling of the company's labor department in 1926, district administrators received strict orders from the governor, under threat of immediate dismissal, "not to assist in any way the recruitment operations" of the new association.[111]

The company's charter itself had been a strategic distancing by the Portuguese government from colonial rule (avoiding the complex financial and practical burdens of overseeing empire). The doubled outsourcing within the company's administration, in its creation of the private association, was a cynical decision by its senior management to devolve responsibility for its coercive labor system onto a private party and thereby deflect criticism from itself. Decision-making high-ranking officials, shielded, to some degree, from the practical and moral challenges of overseeing and implementing a forced labor system, were close to the heat of the international political debate over what benevolent forms colonial rule might take. After profits, their principal concern was that company and Portuguese rule be seen as a successful and respectable form of colonialism.

The tactical separation of forced labor recruitment from state authority did not last long. The association faltered badly in recruitment; at the close of its first campaign, in 1926, its director reported that in Sofala, Govuro, and Mocoque (where the company's native labor department had conscripted more than 2,300 men the year before), the association "had yet to manage a single man." The results were no better in Mossurize (1,393 conscripts in 1925), in Gorongosa (1,716), and in Manica itself, where the recruiter spent fourteen days in the bush "without managing a single recruit."[112] In five months of operation that year, the association secured only 1,006 workers; although the number rose to 5,600 for its first full year of operation in 1927, it was a scant fifth of the figure the company labor department achieved in 1925.[113] During the second campaign, its recruiter in Moribane, long established as a labor reserve for white farmers and miners in neighboring Manica and Chimoio, collected only six recruits out of a male population of 5,700. The recruiter warned that in the absence of "repressive orders . . . the Association would be unable to survive."[114] His counterpart in Chimoio wrote that "everything was on the road to ruin."[115]

Even before receiving these discouraging reports of failure, the association's director, Armindo Gonçalves Forte, appealed to the company governor for assistance: "With the aim of intensifying recruitment of workers and also to eradicate the native's erroneous understanding of the new labor system in the Territory, we take the liberty of suggesting to your Excellency that measures be announced to establish the compulsory nature of work." Forte worried that "among the natives there prevails, and is becoming ever more strongly rooted, the idea that they are not obliged to work."[116] Forte was not wrong in his assessment. Many Africans understood the shift in the labor regime and were acting accordingly. When the association recruiter in Chimoio interrogated those he considered potential recruits, examining their pass books and inquiring why they had not met the obligation to work, one answered, "I have paid my tax and don't need to work; the Company can no longer force me to work when I have paid my tax." When the recruiter suggested a labor contract, they "laughed it all off."[117] The association's agent in Moribane, making the rounds of various chiefdoms in search of potential workers and explaining his purpose "in their own language," found that "my words did not suit their mindset, and their understanding, as they say, was: 'EAT, DRINK, and DANCE. Work—that is for [our] women on their own GARDENS and nothing more.'" In a letter to the company's director of native affairs, Forte complained that the "legal and moral obligation to work" had become a "dead letter."[118]

The director of native affairs, António Cardoso de Serpa, attributed the association's poor results to a lack of "indispensable preparation and propaganda among the natives" in the transition from the company-operated native labor department to the private association. The League of Nations had recommended the *"progressive"* elimination of forced labor for private purposes, but the company had mistakenly taken a different, and "very abrupt," approach. The administrators, fearing for their jobs (and no longer receiving native labor department payments for each worker conscripted in their district), "withdrew themselves completely from the problem of native labor," with the result "a crisis of workers that threatened to ruin entirely agriculture and all the existing industry in the Territory."[119]

Cardoso de Serpa sent swift instructions to the company's district administrators, detailing the means they could and should "make use of to convince the natives to dedicate themselves to work and to avoid idleness." The phrasing for "make use" was *"lançar mão,"* which may also be translated as "seize upon."[120] The instructions reinforced earlier admonitions in which he urged district administrators "to destroy in the native's mind the idea of the legitimacy of idleness. That idea, once made a rule, would give the black race a unique moral right and would possibly result in impediments to the development of regions where his labor is indispensable." The administrators must "spread and plant within the mind of the natives the notion that they must work."[121]

Early in 1927, to ease identification of those who had not labored to the company's satisfaction, the company ordered 100,000 pass books. Possession was mandatory for all male Africans over fourteen. The company charged a $30 *centavo* fee for each pass book, and instructed chiefs to ensure that everybody had one.[122] Sold with a tin carrying case, the pass book included a photograph and recorded the bearer's identity, occupation, wage history, record of labor contracts, tax payments, and place of residence. No one without a pass book was permitted to work outside of a home district. Cardoso de Serpa called the pass book "the native's safe conduct"; Africans had a different opinion.[123] Some former forced laborers explained to me, many years later, that "whoever had met [the company's demands], it was written in his pass book, 'six months.' When you didn't have [those] six months, off you went."[124] Still, some Africans realized that, though they could not avoid carrying a pass book, they could subvert its intended purpose by taking on different names, thus making it harder to determine their identity and whether they had met the company's demands. In response to the common practice (and indirect evidence of its success) "of people changing their names when outside of their district and even taking on assumed names to undermine oversight by the authorities," the secretary general instructed all district administrators to spread "propaganda to get the native always to use the name given for the census in his home district."[125]

That same year, in May 1927, the company paired the pass measure with an increased economic burden, doubling the hut tax levied on each dwelling to 9$00 *escudos* (£2 at the company's exchange rate). The increase was the first since 1909, with the penalty for failing to pay a sentence of forced labor sufficient to produce, at local rates, one-and-a-half times the tax liability (13$50 *escudos,* or £3). Company administrators and police, no longer officially involved in labor conscription, remained in charge of tax collection. Its aim, so Cardoso de Serpa put it, was "to force them [Africans] to put themselves in touch with our civilization," an aim transmitted to administrators as the "absolute necessity to create needs for the native, to get him to offer his services more readily, and with the aim of mitigating however possible the labor crisis in the Territory."[126]

Cardoso de Serpa, in an effort "to resurrect in the native's spirit the moral obligation to work," issued a circular listing the means of enforcement available to district administrators, among them use of police agents or African chiefs; repeated pass book examinations, including collective inspections, with groups of men compelled to produce their books in front of the community; summoning those who had not yet met the obligation to work, and to admonish and urge them to obey; forcing those who did not obey to work in the "general public interest"; and, finally, sentences for vagrancy of fifteen to ninety days of "correctional labor" paid at convict rates.[127] Provoked perhaps by one labor recruiter's complaint of district administrators' "passive resistance," the circular ended by expressing the company's hope that local administrators would "dedicate all their attention, energy, and action to the resolution of this important problem."[128]

Cardoso de Serpa's circular was one of many that sought to "reduce the rigidity of standing orders and to lead district administrators to interest themselves once again in the problem of native labor . . . [and] to induce the native to seek paid work, to acquire the necessary means of subsistence, to improve his social condition."[129] Its language, identical to the original 1899 labor law, was no coincidence, and the message to district administrators was clear if disguised: they were no longer solely in charge of mass conscription, but they were to pressure Africans to accept the native labor association's contracts.

The formal prohibition of company personnel's efforts to force Africans to work for private employers did not put an end to the practice; it simply drove it underground and employed a system of regulations to institutionalize it, as is apparent in confidential correspondence exchanged among the employees of the company and the association. In an intensified labor sweep, Cardoso de Serpa instructed the administrator in Moribane to conduct a pass book examination. All who had not yet met the obligation to work (or did not possess a pass) were "to be turned over immediately to the Association."[130] The agent in Chimoio District wrote to his superior that orders had gone out to all the districts for "the capture of all the natives who do not have the required four months of labor recorded in their pass books." He expected the company to deliver from 600 to 800 workers.[131] The association's director informed the labor agent in Neves Ferreira District that the governor had "reminded" the district administrator there of "the convenience of sending the [association] 300 workers destined for agricultural work."[132] The agent in Gorongosa received an identical letter notifying him that the district administrator would deliver 200 workers for the same purpose.

Cardoso de Serpa pointed out, in his 1927 report, that "it is quite rare to find natives in the Territory who might resist the advice or the methods of persuasion used by the authorities to set them on the road to work." Those who did resist faced beatings, imprisonment, and the prospect of being marched off to Beira for work in the city's sanitation brigades to collect and haul night soil, or of being sent to cut mangrove trees in the coastal swamps, working submerged in the slimy mire.[133] The numbers supported his optimism; the tally of Africans who "spontaneously offered their services" had more than tripled to top 108,000 that year.[134]

Company administrators worked carefully to conceal the practices that had long enslaved Africans throughout the territory, rewriting the history of their past activities and obscuring the reality of the present. Writing the key circular that instructed district administrators in the new procedures of conscription, the secretary general made clear how little the company intended to change. On the elimination of the company's native labor department, when an early draft of the circular referred to a "transition from the forced labor system to free labor," the secretary general suggested replacing that telling phrase with "transition from the system of recruitment by the RTI [native labor department] to the current system," because "it is obviously inconvenient for it to be said that there existed a system of forced labor."[135] He denied the existence of coercion, either past or present, and went on to claim that "labor is as free today as it was yesterday," actually a true assertion since African "recruits" faced nearly the same degree of violence and menace as they had under the company labor department—it was as "free" as that today.

## Forced Labor's Menace: A "Terrible Lion"

From its earliest years, the company enforced its self-ascribed right to levy taxes and labor with a policy of stark terror. In 1896, when the company began operations, some who held out had seen their huts and fields burned and their goods seized. Company forces engaged in such "violence, depredation, and barbarity" in one district that, according to the company's managing director, widespread consternation spread in the surrounding regions. The killings produced the opposite effect among much of the African population: "That is, they won't work, they won't pay the hut tax, and they won't obey the authorities."[136] In one chiefdom, those who hid were captured, and nine received floggings of fifty strokes each. Six of the chief's *madalas,* or elders, were captured and executed. The company's forces did not bury the bodies, but decapitated them and paraded the heads "around the surrounding villages as a demonstration of the consequences of resisting the company's demands."[137] Menace alone could be sufficient.

Tax revenue extracted from Africans established an immediate cash flow, though its secondary, if no less important, effect was to drive Africans into the labor force, since anyone who lacked the cash payment could, under law, be forced to work. Company administrators were aware of the unholy trinity uniting tax collection, labor mobilization, and violence. The administrator in one Zambezi Valley district, thwarted one year in his effort to meet the demands for forced laborers, threatened in September not to lend foodstuffs from the company's stocks during the upcoming lean months before the harvest. When the holdouts still balked at company service, he noted grimly, "Those who have not yet paid their tax, I have put them between the sword and the wall."[138] Another administrator, writing of famine that "laid waste" to Moribane District, driving all of those physically able in search of sustenance, noted that people had slaughtered all their goats and pigs. Of their relatively abundant flocks of chickens, he said, "there was only a memory." Still, famine relief came only when "he saw himself forced to supply it" to avoid emigration to Southern Rhodesia's neighboring Umtali District, where the British had helped the population to survive the killing drought.[139]

When the company's first governor, Joaquím José Machado, toured with a group of armed Portuguese volunteers, his arrival "immediately resulted in an easy initiation of hut tax collection."[140] The effect of the early theatrical acts of violence was such that, even five years after Machado had left the territory, African residents submitted to company demands rather than "raise Machado's ire," as the administrator in Moribane put it.[141] Menace was further reinforced by action. Outright execution became rare, but the company's police used the *palmatória*— a wooden paddle whose perforated surface reduced human flesh to a bloody pulp—to secure compliance with demands for taxes and labor. No one, not even chiefs, was exempt from such assaults.[142]

The *palmatória*, eponymously named for its use on palms of the hands and soles of the feet, was a simple but cruelly designed device. When the *palmatória* struck a flat fleshy surface (hands or feet, sometimes the buttocks), the blow forced the flesh into the holes: pulling the paddle away could remove some flesh with it.[143] Multiple strokes left a bloody and ruined mess. The paddle inflicted intense pain though it was never fatal, substituting humiliation and outraged flesh for death. After one administrator in Moribane, Philippe da Silva, unleashed the armed company police for recruitment with such abandon that he earned a reputation as "the terror of Moribane," the commissioner for native affairs in neighboring Manica suggested that da Silva was not responsible for the "villainy" of the police. The African population remained unconvinced. He was, they said, "a terrible Lion."[144]

Such menace and violence came as well at the hands of white settler employers, a reality the company's inspector general acknowledged in a confidential letter to the governor, where he noted that ensuring employers' access to African labor was "very much to be desired," and so it might be "convenient to turn a blind eye toward certain excesses of severity."[145] Abundant physical abuse was perhaps the greatest excess of all power wielded by the white colonists who had come to make their fortunes. One employer, Paul Bindé, a French national who held a concession for wild rubber collection in Moribane, earned especial dislike from the men the company sent to him. "If, as I said," the district administrator there reported, "the blacks are reluctant to work for anyone, no matter who it might be, the idea of working for M'zungo França (as they call Mr. Bindé) is . . . all the worse."[146] One Manica farmer beat his workers with such regularity that his farm came to be known to workers as "Chigodore," a name derived from the Shona ideophone *godo*, "of striking on the head with a stick."[147] Both small-scale prospectors, hoping for a quick find that would allow them to sell out to a larger operation, and larger mining companies, anxious to prove the "payability" of their claims to their impatient investors, were ruthless in the means they used to achieve their ends.

Even Philippe da Silva, district administrator in Moribane, known by Africans as "the terror" of the district, reported the effect of such abuse. An employer earned a poor reputation, he said, especially if he "always goes about provoking and shouting at them, because the black is troubled by this much more than a wallop from time to time." Da Silva's relative assessment may have been less than completely accurate, especially his claim that "many [employers] who don't skimp on using the *palmatória* and, at times, the hippo [whip], pass as much better people than the other who work with the tongue and nothing more," but the assertion that "*M'zungo* who often shouts at them, who always bears a stormy look, who grows angry and jumps up-and-down without reason . . . is always bad," rings true.[148]

Forced laborers reported that violence increased toward the end of the month when the deadline approached for employers to pay the company for the conscripts they used. If abuse had reached an intolerable level, workers might even flee before receiving their meager pay—an effective cost saving for often cash-strapped employers. Or, as one sarcastic critic of their practices mimicked their supposed calculations: "These workers have fled? Ah, good—one need only write a letter to the Administrator and he will arrange others to take the place of these. And even better—these have already worked fifteen days and fled without payment. This is what's gained: fifteen blacks, that's fifteen times fifteen *tostões*, or as one says £5. Better!"[149] Other cost-cutting tactics included imposing fines or discounting days worked for imaginary infractions, and compelling workers to purchase blankets or other items at inflated prices. Some employers, such as the boom-and-bust miners, might hope to drive their workers away only as a last resort during a bust period rather than as part of their standard operating procedure.[150]

When four men from Sena fled from rail line maintenance work in July 1929, they reported much of the usual raft of abuses from their Portuguese overseer, such as undercounting their days of work, prohibiting them from drinking water or relieving themselves while at work, forcing them to work on Sundays, and setting unreasonable daily work tasks (thereby creating a pretext for discounting a day's work). In listing the reasons for their flight, however, the inspector from the department of native affairs reported as well that the overseer "had treated them as contract workers before all the other *voluntários*."[151] That comment, fleeting but typical, spotlights the theater of the workplace, where status—and the associated pride and shame—played a role in the struggles that occurred there. The disrespect and lack of honor that came from modern enslavement did not always leave visible marks, but they were keenly felt by those upon whom they were visited.

The violence associated with forced labor became, for many people, the hallmark of company rule; the *palmatória* became a symbol of the forced labor regime, the company's "way of educating people." It was an all-purpose education, as some reported even more than half a century later while recounting to me the suffering they associated with the company's labor system: "If you were a shepherd and an animal went missing, you must get the *palmatória*. If you were a cook and the food didn't turn out well, you must get the *palmatória*. If you were a laborer at work and anything was not quite right, you must get the *palmatória*. If the chief didn't manage to collect all the tax, he must get the *palmatória*. That is to say, whatever shortcoming there was meant getting the *palmatória*."[152] No "shortcoming" was too minor to provoke a beating. One group of conscripts reported, in 1908, that when they paused at work to relieve themselves, they were beaten with fists, and when they paused again, whipped with the *chicotte*, the hippo-hide whip, which flayed the skin.[153] It was scarcely a less terrible punishment than the *palmatória*. But "M'zungo França," the French rubber concession holder, recognized an important difference between the two instruments of punishment, and asked the administrator to beat his workers with the *chicotte* rather than the *palmatória*, "which would spoil their hands for work."[154] His assessment was correct, given a doctor's description of the damage done to one workers' ruined hands, "which had circular bruises on the palms, approximately half an inch in diameter and with some swelling on the back side of the two hands."[155] In this "education," Africans learned a simple lesson: the company's demands for labor were to be avoided whenever possible, for once conscripted there was no way to protect themselves or to protest their predicament to an official source.

Driven out of their homes by police and chiefs and watched over by whip-wielding employers, these "modern slaves" of imperial Portugal, as a British critic of Portuguese labor practices dubbed forced laborers, could hope for little more than survival.[156] Small wonder that an administrator described people's surrender to the labor regime in these words: "For the Company's work, under the orders of its officials, they come, with no matter how much ill will, avoiding as much as they can, resisting passively with great delays, but they come, because in the end it is the Company's work."[157]

# 3

## The Critiques and Defenses
## of Modern Slavery

### From Without and Within, Above and Below

AVID LIVINGSTONE TOOK PORTUGAL TO TASK, IN the 1860s, for failing to eliminate slaving in the areas of Africa to which it laid claim. Had Portugal ever had "a vestige of desire to promote the amelioration of Africa"? He accused Portugal of being an "effete nation" engaged in the "murderous traffic in man."[1] With the passage of the antislavery Brussels Act in 1890 and the resulting more effective coastal patrols, and with greater European control of African territory in the closing decade of the century, the number of slaves exported from Africa did drop, yet the colonial powers, especially Britain and France, turned a blind eye to persistent slaveholding, typically, by slave-owning African elites whose cooperation colonial officers sought.[2] Abolitionist campaigners' earlier references to "Arab" slavers, by which they meant "Muslim," had diverted attention from European Christendom's own history of slaving.

In 1905, British journalist Henry Nevinson, writing in *Harpers'* magazine, fiercely criticized Portuguese labor practices. Nevinson hoped for British reaction against what he called "A Modern Slavery," since the British cocoa producer, Cadbury Brothers, was a principal buyer of cocoa from Portuguese Africa. "Appeal to England is no longer possible," he wrote. "Since the rejection of Ireland's home-rule bill, the abandonment of the Armenians to massacre . . . she can no longer be regarded as the champion of liberty or of justice among mankind. She has flung away her noble heritage. She has closed her heart of compassion."[3] In Portuguese labor recruitment, "slavery exists almost unchecked. . . . The islands of San Thomé and Principe have been rendered about the most profitable bits of the earth's surface, and England and America can get their chocolate and cocoa cheap."[4] To Nevinson, "The difference between 'contract labor' in Angola, and the old-fashioned slavery of our grandfathers' time is only a difference in legal terms. In life there is no difference at all."[5] The Foreign Office was more concerned with access to southern Mozambican labor for South African gold mines than with protecting Africans on cocoa plantations.[6]

In response, the British and Foreign Anti-Slavery Society's *Anti-Slavery Reporter* promptly called Portugal's colonial labor laws a "shameless farce."[7] Portugal issued a formal rebuttal: "The Portuguese Government has always taken special and attentive care to protect and favor the natives in its colonies, seeking to inspire them with an understanding of the duties of work." The labor code requirement was intended "to improve their social condition." Portugal had not "for a moment forgotten its high duties as a colonial power; on the contrary it has sought to fulfill them sincerely and loyally in the interest of civilisation and humanity of which it has been from remote times the most courageous defender and champion."[8] Feeling the heat of scandal, Cadbury Brothers stopped buying Portuguese cocoa, replacing it with a supply from the British colony of the Gold Coast, and the latter-day abolitionists subsided.[9]

Within the territory itself there was virtually no public debate on Lisbon's forced labor and few open challenges to the company's "paternal guardianship."[10] The limited, and muted, dissent expressed, especially by district-level officials, was entirely an internal affair. One European resident wrote, in the *Revista de Manica e Sofala* (*Manica and Sofala Review*), of the need to "promote Africans' moral and intellectual development"; without company labor requirements, local officials would be "unable to provide the natives with the protection and tutelage that will make them progress in moral and material terms."[11] Guillaume Vasse, a French national resident, reported that the "Company's relations with the natives are wisely regulated in every respect. . . . The number of working days required of them by the Company, the mode of recruiting labour, the method of payment and rate of pay—all these are strictly and carefully defined."[12]

At the same time, the company instructed its district administrators to "protect employers' interests and . . . to use the persuasion and moral authority they possess to get the natives to do the work necessary for the Territory's general well-being and its agricultural, commercial, and mining development."[13] The inspector general wrote that "the smallest suspicion of difficulty in the native labor question always results in the worst impact on foreign capital investment in the Territory."[14] The company governor's 1907 report defended the company's policy: "Prolific proof isn't needed to gain an appreciation of the practical results produced by the company's methodical and persistent effort in educating the native for work, an effort which consists of taking him to centers of work . . . and of convincing him that he must improve his conditions of existence through work."[15]

British missionary John Harris's book of 1913, *Portuguese Slavery: Britain's Dilemma,* called the practice by its name. He and his wife, Alice, had more than a decade's experience campaigning against atrocities in the Belgian Congo, their message condensed in the lines of a "Congo hymn":

> Britons, awake!
> Let Righteous ire
> kindle within your soul a fire,
> let indignation's sacred flame
> burn for the Congo's wrongs and shame.[16]

*Portuguese Slavery*'s opening chapter, "To the British Public," declared, "It is your business." Slavery "is in the warp and woof of Colonial Portuguese character."[17] He drew on evidence collected from travelers and missionaries to Portuguese Africa that accused Portuguese government officials and employers. He pointed out that officials cited labor laws as protecting Africans' interests while engaged in the most serious abuses themselves.

Alfredo Augusto Freire de Andrade, Portugal's general director of the colonies (previously, governor-general of Mozambique, and earlier, company administrator of Manica District and director of its mines department), opened a defense. "Life in the tropics was so easy," he wrote, with "these lazy, indolent, inactive Africans" unaccustomed to steady work. Freire de Andrade asked, "Should the native be left to his natural inertia, deprived of all civilization, or should one attempt by humane and just means to compel them to work?"[18] His response amounted to little more than blank denial and the suggestion that absent compulsion, Africans would work little or not at all.

Portugal was soon saved further criticism or need for self-justification by the outbreak of World War I and the spread of the battlefield to African territory. The British, with their own laws authorizing forced labor, now conscripted tens of thousands of West Africans for carrier service. Some Nigerian carriers, taken in 1918 to support British troops in combat against German forces in southern Tanganyika—just across the Rovuma River from Mozambique—were treated so poorly that, as one British doctor reported, "driven by hunger [they] were eating roots, leaves and berries and in consequence a large number of cases of alkaloidal poisoning occurred through which several men lost their lives."[19] In northern Mozambique itself, which saw a German invasion, African porters and troops fared little better. The Portuguese conscripted tens of thousands for service, many of whom suffered so much that some claimed "they were treated as cattle," and others, in reaction, developed pro-German sentiments.[20] Between battle and the associated devastation on noncombatants, the African death toll in northern Mozambique was perhaps 50,000 people.[21]

## Investigations of "Natives Working under the Hippo Lash"

In 1924, Edward Ross, a University of Wisconsin sociologist with eugenicist views, had traveled to Mozambique and Angola at the invitation of a missionary group to collect data for his *Report on the Employment of Native Labor in Portuguese Africa*.[22] The London-based International Missionary Council had financed a substantial portion ($1,650) of his expenses to investigate "harrowing accounts" of labor abuses and to collect evidence that might be put before the just-created Temporary Slavery Commission of the League of Nations.[23] (Ross would subsequently inquire into the possibility of appointment to the commission, writing, "I have become very much interested in the treatment of natives by powerful people. . . . I don't mind saying that I would love to make investigations as I did in Portuguese Africa of the treatment of the labor of the backward races."[24]) Ross spent most of his time in what he called the "Dark Continent" in Angola, and in Mozambique he traveled through the company's territory.[25] He investigated the public administration of Portugal's colonies, but did not spare the local South Asian merchant community, "pure parasites" who held "the world's record as leeches."[26]

Ross's *Report*, published in 1925, documented abuses ranging from "state serfdom" to systemic physical abuse, theft of wages, and the use of state administration to compel Africans to work for private employers, with raw descriptions of "unpaid conscripted natives working under the hippo lash."[27] Ross cited a number of interviews he conducted with Africans. One in Angola told of a group of women at work on road construction, some carrying babies on their backs:

> Some days she comes, some days her husband comes. Sometimes after the men are taken from the village, they take some of the women. Some men were taken to Catete on the railroad to work in the cotton fields. They may have to stay two or three years as contracted laborers. Some of them have been sent to work on sugar plantations for a six-month's term, but under various pretexts the time may be prolonged to seven or eight months. The planter told them that he had "bought" them of the Government, that they were his slaves and that he did not have to pay them anything. They got only their food and a receipt for their head tax.[28]

In an interview with a group of "Ambaquista" villagers, Ross paraphrased this bitter testimony:

> They say that in the time of the [Portuguese] monarchy (before 1910), although they were slaves, they were better off and got more for their work. Their lot is getting harder. Things got abruptly worse for them in 1917–1918. The Government makes them work but gives them nothing. They return to find their fields neglected, no crops growing. They would rather be slaves than what they are now. As slaves they have value and are not underfed, but now nobody cares whether they live or die. This Government serfdom is more heartless than the old domestic slavery, which was cruel only when the master was of cruel character. Now they are in the iron grasp of a system which makes no allowance for the circumstances of the individual and ignores the fate of the families of the labor recruits.[29]

When an Angolan "elderly carpenter and early mission convert" remembered "some of the planters had hundreds of slaves, I ask, 'are conditions for your people better than they used to be or worse?' He replies, 'Twelve years ago when there was slavery the slaves had all the hardships while the free negroes were not badly off. Now we are all slaves.'"[30]

Ross's *Report* declared that "blacks here [in the Mozambique Company's territory] tell the planters that they are just slaves of the Mozambique Company."[31] "Cowed and discouraged the natives will have no incentive to acquire skill. As life becomes harder for them, the shoots of the higher civilization among them will wither." Ross reserved his strongest language for the colonists: "These unscrupulous and cruel whites will go about in motor cars, snatch comely black maids to gratify their lust, intimidate the blacks with the palmatoro and chicote, and maintain handsome motor roads, plantation homes and government buildings with unrequited native labor. In the use of machinery, the applications of science to industry and the adoption of luxuries, this regime will look like civilization; but in reality it will be but a veneered barbarism."[32]

Ross's missionary backers' covering letter to Ross's *Report* offered some palliative comment: "We have no desire to criticise unfairly or otherwise to embarrass the Government of Portugal. We recognize the heroism of its early pioneers in Africa and the great achievements of Portugal in the development of its colonies."[33] Ross's stark *Report* did not have the impact he and his missionary backers hoped for. The Temporary Slavery Commission of the League of Nations decided to accept information only from official sources; it did not consider the Ross report such evidence.[34] The league queried the U.S. Department of State about Ross's "good moral character," at first, receiving no reply at all, leading to a *New*

*York Times* headline, "Washington Delays League Slave Case."[35] The following day a reply came from U.S. Secretary of State Frank B. Kellogg: since Ross was not a government official, the Department of State "was not in a position to express an opinion."[36] (The *Times* itself had shown an interest in "the important problems of the Dark Continent," noting that "while the old-fashioned export of human beings as an industry is restricted to a few places, it has continued elsewhere under other names, as 'indentured labor,' or 'contract labor,' or 'compulsory labor,' all of which in black Africa mean slavery of one kind or another."[37])

In Portugal, the Portuguese colonial establishment pointed to Ross's lack of knowledge of Portuguese and his consequent reliance on interpreters, and to what they implied was naïveté in believing what Africans told him. A suggestion appeared in the Colonial Ministry's in-house organ that any labor abuses could be attributed to African police who, "with little civilization . . . tend to abuse their authority."[38] One individual, who, Ross's backers suspected, was a company representative, contacted the League of Nations with an offer to come to Geneva "for the purpose of contradicting evidence."[39] The Portuguese delegation to the league's Temporary Slavery Commission sought to draw a semantic distinction between "obligatory labor" and the "obligation to labor," the former prohibited, the latter necessary to combat Africans' belief in "a right to laziness." Moreover, African labor was essential: "the region's economic development could only be brought about with the knowledge, capital, and work of the civilizing race in cooperation with the natives' labor."[40] The Portuguese response was neatly captured in the title of an article by a colonial ministry official that appeared in the ministry's *Bulletin:* "The Portuguese Are Not Incompetent Colonizers." That article dismissed as a falsehood that "the slightest of breezes would sweep away" any suggestion to the contrary by those ignorant—or who "might feign ignorance"—of Portugal's colonial history. The counterexamples offered, however, were flimsy evidence: the Portuguese outposts in the Azores, Madeira, Cape Verde, São Tomé and Principe, Macão, and "our India" (an aggrandizing reference to tiny Goa), as well as idiosyncratic claims to New Bedford, Fall River, and Taunton as "important colonial centers" in North America.[41] The author inquired "why this campaign of discredit [was] mobilized against us," and suggested that critics (who would do well "to consider their own conscience") did not have "the daring to tear us down" before the League of Nations, "a noble and impartial institution."[42]

## The League of Nations: Playing "the Antislavery Game"

Despite Portugal's sensitivity to foreign criticism of its colonial labor practices and concern over the League of Nations' investigations, naked self-interest on the part of each of the colonizing powers would, in the end, greatly circumscribe the reach and the effectiveness of the league's actions. Newly created in the aftermath of World War I, the league first took up "The Question of Slavery" in 1922, and asked member states to report on legislative and administrative measures taken to suppress slavery. Portugal pointed to its record in Africa as a triumphant success, with only indirect reference to "calumnious accusations" on its reputation as a colonizing power. Its fifty-eight-page justification of its labor policy and practice, issued in 1924, opened with a remarkable claim: Portugal was "one of the first States to solve the intricate problem of the utilisation of Black labour."[43] Admitting that "restrictions in connection with labour" would be hard to eliminate, it defended any delay, because "wherever a buyer is to be found, there will always be a seller to deliver the goods." Portugal compared the difficulty of banning forced labor in Africa to outlawing liquor in the United States: "A striking example of this is furnished by the situation in which prohibition has brought about in America, rich and powerful country though she is."[44] It simultaneously assured the league that Portuguese laws respected "individual liberty" and the "principles of justice and equality for all," and questioned "whether certain philanthropic ideas are not sometimes as applied to the negro races of Africa, likely to produce an effect contrary to that intended." "Bitter disappointment" could follow from failure to "convert the native of the bush . . . into a European." To guard against such unintended consequences, the "negro has to be civilised by his labour and must be made to co-operate by this labour in the process of civilising himself and developing tropical Africa."[45] Its report to the league, "The Question of Slavery," seemed oblivious to its inherent contradictions.

All of the commission's twenty-one meetings in Geneva, with protracted discussions and negotiations, were closed to the public, though the proceedings were carefully documented in the meetings' minutes. On the question of forced labor, which the commission called "perhaps the most difficult of the problems before it," the draft convention the commission produced stated that the signatory parties should "take all necessary measures to prevent compulsory or forced labour from developing into conditions analogous to slavery." Such practices ought to be used solely for public purposes, but where "compulsory or forced labour for other than public purposes still survives, the High Contracting Parties shall endeavour progressively and as soon as possible to put an end to the practice."[46] It did not propose direct prohibition of forced labor. All the commission members, save Harold Grimshaw (an official at the International Labour Organization) and Louis Dante Bellegarde (a Haitian delegate to the League of Nations), were representatives of empire, and had to know that each empire in its own way depended on such labor.[47]

The Portuguese representative, Alfredo Augusto Freire de Andrade, told the gathered parties that he had always insisted that it was necessary to induce the natives to work for the development of their territory. The demand for native labour, however, must be proportionate to its capacity. There were certain native races who were absolutely incapable of labour. If natives were willing to work on their own fields or to take service with individual employers, he did not think they should be compelled to work in other ways. If, however, they were entirely idle, they must somehow be persuaded to work, at any rate, for a certain definite period in the year.

His views on the matter were shared by the representatives of missionary societies with whom he had frequently discussed the question. He could not agree that all forms of persuasion, even moral persuasion, should be regarded as involving forced labour. The Director of the International Labour Office had himself stated that there was certain work to be done in native territories and that the natives must be persuaded to undertake it. He would ask Mr. Grimshaw whether he maintained that natives had a right to abstain from all labour. If such a right was not recognised, the question arose what form of persuasion should be brought to bear.

Mr. Grimshaw agreed that the native had no right to abstain from all labour.[48]

None of the commission members expressed a contrary view; "there was no question of the Commission being opposed to the encouraging of natives to work."[49] As for forced labor practices, the commission judged that they were sometimes a disguised form of slavery to be avoided unless impossible.[50]

Nor were any of the league members represented on the commission—Belgium, Britain, France, Italy, the Netherlands, and Portugal—willing to commit wholeheartedly to far-reaching changes in the practice of forced labor. But Britain was well aware that slaveholding persisted in parts of India and Burma; its Colonial Office was unable and unwilling to enforce complete abolition there. France had yet to abolish slavery in its Moroccan protectorate, and Belgium could not claim to have eliminated all slaveholding in the Congo. Portugal itself sought to avoid or delay any scrutiny. In the end, the commission members, as Suzanne Miers puts it, "used their report to play the antislavery game for the benefit of their own countries."[51] Chattel slavery was abolished in regions under control of the European powers in Africa, existing only in independent Ethiopia and Liberia and in the interior reaches of the Sahara, where the writ of law could not be expected to reach.

The league's Temporary Slavery Commission's final Convention on Slavery—that "all forms of compulsory or forced labour should be prohibited except for essential public works and essential services"—was watered down, with its assurance that member states "remain free to define what they understand by 'compulsory labour'" and by the term "essential public works and services."[52] The commission called the "obligation placed on the native to work on his own land, for his sole benefit," a matter "in which each State would exercise its own discretion," while acknowledging that "indirect or 'moral' pressure" on Africans to work for private employers might be "tantamount to compulsion." It urged "prudence on the part of the administration."[53] And thus was the league's Convention on Slavery passed, with no effective measures to repress the practice of forced labor.

When the commission solicited comments from member states on its 1926 Draft Convention on Slavery, Portugal replied with the claim that there "is not and never has been any race prejudice in our colonies or in the mother-country." Moreover, it suggested that "efforts have very rightly been made to abolish all kinds of slavery everywhere, but it has frequently been forgotten that race prejudices place their victims in a far worse moral position than forced labor can do. It is cruel and inhuman to teach a man and raise him through education to a higher level, if possible, than that of most other men, if afterwards he is always and at all times to be ostracised and perhaps subjected to every sort of humiliation." Portugal also offered the false statement that "Europeans and persons born in the colonies have the same rights under law." A policy of equality by "law and custom," Portugal contended, had allowed it to maintain its "Colonies with the support of their natives," free from unrest or rebellion.[54]

The shift in focus from slavery to racism as the evil necessary to attack, perhaps a diversion, was also a thrust at the Union of South Africa, the assertion of the legal equality of the races a barely veiled reference to South Africa's legislated racial inequalities. The assertion of race prejudice's moral harm could, by extension, be seen as an open rebuke of the Union and Britain. Anti-British sentiment was still strong within Portugal's colonial establishment, and Britain's representative at the league was the former representative from South Africa and a close associate of Jan Smuts, who as South Africa's prime minister had earned Portuguese enmity through his efforts to maintain a British stranglehold on Mozambique's port of Lourenço Marques.[55]

Portugal's rebuttal continued that because "under Portuguese law the colonial native has the same rights as other citizens, it is only fair that he should have the same duties." Chief among these duties was "an obligation upon all citizens to work for the advancement of civilization and the continuance of progress." Accordingly, in the colonies, the "ethnologically backward native peoples . . . must cultivate their lands and exploit their resources." It was the burden of the "colonising race" to "use every means that is not inhuman or dishonest or cruel to induce the native to work for the good of the community."[56] Such endeavors were "in the general interest of mankind." Portugal's defense was mute on the means by which it "induced" Africans to work. Portugal reiterated the African's "legal and moral obligation to provide for his own maintenance and . . . to improve his social status by his labour." In compelling those who failed to meet that obligation to work, "what we have done is what we see all other civilised nations doing. If there is to be freedom to work, there must not be freedom to do nothing." Portugal declared that "the law of labour is a law of nature which no man may escape"; it "would obviously be an unsatisfactory state of things if one section of society lived at the expense of the other." Portuguese legislation only confirmed "this natural law, by treating all Portuguese, whether white, black, yellow or copper-coloured, on the same footing."[57]

The lesson for "civilised nations" was, Portugal concluded, that no speedy end to forced labor was possible or sensible: "for a long time yet the native will have nothing to contribute to the progress of his country except his labour, which is the more essential because, at least for the present, the European is incapable of hard manual labour in a tropical climate." Thus, the "civilisation and progress of the natives and the development of the colonies must go forward side by side, and cannot be separated."[58]

Despite the weakness of the league's actions, company officials worried because they saw their forced labor system as a public relations and political, rather than moral, dilemma. António Cardoso de Serpa, the director of native affairs, lamented in 1927, "If we don't develop our colonies, a task for which African labor is indispensable, the economists will come and say that we don't have the right to keep [the colonies] . . . if we try to get the native to contribute his labor to develop the land in which he lives, the philanthropists will accuse us of using a form of disguised slavery. It is not easy to reconcile these two principles, much discussed in the League of Nations."[59]

In the years immediately following the slavery convention's adoption, British critics pushed for a second convention to address the disguised slavery of forced labor. Such a convention would pose a threat to all the colonial powers, and at a time when Portugal had good company in its reliance on forced labor, especially in Africa, where colonial administrations depended on it and condoned African authorities' use of it as well.[60] The league delegated the task of drafting a convention to the International Labour Organization, but Belgium, France, and Portugal each worked, with success, to limit any restrictions on specific practices. The final agreement, which produced the 1930 Convention on Forced Labor, contained a number of exceptions and ambiguities that reduced its effectiveness. Worse still, those states that ratified it committed themselves only to "suppress the use of forced or compulsory labour in all its forms within the shortest possible time period."[61] In the end, the 1930 Convention on Forced Labor failed to compel member states' compliance. Of the colonial powers, only Britain and the Netherlands adopted it promptly; Italy waited until 1934, France until 1937. Belgium did not sign on until 1944, Portugal until 1956.[62]

In 1930, Portugal did issue a new colonial labor code that was to remain in place for the remaining dozen years of the company's control. Although it began with the boast that all previous legislation had upheld "the principle of free labor," it admitted that, until recently, "coerced labor had been resorted to," but only because it had been "indispensable to dislodge them [Africans] from idleness."[63] It further boasted that, thanks to this policy, "the native has progressively been losing that instinctive reluctance [for work]." The code included provisions seemingly designed to discourage those who might criticize Portugal's labor practices, with fines (from 500$00 to 5.000$00 *escudos* for Europeans, or correctional labor from one month to one year for Africans) for anyone who "might harm the honest work of recruiters or the order and discipline of the native labor regime." Singled out were those who might "spread among the natives, in regions of recruitment, rumors tending to discredit the recruiters or employers, planting in the minds of natives unfounded fear of harm or danger."[64] It set fines of 2.000$00 to 20,000$00 *escudos,* or correctional labor for up to two years and expulsion from the colony, for public speeches, declarations, pamphlets, books, newspapers, photographs, and other publications, either for sale or free public distribution, that "might spread false information, seeking intentionally to prove the existence of slavery or slave trading, or contribute to the disrepute of native administration in Portuguese colonies."[65] The much-feared secret police of António Salazar's authoritarian New State, from the 1930s on, tightened Portugal's grip on the colonies. Public critics of its subcontracted slave labor would, in consequence, be few for decades to come.

## The Company's Own Critics: "Barbarous, Cruel, and Hateful"

The Mozambique Company administration, like Portugal itself, responded to criticism from its detractors and from servile laborers with denial or self-righteous indignation and rarely amended its practices. Few direct protests from Africans and African workers against the labor regime have survived, but stinging denunciations from some white observers within company ranks did survive and are preserved in the reports and letters of the extensive company archives now in Maputo.

The internal debates included protests from internal investigating commissions, sometimes created in response to dissent from within the administrative ranks. So, too, some company administrators called the work of rounding up Africans as "an insane undertaking"; others objected to private employers' abusive labor practices, not the system itself.[66] An official who wondered whether a farmer's ill-treatment of her workers was a consequence of "wickedness, stupidity, or lack of conscience . . . which merits our most formal condemnation" did not venture beyond warning that any further complaints of this sort would result in a cutoff of her labor supply.[67] Another hastened to state that he made no "judgments about recruitment of natives" lest his "words be misinterpreted" or he be suspected of, "harboring any ill will toward this work [labor recruitment]."[68] But some protests from officials in the middle ranks of the company bureaucracy questioned the system and warned of its consequences. While they may have rejected the charge of slavery from colonial critics, they had misgivings about the labor regime and their own role in its operation. They may have granted Africans' "need" for discipline and for colonial authority, but a number, in letters and reports to their superiors, expressed an ambivalence of mind, some questioning the moral and the logic of the system they were helping to maintain.

The company's own inspector general, in an assessment of the labor department's operations, spoke of the "barbarous, cruel, and hateful" abuse that "brutes" (he meant employers) visited upon workers the company delivered to them.[69] When white farmers' African field workers had no more than maize flour to eat, even some of the company's officials objected.[70] An administrator in Manica maintained that the company had an obligation to see that workers received "the nutrition their bodies needed . . . [and that] they deserved no less than a donkey, mule, or horse, for which the food provided contains the essentials of life." Workers, he said, had a far higher standard of living at home in their own villages.[71] Only occasionally, however, did company administrators suggest a defense of Africans' rights. One such administrator was Alfredo Augusto Freire de Andrade, a well-connected member of the company's administrative ranks who would go on to become governor-general of the colony of Mozambique and, later, director general of Portugal's colonial ministry and representative on the League of Nations Temporary Slavery Commission. In 1900, Freire de Andrade, then Manica's district administrator and director of its mines' department, said that "it is not fair to send men here [for mine labor] who have just finished [rubber] collection; the natives, seeing that the Company does not respect the contract, and that they are being pursued to collect rubber, work they don't like . . . abandon the district."[72] Serial conscription of men on consecutive contracts was not only unfair but could backfire. Freire de Andrade protested, "We have natives here . . . contracted for 3 months and who are found here very much longer, always asking to go home to rest, and who we have kept until we could find substitutes, which has been impossible."[73]

Freire de Andrade understood that Africans' reluctance to work in Manica had little to do with laziness and much to do with realizing that the company was ignoring the terms of its pseudocontracts. Still, within a year Freire de Andrade—both district administrator in Manica and director of the mines department—was responding to reports of African criticisms of the labor regime's excesses with the comment that "it all depends on the meaning given to the word *excessive*, because for the black all work is excessive."[74] Africans objected to concession holders' use of violence to "force them to work more than they are able, or, at least, more than they imagine they are able."[75] Responsible for the mines' development, Freire de Andrade was, no doubt, especially eager to ensure a steady flow of African labor to Manica to supply the gold mines. His notions of fairness may have contributed to his wavering embrace of company conscription, though it soon firmed up in view of his interest in the mines' development.

A fellow administrator, António Felippe da Silva, in neighboring Moribane, an undeclared labor reserve for forced African laborers, lost patience with the work of seizing unwilling African conscripts and declared it a mistake. "It tires the body and the spirit, makes one lose patience, even Job himself, the model in matters of patience, would lose his as well if he were to return to this world and be obliged to such work, even if it were certain that he might lose the honor of having his name mentioned in the Bible."[76] The practice was, he said, "an administrative mistake." Da Silva tried to convince his superiors to stop forcing Africans to work for private employers, especially colonists who beat and starved their workers and withheld their wages.[77] He insisted that employers' abuses caused "damage up and down the line: [tax] revenue falls, the influence of authority is lost, and our power over the natives becomes a fiction."[78] A decade later, in 1912, the company's own director of native labor would criticize employers who worked company recruits to death because, when they fled "or even died . . . without bringing in even five shillings in fees," the company was left with the unrecouped costs it incurred for transportation and recruitment fees to chiefs and district administrators.[79]

Da Silva's protests seem to have come from his perception of conscription's negative impact on the company. He was, ironically as it happens, widely feared among the people of Moribane, and in nearby Manica, the district administrator reported that he was known by the nickname of *Chigunda M'Pungo*, or "Leg-Chopper," after nearly cutting off the leg of a district resident.[80] Whatever his motivation, da Silva's criticism of the labor system fell on deaf ears; the company's inspector general scrawled a blunt response across the cover of da Silva's report: "The ideas and language of this report are such that it does not bear serious examination. Its only value is to prove that it would be to the Company's advantage to relieve the author of his duties." From a middle-ground position, compelled to confront the practical challenges of enforcement, officials like da Silva saw clearly the consequences of the orders that came down to them. The limitations—political, economic, and moral—of the system were most evident from where they stood, but they rarely, if ever, succeeded in conveying their perspective farther up the administrative ladder.

The most persistent critic within company ranks was José Luiz Ferreira, who served as district administrator in Moribane from 1909 to 1928, when the district was little more than a labor reserve for workers to be dispatched to the mines and maize farms. In his 1915 census report, Ferreira wrote: "Reluctance to serve on contract grows ever stronger among the natives, and only the respect they have for the authorities compels them to show up when called for that purpose."[81] The following year, as the company prepared to double its forced labor service contracts from six months to a full year, Ferreira warned his superiors that, in Moribane, "if recruitment for half a year is difficult, much more so will it be for a full year."[82] When the company made the change to a full year three years later, other administrators echoed Ferreira's concerns, the Mossurize administrator warning that imposing the yearlong contract would be a "disaster." The Mocoque administrator reported that news of the change provoked "great discontent," and, as it was, he could produce conscripts for six-month contracts only with "great exhortation and promises of punishment."[83]

In 1919, ten years into his service in Moribane, Ferreira proposed that the yearlong contract "not be suspended temporarily . . . but rather eliminated absolutely." A yearlong contract "might be logical if all the tasks undertaken—whether in agriculture or in mining—required specialized skills, whereas the work for which contract laborers are destined is not specialized at all . . . but rather is limited to agricultural tasks which all natives learn from childhood in their villages."[84] He based his objection on the logic of labor efficiency, a rationale that echoed Portugal's own colonial labor code, which had justified forced labor as the only way to achieve productive economic activity, in view of what the labor law's authors saw as the "natural inferiority [of] the half-savage African."[85] Ferreira himself did not express his views on the question of racial inferiority, but a humane perspective surfaced toward the end of his proposal. The yearlong contract should not be imposed since "the contract is repugnant to all natives. Many times I have said it and once more I put it in writing. All recruitment, for the native, represents violence." Conscription was of little utility if it created "an unnecessary and general ill will among the natives."[86] Stationed as he was in a border district, Ferreira would have been all too aware of how discontent could lead to out-migration. His was the classic dilemma—caught between meeting his responsibilities and coping with the attendant political and economic costs that were sure to follow.

Ferreira had picked up, though without referring to it, the critique Freire de Andrade had made nearly a quarter century earlier when the company failed to keep to the terms of its "contracts." Of a contingent of 335 workers sent to work on maize farms in 1924, about 220 abandoned work the next year, before their replacements arrived, but only, Ferreira said, because the replacements were late and the first group had been kept past the period for which they had been contracted: "It is true that agriculture has its needs," but "it is also true that what has been undertaken must be adhered to, and in my opinion, the latter takes precedence over the former. That which has been agreed to must be carried out."[87] Ferreira's was a rather radical claim that Africans' rights ought to take precedence over Europeans' perceived needs. Nor did he seem to mind his maverick status within the company administration, seeing himself as something of a prophet proclaiming the truth, as he wrote in his first semester report for 1920 that, "without doubt, I am, as one says, crying in the wilderness."[88] He pursued it further and, later that year, cheered the League of Nations' decision that state authorities such as himself should not conduct labor recruitment for private employers. He wrote, in a 1925 report, that "it was with no small pleasure that I learned of" the league's ruling against government involvement in labor recruitment activities.[89]

After the company abolished its native labor department in the wake of the League of Nations' investigation of labor practices in Portuguese African colonies, Ferreira's report for 1926 carried an almost celebratory note. He "congratulated [himself] for having put an end to forced labor . . . [and] offered respectful reverence to the Governor" who issued the order. He referred to "the many years [he] had pursued a campaign against" the existing system of forced labor, citing his prediction of 1918 that the system could not continue.[90] His campaign and his past criticism had "earned [him] the slur of a negrophile," Ferreira said calmly, but "it didn't trouble me as my conscience rested well.[91]

Ferreira's letters and reports reveal that the international debate over what forms of labor were considered acceptable in a European-dominated Africa had circulated not only between London, Lisbon, and Geneva but also extended to the backwoods of the Mozambique–Southern Rhodesian borderlands. His words suggest that he largely shared the principles behind the system he helped operate, above all a belief in African inferiority and incompetence when it came to making decisions about work. Yet if those participating in the conversation agreed on the underlying principles, the very ambiguity contained therein made it difficult to maintain coherence as the conversation stretched out over time and space. Consensus there may have been on the supposed benefit of European colonial rule; no such consensus existed on how such benefit should be made concrete, or to what extent it might justify a measure of coercion and brutality. Ferreira was the most consistently dissident voice. Freire de Andrade, perhaps, personified more the ambivalence and ambiguity, as expressed early in his career, in his admission of a basic lack of fairness in the company's contracts, even though, as district administrator, he imposed them. As Freire de Andrade rose through the colonial hierarchy, and he moved far from that middle-ground position to an exalted height, representing Portugal in Geneva, his view became more two-dimensional. Now seemingly less concerned with fairness for Africans, he showed little of the frankness he expressed two decades earlier in Manica, and in Geneva, defending Portugal's interests before the world, was complacent about the coercion necessary for "persuading" Africans to work for settlers or for the state. Frank talk, such as there was, remained the stuff of the men in the middle and their internal correspondence and memos to senior officials whose orders they followed.

## African Critiques of Forced Labor: "Slanderous Propaganda"

Africans' critique of forced labor was no less pointed than that of Ferreira, but, mindful of the menace they faced, its appearance was considerably more oblique. Actions often took the place of words. When the rains failed in 1902 and crops withered in the fields, Africans in Manica asked the district administrator for famine relief, whereupon the administrator told them they were welcome to maize flour from the company's stocks as long as they paid for it in labor. Only one African accepted the offer, the rest preferring to forage in Manica's hills and forests for "famine foods"—such as wild roots, time-consuming to prepare and without the flavor of cultivated crops—rather than surrender even that measure of freedom to the company.[92] Seven years later, when drought struck the Zambezi Valley district of Sena and the district administrator threatened to withhold food relief, the African population informed him that they preferred "to eat roots and wild fruits than to go to . . . Manica where they would die."[93]

Forced laborers at work in Manica or elsewhere had only limited opportunities to protest openly; many were hundreds of miles from home and could communicate neither with their African coworkers of different ethnic and linguistic backgrounds nor with Portuguese-speaking officials. They could register a protest with the local secretary for native affairs, but to leave the field to go to the secretary's office in the district center took some desperation. In Manica, it was a journey of ten miles or more, and workers en route risked seizure by any white man they met, since company regulations permitted employers to capture workers who had fled or "showed clear intentions to leave work." Employers were, however, forbidden to secure the *capturados* with handcuffs, fetters, or neck yokes, practices apparently common, one assumes, in light of the regulations banning them.[94]

Further, at Macequece, the district center, protesting workers would have had to speak through an interpreter who might have been unfamiliar with their language or a member of the much-feared police force. Even some complaints faithfully and accurately transmitted were ignored, or worse—an appeal to the company administration could bring further punishment.[95] João Pery de Lind, the district administrator in Manica who went on to become the territory's longest-serving governor, ridiculed workers' "daily pilgrimages" to his office to register complaints he considered as fabrications.[96] When a group of twelve left Manica in 1908 to walk to Mossurize, 150 miles distant, to protest beatings by their employer and the district administration, the administrator in Mossurize dismissed their charges of unjust punishment as lies and ordered them to walk back to Manica.[97]

Sadzungira, a chief from Gorongosa, took a rare open stand in 1928 against the contracting of his people when, so a labor agent reported, the treatment of one contingent, composed mostly of children, "resulted in many having died and others returning to their villages crippled." When the agent sought to contract more workers, Sadzungira flatly declared he "would not supply any natives . . . as long as we did not inform him of what happened to two boys from the previous contingent." The agent, who knew that the two had died in a hospital hundreds of miles distant, reported to his superior that "satisfactory results" were unlikely.[98]

Company conscripts from Mossurize "complained constantly," according to the district administrator there, about receiving wages in depreciated Portuguese silver. "Among them prevails the belief," he noted, "that we keep the gold we receive from the employers who use them so as to pay them in silver."[99] Many African men in Mossurize knew from working in South Africa's mines of the difference in currency values and believed, quite correctly, that the company was engaged in currency arbitrage at their expense. Their counterparts in Moribane, also with mine experience, had a similar view of contract labor under the native labor department, "seeing that it paid little and this little bit in depreciated currency."[100] When post–World War I inflation eroded the value of silver even more, Africans "became reluctant to accept it, fearing that from one moment to the next it might be worth even less." Or, as the director of native labor put it, "the native knows very well the value of the pound."[101]

In one of the few instances in which Africans' protests did produce results, laborers from the Zambezi Valley districts of Chemba and Tambara reported, in 1923, that, while working on maize farms in Manica and Chimoio, they had been beaten, received poor and insufficient rations, and denied rest and medical care. The administrator from Chemba acknowledged that the "effect this had could not be worse," causing "rumors to fly that many had died . . . with others left blind and lame due to the ill-treatment they received."[102] His counterpart in Macequece took the unprecedented step of overseeing an investigation, the results confirming that some of the district's farmers beat, ill fed, and poorly housed their workers, and forced them to work at night and during official hours of rest.[103] When the administrator warned Manica's employers against such "abuses and infractions," the district's farmers wrote to the governor, denying all the charges, attributing the report to Africans' "laziness," and tarring the administrator as rude, disrespectful, and unbalanced.[104] The governor took no action against the farmers and transferred the administrator out of Manica District.[105]

In Macequece, after a man named Dick advised eight newly contracted workers in 1928 that they should refuse to be "recruited" because to do so was "to be sold," four of the eight attempted to back out of the contract. Dick was sent to the district administrator for unspecified "correction."[106] Another man warned others in neighboring Chimoio District that if they found work on their own as *voluntários*, they would be better paid, could avoid physical abuse, and need work only as long as they chose. A labor recruiter complained that the man's words made "the contract odious," and the company imprisoned the man.[107] In Moribane, in 1927, a man named Zaba spoke words of "slanderous propaganda," in the words of the labor agent there, warning contracted laborers that they were to be sent to work in the mud. The laborers fled, probably because, as the director of native affairs reported, Zaba's warning carried more weight "than a thousand words from a white man."[108] Zaba had spoken out at a time when Portuguese colonial labor practices faced international scrutiny, and the company's subsequent, if momentary, wavering may have emboldened him. Before long, words like Zaba's became an offense punishable by a sentence of correctional labor of up to two years.[109] Such denunciations and warnings failed to move those who oversaw the system, but they bear witness to Africans' sense of enslavement and their willingness to risk the consequences of protest.

# 4

# Mobility and Tactical Flight

## Of Workers, Chiefs, and Villages

THE GAZA EMPIRE, FOUNDED BY REFUGEES FROM warring that followed the Zulu state's expansionary conquest in present-day South Africa, occupied much of Mozambique south of the Zambezi River from the 1830s to 1895. Before Gaza was vanquished by Portugal, its soldiers made regular visits to villages in central Mozambique to demand tribute in animal skins, livestock, and, sometimes, people, usually conducting such raids during the dry season, when movement was easier and because, in the post-harvest period, people would be concentrated in their villages.[1] Raiding parties raised plumes of dust, advance signals to villagers in the higher-lying valleys, where lookout posts could spot the rising dust. If signal fires or a drum raised the alarm, many villagers abandoned their huts and hid in mountaintop refuges.[2]

When, in 1997, I asked people in Manica what they knew of Gaza's past over-rule and how local communities had responded to it, several told me the story of the village of Munzongo. One day, people of the village, grown weary of danger-ous hide-and-seek from predatory raiders, prepared a poisonous beverage from the root of the arum lily, or *nzongo,* filling numerous drinking pots with the liq-uid. Then they left the pots in plain view and took flight. When the Gaza soldiers arrived in the empty village, tired and with dry throats, and saw the full drink-ing pots, they slaked their thirst, and died one by one.[3] Munzongo means "place of the poisonous root." The people of Munzongo, outmatched in weaponry and numbers, had used what they had: knowledge of local plants and familiarity with the mountainous terrain. Villagers' tactics of response changed little (though without the poison) as Portugal and the Mozambique Company replaced Gaza as the imperial power in the region. As others had earlier, villagers arranged not to be in the vicinity when company raiding parties came. Africans in Manica knew that when they faced uncompromising demands backed up with pillage, violence, and the threat of violence, their first and most effective counterstrategy was to melt into the hills.

In the aftermath of the "Scramble" for Africa, in which rival European powers vied for control over African territory, both the Mozambique Company and Cecil Rhodes's British South Africa Company hastened to demarcate their territorial claims. But European designs could not eliminate Africans' mobility and their sense of flexible territorial divisions. Although Portugal's and Britain's treaties of the 1890s "fixed" the borders between Portuguese and British companies, imposing a new political geography by creating administrative divisions within a single colony, or dividing adjoining districts, Africans used one against the other and drew on a reservoir of memory of earlier marauders to contest the enslaved labor that accompanied colonial rule.

## Borders and Borderlands:
## "Several Chiefs Have Fled, with All Their People"

In Manica, where the Mozambique Company's activity was most concentrated, a district administrator remarked: "Manica is simultaneously the district with the greatest demand for labor and where the population in scarcest."[4] The paradox was a consequence of Africans' tactics of evasion. Many parts of the territory were far less densely populated than Manica, but villagers there employed the most effective defenses against colonial control. Relocating a village was one of the first and most effective tactical moves to avoid the company's tax collection and labor conscription.

Manica's district administrator, hunting for Africans who had fled to high mountain redoubts along a bush path that "traced the steepest of slopes along which one false step would mean a fall of fifty meters," discovered exceptionally fertile—and well-watered—soil.[5] He wrote in the log of his eleven-day journey, "But the blacks? The truth is that the blacks [are] missing."[6] The lands were "depopulated." The inhabitants of a small village, "as hidden as could possibly be imagined," had "without doubt selected its location in hopes of dodging tax payment and the police who sought them for service."[7] Perhaps fearing a superior's reprimand for having provoked the villagers' flight, the administrator blamed the unsettled borderlands on the neighboring British colonizers: "Anglo-Saxons rob and mistreat in an almost unbelievable fashion."[8]

In 1896, the Manica District administration recorded an African population of 1,289; three years later the census topped 3,100, reflecting a growing bureaucratic ability to compel people to register. Nonetheless, women registered outnumbered men by 1,255 to 692. The men, aware of the direct connection between census taking and seizure for forced labor, were hiding in the bush.[9] In Gorongosa, too, the administrator reported, with concern, that many men were hiding out in the bush to escape conscription.[10] Just as past generations had sought safety from Gaza raiders by crossing the boundary that separated the settled space of the village from the protective bush, so crossing that divide offered once more at least temporary refuge.

Other villagers devised an alternative tactic: camouflage. Since the district secretary homed in on huts to record the population and demand payment—a hut tax (levied on each dwelling) rather than a head tax—some villagers disguised their huts as granaries. The secretary, and often even the African *cipai* (a policeman, usually not a local), could not distinguish one from the other.[11] The district administrator noted with annoyance, "They hoodwink the tax-collector with ease, while there are others who hide their huts far from the villages . . . managing easily to elude us."[12]

Even before white farmers unable to work their land without African labor turned the region along the rail line into a primary destination for the company's modern slaves, the administrator in Chimoio wrote to his superior in Manica of his careful balancing act between sending the police out on recruitment sweeps and maintaining the African population. His letter opened with a reference to the "frequent flight" of villages, detailing the loss of more than 300 taxpayers in the 1902 census. He lamented recent orders to send 250 men to Manica, beyond the 300 or so already working for the company in Chimoio, who had been acquired only through "a true struggle." The administrator advised his superior that he had "no desire whatsoever that any responsibility, however small, should rebound upon me for the abandonment" of the district. He warned that, "should we continue in this fashion, I shall one day have the unhappy occasion to announce that the country is depopulated."[13]

The Chimoio administrator's counterpart in Moribane met similar tactics when 150 conscripts, returning from a stint as rubber collectors, spread the news of their miserable experience, whereupon "several chiefs have fled, with all their people."[14] The administrator reported: "Seven villages in the chieftaincy of Macuio are abandoned, in the lands of the chief Muitanda there is not a single black and the chief himself fled, leaving abandoned his fields which I myself saw invaded by hundreds of monkeys. It is a shame to see the success of tens of people completely lost to them but taken over by the monkeys."[15]

Tactical flight was especially effective along the company's more than 600-mile frontier with British-ruled Southern Rhodesia, where the border had split many communities and chiefdoms of shared language and ancestry. In other regions, where the border followed the landscape of rivers or mountain ranges, much like the boundaries of communities or polities in times past, the borderlands offered convenient cover. As Manica's district secretary discovered, in the chiefdom of Machipanda, people lived on the British side of the border but planted their fields in Mozambique Company territory, thus "paying the hut tax neither to us nor to the English."[16] Company administrators tracked cross-border movements as vigilantly as they could, paying closest attention to chiefs, many of whom had attempted to elude the competing colonial powers who had sought their submission (see illustration 18). Some chiefs crossed from Portuguese into British territory (others in the opposite direction), even abandoning ancestral lands to avoid pursuers.[17] Nor did borderland residents hesitate to move from one imperial sphere to the other. The company sometimes found such mobility suited its own interests; accordingly, when, in 1903, the British South Africa Company doubled its tax (a head tax rather than a hut tax) from ten shillings to a full pound, the Mozambique Company shrewdly held its hut tax at ten shillings, expecting, as the administrator in Moribane put it, that "in these conditions a large number of natives will cross into the Territory of the Mozambique Company," as, late that year, they had done even before the tax hike went into effect.[18]

One mines department director suggested that the company establish a treaty with the British "so that the [Africans] might not be able to pass from one side to the other of the frontier according to their wishes, which has produced here in Manica curious situations. A native chief puts himself on one side of the border while his people are found on the other; there are natives who do something similar in sending their wives to settle to the east of the dividing line while they remain to the west; and still others who live alternatively on one side or the other." By such tactics, the mines department director wrote with some grudging admiration, people could reduce their taxes or avoid paying them altogether.[19] As with any other porous barrier, cross-border movement could go in one direction or the other, a reality recognized by an administrator who saw the tax burden as "only one of the factors that can contribute to stimulate migratory movement, either for or against us."[20]

As the company's conscription efforts intensified, the border increasingly served as an escape route. When, in late 1910, the administrator in Moribane sought to round up a final five men to complete a forced labor gang quota of twenty-five, ten entire villages decamped to Southern Rhodesia. "They say, and it is true," he explained to his superior, "that when the last contingent returned home [the previous month] in November, they were told that they could go rest and would not be called for work, while a week later the police showed up conducting a recruitment."[21] Moribane's borderland location—it abutted Southern Rhodesia to the west and the vast and underpoliced company district of Mossurize to the south—combined with the company's intensified targeting of Africans for forced labor to generate a stream of out-migration. It was commonplace for the administrator there to report the local population heading toward the south of the territory and westward over the border into the British colony. The administrator in Moribane pointed out to his superior in Manica that "the cause of the flight of these natives is well known: their hatred for work. They say that in the districts of Mossurize and Buzi and even in English territory, there is no work [requirement]." In fact, Africans there toiled hard to wrest a living from the soil and resented being forced to work for others, especially in rubber collection service, work they regarded as "an abomination."[22]

Somewhat farther south along the border with Southern Rhodesia, the administrator from Mossurize wrote of the "dangers of the emigration of our natives to English territory, these difficulties are permanent." Referring to his previous correspondence and reports, he reminded the governor that "the native of this region has the greatest repugnance [to forced labor in Manica]. . . . I have constantly recruited natives for the mines and pressed the chiefs to supply people for Macequece, and for this reason this year I do not have the increase in huts that the district ought to have, because many natives, to avoid serving in Manica, emigrated to . . . English territory."[23] A few months later, he tallied nearly 150 households that had migrated to Southern Rhodesia, the chiefs reporting that their people had left "owing to the constant requests for workers for Manica and the trifling salaries" they brought home after five months' absence.[24]

The porous frontier was only one such frontier; central Mozambique was scored by many boundaries, each with its own borderland. Along the northern and southern reaches of the territory, Africans could look across the Zambezi and Save rivers into lands Portuguese-governed but not company-ruled. For those in the company's southern districts of Mossurize and Govuro, the Sul do Save (comprising the southern provinces of the colony) was governed by the Portuguese colonial state no less exploitatively than by the company itself, and under the same labor code, if with a thinner presence on the ground. More important, southern Mozambique was along the path to South Africa's Witwatersrand, where earning opportunities were far beyond those available in Mozambique, despite the rigid racial hierarchy of the labor market and the workplace. At the other end of the territory, the African population had only to cross the Zambezi River into territory where the Portuguese colonial state governed with a harsh but somewhat looser hand. In Gorongosa, increasingly a target for the company's conscription activities, the administrator confessed, "My fear is that they—as their belongings weigh little and their housing costs nothing—they will take off for the lands of Zambezia."[25]

## To Combat the Company's "Nightmare": Deportation, Extended Labor, Beatings with the *Palmatória*

When Africans left for British lands, it was a triple blow to the Mozambique Company: loss of laborers, erosion of the tax base, and concrete evidence that Africans preferred life under British rule than under Portuguese rule, an always sore point for nationalists within company ranks. The secretary general termed Africans' flight a "great loss," a "devaluation" of the territory. The inspector general put it more plainly: "Our native population is not large and as they represent one of our chief sources of revenue every endeavour should be made to make them contented to remain in the territory."[26] The governor, imagining his administrators' thinking, summed up their challenge: "If I don't supply natives, it will contribute directly to the ruin of the businesses that request them. If I do supply them . . . I will see fleeing from my district hundreds of head or hut taxes, and I will have eliminated important sums of the company's budgeted revenue, whose amount I cannot calculate."[27] One newly appointed (and, as it turned out, short-serving) administrator in Gorongosa described recruitment for Manica as "the nightmare of my existence as administrator of this district, for I don't know how to explain this refusal for work in Macequece. I have to enlist in this passive war and go on supplying workers for Manica in homeopathic doses, employing gentle methods so as not to set off an emigration such as that which already took place in the lands of Maringue."[28]

The company resorted at times to severe means to counter African mobility, including long stints of "correctional" labor or deportation to São Tomé (long distant, off the west African coast), where forced laborers from all corners of Portugal's far-flung empire—including some from lands as distant as southern China—were dispatched to work on cocoa plantations in what often amounted to a life sentence.[29] Other responses were more prosaic, such as beatings with the familiar *palmatória*, the perforated wooden paddle. But aware that Africans might flee or "tread lightly when they hear that labor recruiters are about," as one district administrator in Moribane put it, the company reached for more effective counterstrategies to solve the "native labor problem," chief among them laws and practices designed to limit mobility. In 1909, it became a crime for any African to leave the territory without permission from the administrator in his or her home district. Unauthorized movements were "clandestine emigration," an offense that carried a sentence of up to twenty months of unpaid "correctional" labor.[30] The district administration in Manica routinely imprisoned Africans, sometimes simply for "not being able to establish their identity" or "bearing passes that did not belong to them."[31] Some who tried to leave their districts had encouragement, so the district administrator in Manica reported, as he sent under guard to Beira seven African men he described as "agents of clandestine emigration." He listed them by name, though because four had been arrested for carrying passes other than their own, it is unclear how he identified them. All had been caught in Manica, most along the border, and he suspected them of attempting to recruit workers for Southern Rhodesian mines.[32] Persons accused of enlisting others to leave faced a double sentence of forty months.[33]

When Rhodesian mines secretly sent recruiters into the territory, a practice the Manica District administrator termed a "scourge," the company lodged complaints with the British administration and fined Europeans—"mostly Greeks and Italians, but also Englishmen"—caught trying to entice Africans across the border.[34] When the clandestine recruiters were African, the penalties were far harsher. Because Africans arrested for such offenses could seldom afford to pay fines assessed, and because company officials were convinced that Africans "didn't consider prison a punishment," they compelled such captives to work without pay, often for the department of public works.[35] The English manager for Mozambique Mines, seizing one African he believed to be a clandestine recruiter in the employ of a Southern Rhodesian mine operator, did not trouble to contact the company administrator, but ordered the man "to be roped and . . . punished by frequent flogging and very prolonged imprisonment as a severe warning to others such who, hearing of such just desserts [sic], may be deterred from repeating this growing and all too prevalent practice on the part of unscrupulous persons who instruct them to come or allow it."[36]

João Mascarenhas Manuel de Mendonça Gaivão, who, in 1911, replaced the influential and well-connected João Pery de Lind as Manica's administrator, urged his predecessor—as of 1912, governor—to take note of the fact that "there is no doubt that the migratory flow has not weakened," notwithstanding the frontier patrols he directed and the new police outposts he had established. It was something of a losing battle, since "the black who might want to emigrate shuns the roads." Like some counterparts, Gaivão urged preemptive rather than reactive measures. The "only truly effective way" to combat the flow, he claimed, "is in the manner of treating him, of feeding him, of paying him. When the native feels better among us than in Rhodesia, the emigration will cease, because, contrary to what many people think, he has love for his land."[37]

Gaivão's assessment was echoed in observations by others farther up the company's administrative hierarchy. The director of the native labor department, following a mid-1914 visit of Sena, a district that had supplied more than 4,500 conscripts annually over the previous three years, wrote to his agent in Manica (where many conscripts had been sent) of "the discontentment which reigns among the native population, due above all to the less than humane way in which some farmers have treated the workers."[38] The effect was to send hundreds of people, "including entire villages," in flight from the territory. The director proposed that his agent might supervise work conditions on the farms in Manica more closely, adding that it was "unnecessary to point out the harm such inconveniences brought to the Company's interests." Likewise, the inspector general reported, their ill-treatment at the hands of Manica's white farmers led "a considerable number of Africans to emigrate for neighboring territories."[39]

In Govuro, abutting Portuguese colonial state-controlled southern Mozambique, the company's administrator emphasized the ease with which people emigrated. Not only was the border region extensive enough to be beyond effective surveillance, but, across the frontier, "they find the same land, the same practices, the same customs, friends, and relatives." Some administrators saw brutality as counterproductive; in Mossurize, the district administrator decided that rather than crush resistance, he would seek to accommodate it. He reported to the governor that "as much as possible I have avoided recruiting many people from the chiefs along the border." His prudence was well-founded, for, when "lately to satisfy the requests for workers for Manica I found myself forced to clamp down a bit more on recruitment in this region, it resulted in the removal [to Southern Rhodesia] of quite a number of huts."[40] Mobility posed such a risk to the company in Govuro that, though it conscripted more than 40 percent of the male population in 1913, none were sent outside the district for fear of triggering outmigration. In some chiefdoms there, located far in the interior and close to the border, leaders complied with company demands for men for close-by rubber collection; efforts to send them farther off for any other labor prompted widespread flight.[41] In response, the company declared fourteen of the district's chiefdoms, with a male population of 1,400, off limits to conscription for the "most violent" of all work, that is, work in the coastal mangrove swamps.

## The New Yearlong Labor "Contract":
## "Great Distrust and Discontentment among the Natives"

Countless recruited workers fled Manica, the patterns of their flight—reflected in meticulous data recorded by the company's labor department bureaucracy—testifying to careful planning more than impulse. Worker flight ebbed and flowed with the agricultural calendar, surging during October, November, and December, when the agricultural labor burden was highest and the pace of work most furious. Over a sixteen-year period, in the months of July through September (the relatively slack period in the annual agricultural cycle), the rate of flight was 5.4 per 100 conscripts. When white farmers drove their workers hardest, during the hot and wet months of October through December, when workers in the fields "suffered the most, exposed to the season's fiery sun and the torrential rain," the rate nearly doubled, to 9.5.[42] One company employee wrote that "Africans were forced to work under the rains and also because, being the most active time for agricultural work, the employers constantly policed their workers, seeking to extract the greatest amount of labor they could produce."[43] A complaint came from one group of farmers that workers' flight at harvest time one year could not be explained since "all in the district these days treat our workers well." True or not, it was tantamount to admission that in other days they treated their workers badly.[44]

Africans targeted for forced labor from September through March would have been especially unhappy, because this was the period when their labor was most needed at home, to support a family, especially important for younger married men under pressure to meet their in-laws' expectations or, perhaps, to produce a surplus of produce to sell on the growing market. Writing of the risk of large-scale flight, the administrator in the southern district of Mocoque mused, "I don't think there will be an exodus from the Territory, but it is not convenient to put the screws to them now, when the natives have [to] deal with their own farms."[45] The administrator in Gorongosa tactfully told the governor one November that, because it was planting season, a request to increase a recruitment demand "struck him as inconvenient."[46] Another local official in the Zambezi Valley reported that the only way he could send one group of 109 conscripts in October, "forcing them to abandon their own farm work," had been to promise an end-of-contract bonus on their return home.[47]

When the Spanish influenza pandemic struck the region during the 1918 growing season, flight was neither strategic nor fast enough to save workers. People began to die in Manica's villages, "possessed by such terror," wrote the district administrator, "that none would appear even to pay their hut tax, in order to avoid contact with the whites, who they believed to have transmitted the disease."[48] The governor prohibited Africans (and Asians) from leaving the district; by the end of October all the territory's schools were closed, and public events of any kind, including religious ceremonies, were banned. Only Europeans with medical clearance had freedom of movement.[49] Still, many African workers defied such orders. The director of mines told of a "wholesale stampede" as workers fled, leaving the mining industry in paralysis.[50] The resort to flight was, said the director of the native labor department, "a means of defense."[51] Many abandoned work and sought refuge in the bush; others died on the road on the way home.[52] The response by one contingent of forced laborers from the neighboring district of Moribane was typical; of its 240 men, nearly all had fled from work in Manica, and, by mid-1919, according to the administrator's accounting, 16 had died from influenza, 49 were unaccounted for, and the remaining 175 had been rounded up and sent back to Manica to fulfill their term of forced labor.[53]

As southern Africa recovered from the impact of World War I and the demand for African labor approached a new peak, the director of the company's labor department fretted, in his annual report for 1919, that his department "would be unable to supply any more" than the 23,439 forced laborers for work that year, and perhaps "unable to obtain even that number, which was . . . greater than previous years. . . . Thus, we must resort to other means to ease the labor crisis."[54] Other means were found. The company doubled the length of forced labor contracts to a full year. Under the six-month labor regime that had prevailed since 1911, African families could lose the labor of their adult and adolescent male members at a time of year when it was very much in need, but under the twelve-month contract that possibility became a dead certainty, threatening the survival of agrarian African households.

Senior company officials who had polled local officials as early as 1909 about a proposed twelve-month contract had learned that many of their own administrators thought the proposed increase "inconvenient" or "too much." The administrator in Mossurize stated plainly what other colleagues only hinted at: "One year was without question too long and would increase the number of natives who flee the work for which they are contracted."[55] When the company instituted the yearlong contract in 1919, from Mocoque came a report that "when it was determined that the contract would pass to twelve months there was great discontentment in the native population, which caused constant flight from their places of work." The long-serving administrator in Mossurize cautioned the governor that "it would produce a disastrous effect among the natives of the district." The people of the district "had been guaranteed in a meeting and in the presence of their chiefs that the contracts would never be for more than six months."[56] None of this was a surprise to those with experience, since when the company had, in 1911, without warning, extended labor contracts from four to six months, many workers had left two months before their contract's end. The company had broken its word, and the workers considered their obligation done, but as far as the company was concerned, they had "fled without a justifiable cause."[57]

Signaling its unswerving dedication to supply forced African labor, a 1919 company circular announcing the change in length of the contract began with the claim, "In tropical climates there can be neither agriculture nor industry without native labor."[58] In 1920, the company's native labor department seized more than 10,000 men for yearlong forced labor contracts. The total number of days worked by the company's 27,184 modern slaves increased that year by 80 percent, from just over 2.5 million to nearly 4.5 million.[59] Thousands of forced laborers fled: from 1920 to 1924, *evadidos* averaged more than 2,100 per year, or 7.4 per 100.[60]

Manica's district administrator, who served a short stint as secretary general when the yearlong contract was introduced, wrote later that he had been impressed "by the nearly universal clamour from the administrators, complaining of the decrease in population and the exodus out of the Territory, owing to the forced recruitments for the RTI [native labor department]." He admitted that the system was "a little violent," that in some districts the percentage of men taken was "very high," and, moreover, that "extraordinary recruitments" had been conducted in certain areas, "which are always poorly received because they violate existing understandings with African authorities."[61]

As administrators predicted, the numbers of *evadidos* reached unprecedented levels, provoking Manica's white farmers to make sweeping accusations against the long-serving district administrators in Moribane and Mossurize, blaming the flight on the "ill will" they "had always shown in recruiting workers." Buttressing the charge, the farmers claimed workers who fled from the two districts "tell their work companions from other districts that they are not afraid to run off, because the administrator of their district will neither catch nor punish them." The farmers maintained that, before sending the workers on their way, the administrators had given them "some advice . . . that provoked their flight." Whereas previously, so the farmers claimed, workers from the two districts seldom fled, now "they were the first to do so . . . some without even knowing the employer for whom they would work." The farmers complained that, in all the other districts, "great care is taken to capture *evadidos*," but that in Moribane and Mossurize, "the fugitives are never captured." Unable to "undo the unfounded suspicions," the administrator in Manica could only explain that recruitment in the two districts had risen greatly over the previous year (in Moribane, the percentage of men taken nearly doubled from 1920 to 1921), and that the increase in contract length to twelve months had caused "great distrust and discontentment among the natives." The director of the native labor department seconded the explanation.[62]

## Africans Voting with Their Feet: "Ai Khona!" (Never There!)

Even when captured and brought to work for the company or for one of the territory's private employers, forced laborers continued to rely on mobility to defend their personal sovereignty. In Moribane, where the company seized forced laborers for wild rubber collection on a privately held concession, an administrator wrote of the flight of a number of chiefs and their followers. After 150 conscripts in the service of the French national concession holder returned to spread the news of their terrible experience, "one of the chiefs who fled . . . to a perch high on the range, with his people and armed with rifles, called down [to the company police]: 'Come here if you can. You don't have anything to do here—I have no dispute with the Company. . . . but to go there to work for Mzungo França, *ai khona* [never there]!'"[63]

As Manica's white settler farming community entered its stage of peak growth, in the years leading up to World War I, the district administrator in Chemba reported, at the height of one agricultural season: "Forty-five fugitive workers showed up yesterday from Manica, spreading to the seven winds that they were badly treated there, so much so that they were forced to take such measures. They might have reason on their side or not, but what is certain is the negative impact this has among the population at large, which is no simple thing to undo in short measure."[64] When he was district administrator in Manica in September 1908, João Pery de Lind acknowledged that worker flight had affected his supervision of the African workforce. More than 1,000 Africans were at work there at the time. Pery de Lind did think that Africans "might need to be punished once in a while," but, worried about employers' ill treatment, he wrote, "I must confess that I am in general less severe not out of soft heartedness, but to instill confidence in them and ease recruitment."[65]

In 1908, the well-balanced interdependence of Manica's settler mining and maize economy had begun to unravel under the combined effect of bad luck and settler inefficiency. Two of the largest mining companies—Mozambique Mines and Manica Copper—already short of cash, had missed payments to their creditors early in the year. Among those to whom money was owed were the district's farmers who had supplied maize on credit to the miners, by then grown dependent on locally grown low-cost foodstuffs to feed their workforce.[66] The cash crunch rippled through Manica's economy, particularly among the white farmers; most lacked the funds to pay the company for their workers, and with crops in the field to be weeded and harvested, could ill afford to reduce their workforce. But the situation was about to worsen. In anticipation of the winter dry season, the high point for mining activity, two other mines—Edmundian Copper, one of the district's largest private employers, and the Paradox Mine—drastically reduced their workforce in the process of installing new equipment, a retrenchment that further depressed the local demand for maize just as harvest time approached, when the farmers otherwise would have expected their situation to improve. Fortunately for them, the company broke its own regulations and allowed farmers to keep their involuntary laborers on credit, in effect, a bridge loan until their finances improved. Manica's district administrator, Pery de Lind, began to earn his reputation as a champion of white farmers' and miners' interests, as he allowed insolvent farmers to pay the company in maize flour for their workers.[67] The farmers, who would have had to scale back their plantings for the coming agricultural year, drew encouragement from his support and, rather than cutting back, planned expansion of their fields.

But in April of that year, East Coast fever, a deadly tick-borne cattle disease, was detected. Pery de Lind's response was immediate and unyielding; he banned all movement of cattle within the district, no doubt reminded of the rinderpest epidemic that had ravaged the region's livestock population a decade earlier.[68] Without ox-drawn wagons to transport maize and maize flour, farmers were unable to get newly harvested crops to market to generate badly needed income— or to pay the company in kind for their workers. In desperation, they began using their laborers as porters to transport maize, since the few voluntary workers they employed would have refused this much disliked work. Loaded with fifty-kilogram sacks of maize and forced to work into the night, human carriers could not equal the work of a span of oxen. The farmers increased their requests for company laborers, forcing them to move even more maize to pay the company for their labor. By mid-September, just days after the new conscripts' arrival in Manica, 112 decided they had had enough and fled.[69]

Of the 112 *evadidos*, 76 came from Sena, the most populous district in the territory, where for more than a decade the company had drawn tens of thousands of forced laborers. People from Sena, by 1908, had a generation's experience working for the Sena Sugar Estates, a vast Zambezi Valley sugar plantation abutting Mozambique Company territory; a British-owned company, Sena Sugar had the right to conscript its own labor force. Backbreaking work, poor and insufficient food, and physical abuse were nothing new, but, the *evadidos* reported, in Manica they had also been forced to work deep into the night, long past the ringing of the bell that marked sundown, the end of the legal workday.[70] Therefore, they had departed for their home districts in Sena. They voluntarily presented themselves to the district administrator there; they had been maltreated, they said, and were willing to accept punishment for their flight. The administrator in Sena sent the evidence the *evadidos* had given to Pery de Lind; their "frank testimony delivered with some indignance . . . led him to vouch for their truthfulness."[71] To extend working time, their employer "had not wanted them to urinate or defecate except right on the spot where they and their fellows were working." "Now, the native," the administrator continued, "however savage, has some modesty in these matters." On their first refusal to obey, they had been pummeled; on the second, their employer lashed them with a hippo-hide whip. On the third day, they went to the district center to lodge a complaint, where each received six strokes with the *palmatória*.[72] Receiving a beating rather than a hearing was more than they would bear, and they had fled. Some asked for a transfer to Sena Sugar Estates, "where, they say, they won't receive such thrashings and can attend to their needs at will."[73]

Even Pery de Lind, the employers' champion, acknowledged that most of the farmers "became excessively demanding and some of them—hot-tempered in character and education—excessively strict."[74] Pery de Lind now ordered for his district native affairs staff to "exercise maximum vigilance" in their workplace inspections; they were to pay special attention to enforcement of regulations on housing, meals, and working hours.[75] He issued other instructions directly to the district's employers, admonishing them to uphold company regulations on worker treatment and pointing out that abusive practices tended to contribute to Africans' "reluctance to service in this district, thus making difficult or impossible [its] development." He warned Manica's white farmers and miners that should workers flee because of employer abuse, the company would not send replacement workers. "Either the native is up to the work for which he was supplied or not," he wrote in closing. "If he is up to it, then nothing justifies the harshness with which many treat them."[76] Within two years, Pery de Lind had become company governor, and his replacement in Manica was pursuing a different policy. When workers fled from Manica's farms, the district administrator ordered that their capture "must be undertaken with all zeal, in light of the incalculable effect on the natives seeing the reappearance of those who had fled."[77] The capture and return was an object lesson, intended, as one labor recruiter later put it, to make "workers understand the impossibility of being able to escape without them or their families being captured to complete the contract period."[78]

More than a decade later, forced laborers from Chemba at work on Manica's maize farms encountered a host of abuses, all in violation of company regulations. Beaten, ill and insufficiently fed, forced to work during mandated periods of rest, and denied medical treatment, a number fled. They were captured and returned to complete their contracts in Manica and Chimoio, and "were nearly forgotten . . . having to work several more months beyond their contract [period]."[79] An official observed "the natives' fear when he told them that they would be imprisoned and returned to the same farm" from which they fled.[80] Another official said, of six workers who fled from Chimoio after being beaten by a farmer there, they "have an enormous reluctance to return to the same boss, with fear of the reprisals that he might carry out and which, in general, are the norm."[81] He issued a directive two weeks later: if the workers were returned to the same farmer, it would be "convenient" for him not to practice the "customary vengeance."[82] The company's standard orders later instructed that captured *evadidos* be reassigned to other employers whenever there was "justified fear that employers might conduct reprisals against deserters."[83]

Employers' vengeful reprisals were only one reason why, for many, flight became less and less useful as a strategic defense against company conscription. Early after conquest, the new borders drawn between Portuguese and British colonies and the internal boundaries between different levels of administration first created fluid borderlands where villages and sometimes entire chiefdoms took refuge. With time, however, the company's reach extended into even these regions, and administrators punished flight from "recruitment" with beatings, sentences of "correctional" labor, or deportation for years of forced labor from which most never returned.[84] The increased pressure and such penalties meant that many conscripts took to their heels only as a last resort, with many of those who fled leaving the killing fields of Manica's white farmers, or because of concern about the impact of their prolonged absence on the families left behind. Personal mobility remained but a vestige of individual sovereignty, and the more successful strategies that Africans pursued involved engaging, in some fashion, with the company and the colonial economy it created.

Porters crossing the Revue River.

Hunting party.

Manica. Ox-drawn "Boer Cart."

Mozambique Company *cipais* in front of the Manica District headquarters.

Mozambique Company labor compound, Manica District.

Mine battery at the "Guy Fawkes" mine, Manica District.

Catholic mission, Macequece, Manica District.

Beira Railway train arrives, Macequece, Manica District.

Homestead gathering in the shade of a Baobab tree.

Mozambique Company employees on the courts, Macequece, Manica District.

Mozambique Company conscripts collecting night soil.

Mozambique Company public works conscripts making bricks.

River-crossing, on return from the mining area, Manica District.

Power generator on
the Munene River,
Manica District.

Processing the maize harvest, Manica District.

Field clearance with cattle-drawn plow.

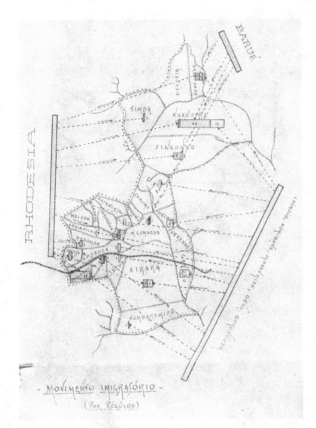

Migratory movement by
chiefdom, Manica District
census report for 1928.

Mule-drawn "Boer Cart."

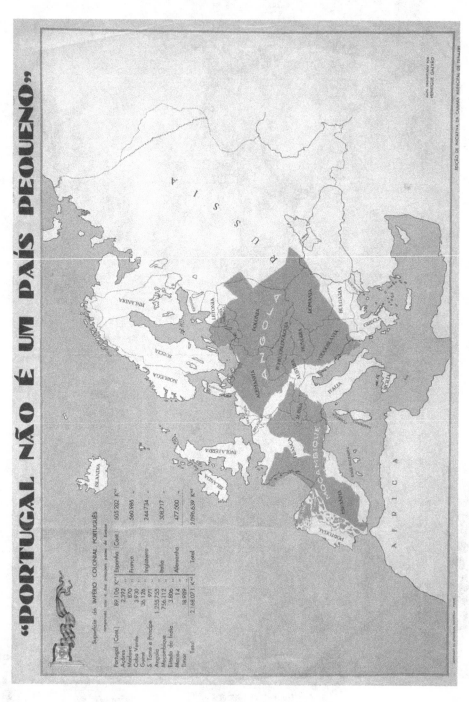

"Portugal is not a small country," ca. 1935, a "greater" Portugal, compared to Europe.

# 5

# Targeting Chiefs

## From "Fictitious Obedience" to
## "Extraordinary Political Disorder"

IN AUGUST 1895, MORIBANE, A CHIEF WHOSE LANDS
lay in central Mozambique's Manica Province, waited with trepidation the
arrival of Ezequiel José Bettancourt, an emissary of the Mozambique Company, which was seeking to impose its authority on the African population.[1] As
leader of large chiefdom in central Mozambique, and with authority over a siz-
able population, Moribane was a prime target. Moribane was aware the company
governor, Joaquím José Machado, had dispatched Bettancourt to win obedient
consent to pay tribute, and, like many other African rulers in their encounters
with European colonizers, Moribane faced an impossible choice: submission or
ruin. He tried a strategy in between. (To many Africans the company *was* "Machado," the man at its head and the power it wielded synonymous.[2]) Moribane
put out a call for hundreds of men in his chiefdom to arm themselves and gather
in his *kraal*; he knew Bettancourt would cross paths with the armed and hostile
men on his journey, and discover their destination. Although a show of force
might rouse Machado's anger, Moribane decided it was his strongest hand to play.

Moribane had for several decades already recognized a sovereign's dominion, but that one came from the African continent itself: Gungunhana, king of
the Gaza empire, who held sway over much of central and southern Mozambique, had sent his representatives to Moribane. Moribane had accepted them,
paid tribute to Gaza, and directed his followers to do the same. But the new
demand, from the Portuguese Mozambique Company, was not African, and it
was, in effect, a demand for a double tribute. Acknowledging one suzerain would

provoke the competing other; compliance with the Portuguese empire builders' ultimatum would bring swift and almost certain reprisal from Gaza, whose soldiers, stationed in Moribane's home village, would resent his receiving Machado's emissary, much less his acceding to his demands. Therefore, when Bettancourt arrived, he found nearly 500 of Moribane's men, armed with rifles, massed there, and distinctive among them Gaza soldiers adorned in animal skins. Bettancourt's own African porters were "infused with visible terror" by Moribane's martial display.[3] At Moribane's side stood the leader of the Gaza military unit, the Gaza elder distinguished by his one eye and by a head-ring to mark his seniority. As the Portuguese envoy approached, the armed men shouted until Moribane ordered silence and demanded to know of Bettancourt "what he wanted and had come to do in his land."[4] Bettancourt replied with questions of his own: why had he been met with armed men, and why, as he traveled on the way, had Moribane's people refused to let him purchase food supplies? The harvest had not long passed, and with people's granaries full to bursting, a surplus sufficient to feed Bettancourt and his porters along their journey could readily have been spared. With his retort, the crafty Portuguese had slipped in an implicit criticism—lack of hospitality to a visitor, a transgression of local norms. It was not his doing, Moribane responded, but by order of the Gaza soldiers.

Bettancourt requested shelter for the night, but Moribane took time to consider; he would talk over the matter with his advisers and the Gaza soldiers. But what did Bettancourt want of him, Moribane then asked. To collect the annual hut tax on each dwelling in Moribane's lands in return for protection from the Mozambique Company, Bettancourt replied. No, said Moribane; he paid taxes only to the Gaza state. Bettancourt disputed Gaza's tax-collecting authority and announced that unless the hut tax was paid to the company, Moribane would face war, and the company's forces would "burn and destroy him" and lay waste to his lands. Moribane refused nonetheless; he would, he said, recognize no authority but Gaza. Bettancourt left the following day.

A week after Bettancourt's departure, Governor Machado authorized a force to expel the Gaza soldiers and to "teach Moribane to pay taxes and supply people for Company works."[5] A month later, Machado ordered rebel villages "reduced to ashes and rebel supporters to be pursued and exterminated." A mixed force of military police and Portuguese settler volunteers arrived in Moribane, as the chiefdom was known, to demand the tax and compel recognition of the company's right to collect it.[6] Some accounts say that Moribane, after a brief skirmish, submitted; others say that he fled and that the company seized his goods as tax and appointed a new chief in his place. Still other stories say the company captured and imprisoned him.[7] In any event, less than a year later, the Mozambique

Company dispatched armed men throughout the territory to collect the tax, and succeeded, in some places, however, not just with a show of arms but with use of arms as well.

In reporting on Moribane's refusal, Bettancourt had complained that "our laughable authority . . . obtains at best a fictitious obedience."[8] Once the company stamped the authority of the Portuguese empire throughout the territory, using tactics not for the fainthearted, and especially after it created its native labor department fifteen years into its rule, the company extended its power and control over rural African communities. Local administrators regularly crisscrossed their districts, seeking out chiefs to ensure they would follow orders and record the numbers of men in each chiefdom considered eligible and "fit" for forced labor. The goal was to make chiefs the local extension of colonial authority and to co-opt them into its service.[9] There was no taking no for an answer; those whose cooperation the company sought had to maintain at least a facade of obedience.

## Chiefs Enforcing Orders "Given by the Musungus"

The Gaza empire's mid- to late-nineteenth-century tax levies and armed raids had been especially oppressive, but even indigenous local chiefs ruled with a measure of coercion and used their authority to extract wealth from their people, often claiming their labor for agricultural work.[10] Chiefs' power was perhaps greater when slave raiding and Gaza incursions made followers' separation from an established chiefdom a riskier venture.[11]

The success of the company's efforts in enlisting the chiefs as "indispensable allies," as one governor called them, was reflected, in turn, in the fear chiefs soon engendered. Before colonial conquest, chiefs' authority, though sometimes great, had been limited by local norms. Now it increasingly became accountable only to the company.[12] *Régulo,* a diminutive form of *rei* (king), was the term the company (and Portuguese administrators all over Africa) chose to refer to these rulers. It conveys the sense of an authority beyond which there is no recourse, a rule shorn of any principle of reciprocity or mutual obligation. There was a clear link between chiefs' authority and the *palmatória*-wielding African police company administrators could let loose if they chose. Followers who disagreed with or resented a chief's orders were careful to keep dissident thoughts to themselves; as one elderly man put it, recalling to me the tension of such relations, "you couldn't even let it show on your face."[13] The role of local enforcer, foisted upon chiefs, corrupted the basis of the chiefs' power, as it was based on an authority derived from mutual obligations. The new role of absolute untouchable rulers the company sought for chiefs was without such a basis. Unable to execute the company's orders as chiefs, they could only do so from a position as strongman, and not all chiefs accepted the mantle of absolutist authority. When some sent relatives and neighbors off for forced labor, "people understood that even the chief, too, was not responsible"; as elderly women and men told me when I spoke with them in 1997, in the end, "power rested with the Company."[14]

Chiefs were, for the most part, no more willing participants in the system than their followers were; but those who refused to realign themselves with the company put their status or even their liberty at risk, especially when their reluctance impeded police labor sweeps. Their status offered no protection from assault; one chief who declared that he "had no people to give" was whipped and bound, regaining his freedom only after the police took his money, his small stock, and the clothes off his back.[15] A chief who hesitated or refused to assist might face a beating, often with the *palmatória*. Continued lack of cooperation might bring imprisonment and even deposal and replacement by a more compliant candidate.[16] Some chiefs resisted indirectly, neglecting to report households or even entire villages to the census taker and countenancing their people's efforts to avoid tax and labor obligations.[17] But despite such evasive tactics, the company extended its reach. The expansion of gold-mining operations, border demarcation missions (Portuguese and British administrators continued to squabble over the precise location of the border), and more mundane mapping activities gradually reduced the number of resisting chiefs and narrowed the spaces in which people could hope to live relatively unmolested, even in the territory's 60,000-plus square miles, which were impossible to patrol by "mere police action."[18] Administrators needed local chiefs to surveil and control the population, which otherwise—as the district administrator in Chimoio expressed it—might "seek refuge in places that allow them to devote themselves to the loafing to which they are accustomed." The company's co-optation of the chiefs often bore success, as the Chimoio administrator discovered one year. Many huts—320—had disappeared from his district, but still the chiefs came almost weekly to district headquarters to report the flight of another village and thus to distance themselves from the actions of their fugitive people.[19] In Manica, chiefs' participation in annual tax collection greatly speeded the process. In 1908, the district secretary reported that more than three-quarters of the tax was paid in the first fifteen days. Laggardly payments, over another month, came primarily from those "who possess huts around Macequece and are not subject to any chief, which makes it more difficult" to collect their tax.[20] The delay from Africans living in or around the district center, with more and better cash-earning opportunities than those who lived in far outlying villages under the more direct control of a chief, pointed to the chiefs' central role in tax collection. When, in the midst of the 1919 census, several chiefs from the subdistrict of Moribane (like the chiefdom itself, named for the chief) fled with their people into the forest, the chief Moribane soon stepped forward to deliver the wayward chiefs and their followers, using his own authority to present them to the company. At Moribane's request, the administrator completed the census on the spot.[21]

Despite such victories, the steady compliance the company sought from chiefs themselves could not be secured by coercion alone. Some administrators, showing an entrepreneurial spirit typical of the first generations of colonial officers, improvised carrots to accompany the stick.[22] In some districts they offered a fixed cash payment, in others a gift in cash or goods, and in still others an exemption from the hut tax.[23] In Moribane's chiefdom, where the company had imposed its authority at gunpoint just three years earlier, the district administrator found the chief cooperative in helping to collect the hut tax in 1898 in view of his receiving $500 *reis* set aside from each tax payment. The chief explained, so the administrator said, the arrangement "was an order given by the *musungos* and as such only when they gave an order to the contrary would he stop receiving it."[24] Several years later the Moribane administrator reported that "several chiefs have fled, with all their people" rather than meet the labor recruitment quota. He seized their chiefs as an object lesson. "I have just caught—after three weeks of trying—Zichiche, the most important, and I hope that the others will return shortly, once they learn that he has been imprisoned and that those who assisted with recruitment received a small payment."[25]

Some district administrators also purchased chiefs' assistance in conscripting workers. In Mossurize, where the company typically sought mine workers for Manica, one administrator, for a time, paid chiefs 1$000 *reis* for each worker supplied. Learning of the practice, his counterpart in Manica fretted that paying some chiefs and not others might "produce a certain ill effect among the natives and even among [other] district administrators themselves."[26] The governor, noting the chiefs' "valuable" role in the conscription system, proposed standardizing the compensation they would receive, given that it was of the "highest importance that the Company have as exact a census as possible . . . from which might be calculated the number of hands available for work."[27] One of the benefits, according to the territory's *Revista de Manica e Sofala* (*Manica and Sofala Review*), was that the company distanced itself from "all that is disagreeable with this process, such as admonishing the natives to pay their tax, the forcible presentation of the laggardly, the denunciation of huts which might be hidden during the census—all this is the burden of the chiefs, who earnestly undertake the loathsome role given to them, beguiled by the handsome cut they receive."[28] The company's investment in the chiefs paid off quickly in what the governor, in his report for

1905, called a "progressive real increase in population." He predicted the rate of growth would accelerate once the tax collection regulations were in full effect, standardizing the census process and the percentages to be paid to chiefs, and the chiefs "become interested in the growth of their own area's population and cease to hide from the census taker some huts as they presently do."[29] Payments to chiefs were fixed at $250 *reis* (one shilling), at first deducted from the company's levy, but in 1911 the company began charging an additional $250 *reis* designated for payment to the chiefs so its own revenue was not reduced.[30]

In establishing the native labor department in 1911, the company enlisted the chiefs in its conscription operations and replaced individual administrators' improvisations with territory-wide standards. Two years later, in a poll initiated by the secretary general, local administrators explained the roles of themselves, their assistants, the company police, and local chiefs in the new vertical bureaucratic hierarchy, exerting downward pressure to force Africans out of their rural communities and into labor service for the company and private employers. Some praised the order that replaced a previously haphazard system, but said bluntly that it could not overcome all problems in those districts that sent the greatest number of forced laborers. One administrator typically gave the chiefs eight days' notice to produce their quota of conscripts, but, revealing the limits to the role thrust upon them, he reported the chiefs seldom could meet the quota, because "the chiefs do not have the moral force needed to compel those people to show up at the district headquarters; lacking the moral force, then follows the need for them to come request police to go do such work."[31]

The labor department aimed to integrate chiefs' authority and influence into its own operations, both in the initial seizure of forced recruits and over the length of its "contracts." Thus, on occasions when conscripts received an advance payment—nearly always destined for tax collection—their chief was designated a guarantor and held responsible for repayment should the *contratado* (contract worker) become an *evadido* (one who fled) before working long enough to pay off the tax advance.[32] The labor department's director proposed paying chiefs for each recruit turned over for a contract, "not only as compensation for the great labor and responsibility required of them in the work of recruitment, but also to induce them to carry out the propaganda necessary for greater acquisition of labor."[33] At the start of the recruitment period for the 1916 agricultural season, the company authorized the labor department to pay chiefs $12 *centavos* for each conscript, in light of the "great responsibility the chiefs assume and the sometimes violent work which requires them to spend lengthy periods of time outside of their villages."[34] But they were to receive the payments only after workers completed their contracts or had died or were sent home on medical orders. The director of the native labor department proposed further that if contract workers fled, their chiefs would receive payment only after the *evadidos* were captured and had completed the term of the contract, a provision, he suggested, that would lead chiefs to take "every care" in counseling contract workers not to flee from their place of work and, further, might motivate chiefs to help hunt down workers in flight.[35]

Two years later, the governor increased the payments—$15 *centavos* to chiefs for each worker sent on a six-month contract and $25 *centavos* for each on a twelve-month contract—but the company's board of directors vetoed the increase, whereupon chiefs from the Sofala District came forward to ask that contract lengths be reduced in light of the "great disorder" the longer contracts had brought to their villages.[36] When, in 1920, the company imposed the yearlong contract over the warnings of many of its own employees, and the numbers of *evadidos* rose, the department began to pay chiefs again for each worker recruited.[37]

When the labor department shut down in 1926, and the director compiled its final report, it included a 142-page listing of African authorities in the territory, with the names of more than 8,000 chiefs and headmen—one for every thirty-five Africans in the territory—and a tally of population figures for each chiefdom.[38]

## Chiefs Bartering Their Followers' Labor: Forced to Work "of Their Own Free Will"

The company's practice of enrolling chiefs as what one administrator would call "a government's best assistants" was not uniform; in some parts of the territory, district administrators had to adapt to the political terrain, which following the outcome of conquest was at times uneven.[39] In sweeping away the two great nineteenth-century Nguni empires and laying the foundation for European colonial rule, Portugal and Britain had scattered the people who lived along the eastern edge of the Great Zimbabwe plateau and fractured lines of authority among chiefs. Only a decade or more later did some of the displaced chiefs begin to return home, seeking to reoccupy their lands. When borderlands chiefs approached the company in hopes of resettling, their overtures received a warm reception from officials, who hoped to tap into the influence chiefs held over the wider population, since tracking down all reluctant hut tax payers or conscripts was practically impossible. Hence, it was with some satisfaction that João de Oliveira Amaral, the Manica District secretary for native affairs, wrote to the company governor, in 1903, that two relatives of the former paramount chief

Mutasa had now settled in the territory, leaving the British colony of Southern Rhodesia and showing "a willingness to help us." Amaral was especially pleased because the two relatives claimed to wield influence over people from Mozambique who had remained in the English colony.[40] When a son of Mutasa, a chief named M'vumbi, requested permission to occupy part of his (now deceased) father's lands within the company's territory, Amaral acknowledged that "he had the right to succeed his father" and granted permission to resettle.[41]

Amaral was writing for his superiors, and may have represented M'vumbi's request as an unequivocal recognition of the company's authority, but the chief had not approached Amaral entirely as a supplicant; his intention was not merely to settle in Manica District but also to secure relief from the increasingly obnoxious demands of European colonizers of any nationality. Just over the border, the British South Africa Company was making life ever more unpleasant in 1904, moving to double the head tax and restricting Africans' access to land, measures designed to drive Africans onto the wage labor market from a poor bargaining position.[42] Worse still, the Southern Rhodesian mining industry was seeking to ensure its profitability by reducing African workers' wages.[43] M'vumbi's move to company-ruled Manica would be an escape from these unwelcome changes, especially if he negotiated his return deftly. To this end, he had brought fifteen families as a bargaining chip and made Amaral an offer: they would leave British territory and settle in Manica District, and, if the company did not conscript them for forced labor, he would use his influence to bring still more from British territory to Manica.

Amaral, no doubt thinking of the increase the in-migration would bring to the district's hut tax receipts—and the 6 percent of that increased revenue he would receive, as the census taker—accepted M'vumbi's offer.[44] For the next year, "none of the people who accompanied him would be called to work, giving them time to establish residence and proceed with field preparation and planting."[45] Amaral predicted the agreement would induce still more to return to their old villages in Manica, including some who had fled in the unsettled late 1890s. Two years later his predictions proved correct. When, in mid-1905, he traveled to the north of the district, he found more than 250 huts occupied by people from English territory, and he believed more "would come if the natives are not pursued too vigorously for Company service." As he had with M'vumbi, Amaral promised the newly settled people that because "their villages and fields were not yet in order," the company would conscript no laborers for the rest of the year.[46] Amaral was acting on his own initiative, but the governor's annual report observed that the territory's population growth that year was a result, in part, of "the paternal manner in which the natives are treated by district staff, from which we saw the entry of natives all along our borders, as much with the Government of the [Portuguese colonial state-run] districts of Inhambane and Gaza to the south as from Zambezia to the north and Rhodesia to the west."[47]

M'vumbi's influence over his followers gave him bargaining power with Amaral, and the concessions he secured would draw more to follow him, and increase his prestige, his authority, and his power, but the returnees themselves knew they were taking a risk, since their exemption from forced labor was only for a year, and, according to Amaral himself, "it should be noted that all these people had once fled from there, owing to police raids in which [the police] had committed all sort of abuses."[48] But police abuses were on the wane, so the people reported to Amaral, and the company's conscription activity "is regulated and from each village leave only the number of blacks that it can supply."[49] They could, of course, always recross the border into Southern Rhodesia or move northward out of company territory into Barué District, an area beyond the company's reach and only nominally under Portugal's control.[50] But they did not mention that to Amaral.

It was, in any case, an opportune moment to resettle in Manica. The London gold market had recently collapsed, and the blow to investment in mining had plunged the region into what the district administrator called a "state of paralysis."[51] It would be several more years before European settlers discovered the potential of Manica's well-watered, fertile soil to produce a bountiful and highly marketable maize crop. Just at the time when Africans in Manica were negotiating their agreements with Amaral, the company's conscription activity slowed. It was a brief respite; within a few years, the governor would refer to the demands for African labor as a "terrible spectre that rears up threateningly."[52]

Early in 1906, seasonal rains rendered much of Manica's road network impassable, as rivers swelled and washed away bridges, and mountain runoff and perennial streams tore out roadbeds and drainage ditches.[53] The district administrator, João dos Santos Pereira Jardím, reviewed the damage with dismay, especially severe in areas of white farming and mining. The roads were a vital linchpin in the district's economy, with the white farming community dependent on them to transport their harvest to market, and the mining industry, now resurgent, similarly dependent on roads to move the heavy machinery for processing ore. Construction of spurs off the main rail line was prohibitively expensive, and none of the district's waterways was sufficiently navigable. The oxcarts used to move the heavy loads had gouged deep ruts in the roads, which would now be in frequent use in the approaching dry winter months, from May to August, when the water table would drop, allowing deep-level mine activity.

The district administration had, in past years, relied on the company's department of public works to conduct the necessary road repairs, employing paid workers, but Jardím considered the arrangement "totally uneconomic." He also considered it morally unacceptable, because, in not compelling local African residents to carry out the work, the company promoted "an acceptance of native sloth." Thus, he sought out nearby chiefs to demand that they send men to clear and repair the roads. All he promised in return was to feed those who undertook the more arduous repair of earthworks. The rest would receive nothing at all.

The chiefs acceded to Jardím's demand, and, two months later, Cesár Augusto Cardotte, Amaral's successor as district secretary, reported that workers had cleared and repaired nearly eighty-four miles.[54] In June and July alone, one group built a new stretch of road just over twenty-five feet wide for a distance of nearly two miles, and by the year's end the chiefs' labor gangs had restored more than 150 miles of roads, constructed three lengthy detours, and erected a new bridge over one of the many rivers that cut through the district.[55] Cardotte noted, with some penny-pinching pride, that this work had been done "without the Company having to spend great sums, having only supplied rations to twenty natives during the time they cleared and repaired the Chua-Chimeze road."[56] He commented that "the natives of Manica are so lackadaisical about work and truly lazy that this labor was obtained simply by their good will, seeing as they were satisfied by the simple promise of not being called by the Company for other work as long as they took charge of road clearance." Early the next year, the rains fell almost without interruption from 29 January to 4 March, with damage to the roads severe and widespread. Jardím wrote that the repairs would require far more workers than the chiefs had supplied the previous year, but he feared that with widespread recruitment, "the population would take to their heels were I to break the promise I made."[57]

The company's conscription sweeps in other chiefdoms for Manica's white farmers had already begun to trigger the flight of entire African villages to Southern Rhodesia. At midyear, the census showed a 30 percent loss in population in chiefdoms along the border.[58] Yet in Southern Rhodesia, the tax burden on the African population was much heavier—as Cardotte noted, the British levied taxes on women and children, not only on men, and in the company's territory the hut tax was effectively much lower. In Cardotte's mind, the flight reflected "the horror that people in Manica had for work" and underscored how incompletely the company controlled the border region.[59]

After Jardím, the district administrator, died in May, his successor, João Pery de Lind, learned of the existing roadwork arrangement and decided to follow in his predecessor's footsteps, noting that many villagers had "refused, finding themselves over burdened with work," and a number of chiefs came to him to complain about the labor levies.[60] Villagers continued to flee, whereupon Pery de Lind, like colonial administrators in other parts of Africa, decided to make virtue out of failure and proposed a bargain, "promising not to ask for their people for [other] work as long as they were prepared to carry out repairs on all the roads at no cost to the Company."[61] The chiefs agreed "from the start" and, according to Pery de Lind, "were satisfied with his proposal." He was no less satisfied; workers had reconstructed two stretches of a road network that had been completely swept away by flooding rivers earlier in the year, and he had achieved substantial savings (spending about a quarter of the outlay of three years earlier). "I have at work repairing the roads no fewer than 160 men to whom I gave only—as a *saguate* [gift]—flour which I also obtained without cost from the fields I had the prisoners tend."[62]

In the next year Pery de Lind and the district's chiefs formalized the agreement as a permanent pact. The *Revista de Manica e Sofala* predicted approvingly that the accord, "made with the natives at their request," would produce "a road network of first order . . . at insignificant cost."[63] The work, so Pery de Lind said, "was not limited, as in previous years, to weeding and smoothing of the road bed," and, in addition, the workers had dug nearly forty-five miles of drainage ditches, widened a number of stretches of road, and reconstructed others to reduce their overly steep pitch. He again noted with pride the savings achieved, reducing the previous year's cost by almost two-thirds.[64] "The natives were pleased, requesting that the deal might continue," and in a sure sign to a district administrator that the African population was "content," the hut tax "was collected with the same promptness and ease as the year before."[65]

Pery de Lind elaborated: "With their docility, respect, and submission to all Company authorities, the natives subject themselves with apparent good will to the work of clearing and repairing the roads with which they were occupied this year, simply because they are allowed to undertake the work by their own free will, in which they can be substituted when tired, which generally happens at the end of eight days' work. Thus, they avoid being recruited by the Company and compelled to work, of which they have great horror, and which in Manica, owing to its special situation, would produce a strong current of emigration to Rhodesia."[66] In addition to cost-savings, Pery de Lind praised himself in countering Africans' "repugnance for work."[67] He considered the deal with Manica's chiefs a victory that might replicate the "conquest that had been achieved over a great number of the natives in the Territory."[68] Of course, it was Manica's chiefs, not company officials, who had produced the laborers who worked on the roads without pay, but it was the company that brought the weight of its authority on the chiefs.

## Purchasing Chiefs' Cooperation: A "Modest and Simple Concession"

Commenting on the road repairs carried out by African workers in Manica, César Augusto Cardotte, the district secretary, wrote to his superior, the district administrator, that "I must say that the native of Manica, being so lazy and thus resistant to work, received this work levy badly . . . but despite the protests all was managed without violence."[69] But the residents of four entire villages had moved across the border to English territory, putting Cardotte's negotiation skills as district secretary to the test. He headed out into the hills in pursuit and managed to secure the return of the four villages, but "it is true," he confessed, that to do so and "to relieve the bad impression that this work had caused, it was necessary to operate with great prudence, visiting the villages several times."[70]

Cardotte had "to speak with all the people," not merely with the chiefs, and had won the villagers over, in effect, with a bribe—"the indispensable gift."[71] Rather than either the standard Portuguese term for gift or present or a Shona word, he used the word "saguate," a term the Portuguese had borrowed during centuries-long dealings with peoples of coastal South Asia.[72] The exchange of saguate had been part of Afro-Portuguese relations in southeast Africa for several hundred years, with Portuguese merchants typically offering cloth or alcohol to African rulers, especially the gatekeepers to Manica's gold trade, in exchange for permission to trade.[73] Less powerful chiefs paid saguates to their overlords and even, sometimes, to Portuguese authorities.[74] At times a saguate was a tribute of significant value, at others little more than a token gift in ritual recognition of a vassal's fealty. But the presentation of a saguate usually indicated reciprocal obligations or uncertain hierarchy, and Cardotte's use of the term suggests that, far from any "conquest" of African labor in Manica, he was carefully bargaining for it. Even if Cardotte could have unleashed the company's armed cipais to compel service, the past several years' efforts to force people in Manica to work had proven the limits of such coercive practices. In writing of his offer of a saguate, Cardotte not only relied on received vocabulary but admitted that force alone could not win the submission the company sought. What he actually offered, Cardotte did not say—though in other situations he mentioned cotton textiles— and the monetary value of the gift was less significant than the fact that he had to offer it at all.

Cardotte—and his superior, Pery de Lind—acknowledged, at least in part, the limitations of the company's claim to the labor of Manica's African population, justifying "the modest and simple concession" by pointing out how easily people might cross the border to elude the company's conscription sweeps.[75] The bargain struck with Manica's chiefs helped the company control the district's African population. Even if that control fell short of the "conquest" Pery de Lind hoped for, it brought important stability. Pery de Lind, in a show of bureaucratic dexterity, made the most oblique of references to this with his statement that it "seemed to me of all convenience to continue in the direction my predecessor had started and so I searched for a way to do away with the troubles that heretofore had existed."[76] His claim to "convenience" was stylistically of a piece with fellow administrators' routine references to the "inconveniences" that resulted from the company's efforts to enslave the African population. The agreement did reduce the district's expenditures on public works, in Manica's mountainous terrain an ongoing and substantial expense, and simultaneously secured company revenue, since a reduction in out-migration of villagers would increase the annual hut tax takings (and contribute to his personal income as well; as district administrator, he received 4 percent of tax collected).[77] His boast, almost certainly an effort to bring his thriftiness to his superiors' attention, downplayed the energetic negotiations in which Cardotte and Amaral had engaged, and the tense mountainside standoff.

Perhaps more important than money saved and revenue increased was the agreement's contribution to preserving the company's (and, by extension, Portugal's) image as a colonial power. Whenever Africans fled from Portuguese to English territory, company officials brooded that Portuguese colonial rule would be compared unfavorably with its British neighbor's. Stemming that outward flow of its population helped avoid an unflattering comparison and further produced "a magnificent road network serving the mining and agricultural region," a network, according to a successor of Pery de Lind, "considered among the best in all southern Africa."[78] The chiefs' labor gangs of what Cardotte had called "truly lazy men" had created roads that were "the envy of all the visitors from neighboring territories"—of the company's rival, the British colonies.[79]

As a result, Manica's administrators renewed the bargain annually with the district's chiefs to provide unpaid labor. They were able to maintain it for nearly two decades. Every year the administrator would summon the chiefs to a meeting to hear instructions and advice from the company, and to receive their pay for assisting the district administration with the census and tax collection. The meetings opened with a roll call of the chiefs, followed by a distribution of the tax shares, sums that for the rulers of larger chiefdoms were more than most African men could hope to earn in a year.[80] After the chiefs received their pay, the administrator delivered his instructions, including warnings to report any forays by Rhodesian labor recruiters; the chiefs also "must always report all deaths or departures from their villages, under pain of being held responsible for the payment of their tax."[81] Thus, chiefs were paid off for supplying the unpaid labor of their villagers, being persuaded, in effect, to serve as the company's labor recruiters.

Pery de Lind's successor, João Mascarenhas Manuel de Mendonça Gaivão, persisted in seeing or describing the labor as freely given. He told the chiefs in 1914 that he "was very satisfied with the work carried out voluntarily by Manica's natives during the last year in repairing the district's roads . . . and asked the chiefs whether they wanted to continue to perform this work for the company free of charge as in past years or if they preferred to be recruited for distribution to employers." The district commissioner for native affairs always recorded the same answer from the chiefs. "All of them said that they wanted to continue the same work as past years."[82] The administrator proceeded to assess the number of workers each chief would supply, basing the levy on the number of men in each chiefdom. Chiefs with the largest population supplied the most workers, just as they received the largest hut tax shares.

Manica's chiefs, like their counterparts elsewhere throughout the territory, had been compelled to meet the company's demands, but the agreement made their chiefdoms more secure, as long as they supplied workers for road repair. By making the agreement, they could ensure that armed company police would no longer descend upon their villages to sweep men up into the company's forced labor net, possibly resulting in the chief being held responsible for his followers' actions.[83] Moreover, if the agreement succeeded in reducing flight from their villagers, the revenue the chiefs received from the company as a percentage of the hut tax would continue to increase. The downside was that they had to deliver their people for arduous unpaid labor. In contrast to the rest of the territory, Manica's chiefs controlled this practice entirely after 1908, thereby assuming a greater role as local enforcers of company power.

For the villagers who actually did the company's work, the agreement spared them from abuse by the district's notoriously brutal white maize farmers, since they did not work for them but dug drainage canals, felled trees and hauled timber for bridges, and constructed roads for the company, all back-breaking work in Manica's mountainous terrain and rocky soil. Also, the work came at a time of year—late April to September, mostly postharvest—when workers might otherwise have had time to rest, to market surplus crops, or find short-term wage labor to earn cash for their tax payment.[84] (The arrival of the planting season in September provided an incentive to complete the work early—in some years, as early as August.[85]) But their work in maintaining Manica's roads was not entirely without reward, for they, like the district's white farmers and miners, would now have ready market access. Nor did the roadwork necessarily conflict with their needs for their own field labor. One year the district administrator reported that work had to be completed before the end of September, "so as not to interfere with the Manicas in clearing fields for the coming planting."[86] The workers also had some autonomy on the job. Cardotte suggested that unpaid forced labor was endured largely because "they can go about conducting this work of their own free will, where they can be spelled as soon as they are tired, which generally happens after eight days of work."[87] Of course, they were not working "of their own free will," though they had some control over the conditions. Another administrator seven years later repeated that men worked with "good will, being free from work in agriculture and the mines, which they detest." Also, the road labor "did not represent a heavy burden for the natives of Manica, because they switch off at work when they wish, it being very rare for a native to remain more than 15 days at work without one or another relative coming to replace him. Aside from this, they work close to their villages and the Company treats them with all humanity, which unfortunately does happen with the majority of farmers and miners in the district."[88] Short-term and close by, work on a road gang allowed some measure of control.

Pery de Lind campaigned tirelessly over the coming years to ensure that thousands of Africans from other parts of the Mozambique Company's territory were dispatched to unpopular toil in Manica's maize fields and mine shafts. Yet chiefs' collaboration with company "recruitment" for labor workers detested proved to be, in the end, little more than tissue-thin cooperation.

## The Consequences of Accommodation: Failed Revolt and "Absolute Misery"

In 1917, the leaders of Barué District—an area originally included in the company's concession but only under nominal control and never handed over by Portugal—rose up against colonial rule in a revolt that attracted widespread support. An administrator in Manica had warned that Africans in Barué could buy arms and powder from itinerant South Asian merchants, and proposed building a military post where his district abutted Barué.[89]

The Makombe dynasty, which ruled Barué, had become increasingly distressed by Portugal's efforts to bring Barué under its rule, first, as elsewhere, with labor conscription. The Portuguese had escalated conscription in the early years of World War I to build a road linking the Barué capital with the rest of the colony. When, in its effort to repulse the German invasion in 1917 of northern Mozambique, Portugal conscripted thousands from Barué for carrier service in northern Mozambique, the Makombe took action through diplomacy and carefully directed threats of retaliation for noncooperation, drawing support beyond Barué itself. Africans in neighboring company districts of Sena, Chimoio, and, above all, Gorongosa joined the uprising, which came to be known as "the Barué Rebellion."[90] Although the rebels' ability to recruit allies in Manica was limited by the small and well-policed border it shared with Barué, those elsewhere who hesitated to join the rebels faced blunt threats: "You are the same as the white men, you will be killed."[91] The Makombe attacks, directed, first, at Portuguese strongholds in the Zambezi Valley, caught company and Portuguese forces off guard as rebels overran the town of Zumbo and laid siege to Portuguese garrisons in Tete and Sena, and were poised to spread the uprising farther, threatening Portuguese control of much of central Mozambique.[92]

Portugal, desperate to regain control, appealed for and received arms and matériel from the British. Paid African soldiers, hired from former rivals of the Makombe, provided a decisive counterforce. In spreading the revolt, the Makombe were isolated from secure supply lines and could not maintain their fighters far from their heartland. Parts of Barué remained in rebellion well into 1918, but most of the surrounding company districts were brought under Portuguese control with devastating force by the end of 1917.[93]

The company's labor regime helped to spread the disorder into 1918. Nearly 1,500 of the labor department's almost 1,800 conscripts in Buzi, several hundred miles from Barué, came from areas in rebellion, most of them recent arrivals.[94] The district administrator from Buzi reported an attempted worker uprising on the principal sugar plantation.[95] About 700 conscripts refused to work, though one group of 66 heeded the administrator's direct order to return; and another group of 114 stated that "they were tired, having worked eighteen months and that they wanted to return their homes." The administrator ordered the police to separate these malcontents from the larger group, whereupon "all the workers present . . . fell upon the police, shouting and attempting to carry off the group of 114." After the administrator ordered the police to fire warning shots in the air, the rebellious workers fell silent, "raising their arms and encircling [the administrator], declaring they would go to work and finish out their contracts."[96]

Once the tide had turned against the Makombe's uprising, the company governor, not satisfied, retaliated, ordering his field commanders to "burn all the rebel villages, destroying all the fields, confiscating all their cattle and taking as many prisoners as possible including women and children. . . . It is indispensable that these actions be carried out as rapidly and violently as possible in order to terrorize the local population and prevent further revolts." British officials in the Rhodesias, carefully monitoring events just over the border, reported that some defeated rebel leaders who were captured with wives, who had served alongside them in noncombat roles, were executed and decapitated, their wives given their husband's heads and sent home with them for all to see.[97] A local official in Gorongosa observed, at the uprising's end, that only half a dozen villages remained intact in that region.[98]

In the hard-hit Gorongosa District, the administrator made vague mention of "military operations and occupation," but Manica's secretary for native affairs, who had participated in those operations, reported "pillaging of rebellious regions" and punishment of persons implicated in the rebellion, a faint reflection of the "deprivation and hard lesson they received" at the hands of company forces.[99] The consequences were evident in a loss of nearly 2,500 people in the first postrebellion census in Gorongosa. Many had fled; others had been killed or died from other causes of death—altogether, more than 10 percent of the precensus population.[100] The devastation in Gorongosa had been especially violent; the district administrator reported that "the disorganization among the natives is enormous, with at least 95 per cent of the old chiefs having died, in such a way that the natives fled in every direction, dispersed and distant one from another, so that there are people from the same village and even the same family who long have not known where each other are."[101] Yet on the third day of the census "the natives came to meet me, encircling my *machila* and accompanying me for a distance of 12, 16, and 20 kilometers, all the while singing and the men taking the *machila* from the *machileiros* to carry; during the night they danced until dawn." The administrator explained the celebration; his arrival reassured Gorongosa's African population, who until then had "considered that the war was not over."[102]

Just as the rebellion came to a close, the Spanish influenza epidemic swept through the territory. A census of Gorongosa in mid-1919—the district's first in three years—found near-total devastation; the quick succession of war, flood, and pandemic had reduced the harvests of 1917 and 1918, and emaciated people had "fed themselves almost exclusively on roots." The administrator reported there were many children "who had little more than skin on their bones, who I would give at most one or two days to last."[103] He found people living in temporary shelters of woven reeds encircled with protective thorny barriers, and "men and women clad miserably with ragged bits of sack and cloth or monkey skins," others with bark cloth; some were completely nude.[104] Almost the entire population were "living as fugitives, in groups of three, six, eight people generally hidden as much as possible," with people "scattered throughout the district. . . . I found one head of family by himself in a shelter on Gorongosa Mountain, later coming across a young son in Meringue, two grown brothers in the lands of Charifumbe, and the mother with the other two young sons in the lands of Sanhaxoco, with one not knowing of the others." To speed his census taking (and later on, his tax collecting), the administrator tried to reunite families he identified and to create new villages by "grouping together groups of families, with no fewer than seven sound men making up a village for which I nominated a chief and designated a spot to build new huts," to replace "an enormous percentage of subchiefs who had disappeared, some in flight and others having fled, while many chiefs had died . . . [resulting in] extraordinary political disorganization."[105]

Ironically, the Barué Rebellion's challenge to the company's dominance and the company's ruinous response had destroyed those chiefs most closely associated with company power. In assessing the loyalty of the few remaining chiefs, the administrator suggested that most able-bodied men in Gorongosa had taken part in the rebellion on orders from the Makombe, while few of Gorongosa's chiefs had "taken up heart and soul with the Barué rebels." Many, indeed, had been compelled to join the uprising. Others took to hiding to elude the company's press gang. The administrator replaced any chief who had not fled from an area the rebels dominated on the grounds that those who remained must have welcomed the rebel forces.[106] He reported no resistance or objections to his selection of new chiefs and formation of new villages. To the contrary, "the native seems disheartened, unraveled, timid, watching themselves, full of dread, humbled, and cursing the war [the Barué Rebellion] that was forced upon them." Before they had lived "happy and with abundance"; now they lived "in the most absolute misery."[107] In bitter irony, rebels who surrendered with their arms or were turned in by others were compelled to undertake unpaid roadwork and brick making, intended for construction of a permanent military post where the road from Macequece, Manica's district center, entered Barué.[108]

If some chiefs' support of the rebellion was an effort to reject their role as enforcers for the company's forced labor regime, it was made in vain. With company control restored by 1919, labor department recruiters descended on Gorongosa and swept up more than 1,000 men for forced labor early that year, then returned for another 1,200, taking a total of 3,776 men, just over 36 percent of the district's entire male population.[109]

Peace, or what passed for peace under company rule, returned, but it was an uneasy peace, the underlying tensions unresolved. In Neves Ferreira, a district hard hit by the rebellion, the district administrator in 1919 said the district's chiefs were less than fully cooperative with his scheduled "recruitment"; one, in particular, Tica, warned he could furnish only forty workers since many had died from "the illness that had gone about," and many others had fled, motivated by their dislike "for being sent [for work] so far from their land." They preferred to work closer to home, where "they might spend the nights at home with their family," impossible under labor department contracts. The district administrator's "retort," as he phrased it, was that "many more people were needed" and that Tica "had better try to arrange them, under penalty of [the governor] becoming very cross, which would be very bad for him, Tica." In an effort to sheathe the fist in a velvet glove, the administrator told Tica that chiefs would be paid 15 cents for each recruit taken on a six-month contract and 25 cents for each taken for a year.[110]

## "Promises to the Natives Must Be Kept Religiously"

More than 10,000 people left Gorongosa District, and more than 58,000 quit company territory, at least temporarily, in the first years following the Barué Rebellion.[111] In Manica, there was an inflow of 1,200 immigrants "in search of refuge," in the words of António Cardoso de Serpa, the district officer for native affairs.[112] The great bulk of the immigrants settled in the northern part of the district, closest to the recent rebellion, tripling the population of chiefdoms there.[113] The immigrants found safety and protection from the company's labor raids under the roadwork agreement.

In 1925, when forced labor practices in the Portuguese colonies came under scrutiny from the League of Nations, unpaid labor like that under the agreement with Manica's chiefs to provide their villagers to dig ditches and repair roads was denounced amid general condemnation of forced labor. Although the league's Slavery Convention of 1926 and Forced Labor Convention of 1930 were, in the end, mostly ineffectual, there was, said António Cardoso de Serpa, a "growing tendency in modern ideas toward voluntary labor."[114]

Meanwhile, however, at the district administrator's annual meeting, or *banja*, in early 1925, the administrator "informed them [Manica's chiefs] that the old system would end, that they would cease to send people to work without pay on the roads, rather they would—like chiefs in all other districts—send workers to the native labor department twice a year, in numbers that would be assigned to them shortly." Compulsory conscription would be reinstated. The chiefs "predicted that there would be flight" in response to the return of forced labor. The administrator wrote, in his report for the first trimester, that "the population decreased considerably, without doubt because of the new labor regime." The final census numbers bore out the chiefs' predictions: the population dropped by almost 2,000, or nearly 20 percent, in what the district administrator in Manica described as "an exodus."[115]

In compiling his census report for 1926, Cardoso de Serpa expressed regret for the decision to end the negotiated bargain with the chiefs, put in place "by the distinguished colonist *Senhor* João Pery de Lind." Breaking the deal with the district's chiefs "was a big mistake"; it "produced the worst results . . . completely disorganizing the native population in the area." To seize African residents for forced contract labor would result in "our having neither forced labor nor voluntary labor . . . and shortly we will have a depopulated district."[116]

The League of Nations intervention finally offered some hope of reform. The company's native labor department, to be abolished later that year in response to the league's pressure, would, so Cardoso de Serpa hoped, "happily create a new labor regime," restore Africans' confidence, and induce them to return to the district from which many had fled for Southern Rhodesia. Such hopes would only be fulfilled, he said, if the company recognized that "it is indispensable that the promises made to the natives must be kept religiously."[117] Later that year, the company replaced the labor department with a privately run recruitment agency, acceding, at least in formal terms, to the league's injunction that public authorities should not recruit African workers for private use. Instead, the company had arranged for a private subcontracting agency to undertake forced labor recruitment with disguised company support. The league's scrutiny had led the company to camouflage even more thoroughly its use of force to compel Africans to work.

The consequences of the company's unilateral decision to break the bargain with Manica's chiefs were immediately evident. Africans in Manica rejected the company's effort to force them into service under the guise of "a new labor regime." A corollary effect, said the district administrator, was that the district's roads "were in a truly deplorable state." The company lacked the labor to maintain them, work "that in the past was done with relative ease."[118] Even a decade later, the company had yet to find a solution, the director of the mines department reporting that district miners could not move goods and "were complaining bitterly of the state of the roads." He himself could not get out to visit the mines, since the roads were in "a ruinous state . . . a true horror."[119] One miner proclaimed that, in Manica, "roads are something that do not exist. There's something they call roads, but that's not what they are. They are only some paths, and even those are in such a state of abandonment, that a miner who might have to get from one end to the other would spend days and even nights, buried in pits and the mire."[120]

Chiefs in Manica, for nearly two decades, with the collaboration of Pery de Lind, had employed a stratagem to balance the company's demands for forced labor so as to serve their own interests, receiving "gifts" and payments, preserving and even expanding their chiefly authority and prestige by ordering their villagers to take part in sustained and unpaid compulsory service. (Even the earlier conscripted workers sometimes received a wage.) During the nearly two decades in which their workers maintained the district's road network under the negotiated agreement, the local economy flourished, but white farmers' demands for forced laborers increased accordingly. Those workers, the company's modern slaves, had come mostly from undeclared labor reserves such as Gorongosa District, where chiefs had little or no leverage to ease the enormous pressure of the company's demands. The Barué uprising of 1917 presented a rare, and illusory, chance to win a degree of freedom from the company's servitude, but chiefs and followers alike paid a heavy price for their effort. In Manica as well, when the company judged the chiefs' cooperation no longer useful, it turned on its allies and imposed on them a similarly unbearable burden.

# Seniority and Subordination

## Disciplining Youth and
## Controlling Women's Labor

THE MOZAMBIQUE COMPANY'S RULE, AS WITH COLO-
nial administrations elsewhere in Africa, introduced rigidly hierarchical
lines of authority. It presupposed a one-way flow of power: from the top
down. Under the pressure of the colonial regime of forced labor, power relations within African societies—between elders and juniors, between women and
men—became more unbalanced.[1] People in relatively more secure positions were
less subject to principles of reciprocity, based on norms of mutual obligation, and
could at times ignore them with impunity.

### Latter-Day Pawns: Labor and Generational Politics

Although within African communities young people were expected to recognize
the authority and status that came with age, nearly always surrendering some
measure of control over their labor, their allegiance was to their parents and
elders, not to outside employers. Unmarried adult children ordinarily worked
within their parents' household, and some newly married men, too, might engage
in labor service to their wife's family, sometimes for extended time periods. As
women and men aged, they gained in status and exercised more control over their
labor, but growing older, in chronological terms, was not sufficient for advancement in social stature; social aging was important as well. Thus, across central
Mozambique, and more widely throughout southern Africa, diverse as the region
was, an individual's status was tied to specific mileposts: achieving economic in-

dependence, marrying, producing and bearing children.[2] Established norms governing the passage of social time were calibrated to prolong a youthful stage, for the longer it lasted, the more benefit older relatives could derive from controlling young people's labor. The advent of colonial rule, and especially the emergence of industrial capitalism and urban development in southern Africa, transformed the political and economic landscape in contradictory ways. Colonial administrators, as a rule, presumed chiefs, and older men more generally, were dominant and could act as an extension of state authority, and thereby relied on them and increased the power they wielded. Simultaneously, and at cross-purposes, colonial efforts to drive younger men into the wage labor market weakened the structure of senior male authority, as some youth earned wages and, with them, gained an autonomy that allowed them to cast off the yoke of obligation to their elders.

In 1901, the Mozambique Company secretary general issued a territory-wide circular reminding local administrators, "when recruiting natives for the Company, have care not to send children or the elderly or those who, by their lack of physical robustness required for work, are manifestly incapable."[3] With both youth and elders seen as "incapable," elders' senior status was denied, and the company regarded them as being just as weak as the young. Similarly, the secretary general requested the administrator in Govuro send eighty to ninety miners for Manica's mines: "the Governor recommends that you choose [the miners] scrupulously . . . it being inconvenient to send worn-out men or excessively young boys."[4] Clearly it had been the practice to seize old and young. Even the influential Augusto Freire de Andrade, later governor-general of all of Mozambique, encountered similar results as director of the mines department in Manica when he found that, in a "special recruitment" for mine workers, workers had been "badly chosen, with many old men and others still children . . . some lacking the strength for such arduous work and others the experience or the knowledge."[5] João Pery de Lind, Manica's district administrator, noted, in 1908, among the African workers sent to Manica "a high percentage of those who completely lacked the sturdiness needed for agricultural labor, some because they were too young and others because they were too old."[6] A year later, he urged the governor to order district administrators to conscript a higher percentage of adult African men "fit for labor," advocating ramped-up "recruitment," since "without doubt the percentage which has been in use to recruit among the village men is far too low . . . and what's more is that it's certain that some contingents contain many adolescent boys."[7] The following year, he found that many conscripts from Sena were adolescents between fourteen and eighteen years of age.[8] The district administrator from Govuro wrote of his last recruitment sweep in 1909 that "these 700 blacks are not all young men; there is perhaps a percentage of 40 percent of men of age and others very young, but it is what can be organized."[9] Conscription, especially in the years before the company created its native labor department, was at times a chaotic activity in which, as one official said, "*cipais* and even white policemen would arrive in the villages . . . and seize" whichever men they happened to encounter, neither knowing or caring who they were, where they were from, or what impact their seizure might have on the villages.[10] The fact that African households depended on young people for their support did not figure in colonial decisions guided solely by the colonizers' own self-interest.

Summoned by district officials to produce forced laborers, some chiefs reported "it was impossible for them to supply another native, since they had only some old men and children in their villages."[11] Although some employers complained that "they wanted the workers to produce the daily amount of work deemed reasonable for a man," others, especially Manica's cost-cutting white farmers, found a powerful incentive to ask for younger workers—the company charged 44 percent less for them.[12] After the labor department was set up in 1911, "recruitment" became an organized endeavor, and chiefs became central in conscript selection. Yet conscription of the young continued, despite a ban on impressing young boys and elderly men into labor brigades. To meet the fixed quotas, police, administrators, and chiefs colluded to send the required number, fulfilling orders in formal if not substantive terms. Pery de Lind's successor in Manica wrote, in 1915, that the department was routinely dispatching "old men without the stamina for work or children whose bodies atrophy under the oppressive burden of agricultural labor."[13]

The seizure of elderly men, perhaps more than anything else, suggested a world out of balance, since, in the territory's African societies, power and status corresponded closely with gender and age. The company's enslavement of those of the greatest prestige struck deeply at the basis of authority in African communities. The impressing of the elderly was largely confined to the opening years of company rule, when methods of conscription varied from one district to another, often according to the personality of local administrators and the nature of their relationships with chiefs. Although local chiefs themselves did yield in sending youth, they would not have countenanced the taking of elderly men. Once the company established its labor department, incorporating chiefs into the conscription process, older men soon faced far less risk of forced labor.[14]

Toward the bottom end of the social and political hierarchy, boys and adolescents, legally protected from labor predation, were, at times, specifically targeted, even by their own communities or families. During the labor department's sixteen-year existence, from before World War I to the mid-1920s, no one was better placed to select male youth than their own chiefs, guardians of senior male privilege. Chiefs may have targeted youth to protect elders. So, too, fathers and uncles, faced with six months or longer as a field worker for a Portuguese maize farmer, or twelve-hour shifts shoveling ore underground in Manica's mines, or cutting mangrove poles, may have "volunteered" their sons or nephews as pawns for conscription. Just as elders of generations past pawned vulnerable young family members in return for food stocks or other resources in times of drought or other hardship, so some senior men offered up their young male relatives so they themselves might avoid the company's labor slavery.[15] The customary support by elders of youth was distorted by the company's demands.

Older men may even have seen additional opportunity in offering up their youth to company press gangers, in view of the lump-sum payment, calculated at 1$000 *reis* for each month of a contract, sometimes received by "recruited" persons and deducted from future payments, such advances paid only when guaranteed by a chief or family member.[16] Senior men or chiefs thus may have compelled their youth to work for the company, laying claim to the payments themselves, perhaps using the cash to meet the company's annual hut tax (assessed for each dwelling), up from $900 *reis* to 2$250 in 1894, to 4$500 *reis* in 1909, and 9$00 *escudos* in 1927, and knowing that older adolescent boys, if short of the minimum age of eighteen for "recruitment," might pass the muster of district administrators and meet employers' expectations, shouldering the workload of an adult man. Some sent their youth into the forced labor system exchanging their productive potential for a one-time payment in time of need, with the expectation that the young person would, with luck, return.[17] Such decisions were not without peril for elders, either; in the territory, on occasions when forced laborers received an upfront incentive payment, the family head (or his chief) became the guarantor; should the youthful worker flee, fall ill, or die, his relatives would be saddled with the debt.

Substitutions of youth for senior men could occur even after adult men had been selected for a labor gang. Company administrators occasionally reported that between the time forced laborers were chosen and their arrival at work, adult men were, in some manner, replaced by younger relatives. A territory-wide circular issued early in 1915 instructed district administrators "to take all necessary precautions to avoid the recruitment of natives who, due to their excessive old age or youth might not be in a state to produce the work that is reasonable to require from contracted natives. Strict instructions must be given to the police who escort the contingents to prevent any substitution of natives during their journey."[18] The guards who accompanied forced labor contingents on the road may have overlooked such substitutions, or missed them, if nighttime darkness cloaked an exchange, or if boys darted from the surrounding bush to join the contingent as an older relative ducked out into its cover, hoping that the handful of guards would not notice the exchange. A decade later, in 1924, the secretary general issued a circular, stating: "It has been verified that some workers have been listed as adults upon recruitment, while later, when reporting to work, it has become clear that they cannot be considered as such, by virtue of their apparent age. These cases can only be attributed to the exchange of children for adults while on the road, which has been proven at times in which those boys have confessed to the exchanges."[19] In 1928, the agent in Manica responsible for distributing contract workers to employers pointed out to his counterpart in Mossurize: "Clearly some natives were exchanged on the road, because some boys arrived here possessing such a build that they could not be distributed."[20] By surrendering the labor of their youth, the older generation itself could dwell somewhat more securely on their rural homesteads, a dilemma widely shared among African communities targeted by labor-hungry colonists and colonial administrations.[21] Reports and circulars that documented the exchange of youth for elders made no mention of the unequal power relations that drove such switches. Confronting the colonial state, older men exercised rights based on seniority to let the heaviest of the new burdens rest upon generations below.[22] Male elders sought to maintain their control over their juniors' labor, to preserve the existing social and economic order, and, at the same time, to stabilize or improve their own position in the face of colonial encroachment.

Youth thus impressed into forced labor had fewer opportunities to gain independence. Seeing the generational covenant at risk of rupture, some might withdraw when elders attempted to direct their labor toward compulsory farm work for white settlers, to many youth a trap that would make them perpetual children. When young men believed that their male relatives might be unable, or perhaps unwilling, to fulfill the implicit bargain by which the older generation provided the bride wealth necessary for marriage and eventual passage into adulthood, youth might compensate for stints of poorly paid work in forced labor contingents on behalf of their elders with more remunerative wage work in a variety of mostly urban or industrial settings.[23] Seeking to lessen their dependence on the fortunes of their fathers or uncles, some youth embraced the opportunity to accumulate such resources on their own, and, in so doing, accelerate the process of growing up in social terms. Engaging in wage labor and thereby accumulating individual wealth was a way to short circuit the established social aging process. In Mozambique and throughout the wider region, they sought to work on their own behalf to accumulate the resources for bride wealth and marriage that would make them men.[24] Some among the older generations regarded reduced control over the labor of their youth as a significant net loss, in material terms, as well as a challenge to or rejection of their authority, in social terms.

Such choices affected African elders most immediately, but settlers and their governments as well, in challenges to colonial control in ways neither expected nor intended. Early in twentieth-century South Africa's Natal Province, the tension inherent in such unequal relations broke through the generational order when younger Zulu men, facing new tax burdens imposed by the colonial government in Natal Province, rebelled against their elders' attempts to compel their consent.[25] These young men bridled at the new tax obligation and at the impediment to their freedom to pursue new economic opportunities. Elders, disapproving of youth's mobility, most especially when it removed their labor from the household, were angered at some youths' inclination to keep their earnings from mine or other wage labor for themselves, rather than surrender them, as custom dictated, to the family patriarch. When the Natal government imposed a new tax on unmarried men, Zulu elders closed ranks with colonial administrators to enforce the obligation, whereupon some youth rebelled, fomenting unrest that culminated in a 1906 rebellion, suppressed by colonial troops but not without roiling rural Zulu communities and exposing unexpected fracturing in the fault lines of power in African societies. The one-way top-down lines of authority on which colonial administrators had been counting proved unstable.

As urban labor demands in southern Africa exercised a steadily growing and inexorable pull on the African population, white farmers in South Africa depended on African labor much as did their Portuguese counterparts in Manica, competing for African labor with the gold mines, which paid far higher wages. Many Africans in Natal found that the only way to remain on what had become white land was to work for its new owners, but senior Zulu men rejected farm labor as burdensome, low paying, and below their station, and brokered the labor of their junior male (and sometimes female) relatives. One official noted that "the kraal [homestead] head is usually exempted if there are other inmates who render service."[26] In return for permission to remain as residents on now-white land, seniors compelled sons and daughters, nieces and nephews, to enter the service of white landholders, working for insignificant wages or none at all.[27] With time and good fortune, elders' assistance would be forthcoming, but the path to manhood was drawn out, and, as one young man remarked, "The bad part of it was that you became a laughing stock to your peers because of the low wages you were receiving."[28] By delivering their juniors' labor to white farmers, older men ensured their use of white-held land for growing maize and sorghum and grazing cattle, the economic underpinnings of their social rank.

The Mozambique Company, like colonial authorities elsewhere, was aware of the respect elders commanded and the authority they wielded, and depended on that respect, while exploiting it. District administrators counted on chiefs to compel followers to contract labor, and on household heads to stand as guarantors for advance payments to contract workers, typically and immediately re-circulated to the company as tax payments, practices that resembled a clause of South Africa's 1932 Native Service Contract Act that gave male African household heads the authority to bind dependents' labor over to white farmers by "contract" for six months annually, guaranteeing senior men's standing as labor tenants on white-held land.[29] And just as senior men in South Africa might face eviction if their juniors did not keep the contract to work for white farmers, so younger men's flight from the Mozambique Company labor contracts exposed their senior male relatives to liability as guarantors.

Benedict Carton suggests that "competing patriarchies" were behind the 1905 eruption of unrest in South Africa's Zulu society, with colonial administrators and male elders dueling for control over young people's productive capacities.[30] Power in African societies in the Mozambique Company's territory was less centralized than among the Zulu, and in central Mozambique relations across generations were insufficiently rigid and one-sided to serve the purposes of the company. A more authoritarian hierarchy would have been necessary. The form of latter-day pawning in which senior African men in central Mozambique engaged was a carefully negotiated strategy that held a middle ground. Older men, in dispatch-ing youthful workers, could ward off the company's demands and preserve their own authority and social status. When the company paid the younger workers at a reduced rate or not at all, youths may have rebelled against their elders' author-ity, considering the bargain broken. In entering the forced labor system under the coercive authority of their elders, they had taken a step, however uncertain and risky, toward freeing themselves from that authority. Some spoke out against this mortgaging of their labor for meager wages, arguing "that they gave the men a run for their money at work [and questioned why] they should receive less than they."[31] They feared that their marriage and independence might recede into a distant future, along with a claim to manhood. Driven by hopes to accumulate the wealth necessary to establish their own adult status, theirs were less efforts to avoid the company's forced labor than, perhaps, to engage it strategically.

## "Forcing the Natives to Work without Distinction of Sex"

When company police swept into villages, their principal targets were men, because of their perceived potential as laborers, and, secondarily, boys, but the police often kidnapped the wives, sisters, and mothers of men whose labor the company sought. The administrator in Moribane reported that when the police "appeared in the bush for recruitment," the district's African residents "abandon the villages and hide themselves with their wives."[32] But hiding in the bush was not practical for self-sustaining farming communities, and women's household-based labor responsibilities (child rearing, food preparation, and field work) made escape an unlikely option. Nor were chiefs' wives necessarily safer: when, at times, some chiefs declared that they could not supply enough men to meet conscription quotas, their wives were taken, some gaining their freedom only after their husbands paid a cash ransom.[33] Seizing women yielded benefits for the company when sought-after men turned themselves in to win their female relatives' release. The police, too, benefited, sometimes by payoffs, holding women until their relatives bought their freedom.[34]

The company's careful documentation of its operations left no doubt that it was standard practice to extract male labor by seizing vulnerable women, counting on affective ties and social obligations and hierarchy to do what coercion of men alone could not. In the Zambezi Valley district of Tambara, the company's administrator reported, matter-of-factly, that kidnapping women, often with the collaboration of a chief, was a routine part of company "recruitment." A chief who failed to recruit the required number of workers could send the police "to track down the men in the villages, or their women, if the men are not found in the villages, thus to force them to go to Manica to work."[35] When, in neighboring Chemba, males fled from labor sweeps, the administrator dispatched police to pick up their wives and mothers and hold them at district headquarters until the worker quota had been met. Then the women were released and "shown the bad behavior of their sons and husbands."[36] But whether such practices were authorized and ordered by a district administrator or were simply freelancing improvisation by company police (as one district administrator in Manica suggested, on learning of the "villainy" practiced in neighboring Moribane), the effect was largely the same.[37]

Nor were such tactics an artifact of early conquest disorder: four decades into company rule, the administrator in Beira's immediate hinterland of Chiloane openly declared that in his twenty-one years in the district, he had always ordered chiefs to turn in anyone who had not paid their tax, men to be sent to work and women to be detained at the district headquarters. It was it "a very old practice," he declared, and "the chiefs themselves acknowledge the necessity of detaining and bringing to headquarters the women of those who are well known as dead beats."[38]

The administrator in distant Govuro, reporting detention of women as a matter of course, said that much of the hut tax was collected only by "forcing the natives to work, without distinction of sex."[39] Women's formal exemption from forced labor did not protect them, simply ensuring that their dragooning fell outside the law, adding to their vulnerability. When the governor sent out instructions in 1911 to all district administrators specifically prohibiting conscription of women "for any type of work," women continued to face the prospect of compulsory work for district-level administrations and for local white farmers.[40] When the company was short of milled grain for conscripts or prisoners serving in Manica's department of public works, police commandeered women to reduce large quantities of maize to flour.[41] It was, one elderly woman made sure I understood, as she described these demands to me, "very strenuous" labor, without access to a mill and compelled to pulverize with mortar and pestle. Other women were forced to labor in the fields for private white farmers nearby—for example, at harvest time to transport maize and other crops to storage.[42] As compensation, the women might receive some salt. In such circumstances, just as with long-term conscription of African men, it fell to local chiefs to turn out the women white employers demanded.

## Contract "Disorganizes the Family": Husbands Absent, Wives "Returned to Their Parents' Homestead"

Kinship relations in African communities throughout the territory, especially those within a household, were freighted with inequality, the conjugal bond created by local marriage practices implying a subordination of women not confined to husband and wife. One older woman, born just prior to the First World War, described to me in 1997 the welcoming of a young bride into an in-law's family: "In the first days, you must arise very early. Light the fire, go to the well, draw water, and come back with it. You heat that water and then as the sun rises, you begin to give [your in-laws] water to wash their face. All the family of that house. And for this, you must also be a disciplined person." The required "discipline" and capacity for hard work extended throughout the day, for a young wife was expected to labor in the fields to cultivate maize, sorghum, and millet. She further explained to me, "Now if you could not manage all that work, you would have to be sent back to your [parents'] house, sent away. . . . If you could manage that farm work well, then they would say 'we have a good young person.'"[43] Younger wives' subordination, especially the expectation that in the early period of their marriage ("the first days") they be at the service of their in-laws, derived from their status as newcomers in their husbands' extended family.

In company territory, as in the wider region, younger women's opportunities to accelerate their social aging in a manner that might preserve or expand their autonomy were far more limited than those for young men, not only because wage labor and commercial agriculture were mostly male spheres of activity but also because while some women did work for wages as well, colonists' beliefs about appropriate gender and work roles limited African women's access to wage work.[44] Also, men's intervening absences for compulsory labor compelled adjustments by those who remained, including, for some women, a decision to quit rural areas for towns to pursue new opportunities and bolster their independence.[45] Young women facing fathers' expectations that they marry might flee to mission stations, where joining a new religious community, together with education, could enhance their social and economic mobility; others, including married women in areas abutting white settlements, might market garden production to colonists. Such autonomy often displeased their fathers and husbands, whose ability to command women's labor was reduced at the same time that labor migrancy took men away from homesteads. They saw women's absence as a threat to the rural life to which they themselves expected to return, and balked at efforts to increase labor migration. In turn, colonial administrators and elder African men collaborated to establish policies and legislation that restricted women's economic mobility. To placate men threatened by women's new autonomy and thereby secure male labor that colonial employers demanded, colonial administrators generally, and especially in Southern Rhodesia and South Africa, passed regulations banning women's commercial activities and defining them as legal minors, subordinating them, formally in law, to their male relatives.[46] In Mozambique Company territory, though, with fewer urban or town settings and even less of a missionary presence, women's mobility was far more limited.

Some company officials recognized that the principle of senior male primacy sometimes served their interest and sometimes not. The district administrator in Sena reported, in 1916, that many households in the district had taken up cotton cultivation in part at the company's encouragement, but still he expressed dissatisfaction: "In Zambezia, the plantings are undertaken by the women and girls and rare is the man who is seen dedicating himself to that. It is enough for it to be said to the native that he will not be taken for work outside of his district as long as he cultivates and presents a certain quantity of cotton, for him to instruct his family to plant it, because the native prefers to stay calm at home to having to remain absent for months at work."[47] Company administrators planned to build facilities in Sena's subdistrict of Chemba to grade and process the cotton, but Sena's administrator was unhappy because, he said, African men were doing none of the work. African men could successfully use their customary gender-based authority to deflect the company's demands and ensure that labor burdens would rest not on their shoulders, but on female family members.

The company's labor regime, however, weighed on relationships between women and men, disrupting gender relations as men became unavailable to fulfill responsibilities. An administrator noted that the start of the planting season was a "bad time" for "recruitment" sweeps because men were attending to their own fields, yet with African laborers demanded by white farmers, the period before the planting season—August and September—was precisely when the sweeps occurred.[48] One district administrator suggested postponing a sweep, writing to the governor that "meeting this request would be inconvenient . . . [because] this is the time in which the natives' agricultural work begins and so they have great reluctance to leave their villages."[49] Even João Pery de Lind, who rarely missed an opportunity to promote employers' interests, advised Manica's farmers one December to reduce worker flight by avoiding ill treatment, because "at planting time such recruitments are very difficult."[50] Writing to the director of the native labor department, the district administrator in Sofala explained that "being absent from their villages for a year creates great troubles for [male contract workers] . . . for it is they who prepare the land for the women to cultivate."[51] The heavier labor of field clearance was considered the responsibility of men, and when they were gone from home, female family members had to assume a greater share of household labor burden, including cultivating foodstuffs for their own families.[52]

Women could compensate for the absence of male labor by inviting neighbors to work parties in a long-established practice of mutual assistance, resorted to in times when a task exceeded the capacity of the hands available.[53] Reciprocity governed the practice; thus those who received their neighbors' help would be expected to provide help when asked—perhaps for the heavy work of field clearance or a crucially timed round of weeding. Such assistance came at a cost of extra labor and for food and drink, since those who came to help expected to eat and drink as well as to work. Millet beer, or *doro*, was consumed while the party worked, with a first beer break after several hours of work, a second sharing of beer with the midday meal women prepared, and a third at the end of the day's work. (The final bout of drinking was called the *madzande*, which, one older man explained to me, was a tongue-in-cheek reference to how difficult it could be to work effectively after having drunk a generous amount of *doro*.[54]) In all, a work party consumed a quantity of beer that took days of preparation. (The six Shona words for beer refer to the multiple stages of brewing—grinding millet, fermenting the milled grain, and boiling the solution; the process also includes the work of the cutting and carrying of firewood and the drawing and hauling of water.[55]) Fetching water or grinding millet might be delegated to younger girls, but the bulk of the labor fell to adult women. One older woman, when I asked who had brewed the beer, replied emphatically, "it was I, *I* brewed the beer."[56]

When men were lost for long stretches of time and returned with little or nothing to show for their toil, their wives sometimes rebelled. The principle of male privilege notwithstanding, mothers might discourage their sons from leaving, and wives might temporarily abandon the conjugal homestead and await their husband's return from the relative security of their parents' household, or even repudiate a marriage completely.[57] As company officials eventually learned, the company overlooked women's roles and women's labor at its peril. However male-dominated African communities appeared, women might defend their interests. Some, perhaps younger, recently married women, who faced such challenges with fewer resources and less social capital, rejected these new and straitened circumstances, even before the company created the native labor department, with its six-month minimum contract. The district administrator in the Zambezi Valley district of Tambara observed, in 1909, that "with workers absent only five months"—four months of labor, plus two weeks travel time to and from the place of work—"they generally return to find their wives [returned] to their parents' house and at times already [re]married, and when they are not married, they have taken up with another man, and do not return very willing to the house of their former husbands, claiming that they cannot stay alone at home."[58] When the labor department was established in 1911, the administrator in Chiloane—nearly 250 miles distant in the southern reaches of the territory—reported that, with forced laborers absent from home, a number of wives "rather than working in the fields, had returned to their parents' homesteads."[59]

When the men reached home at the "contract's" end, so one administrator observed, "they had nothing to eat nor any means of paying their taxes," for their fields had been uncultivated. A *contratado* then "has the following chores to do: locate his wife at her parents' house and present a gift to his father-in-law; put his hut in order; buy or beg from family some food to eat or some seeds for planting, for his wife has generally abandoned her husband's homestead in leaving for her parents; and buy cloth for himself and his family, for generally their clothing is in tatters."[60] Few forced laborers came home with enough cash to take care of even the most basic of necessities, affecting an extended network of relationships laden with status, prestige, and power.

The administrator from Neves Ferreira wrote to the governor at the start of the planting season in 1921 that the new yearlong contract was "not a good idea," because workers disliked the extended absence from their families. Some men found their fathers-in-law had tried to marry off their daughters while they were gone, despite the usual arrangement in which matrimonial planning and negotiations were undertaken jointly with a young woman's father.[61] This usurping of men's sovereignty within their household and community struck at the foundation of their status as fathers. The effect could be disastrous, undermining their identity as adult men, which depended on their authority as a household head.

For many young women, it may not have mattered greatly whether their fathers were directly involved in discussions over their matrimonial future, for the would-be brides generally had little say in marriage negotiations. Yet when their young male peers, lovers or not—those of an age most likely to be swept into the forced labor system—were also lost to them, they faced the greater likelihood of being married off to an older man. One elderly woman, speaking to me in 1998, recalled the words of a song that appeared to counsel reconciliation with that fate, suggesting there was benefit in marrying a *madala,* an elder past eligibility for conscription, and little point in waiting for a young man who might die or be maimed while working a forced labor contract.[62]

With women's narrower opportunities to acquire cash, a husband's prolonged absence or worse, desertion, might auger great hardship.[63] Labor exchanges, supported by women's beer brewing, could compensate, but households that benefited from the infusion of men's wages, sometimes invested in livestock and plows, were less likely to cooperate with poorer women who had fewer resources to offer.[64] The death or maiming of a contract worker could result in impoverishment for those left behind. One senior company official remarked on "women's well-known reluctance to give willing consent to their male relatives' emigration to the Transvaal," even though they returned flush with wages from South Africa's better-paying gold mines.[65] Nor was such reluctance confined to the territory; in neighboring Southern Rhodesia, a Native Affairs Committee report noted that "women frequently adversely affect the labour supply, as they refuse to allow their sons to proceed to work lest they should die or be injured in the course of their employment."[66] In the Mozambique Company's territory, men's departure on company contracts must have prompted a foreboding in wives and mothers.[67]

Particularly during the Great Depression, such privations were significant enough that the company could not ignore them. Under company law, unmarried adult women and widows were liable for their own tax, and women temporarily widowed because of male absence on labor contract or as migrant labor had to assume alone the survival of their household. When the director of native affairs, António Cardoso de Serpa, tracked tax payment rates throughout the territory as the Depression intensified, by 1932, he found the decline impossible to ignore; the tax in relatively well-off Manica was only two-thirds paid up even by April of the following year.[68] He proposed a tax reduction for female taxpayers: "It is neither fair nor reasonable that female contributors, who in the Territory do not do wage work and who have great difficulty in obtaining cash, should be subject to the payment at the same rate which falls on any young and vigorous man."[69] The following year the company scaled the tax liability back to its pre-1927 level of £1 for widows and unmarried or divorced women, who, according to Cardoso de Serpa, "were almost entirely without possibilities for earning money to meet [the tax] burden."[70] The next year Manica's district administrator commented on the growth of tax exemptions, mostly among "those unable to pay, due to old age," and "some women who were exempted due to the crisis."[71] The district adminis- trator in Manica wrote to Cardoso de Serpa for guidance on who should qualify for the reduction—should prostitutes receive the discounted rate or did it only apply to "women who lived by their honest labor"?[72] Cardoso de Serpa deferred to the governor, who said the reduction "should not apply to native women who dedicate themselves to prostitution," then, apparently having second thoughts, reversed himself; it "should apply to all widows and single and divorced women without any restriction."[73] His second thoughts might have been influenced by the fact that the query came from the district administrator of Manica, which had the third-largest European population (after Beira and Chimoio) in the terri- tory and the largest "foreign" (that is, non-Portuguese) European population, including many Britons who worked in the mining industry.[74] Also, the district center, Macequece, a mere twenty miles from Umtali, Southern Rhodesia's third- largest city and mining center, did not have the strict color bar that prevailed in the neighboring British colony. Like Lourenço Marques, a destination for white men from South Africa seeking African female companions, central Mozam- bique drew white settlers from Southern Rhodesia. For some women without male support or social ties, prostitution might generate the income to satisfy the company's demands.

When, in 1920, the company extended the period of forced servitude of Afri- cans to a full year, the governor said the contract "disorganizes the family." For fathers and husbands who slaved in Manica's maize fields or for other employers in the territory, the theft of their labor power had consequences for all members of a household. The ordinary balance—even a balance founded on a measure of inequality—was no longer possible. As the district administrator in Manica sum- marized: "The twelve-month contract throws native families into disarray, spoil- ing their agricultural endeavors, contributing to lower birth rates and causing many divorces."[75] The unprecedented number of *evadidos* the labor department recorded in the wake of the imposition of the twelve-month contract no doubt reflected some workers' efforts to save themselves from Manica's white farmers, but just as surely reflected attempts to preserve or salvage their family life.

# 7

# An "Absolute Freedom"
# Circumscribed and Circumvented

## "Employers Chosen of Their Own Free Will"

ANY AFRICAN MAN BETWEEN FIFTEEN AND SIXTY could, by law, avoid the Mozambique Company's forced labor roundups if he found work on his own, practiced a recognized profession (for example, as a teacher or tailor), or cultivated land of a specified minimum area. Many men and older boys struggled to exercise their paper right to choose how to assign their labor power by finding wage work on their own terms before the press gangs arrived. But though the regulations of the Portuguese colonial ministry and the company governor declared that Africans had the "absolute freedom" to choose how to fulfill the legal obligation to work, the company forced Africans to exercise that "freedom" of choice.[1] First declared in its 1899 labor code, the right was restated by Portugal in its final colonial labor code of 1928: the law did not "release them from meeting the moral obligation to work."[2] Though the decree acknowledged the "unity of the nature, origins, and ends of all human beings," it did not implement it.[3] No unemployed white man in the colonies was rounded up and marched off in a press gang.

## The Territory's *Voluntários:* Finding "an Employer That Suits"

Because colonial rulers, in general, and the Mozambique Company, in particular, assumed that Africans would not work in the absence of coercion, they employed administrative machinery backed up by violence or menace to round up the necessary workers, often to undertake tasks white farmers failed to or were unable to handle on their own. A truly free choice of employers would have meant that the company, many settlers, and other white colonists would have had to manage without captive labor.

João de Oliveira Amaral, Manica's secretary for native affairs in 1902, complained of the tactics some Africans devised to avoid long terms of service under the company's control. Amaral considered the people of Manica "the worst of the Territory," because they would take a job (and avoid the roundup), then leave the post to switch to another job every week or so. "A white proceeds to train a given black for seven days and on the eighth is left without him. I have done all I can to keep the Manicas for the length of the contract, but I am convinced that nothing can be done with that race of people."[4]

A successor to Amaral in Manica, António Cardoso de Serpa, who shared Amaral's contempt, wrote in 1921, "The so-called voluntary natives do not engage in regular work." Cardoso de Serpa elaborated: "In fact there is a large number of natives who, when recruitment occurs in the districts, go find work as *voluntários* to avoid the contract and then, once the period of recruitment has ended, continue their devotion to vagrancy."[5] After service as district administrator in Manica, Cardoso de Serpa served a brief stint as secretary general in 1921, in that post reading correspondence from fellow administrators throughout the territory. "Many of these *voluntários* constantly go about changing their residence and their employer," he wrote, "and as soon as they face urgent work that requires a sustained effort, they move on elsewhere to find easier work or better pay."[6]

If some, even most, white administrators saw laziness and mendacity, Africans themselves may have seen logic and strategy in their behavior. One company administrator who understood Africans' decisions more astutely than any other in the available records was the long-serving and self-confessed "negrophile" in Moribane, José Luiz Ferreira.[7] Ferreira's comparative isolation in a backwater post, overseeing one of the company's undeclared labor reserves, may have given him clearer insight than that of most of his counterparts. His district bordered Manica and Chimoio, making it a default supplier of labor conscripts for the mines and the maize farms, but, abutting Southern Rhodesia and the territory's southern districts, the district fell within the arc of South African mine recruiters' travels, thus providing an important work option that could save Africans from the company's own "recruitment." When the company raised the annual term of the forced labor contract from six months to a full year, Ferreira, in 1920, wrote to Cardoso de Serpa, then district administrator in Manica, explaining the African perspective. They could see that "to be contracted pays little, and even this little in a depreciated currency, and what's more," that they would have "to work for a fixed period and to serve an employer" not of their own choosing. "While on the other hand, voluntary work is paid in good currency, one can find an employer that suits, and, besides this, one can sign up for as long as one likes." In his opinion, "it is obvious that the native is not irrational . . . does not hesitate to avoid forced labor however possible."[8]

Cardoso de Serpa noted, in his tax collection report for 1916, that "the natives of Manica have a great preference for mine work and as Drivers (of cattle), and there is no lack of these positions in the region itself."[9] Finding work on their own, they left the higher-paying but dangerous underground mine work to others, and chose to remain on the surface, sorting crushed ore or cutting and carrying wood for shaft timbers or fuel. Others worked for the alluvial outfits that churned the sands of Manica's rivers in search of the fine grains of gold deposited there, or sought employment at the "Edmundian" copper mine, with its reputation for paying its workers on time "and treating them reasonably," and for failing to "resort to sophistry aimed at forcing its workers to flee on the eve of payment."[10]

Cardoso de Serpa had come to understand why many men preferred "mine work to any other, offering the best compensation."[11] For those in Manica who lived near the mines, the work there allowed them to live at home and avoid their employer's food and housing, both the source of perennial worker complaints. Their wages went toward their taxes, generating an income stream so steady that even when World War I disrupted the industry in 1915 and many of the district's mines "reduced their workforce to what was strictly indispensable," the secretary of native affairs predicted little difficulty in completing the year's tax collection.[12]

The secretary general, António de Sousa Ribeiro, expressing disapproval about African workers' freedom of choice, protested that to "allow the natives the choice of employers, without any restriction, would not be a good idea, because there are certain tasks—for example, stump pulling—which the natives don't much like, thus it is natural that they would only offer themselves at farms with fields already cleared and where consequently the work would be lighter. This would have a bad effect on the natives and could even produce a certain disorganization in the labor supply."[13]

The many from Manica who went to work, voluntarily, for the district's white farmers virtually never worked in the fields, which were full of seized laborers, but took jobs as drivers, "work which they preferred to any other."[14] Drivers possessed skills not readily found, and white farmers made a special effort to attract and retain these workers. The low rates they paid for the company's conscripts enabled them to offer attractive salaries to these skilled workers, with premium monthly salaries of £2 or more. They guided cattle-drawn plows though maize fields and piloted the dozen or more oxen that made up the "cattle trains" that drew wagons of harvest to the railhead, both vital to the white farmers, tasks for which the district administrator reported men from Manica had a "special apti-tude."[15] The director of the labor department observed that workers from Mori-bane, too, were "very much sought after" by Manica's white farmers, for work with draft animals and plows and "other work [requiring] more trust."[16] These Africans' key role in maize production protected them from abuse by the farm-ers. Such work also offered an opportunity to hone skills for later use on farms of their own, and to accrue savings from wages, often invested in cattle and machin-ery. Many Africans were acquiring "through work the means for a more prosper-ous existence," as the injunction in the labor law had urged.[17]

As for those unable to find work on their own before the native labor depart-ment's semiannual sweeps, the inspector general noted that in the department's last years of operation, they never ceased efforts to avoid the roundups: "Gener-ally, the black goes for 'contract work' unwillingly, with an aversion that prompts them to shun it however possible, it being necessary at times to send police into the villages to force them violently to work."[18] By 1925, there were more than 64,000 company *compelidos* (forced laborers) and just over 40,000 *voluntários*.

### Joining the Migrant Flow: "It Is Better to Go to John"

Even before the last decade of the nineteenth century, when the South African Chamber of Mines developed its regionwide labor recruitment system, men from southern Mozambique had long trekked to South Africa, some as early as the 1860s, or had shipped by boat to work on sugar plantations in the English colony of Natal.[19] With Johannesburg's (known to some as "John") emergence as an in-dustrial center in the 1890s, there was a large and steady flow of men that inten-sified after Portugal's 1899 colonial labor law made them vulnerable for forced labor. Southern Mozambican men could avoid Portugal's forced labor dragnet by such migration, through the system established by the mine owners' Wit-watersrand Native Labor Association and authorized by an agreement between Portugal and the Transvaal Republic (as later, with the Union of South Africa).[20]

In southern Mozambique, Portuguese colonial officials governed under the same metropolitan labor law of 1899 that authorized the company's forced labor, with Portuguese state-controlled southern Mozambique and company-run cen-tral Mozambique existing side by side as Portuguese possessions. Portugal had retained direct administration of the southern portion of its southeast African colony, partly because outsourcing this parcel as well might have undercut its as-sertion of sovereign rule, but also because South African reliance on the port of Lourenço Marques, together with the capitation fees paid to the Portuguese colonial administration for Mozambican migrant laborers in South African mines, generated a strong revenue source that Portugal saw no reason to share with a private company.[21] Since the Mozambique Company's quasi-sovereign status gave it the right to govern African labor on a wholly separate footing, it jealously guarded its pool of African labor. Its forced recruitment monopoly within the territory itself excluded all others. It policed its borders with neighboring colonial administrations, Portuguese or British, and turned away all South African and Southern Rhodesian requests to recruit within company territory. Company laws against "clandestine emigration" prohibited Africans from leaving the territory without permission, and, with penalties for violating these laws of up to twenty months of forced labor, the company effectively denied to many African workers within its borders the right to exercise freedom of choice.

In contrast, southern Mozambique served as a massive labor reserve for South Africa, most especially for its mining industry.[22] Portugal leased these African workers to South Africa's Chamber of Mines, rewarded by a steady cash flow of wage remittances—holding half of mine workers' salaries in trust for payment only on their return to Mozambique. The Portuguese colonial administration received, in addition, a direct payment for each worker recruited by the Witwatersrand Native Labor Association for the Chamber of Mines.[23] Although life on South African mining compounds was often harsh and mine work dangerous, it paid wages at a rate that exceeded almost any in Mozambique. In consequence, by the close of the nineteenth century, more than 70,000 men from southern Mozambique were choosing to go to work in South African mines every year; they comprised three-quarters of the gold mines' workforce, a level sustained throughout most of the twentieth century under successive agreements between Portugal and South Africa.[24]

Despite the Mozambique Company's ban on South African recruiters, some clandestinely breached the border separating company territory from southern Mozambique (where they operated freely) and signed up workers from the territory's southern districts of Mossurize, Govuro, Mocoque, and Alto Save. The governor complained that those regions were "a vast field of action for buccaneers from the Transvaal, and one of [Wenela's] labor reserves. . . . They recruit workers, steal the natives, and, finally, are the true rulers of the country."[25] Even as far north as Manica, the district administrator once wrote of his suspicions that a Transvaaler he knew as "Bodo J. Dangers" was responsible for the disappearance of a group of thirty workers from Moribane en route to Manica.[26] Recruiters from the Rand (as South Africa's gold mining region was known) remained active in the wider area over the long term, some setting up "a cordon of encampments" just over the border in southern Mozambique, from which they could operate openly, for the express purpose of luring men from the territory.[27] Some were bold enough to drive their trucks across the border into the company's concession, the more easily to carry off the workers for the Witwatersrand.[28]

Thousands of adolescent African boys and men from the territory joined the migrant flow, with great numbers making the journey independently of the South African recruitment network. By 1901, the company's administrator in Govuro wrote that hundreds of men were at work outside the district, with many "setting off for the Transvaal or Rhodesia, where they remain, sometimes for years."[29] Writing from neighboring Mossurize, his counterpart pointed out that "the difference between salaries in Manica and Rhodesia is not so great and if they still emigrate there [Southern Rhodesia] it is due to forced recruitment for Manica, which every year takes a large number of natives whose work is used for agriculture, leading them to detest the region of Manica."[30] Another administrator left no doubt about the role played by the company's contract labor in the exodus; he reported that the district's "chiefs declared that most of the natives who left for the Rand did so after their return from Chimoio, Manica, and Beira, with only a short stay at home."[31]

One group of men from Mossurize explained their decision to the district administrator in stark terms, telling him, "after all, the *muzungos* of the farms continue to give us drubbings and so it is better to go to John [Johannesburg]."[32] Thousands went to work on South Africa's gold mines—Ferreira called these "the best school" for mine work, even though drubbings were abundant there as well.[33] One former miner recalled, "I noticed that the white man knows how to beat up a black person. We were beaten, we were beaten . . . a fist would go up here, the fist would go up here. We were beaten with a *klap* [lash]. We were beaten."[34] There was physical brutality at "John," but braving the violence of South Africa's mines might mean returning home with the means to pay for bride wealth and to establish themselves as independent men, heads of households. A field worker in central Mozambique would be lucky to survive with even the amount needed to pay his hut tax.

Those who traveled independently of the established South African recruitment networks showed a perseverance that testified to ambition, desperation, and courage. Setting off to walk many hundreds miles was not a decision to take lightly. Dry season travel meant facing freezing nighttime temperatures while sleeping out in the rough, and a journey during the rainy season risked falling ill with malaria or fording rivers and streams swollen with floodwater. Exposure, illness, and exhaustion could reduce migrants to a weakened state that undercut their earning potential if they were fortunate enough to survive. Some died en route, freezing to death, sleeping with only a thin blanket's cover or falling prey to animal predators.[35] They faced dangers from humans as well, especially detection and arrest by company or Portuguese colonial police, or encounters with unlicensed South African labor recruiters, little more than man catchers who would capture migrants before they reached the mines and bind them over to employers to be held captive in conditions no better, and sometimes worse, than on the wretched farms in Manica.[36]

The company's own inspectorate in central Mozambique, suggesting that it might decide to reverse the trend by providing tempting competition, proposed, in 1909, that if the district administrator in Govuro "were able to induce a group of natives from his district to contract for work in Manica and *if these were properly paid,* it might be possible to establish, within the Territory, a countervailing force to well-paid mine labor in the Transvaal and Rhodesia."[37] But the proposal was never enacted, and the company had little success, since neither it nor most of the territory's private employers were willing to pay African workers "properly," and not even its native labor department could provide the necessary counterweight. Governor Pery de Lind noted, several years later, that Africans in Mossurize "mostly tend to find work in the Transvaal mines where, as is known, the salaries are relatively high, and those within the Territory cannot in any way compete."[38] Nor did time reverse the trend, for, by the mid-1920s, the inspectorate still reported the "recruitment of natives from the south of our Territory is impossible to manage, seeing as they go to work to the Transvaal whose mine salaries greatly attract them."[39] By the 1930s, some company administrators seemed resigned to the southward "clandestine emigration," one observing that nearly all migrants ended up in the Transvaal, "where they are long used to going for many years now, despite all the efforts made, also for many years, to prevent them from doing so."[40]

For the most part, company administrators themselves did not see such African workers as the rational decision makers José Luiz Ferreira had described; they did not view it as strategic choice. One administrator explained emigration to the Transvaal as simply "an ancient tradition of the race," despite its recent emergence during the period of the development of South Africa's industrial capitalism and the company's best efforts to prevent it.[41] Calling for the company to "combat" this outward flow of labor, district administrators and settler farmers supported repressive measures against Africans' migrancy, including proposals to impose fines (scaled to length of absence, with progressive punishment for returned migrants—the longer Africans were gone, the greater their savings were likely to be) on returning mine workers. Decades of such "combat" notwithstanding, it was a struggle the company lost to the migrants, whose treks southward never ceased.[42]

In the words of one administrator in Mossurize, the outflow was a "spontane-ous" movement that "long ago penetrated the traditions of the races who live in this district."[43] In that district, the administrator wrote, at the end of the 1930s, "it would be difficult to find an adult man who had not gone to work on the Transvaal at least once." "The boys, ever since they were little," were accustomed to hearing "marvels of their elders' travels to the Rand, [and] scarcely before they feel strong enough to endure the harsh work of the mines, they put themselves on the road, knowing that until they do, they will not be seen as real men." He pointed out that starting a family, "the highest aspiration of all the adolescents," brought bride wealth costs that would take years to save in the territory.[44] He was correct about that, at least.

## Finding "New Methods ... to Elude the Authorities"

Rand-bound migration was not an option for most Africans in the territory, and those from remote areas, such as the upper Zambezi Valley area, far from the Rand and from any of the territory's own centers of commerce, had fewer ready opportunities to avoid serving as a *contratado*. For some, the distance to South Africa was simply too great—the densely populated south bank of the Zambezi River was another several hundred miles distant—and passing through well-traveled and well-policed areas was a risk. So, too, mine labor, especially under-ground, was dangerous and debilitating.[45] Contrary to the belief that some Afri-cans migrated "by nature," many pursued it, despite its danger, as in their own interest. Others embarked as on a rite of passage that had little to do with mining itself.[46]

Among the African population, others created work opportunities of their own; one such came in the latter part of the 1920s, in the wake of Edward Ross's report on abusive labor practices in Angola and Mozambique and the accom-panying, if short-lived, League of Nations' scrutiny of labor practices in Portu-gal's African territories. The company, in response, briefly, and partially, subcon-tracted its role as labor conscripter, passing that task on to a private association, the Native Labour Association of Manica and Sofala. When the association struggled to fulfill employers' requests, Africans, observing that district admin-istrators and their armed police were temporarily sidelined from recruitment, exploited the resulting uncertainty.

Africans' resistance to the association's contracts, initially made without com-pany administrators' menacing participation, caused the Native Labour Associa-tion to founder, imperiling the existence of the territory's white farmers, many of whom were its members, entirely dependent, as they were, on coerced contract workers.[47] In 1926, at the close of the association's first four fruitless months of operation, its director, Armindo Gonçalves Forte, sounded a note of concern about what he considered "the native's attitude . . . that he is not obliged to work." Reviewing the Native Labour Association's meager results throughout the territory, Forte could point to only a single strong area of operation, Chemba, where the company's agent had contracted nearly 1,000 men. Of those, 500 had been sent for agricultural work; he hoped their timely arrival in the maize belt might "ease the critical situation of our members."[48]

Chemba was, in some respects, a likely source of labor for the white farmers; during the company labor department's last five years of operation, from 1922 through 1926, an average of nearly four in ten men or boys from Chemba were taken as company *contratados* annually, with thousands sent to Manica's maize farms.[49] The private labor association and its modus operandi were new, but thousands (fewer than as forced laborers) from Chemba had worked in the past as *voluntários* and knew how poorly contract labor compared. The Chemba workers were about to challenge both the association's survival and the company's ability to maintain its authority. Shortly after reaching farms in Manica and Chimoio in late 1926, some conscripted workers from Chemba charged that the work did not conform with the terms explained to them when recruited, and insisted that those terms be honored. Forte, writing to the company's administrator in Chemba, who had overseen the workers' recruitment, stated firmly that "the workers' allegations cannot in any way be true." He asked the administrator to send "one or two of the chiefs of greatest prestige" from Chemba to the farms, to keep the men at work.[50] Yet within days, Forte sounded close to panic, reporting that great numbers of Chemba workers were now in flight, "which could lead to certain financial ruin for the Association."[51] The association's agent in Chemba had found many workers only by offering advance payments on their contracts, a risky practice but one the association approved and one the district administrator encouraged, most likely because he could count on collecting it quickly in the form of hut tax payments. The agent in Chemba who sent the workers attributed their flight to the "natives' knavishness," a charge the district administrator there rejected. "The knavishness cannot be attributed to the natives," he said, suggesting the agent himself needed closer supervision.[52]

Six of the workers from Chemba reported they had fled a farm in Chimoio after the farmer beat them with a bamboo rod and undercounted the number of days they worked, for the purpose of withholding payment.[53] Two other men fled a farm near Macequece before meeting the farmer himself, proof, Forte suggested, that "they fled without any reason," or at least none related to the work, since they had not yet started.[54] Even on farms where no abuses were reported, the association's recruits encountered numerous *voluntários*, better treated and well paid, some working at skilled positions, others mere field workers like themselves who had sought out work on their own. The unequal conditions for the same work were surely galling.

Workers' efforts to create for themselves a "more prosperous existence," as Portugal's colonial labor law put it, undercut the attempt of the Native Labour Association to carry on the company's labor regime on a private basis. When the association initially faltered in meeting demands for workers, the farmers hired job seekers who had turned up at the farms and agreed in their desperation for labor to demands for higher wages. Forte, unwittingly echoing Ferreira's earlier observation about the benefits of work as a *voluntário*, reflected somewhat bitterly that "in these conditions, it is obvious that the native, having an offer of more pay and shorter term of service," would not hesitate to abandon a prior obligation to the association. Employers' pursuit of what the director of native affairs called a "disloyal competition," together with what Forte condemned as workers' "lack of scruples," created something approaching a free market in labor in which the association could not keep afloat.[55]

Through the first several months of 1927, scores of workers from Chemba continued to flee the farms to which they had been sent; by early April, 170 had fled, and, according to Forte, the numbers "were mounting every day . . . which represents for this Association a loss of about £500."[56] Forte had his own interests at stake as a minor shareholder in the association and was under pressure from association members who pressed him to make good on the workers they expected.[57] The manager of Andrada Mines in Manica wrote of the disappearance of two workers sent by the association, and, inquiring about another, asked whether the authorities might "arrest him and send him to you after punishment. . . . We would ask you . . . to treat this matter as urgent. Our Head Office is enquiring into this and point out, quite rightly, that the desertion of these two boys is a monetary loss to the [mining] Company. In the case of 'Nazaro' we have paid his recruiting fee, all expenses bringing him here, his repatriation fee and Hospital fees, and now seemingly we are not to have the benefit of his work." Still another worker "was taken to prison on the 12th of March and died in Macequece on 14th March, we had possibly 3 days work from this boy and yet had to pay all expenses as in the other two cases." The manager closed his letter with a request for a partial refund of the recruitment fee the association had charged.[58]

Forte and his association were concerned with their financial losses, but also, as Forte said, with other losses "of a moral character, as it might be undermined . . . by the farmers' lack of confidence . . . and finally by the ineffectiveness of our efforts to capture the *evadidos*."[59] Forte's agent in Chimoio, suggesting that some workers had invented charges of ill-treatment to justify their flight, urged the association and the company to take a hard line, returning any *capturados* to the same employers, since otherwise "in no time anarchy will reign among the natives."[60] Without such measures, he believed, they ran the risk of triggering the flight of laborers still at work. Forte asked the administrator in Chemba to return the *evadidos* by force to complete their contracts, or, at the very least, to imprison them or their family members.[61] As with the farmers' abuse and the workers' subsequent flight, the request for collective punishment—a practice in which company officials were well versed—was the predictable next step in the conventional script.

Yet when the administrator in Chemba summoned the district chiefs to prepare to capture the *evadidos* (or failing that, their relatives), the response suggested that the Chemba workers had taken steps in an entirely different direction and departed from the script. The chiefs reported "the workers in flight had not returned to their villages and that a large number" were not to be found within the district; they could be sought out in the agricultural region along the rail line or in Beira.[62] Forte complained directly to the company native affairs department about the "impractical" suggestion and pointed out the "plain impossibility of recognizing [the *evadidos*] among the 20,000 natives at work in Beira and along the rail line." He proposed that some chiefs and relatives in Chemba "be captured and sent to the work sites" from which the contracted workers had fled, in hopes of tracking them down.[63]

To do Forte's bidding, the district administrator in Chemba helped to locate a man named Canivete, whose son, Michone, had been sent by the association to Chimoio. Canivete embarked on an odyssey through the districts of Neves Ferreira, Chimoio, Manica, and Buzi in search of his son, the association footing the bill for his travel costs. He could not find his son and learned only that he had been in Buzi but had decided to return home to Chemba. Forte asked that the son be found and either be forced to complete his contract or reimburse the association for the costs of his contract and also for the costs of his father's travels.[64]

The Chemba workers' new strategy—aimed not at avoiding work but, as association officials soon learned, at finding better employment—and their tactical innovation in its pursuit became apparent as other relatives and chiefs began to report on the whereabouts of the *evadidos*. The association's agent in Chimoio wrote that "just today I managed to muster some of the *evadidos* who had been captured by the chiefs and relatives who came from Chemba for this purpose."[65] Far from hoping to return home, they had not even left the area; some were at work for the Beira Railway Company and others, in Manica, for Andrada Mines. Still others had put to use what Forte called "new methods . . . to elude the authorities." The agent reported that one *capturado* had been found near Chimoio with a new pass book; he had "gotten rid of the one he brought from Chemba, and upon being captured he had completely false identification, given that previously his name was Jack."[66] Nor was the erstwhile Jack the only one to realize that the pass book could be used to undermine the bureaucratic control of the company. The agent reported on his own success, fleeting as it turned out, in capturing a group of *evadidos* with the assistance of chiefs, village heads, and relatives from Chemba, but in response, twelve of the *capturados* countered with a move "that can not be checked . . . fleeing anew into the bush and leaving their pass books with the chiefs."[67]

The results from Manica were only marginally more promising, the association's agent reporting that ten village heads from Chemba also had arrived to search for their wayward villagers and discovered fourteen at work as *voluntários*. The police found that "they had made false declarations to acquire new pass books and flee from work," detained them, and took them to court, where they were convicted and sentenced to sixty days in prison.[68] For the few *evadidos* who were caught, scores more remained at large, able and willing to shed one identity and acquire a new one.

Forte's agitation peaked as it became clear just how completely the people from Chemba were outmaneuvering his association and the company. In justifying his call for severe punishment, Forte reiterated the charge that the Chemba workers had fled without cause, and that it was a "premeditated act." In a letter to the director of native affairs, Forte could barely conceal his frustration behind the opening formulaic politesse ("We take the opportunity to request Your Excellency deign to call the attention of Mister District Administrator of Chemba District") before relating his latest encounters in tracking down the *evadidos*. He had sent from Chemba the fathers, cousins, sons, and brothers of nineteen workers who had fled, but now learned that these relatives "had run off as well, after having—at our cost—traveled and eaten as much as they liked." That these were forward-thinking strategies no doubt heightened his displeasure, and his indignation, at the very real possibility that Africans had taken advantage of him.[69]

Neither the association nor the company had a ready response for workers' nimble planning, in which they, with chiefs and family members, colluded to use the administrative infrastructure of recruitment to their own advantage. The workers thus subverted the system's bureaucratic rationality, turning the reliance on decentralized decision making against itself, aware that their tactical advantage in mobility could reduce the system's capacity to maintain control over long distances. They foresaw that the company's dependence on chiefs might prove self-defeating when the enforcers proved less than capable or reliable. In so doing, they manipulated the same system that had long controlled their labor, and thereby often secured better-paying work that might allow them to improve their social condition.

## A "Fateful Salary Increase" and "Depressive Crisis"

African workers' ability to choose among wage-paying employers depended vitally on the reduced level of coercion during those few years at the end of the 1920s, but also, as Cardoso de Serpa said in 1929, on the territory's "continuing development . . . [with] labor demand being much greater than the supply of workers."[70] Following the company's 1926 abolition of its native labor department, the "abrupt change in native labor regime [and the] intense search for workers," in the association director's words, led to "a fateful salary increase," one to which they resigned themselves "not without some repugnance."[71] Unable to rely as dependably on the coercion of the past thirty years, employers now offered *voluntários* monthly salaries ranging from thirty to forty shillings—even mere field workers were refusing pay less than twenty-two to twenty-five shillings monthly, or roughly a third to half again as much as the salaries the association offered.[72] Other employers, such as Beira Railways and firms that handled cargo at the port, offered monthly wages of twenty-seven shillings, and, Cardoso de Serpa added, with "work conditions much less heavy than those in agriculture (only eight hours of work daily and days off on Saturday afternoons and Sundays)."[73]

Soon, however, the Depression hit the territory hard, eliminating investment, tightening credit, and driving down prices for agricultural commodities like maize. The disaster affected all parts of the territory's economy, not all at the same time. Mining, long sensitive to capital market volatility, felt the effects first. The director of mines remarked, in his annual report for 1929, that "the pronounced depressive crisis . . . reached a highest degree: mining production was insignificant, the abandonment of the mine field obvious," and that the mines department, reliant on production-generated fees, could barely cover its costs.[74] The following year, white farmers in Manica and Chimoio faced "an enormous fall in prices for their products and a lack of buyers." Some, unable to afford even the below market rate for coerced African labor on which they depended, tried unsuccessfully to pay the association in maize flour, and then stopped farming altogether.[75]

The enormity of the Depression's impact was evident in the director of native affairs' observation, two years later, that, "the abundance of native labor in the Territory was growing worse from one day to the next."[76] The director's assessment was matched by that of a manager from the Buzi Company's sugar operations, who wrote to the association director that "unfortunately . . . voluntary labor all over is in search of work and is abundant," explaining his limited interest in hiring contract workers.[77] The suggestion that a plentiful supply of African labor was an unfortunate problem signaled just how completely the economic crisis had overturned the established order. A superabundance of African work-seekers, with a consequent downward pressure on wages, was exactly what the company had unsuccessfully sought to achieve with its conscription efforts over the past thirty years.

The global economic crisis reversed the long-standing dynamic of the territory's labor market, in which most employers' demand for labor had been so insatiable that they would accept nearly any worker, no matter how limited his physical abilities, giving him up only if too weak or ill to be of use. Now, the administrator in Manica reported, "employers examine their workers carefully and reject all those who don't appear to be in good physical condition."[78] While, in years past, those charged with recruitment had counted on famine to ease their task—convinced that people would accept a contract rather than starve—employers were now so discriminating that they rejected any workers who, owing to "greater age or lesser physical condition, don't offer a guarantee of a good return on their labor."[79] Some workers, he noted, were "not entirely unable to work, [but their] abilities were diminished such that, given the current labor demand in the Territory," they could not find anyone who would hire them.[80]

By 1931, salaries had fallen by half across the board, and the director of native affairs observed the "abundance of workers being of such a nature that they spontaneously offer themselves for work at inferior salaries."[81] Little more than a year later, toward the end of 1932, work-seekers faced an even worse market: agricultural labor within their district of residence paid 1$68.5 *escudos,* with a premium (2$19.375 *escudos*) for those willing to work farther from home. Even workers with specialized skills could expect no better than 2$70 *escudos.*[82] At such meager levels, especially for agricultural labor, even if workers received their entire salaries—a far from certain outcome given many employers' insolvency—and even if they "exercised a rigorous economy with the wages they received," the district administrator pointed out, "at the end of four months of work, they would be left with only 1$80 *escudos* after having paid their tax, if they had only one tax to pay." It was still worse for those, with family members starving after repeated drought years and locust infestations, who used their wages to send food home, and would be unable to meet their tax obligations to the company.[83]

The result was an amazing contraction in the territory's African workforce from an all-time high of more than 138,000 (conscripts and voluntary workers together) in 1928, to slightly over 73,000 in 1932.[84] Employment numbers stayed low, rising only slightly, to 79,000, in 1936.[85] Territory-wide, the impact was evident in African residents' inability to pay the company's hut tax. Cardoso de Serpa noted with concern that a large group of people from the territory's southern districts traveled to Beira to the Portuguese government representative "to protest against the hut tax rate . . . asking that their complaints be communicated to the Government of the Colony and of the Republic." In one area of Sena, some residents, taking matters into their own hands in 1932, moved into neighboring territory under the direct administration of the Portuguese colonial state—where the tax rate was about a third of the company's—for the express purpose of lowering their tax burden.[86] In other parts of Sena, people defied the administrator's order to enroll in the tax census, and in the southern districts, some openly announced they would pay only 75 percent of the tax, since they could not raise a greater sum. District administrators assured Cardoso de Serpa that the protesters were motivated by straitened circumstances and not by any "ill will," but he fretted about "a spirit of indiscipline and unrest among the native population."[87]

Even in Manica, whose economic prospects were better than most, the population struggled to "relieve their economic penury," and, in the depths of the Depression, Cardoso de Serpa worried that, with no public works to which tax debtors might be sentenced, such "impunity" might lead others to follow their example.[88] The portion of the district's population declared exempt from the tax—the elderly and those physically unable to work—climbed steadily through the middle of the decade, from just 5 percent in 1927 to 11 percent in 1931, 16 percent in 1932, and 18.7 percent in 1933. It hovered at 25 percent from 1934 to 1938.[89] Manica's district administrator, António Fernando de Oliveira Tavares, attributed the rise in exemptions not only to greater selectivity among employers, which reduced some people's earning potential, but also to the fact that "many natives, in plain condition to be exempt, were not [exempted in the past], with their relatives paying their tax. Now the conditions of life are different and many natives come asking for exemptions, which cannot be refused due to their obvious infirmity."[90]

## "Duty to National Sovereignty": Meeting "Nonnegotiable Needs for Labor"

In Manica, and, specifically, within the mining industry, the resurgent demand in labor that emerged toward the end of the 1930s did not herald good news for African workers. In early 1937, the director of the mines department wrote that "the small mines have suffered immensely with the lack of labor, with some at risk of closing and others reducing production." The director, advocating for mine operators who were having difficulty finding African mine workers, especially for underground work, encountered a curious lack of support from Manica's district administrator.[91] In his "desperate struggle to ensure that the Mining Industry might be an important element of progress within the Territory," the director complained that the district administrator was "making light [of the problem]— 'miners, pantomimers,'" he had said.[92] The company should "create needs that can only be satisfied through work," the director wrote, "and impose the obligation to work on all the people."[93]

In a letter to the managing director in Lisbon, the governor stated that he was searching for a way to "overcome the lack of labor"; he had convened an internal company commission of senior administrators and select district administrators.[94] The commission reported that many Africans still found it hard to pay their hut tax; it expressed concern about the potential impact uncollected taxes might have on the African population's respect for the company's authority. It rejected the idea of a tax cut, however, concluding that the current tax levy was "a social and moral necessity." The territory's economy and, especially, white settler colonists had "pressing and nonnegotiable needs for labor." The tax served to "create needs for the native, to drag him from the atavistic and degrading vice of laziness."[95]

Signaling a new turn in company labor policy, in advance of the next agricultural season, the director of native affairs instructed the district administrator in Gorongosa to round up 250 workers for public works because "almost all the voluntary workers are at work in various private employers and it is not possible to obtain the volume of labor needed for public works."[96] The district administrator in Gorongosa declined to comply: "it is not convenient to force the population further."[97] The reply touched off a flurry of correspondence from the governor on down that made clear the ongoing camouflaged coercion.

António Fernando de Oliveira Tavares, now director of native affairs, thought the district administrator's reply suggested that "the population has already been forced, though without saying how, nor when, nor by whom."[98] The term "to force" was commonly understood to mean "to 'oblige by force,' 'compel,' or 'use violence.'" Tavares argued the administrator's words did not "in reality correspond to what legally is done and should be done, which is to try to bring the natives to fulfill their moral duty to work . . . to improve their conditions of life and contribute to the general interest of humanity."[99] The volume of correspondence generated in response reflected the anxiety of the company to meet the letter, though not the spirit, of the law.

As Tavares saw it, "acts of god" had led to "public calamity," with back-to-back locust infestations in 1937 and 1938, in combination with drought in one year and flooding in the next, almost certainly his intentional evocation of the sort of circumstances in which the 1930 Forced Labor Convention authorized forced labor.[100] He underscored the importance of protecting Portuguese national interests, especially a notable agricultural reexpansion in Manica and Chimoio, long the centers for Lisbon's settler farmers, and a Portuguese-operated sugar factory in Buzi. He looked with favor on any and all advice or "persuasive methods" district administrators might use to get Africans to seek work on their own. Administrators "should not back away from the orders and other methods which might be necessary to force [Africans] to uphold contracts legally and voluntarily made"; just how voluntarily the labor contracts were was not considered.[101]

In 1939, two weeks before Germany invaded Poland, Artur de Barros Lima, the company's director of native affairs, wrote to the governor to offer his thoughts on the "native problem" that could not openly be stated in his instructions to district administrators. Cotton cultivation was of growing importance, since Portugal's textile industry hoped to benefit from the then-booming world market. Barros Lima pointed out that forced cotton cultivation had "transformed [the Belgian Congo] in short order into one of the best agricultural trade centers." He listed a number of colonies in Africa and farther afield—Tanganyika, Nyasaland, Rhodesia, Kenya, the Seychelles, Samoa, Papua and New Guinea, Fiji, and French West Africa—all of which permitted forced cultivation without running afoul of the principles established by the League of Nations Forced Labor Convention of 1930.[102] The company's administration left little doubt of its contempt for those principles, one report referring to France, Portugal, and Belgium as having had the "good sense" not to ratify the Forced Labor Convention, whose supporters were, to senior company officials, "puritanical theorists."[103]

Writing to the territory's local administrators, Barros Lima repeated the governor's orders to ensure that their census numbers were precise; without an accurate count of the population, and, specifically, of the number judged "fit for labor," the company would not know whether "there might be natives who are not satisfying their duty to work. We ought to avoid, now more than ever, at a time when the general interest of humanity imposes, if one might not say sacrifices, at least the strict fulfillment of the duties born by all, that any lack of labor in the Territory be reduced if it cannot be eliminated."[104] Barros Lima further explained that while some might be physically or legally exempt from contract labor, "as with women in certain cases," they were not exempt from the moral duty to work, and could meet it by working on their own, for example, in cultivating cotton.[105] Any "sacrifices" would be borne within the African population, not elsewhere.

As wartime needs stoked the global economy, especially for goods such as sugar and cotton, the company returned full-bore to forcing Africans to work. Citing the old rationale of Africans' "atavistic aversion to work," Barros Lima

later wrote that "it is necessary to bring the native to meet his duty to work, because the expression 'lack of labor,' is no longer commonplace and must be substituted by that of 'lack of will to work.'"[106] The first native affairs circular of 1940
reminded district administrators that timely hut tax collection was as important
as ever; it cited the 1892 regulations authorizing stints of forced labor at 150 percent of the tax rate for tax debtors. The administrators were to engage in "intense
propaganda" to induce people to work, and "chiefs were to be ordered to turn in
native debtors under threat" of having their payments to themselves reduced "if
they don't use all their efforts toward this end."[107] These orders were justified by
what Barros Lima called Africans' "duty to national sovereignty," but, above all,
by the necessity of "getting them to fulfill their moral duty to work, contributing
to the general interest of humanity."[108]

The forced cotton cultivation to which the director of native affairs referred
marked the expansion of a vast scheme that, over the next two decades, would
burden nearly a million Mozambicans (in the territory and elsewhere) with the
task of cultivating cotton for Portugal. Portugal's dictator, António Salazar, took
the position that the African colonies should serve the interests of Lisbon; forcing
Africans to produce cotton for Portugal's textile industry was part of that plan.
The company's charter was due to expire in three years, but the colonial ministry
required that it take part nonetheless in the widely unpopular cotton scheme.[109]
In many areas, implementation was possible only by grafting it onto the coercive
administrative machinery for forced labor. Cotton cultivation, burdensome in its
tasks—and often imposed on female cultivators—stole time from tending food
crops, thus undermining rural communities' food security.[110]

Africans selected for the forced cotton cultivation program recognized the
uncertainties of farming and the fixed low prices imposed by the cotton regime.
Early in 1942, a local administrator from southern Manica wrote to his superior
in Macequece with an urgent request for maize and sorghum seeds. Drought had
all but wiped out the year's plantings, and another year of famine would be devastating to cotton cultivation "begun so auspiciously" the previous year. The problem was not the lack of rain for the cotton plantings, but, so an offhand comment
on the effects of malnutrition and starvation acknowledged, "without sufficient
food the native does not work as might be desired [and] reduces to a minimum"
the cotton plantings. The African cultivators of whom he spoke stated the obvious: cotton "is not a thing which is eaten."[111]

The company's last pronouncement on forcing Africans to work came in a
July 1942 report, written on the eve of its charter's expiry. It opened with a reference to Portugal's labor code: Lisbon "neither imposes nor permits the natives of
its colonies to be forced to any type of forced or coerced work for private ends, but

it does not release them from the moral duty, which necessarily belongs to them, to seek through work the means of subsistence, thus contributing to the general interests of humanity." The government held the "right to urge them to work for themselves . . . and to oversee and charitably protect their work under contract." The report suggested it was time for a clearer definition of what "is understood by the 'moral obligation of work.'"[112] That definition would include "directed cultivation," a "euphemism," so the author of the company's report suggested, in use by "free nations and among free peoples [to] disguise the compulsory nature of certain cultivation."[113] Forced labor was authorized under Lisbon's Colonial Act and the company's charter, but in the present emergency, "neither the *voluntários* nor the [tax debtors] are enough to meet the needs which Humanity requires. Why shouldn't we go further?" The report argued that, though the Native Labor Code barred forced labor for private ends, the company authorized it for public purposes in "urgent and special cases," one of which was to respond to acts of God or public calamity, such as fire, flood, severe weather, invasion of locusts or other pests, and epidemics. "That we are at the present moment facing an act of God cannot be doubted. That we are victims of one of the greatest cataclysm[s] which might come to conquer Humanity, as is war, visiting its economic flux on the Portuguese Nation, also cannot be doubted." Even the Geneva principles, expressed in the 1930 Forced Labor Convention, "do not scruple in permitting forced labor to prevent famine."[114] The report pointed to a recent law in Southern Rhodesia that authorized forced labor.[115] "All must come together to put the specter of famine among the natives to flight. . . . We shall force the native to cultivate rice. The authorities lack neither the force of law nor the force of reason. If 'in the heat of battle you don't clean your weapons,' as the saying says, even less can one cross one's arms in the face of a threat that menaces all." The company's final recommendations left little doubt of what was to come: "Hands to work and seed to earth, for the good of the Nation."[116] The last phrase, *"à bem da nação,"* in Portuguese, the Salazar regime's all-purpose salutation more and more commonly used through the 1930s, signaled a ritual recognition of the dictator's authority and suggested that any individual interest must be subordinate to that of the nation.

# 8

# Upward Mobility

## "Improvement of One's Social Condition"

THE IMPRINT OF *SALAZARISMO*, THE NAME BY WHICH dictator António Salazar's ruling ideology became known, was evident as early as 1930, when he added the post of minister of the colonies to his powerful primary role as minister of finance. The Colonial Act of that year, the foundational document for his management of the empire, asserted that part of the "organic essence of the Portuguese nation in fulfilling its historic role is to occupy and colonize overseas domains and to civilize the populations there, exercising as well the moral influence to which it is linked by the inheritance of the East."[1] For Salazar's Portugal, civilizing Africans and exerting a "moral influence" were intimately linked to the trinity of "God, country, work" to which all of its subjects were bound.

Portugal, along with the rest of Europe's colonial powers, was preparing to strut at the International Colonial Exhibition in Paris, due to open in 1931. Planning began in Portugal and throughout Mozambique several years earlier, so that exhibits of the colony's agricultural, industrial, and engineering accomplishments "might correspond to the grandeur of its resources," as the governor-general put it in 1928.[2] Mozambique's planners were charged to present to the pan-European and worldwide audience the state of the "physical, moral, intellectual, and social development of the natives." In the Mozambique Company's territory, from the governor down to the lowest district secretary, officials strove to fulfill Lisbon's call for "a complete demonstration of the civilizing work, both past and in progress."[3]

To accompany its exhibits in Paris, the company sent a slim pamphlet on the territory's history, tellingly subtitled *Conquest and Occupation,* closing with a declaration of Portugal's "Accomplishment of a Historic Obligation."[4] In the four centuries since Portugal had reached the East African coast, so the pamphlet boasted, no enemy—neither the "unhealthy climate" nor the "rebellious and bloodthirsty nature" of the region's inhabitants—had kept the Portuguese from maintaining their place. "Recalling the glory and the sacrifices of past generations, the Portuguese now, possessed by the spirit of the times and aware of their responsibilities, search without cease to fulfill a mission born of civilization." The development of Manica and Sofala, "undertaken for the most part during the last thirty years, is irrefutable proof that Portugal has not forgotten the obligations imposed by its history."[5]

António Cardoso de Serpa, as director of native affairs, drafted the company's monograph on "native policy," one of a dozen short publications sent to Paris to accompany scale models, agricultural samples, and art work from the territory. In it, he wrote that "the conditions of native life in the Territory are the most fortunate and favorable to the progress of the indigenous population. The company had progressively established complete control over all the territory, liberating the natives from the raiding, internecine warring, and atrocities practiced under the absolutist rule of the original native authorities, conditions which had been for centuries the normal state of human existence throughout Africa."[6] Company policy, based on "modern colonial science," aimed to improve the "material and moral conditions of native life, bringing them to evolve within the limits of their rudimentary civilization, so that they might gradually and smoothly bring about the transformation of their particular customs and practices."[7] Africans thus "transformed"—who could speak, read, and write Portuguese; who ate with cutlery at a table; and who dressed in Western clothing and slept on a mattress—were "considered *assimilados* [assimilated] and, as such, were subject to the same laws and regulations as those in place for Europeans."[8] Cardoso de Serpa described company policy as one of "cooperation," most especially with those Africans who by "example and customs distinguish themselves from the rest of the black race."[9]

## Education and the "Fuel of Social Evolution"

In 1926, when the company sensed incipient international criticism of colonial forced labor practices and abandoned its labor recruitment monopoly, it abolished its native labor department and reallocated its functions. Henceforth, district officials were to recruit workers to meet the company's labor needs; a new private labor association would attend to private employers' demands. The labor department had collected demographic and other data on the African population; now, this and other work were delegated to the company's new department of native affairs. Cardoso de Serpa, who had served in Manica's district administration for nearly two decades, became the first director of the department. An "indispensable complement" of the new department's operations, so the Lisbon-based managing director explained to the governor in late 1928, would be "social support" to the African population.[10] This policy shift implied that Africans might be viewed as something more than a source of labor and tax revenue; Cardoso de Serpa observed, in his 1929 report, that, following the "Great War," the Treaty of Versailles, and the establishment of the League of Nations, international agreements "had imposed new methods and rules of colonial administration on the colonizing peoples." Its guiding principles were, first, that "the natives of the colonies should be considered as human beings and not as simple animals, with their education and well-being a sacred mission that Civilization delegates to the colonizing peoples"; and, second, "Humanity needs the unexploited wealth of vast colonial regions, demanding speedy development from those who hold them." For Cardoso de Serpa, "all modern colonialism turns around these two principles"; his report accordingly offered a number of proposals, most focused on expanding African education and on supporting Africans' market-oriented farming, pointing to "how we might promote the education and well-being of the natives and the development of their capacity for work, so that they might obtain the necessary means of subsistence and contribute to the general interests of humanity."[11]

As district administrator in Manica earlier in the 1920s, Cardoso de Serpa had observed a range of Africans' encounters with colonial rule: forced laborers who struggled, fled, fell ill, fled, or died; chiefs who, for the most part, cooperated with company demands and policies; small-scale market-oriented farmers who benefited from commercial sales of their harvests; and the *voluntários*. Yet Cardoso de Serpa took as a given Africans' "backward state of civilization" without the "slightest vestige of literary culture," and with only "rudimentary ability and technical knowledge of agriculture and crafts." The company should provide instruction "appropriate to their mentality," in the manual trades, in moral education, and in the Portuguese language, the "necessary and gradual stages leading to a more accomplished civilization."[12] Toward this end, he suggested building school workshops in more densely populated districts to teach basic literacy and arithmetic, as well as crafts, trades, or farming, in accordance with available resources and the local population's "disposition."[13]

An important force for "civilizing action" had existed in Portugal's colonies long before the company's arrival in central Mozambique. Religious missions—Portuguese Franciscans, in particular—had been prominent in Portugal's sixteenth-century exploits, most notably in unsuccessful efforts to convert and conquer the rulers of Monomotapa, who controlled the region's gold-bearing lands.[14] In more recent times, missionary activity had fallen off; in the decades immediately prior to the 1920s, Portugal had done little to promote missionary activity in the colonies, concerned first with conquest and, subsequently, with building the foundations of a colonial economy. The company provided little material support to missions, and after the fall of the Portuguese monarchy in 1910, subsequent republican governments had been hostile to all religious orders. Only with the rise of António Salazar's rule in 1928 did Portugal, once again, fully welcome the Catholic church, with its well-formed administrative infrastructure and top-down hierarchy, both at home and overseas.[15]

Cardoso de Serpa himself urged a reinvigoration of mission work: only missionaries, with their "spirit of abnegation and sacrifice, free from all material interest, could educate natives" and fill the gap in familial education, which, among Africans, was "rudimentary in organization and morality." Among all the Catholic orders in the territory, Portuguese Franciscans were most active, but Cardoso de Serpa still lamented that their numbers were insufficient for the expansion in African schooling he envisioned. Cardoso de Serpa proposed increased company support for Portuguese missionary activity in the territory, as a necessary component of social support to Africans and as an aid in countering the "pernicious denationalizing influence" of Anglican, Scottish, Swiss, and Americans missions, "which preached their dissolute and dangerous principles" in other parts of Mozambique and along its borders.[16] Cardoso de Serpa's opposition to non-Portuguese and, particularly, Protestant missionary activity was in line with the Salazar government's xenophobic attitude toward Protestant missionaries, which neared paranoia.[17]

Cardoso de Serpa recommended that at existing mission schools throughout the territory, the company set up small farms, where African "students could learn our agricultural methods and for the testing of various crops that might be most suitable to spread among the natives." These projects would "prepare the field or, rather, domesticate the native population," and ready the path for the "civilizing mission."[18] In addition to educational and vocational instruction, the company should stimulate Africans' economic advancement, "which constitutes, so to say, the fuel of social evolution."[19] Africans must be brought to "work productively, to increase their well-being, and for such, the administration, on which this educational action is incumbent, must endeavor to perfect and intensify native agriculture." Cardoso de Serpa suggested company intervention in seed selection, agricultural instruction, and irrigation; in introducing modern equipment; and in methods of marketing and sales, "guaranteeing" the sale of harvests under the best possible conditions, thus "encouraging them to continue the development of their husbandry," and removing what he considered one of the "principal obstacles" to the growth of African agriculture throughout the territory: the middleman role of Asian merchants, "scattered throughout the districts, who purchase African produced goods at insignificant prices, paying them generally in knickknacks without value."[20] (Asian merchants used their market leverage in isolated outlying districts to drive hard bargains with African farmers; the company ensured its own profits from some African producers by imposing fixed low prices and by barring Africans from selling to any other buyer.) All such efforts, Cardoso de Serpa explained, would enable the "improvement and moralisation of the habits and character of the native populations, spreading the teaching of manual trades, agriculture, moral education, and the Portuguese language," all necessary for Africans' progress and evolution to a "more perfect civilization."[21]

António Fernando de Oliveira Tavares, Cardoso de Serpa's immediate successor in Manica, shared his belief in the need for European tutelage. Oliveira Tavares made the case for an energetic approach: "as history teaches us, the advances of civilization are achieved without excessive tolerance, yet applied fairly. Patient and persistent propaganda, with sanctions for those [who] cannot be brought along by persuasion and who do not respond promptly." Oliveira Tavares reminded his readers that only with "vigorous measures was it possible to pacify the population of the Colony, to end such savage customs as severing a thief's hand, or to put an end in English India to the barbarous practice of burning alive surviving widows on the pyre in which the mortal remains of their husbands were incinerated."[22] He and other company officials charged with implementing the company's vigorous measures saw a seamless narrative of "progress" based on "modern" farming, village resettlement, European schooling, and adoption of European cultural norms and practices.

## A "More Prosperous Existence": African Commercial Agriculture and "an Appetite for Money"

Although the territory's African population was overwhelmingly agrarian and dependent on raising crops of their own to meet their material needs, most officials paid little attention to African farming during the first three decades of company rule other than to comment on Africans' "large and bountiful" fields. But, as it turned out, Africans' success in commercial farming, combined with white settlers' failure, led to freedom from forced labor, to upward mobility, and to development of a small, but distinct, African elite.

In the years before a commercial maize industry developed in Manica and neighboring districts, provisioning the local labor force, company officials had lamented that African farmers did not plant more extensively, "so as to be able to sell their production," which "would be good for us and for employers" dependent on costly imported rice to feed their workers. The administrator in Chimoio remarked, "we would not be so exploited by the *monhe* [South Asian] to whom we pay 26, 28, or 30 shillings for each sack of rice."[23] (Envious about the commercial acumen of Mozambique's South Asian merchants, company officials disparaged their success and reviled them as "bloodsuckers" of gold.[24]) The administrator in Chimoio complained that "the native, despite his large '*machambas*' [farms], plants only what is necessary for his nourishment and for his beer. . . . I have tried to make the natives see the convenience and the profit they would earn . . . but I have achieved nothing."[25] João Pery de Lind, Manica's district administrator before becoming the company's longest-serving governor, dismissed African farming with the comment, "there was nothing worthy of mention."[26] His successor, João Mascarenhas Manuel Mendonça Gaivão, though a voluble and critical commentator on Manica's white farmers, derided African cultivators' agricultural methods as "the most primitive."[27]

Africans in Manica cultivating a variety of crops avoided what one company administrator called the "uselessness of the white settler" afflicted with the "vice of maize monoculture."[28] Africans planted millet, sorghum, cassava, beans, sweet potatoes, and peanuts, and some maize, though "almost exclusively destined for sale."[29] White farmers offered no competition in the millet market. African cultivators sold it to Asian merchants, who then exported it to Southern Rhodesia, where mine operators bought it to brew beer for African mine workers. In some years Manica's African cultivators received twice as much for their millet as for their maize and earned more than enough cash to pay their taxes.[30] According to a district secretary, maize was mainly planted for sale, "the proceeds of which were used to meet" the company's tax.[31] The company provided assistance to white maize farmers—cheap African labor, free seeds, storage facilities, subsidized fuel, and, above all, cheap credit—and no assistance to African farmers, but Africans' surplus production generated the cash to pay the company's tax—a vital symbol of its authority and a significant source of revenue.[32] In years of good harvests and strong prices, the district secretary could close the year's tax collection promptly "without having to use any violence whatsoever in the process."[33] Nor was Manica unique in this respect; the administrator in Sena reported that people from Tambara "do not need to leave their land to pay their taxes and clothe themselves and their women," since the subdistrict exported a peanut crop valued at a third more than the annual tax revenue, "to say nothing of beans, sorghum, rice, etcetera." Tambara was known, said the administrator, "as the granary of the Zambezi [Valley]."[34]

Those company personnel who derided African farmers' technique pointed to their use of hand-held hoes and scoffed at the placement of seeds in an "insignificant hole" just below the earth's surface.[35] But by 1920, district administrator António Cardoso de Serpa remarked that the postwar boom in maize prices "has interested them in maize cultivation, with some natives, though still a small number, starting to use plows." In Manica, in 1920, Africans harvested nearly 1,000 metric tons of maize, and, in neighboring Moribane, sold about 500 metric tons of surplus maize.[36] The governor noted approvingly that Africans in Zambezia had expanded their plantings and raised their asking prices "in face of the demand, which indicates an appetite for money." In Chemba District, Africans harvested almost 700 metric tons of cotton in 1921 (which earned them nearly £6,000); the governor estimated their harvest for 1922 at triple that amount.[37]

Manica's African farmers had largely been sheltered from forced labor by agreement between chiefs and the district administration. Even before Cardoso de Serpa's plans for company "transformation" of African farmers, he remarked, in 1926, how those in Manica had diversified their activities, "with some now today producers of large quantities of maize, fruit, livestock, tobacco and various other products."[38] By the later 1920s, these African farmers had compelled the company to acknowledge the importance of their economic activity. Their success, coupled with the pressures of the Great Depression, led the company to break racial ranks and abandon the white settler farmers it had long supported. Cardoso de Serpa, appointed director of native affairs late in 1926, signaled the shift the next year. Like others before him, he believed Europeans were "not up to the task of fierce field work."[39] Thus, the company should not hope for white settler farmers' success, but, rather, support small-scale African cultivators and European-managed large-scale plantations. While the company should not abandon existing European colonists (though it would soon do just that), "we must turn our attention above all to the large businesses and African-produced crops, which offer more secure results and do not require the onerous financial sacrifices that the Company has made." The company should help Africans select quality seeds, drill boreholes for irrigation, and, among those who kept cattle, promote the use of plows.[40]

By 1931, Manica district administrator António Fernando Oliveira Tavares was observing that "the reduction of agricultural activity on the part of the Europeans corresponded with an intensification of native agricultural activity. The number of natives who farm with correct methods, using animal-drawn plows, increased, and it is to be hoped that the harvests will be encouraging."[41] Oliveira Tavares reported his dutiful "propaganda pushing the intensification of native agricultural activity," and noted that the number of formally designated African "farmers" who used "relatively improved methods" had increased to seventy-four (up from twenty-nine in 1928).[42] His report recorded growth in Africans' livestock holdings, which "might be attributable, in part, to the constant propaganda made among the natives that they seek to increase their possessions."[43] Thus boldly claiming Africans' success as a consequence of his own activities, Oliveira Tavares urged that "everything should be done" to help Africans market their crops. "A considerable number" were growing garden crops, selling their produce partly in Macequece, and especially across the border in Umtali, the center of Southern Rhodesia's mining industry and home to a large British settler community.[44]

The steady expansion of commercially oriented African farmers continued, even amid the intensifying hardships of the Great Depression, and as Oliveira Tavares had suggested, this development of African agriculture continued to employ "a considerable number of workers," of no small importance in the face of the Depression's impact, to the good of the district overall.[45] Oliveira Tavares's district secretary said, several years later, that Manica's African farmers "contributed enormously" to the district's financial stability even as revenues fell overall: marketing assistance from the company had brought one group of farmers income of more than £740, "an amount that almost in its entirety entered the coffers of the C. [Companhia de] M. [Moçambique] as payment of the taxes of the farmers, their families, and workers."[46] The secretary urged the company to undertake all measures to "create native wealth and to improve his social condition." Oliveira Tavares, meeting with Manica's chiefs to distribute their portion of the hut tax collection, urged them "to use all of their efforts so that the natives of their lands develop their plantings, endeavoring to produce not only what was necessary for their own needs but still more beyond that amount, to sell and easily pay their tax and buy what was necessary to clothe themselves and their families, with decency."[47]

Throughout the 1930s, the white farming community all but disappeared, while the number of commercially oriented African farmers in Manica continued to grow, increasing fourfold, to 226, in 1937.[48] One group, close to the rail line and the hub of missionary activity, sold the company more than 400 metric tons of maize, and thus, in the opinion of district administrator Mario da Costa, they were "worthy of the protection of the Government." In all the territory, Manica had "the greatest number of native farmers working methodically with cattle and plow."[49] Beyond the growing numbers of market-oriented African farmers, the company's livestock census showed a remarkable concentration of cattle there; from the late 1920s to the early 1930s, Manica recorded about a fifth of all African-held cattle in the territory. In the southern part of the territory, returning migrants from South Africa's gold mines annually repatriated impressive sums available for investment in livestock. Without similar access to mine wages, and despite never being even as much as 3 percent of the territory's African population, Africans in Manica nonetheless held more than 20 percent of the territory's African-owned cattle.[50]

The company, with a great incentive in cultivating an African farming elite, now created a regulatory carrot: any African man who sold thirty sacks (three tons) of maize or twenty sacks of beans or peanuts would earn an exemption as a "farmer" from the requirement to work. The exemption would be noted in their identity book.[51] The importance of that achievement, central to one's well-being and to social standing, was to echo in laborers' comments even seventy years later. One elderly man recounted to me, in 1997, how, "when the dragnet came, if a person had not reached the limit, he would seek out his friends who had some maize to fill those sacks and send in his name . . . to be able to escape forced labor."[52]

## Adopting the "Public Customs and Practices of Europeans"

For the authors of the company's laws and regulations, the narrative of African progress began with attempts to cultivate an appreciation of the value of labor. Even before passing its first labor regulations, the company required chiefs to send adolescent boys and girls to administrative posts to perform unpaid "light work," such as maintaining the surrounding foot paths and cultivating small plots of land for their own sustenance, the intention, as the governor put it, to "habituate all the natives, from childhood, not only to work but also to the company of whites and contempt for laziness."[53] (The statement betrayed an ignorance of the fact that African children already routinely engaged in work that helped sustain rural homesteads, such as guarding ripening crops from bush pigs and monkeys, fetching water, or grinding maize meal.) Manica's chiefs, with some prodding, sent a dozen to twenty young boys to Macequece each year to engage in what the administrator called "light cleaning" tasks and to attend school to learn Portuguese.[54] Manica was unique in this; until the late 1920s, it possessed the territory's only schools outside of Beira, even though the company's charter stipulated responsibility for education in the territory.[55]

The company had long discouraged education for Africans, investing little in schools, giving scant attention or support to the Catholic missions in the terri-

tory, and, in particular, actively obstructing Protestant mission efforts at education. Representatives of the Congregationalist American Board of Commissioners for Foreign Missions, active in the wider region since the 1830s, attempted
to start a mission in company territory but found it an openly hostile environment.[56] Its ill-fated Beira-based project, which began in 1905, lasted fewer than
two years, after company police's continual raids on the mission school, seizing students, beating them, and sending them to work on chain gangs. When
the American Board's Beira representative appealed to the company's inspector
general, a Briton he believed would have an "English sense of fair play in the matter," he reported the following response: "We all, Portuguese and English, like you
personally . . . but why should you waste your time here? We are opposed to missionary work and missionaries in this territory. It is your business to teach the natives their 'rights'. You will see things which you with your ideals will call 'slavery'
and which you must and will make a fuss about. We are here to get labor from
these lazy people. We are going to force them to do it if necessary. You will make
trouble, and though we have nothing against you, we do not intend to have you
or your work here." A second board effort from 1915 to 1917 encountered similar
and equally stubborn company resistance.

Soon thereafter, speaking Portuguese and becoming habituated to "the company of whites" took on a new and different meaning. In 1921, the company im-
plemented a decree from Lisbon that declared: "the laws which regulate the exercise of civil rights of Europeans in the Portuguese colonies extend to natives who
adopt the public customs and practices of Europeans and who submit themselves
to the laws and regulations imposed upon European individuals of the same
social level."[57] In view of the gulf between African and non-African legal status,
the decree had great, if ambiguous, potential to affect Africans' formal standing,
especially among elites. It took another six years for Portugal to clarify what to
"adopt" European customs and practices actually meant. The 1927 law backed
into an explanation of "assimilated" status by specifying the obverse, defining as
"native . . . individuals of the black race or descended from it who do not satisfy
all the following conditions: a) speak Portuguese; b) not practice the customs and
practices characteristic of native habits; c) practice a profession or work in commerce or industry or possess goods from which they support themselves."[58] The
law did not define what "native habits" were to be shunned, but, in practice, an
aspiring *assimilado* had to eschew polygamy for a single wife; practice Christianity to the exclusion of ancestor veneration; acquire and use utensils rather than
eat with one's hands; live in a square or rectangular house of European design,
rather than the typically round hut of mud or clay and reed thatch; and wear shirt
and trousers (or blouse and skirt) rather than a single cloth garment that left the

chest bare. Thus, speaking Portuguese, publicly displaying the adoption of European customs, and having a profession (such as the company's "farmer" designation) could, at least on paper, allow an African the same rights available to Europeans, primary among those rights, the right not to be subject to forced labor.

Among the most easily verified of the requirements, the ability to speak Portuguese could be acquired more readily in Manica than in the rest of the territory, since in 1927, the same year in which the company published the requirements for "assimilated" status, a third of the territory's schools were in Manica. The combined average daily attendance of the district's nine schools was no more than 184, but that was more than anywhere else in the territory outside of Beira (where the equivalent figure was 406).[59] Cardoso de Serpa, the director of native affairs, was displeased that only three schools in all the territory provided an education he deemed "useful and adequate to the native mentality." One offered instruction for men in arts and crafts—carpentry, masonry, and the like—as well as basic literacy; a second taught women literacy, sewing, and other domestic skills, so that they might become "good housewives"; and a third provided literacy and agricultural training. The territory's other schools supplied what Cardoso de Serpa called "literary" education, which he dismissed as "obviously not the most useful for the native in the state of civilization in which he is found."[60] Africans who focused on literary studies "aspire only to be bureaucrats or office workers, and, when they don't find work of such nature, they dedicate themselves to idleness . . . considering manual labor to be beneath them."[61] Too much civilization, or perhaps civilization of the wrong sort, was to be avoided. Cardoso de Serpa agreed more with the architects of "native" policy in South Africa, who openly advocated a purely vocational education for Africans, based on the conviction that, as one British official put it in 1899, "the vast majority of the natives of South Africa will be hewers of wood and drawers of water to the end of time."[62] Such thinking foreshadowed the restrictive policies of apartheid, which emphasized practical skills training for Africans, because, as South African prime minister Hendrik Verwoerd would argue, instruction in literary or scientific fields would simply show the African the "greener pastures of European society where he is not allowed to graze."[63]

By 1929, Manica had fifteen schools, all mission run, all in the central part of the district, and all open to male and female students, except the exclusively male Freire de Andrade School (named for the famed colonial official, once Manica's district administrator) in Macequece.[64] Throughout the district, average attendance was higher for males than for females, but not substantially so. Yet while the Franciscan missionaries who ran the schools did not discriminate in admitting women and girls to school, they did not teach them the same curriculum; of the students who learned to speak, read, or write Portuguese, close to 85 percent were men. The numbers were similarly lopsided in the rest of the territory.[65] This disparity, as well as a male bias for those considered to practice a profession or work in commerce or industry, meant that assimilated status and its benefits could come only from male initiative. Indeed, the decree that specified the requirements for "nonnative" status implicitly acknowledged as much, since a subclause specified that the status could extend to the wives and children of "nonnatives," with no provision for a woman to qualify on her own.[66]

During the 1930s, administrators were far from sanguine about the status of local chiefs, the African leaders the company had long embraced. Manica's district administrator recommended, in 1933, that "many of the chiefs be deposed and replaced with others of prestige, who will be respected and who will comply the orders and instructions of administrative authorities." Replacements should be "the strongest and have necessary prestige," but the company should take great care in selecting new chiefs to ensure that those chosen "have the ability to command obedience and respect for hierarchical contradictions within their social environment."[67] Three years later, there had yet to be any change, and the new district administrator remarked that "the prestige of some native Chiefs is fairly precarious, which is explained largely by their advanced age," which left them without the energy required to impose their counsel on their followers.[68] A commission convened in 1936 to study the role of chiefs in company administration suggested reshaping the balance of authority so that chiefs remained sufficiently under company control but still "prestigious" enough to command obedience from their followers. The commission recommended that chiefs be required to wear a uniform while undertaking their company duties, thus to "put an end to the inappropriate and at times miserable manner in which [chiefs] generally appear, without the slightest distinction by which they might demonstrate the nature of authority."[69]

Manica's district administrator, Mario Augusto da Costa, found Africans in his district, so he said, in nearly the same condition "as that in which Fr. João dos Santos encountered them: savage, lazy, worthless, and with the smallest evidence of love for work or basic desire to meet the most immediate necessities."[70] Costa was especially offended by the chiefs' bearing; some "seemed like wild dogs: unclean to the point of filth, unshaven, nearly nude, wholly lacking mettle." "With the patience of a saint," he urged them to clothe themselves and their families, though, left to themselves, "from the chiefs to the lowest black they prefer to go about nude."[71] Costa instructed his police to patrol the district center, Macequece, and seize Africans clad only in feed sack remnants. Oblivious to their economic distress in the midst of the Depression and blind to some settlers' practice of providing nothing other than feed sacks for worker clothing, he "called them in and scolded them to compel them to dress themselves."[72]

Although chiefs in central Mozambique had remained close to the company and its labor regime, in Manica an African elite of another sort had achieved more autonomy and showed a closer European influence. Even as early as 1926, the district secretary remarked, "The native population of Manica cannot be compared with that of the other districts of the interior."[73] A local pastor praised them in these terms in 1938:

> No part of the Territory offers a field so ready to be domesticated, a native population so prepared to assimilate our civilization, such as this region of Manica.... The native of Manica is, within the Territory, that which presents the best qualities and disposition to be made into a civilized people. The women here and above all the girls in our schools dress as Europeans, decently, and even with style. The idea of the value of thrift and of work, as opposed to what exists almost everywhere else, is already lodged in the minds of many natives here, among whom are found true yeomen farmers, using scores of cattle, iron plows, water-driven mills, raising large herds, pioneers in cultivating garden crops such as greens, strawberries, flowers, etc., which they sell to the Europeans, with it not uncommon for them to harvest 200 to 300 sacks of maize.[74]

This African elite-in-the-making had perhaps heeded the district administrators' exhortations of the past decades to "clothe themselves and their families with decency" and "live in greater abundance."[75]

The Manica pastor's distinguishing of women of "style" from "true yeomen" suggested a group of male producers and another of acquisitive females. His description may have grown out of the Victorian outlook that predominated in colonial societies in Africa, perhaps all the more so for a Portuguese priest; still, it failed to capture the true process of change. What neither the pastor nor the majority of company officials grasped was that the affluence they heralded depended on practices of which they greatly disapproved and sought to eliminate. They saw greater abundance as a proof of their own success in "civilizing" Africa, whereas the "civilizing" was partly a consequence of women's beer brewing, a practice company officials had long condemned as wasteful and sought to suppress. Manica's African "farmers" emerged as the force they were in the 1930s in part through industrious beer production and occasionally prodigious beer consumption.

Company officials had long misunderstood the place of beer in the agricultural production process: two decades earlier, Manica District administrator João Mascarenhas Manuel Mendonça Gaivão condemned Africans' "imprudence" in using part of their grain harvest to make beer, "passing days upon days in their habitual parties and continual drunkenness"; he worried that such alcohol use might "lead to a weakening of the race."[76] Speaking with Manica's chiefs in 1916 when irregular rains seemed to presage below-normal harvests, Gaivão urged that their people "abstain completely" from brewing beer and exercise the greatest parsimony "so that their food stocks might last until the next harvest, and so that drunkenness might be avoided."[77] Gaivão reminded the chiefs, in another meeting, that "the sale of kaffir drinks [beer] was expressly prohibited and that they should inform the natives under their rule of this order so that drunkenness might be avoided, and to put an end to the great disorder there had been in some of Manica's villages during the year." An additional benefit was that "agricultural and mining works would [not] be undermined with secret sales of [beer] in the labor compounds, as had sometimes occurred."[78] His, or any other official's, perception of rural economic life—viewed from horseback if he could afford a mount or from *machila* (a traveling hammock carried by African porters) otherwise—failed to grasp that brewing and drinking millet beer was important to agricultural productivity. Not until 1928 did the district administrator, António Fernando de Oliveira Tavares, begin to notice a connection between beer brewing and larger-scale African farming. He said that food stocks would meet people's needs, "even given the practice of using part of the harvest to make the 'beer' with which they pay for help in farm work."[79] The following year he pointed out that part of people's harvest "is always consumed in making fermented beverages (*pombe*) which the natives use to pay others for help in field work."[80]

Those who achieved designation as "farmers," just as those with the *assimilado* status most typically acquired by urban dwellers (who were most likely to attend school and acquire the linguistic and cultural knowledge required for assimilated status), were, by definition, men, based on an assumption that such achievement was exclusively their province. But since women brewed beer and worked in the fields, their labor formed the basis of men's material success. In both rural and urban settings throughout southern Africa, female beer brewers and shebeen queens (operators of informal and often illegal drinking establishments), sometimes wealthy and influential, were nearly always excluded from formal recognition of their accomplishments and contributions.[81]

Toward the end of the 1930s, the company inspector celebrated the work of the Franciscan fathers who served in the territory. In his report he wrote that "today, Portuguese missionary activity in Manica is in clear prosperity." He spoke approvingly of Macequece's day and night schools, an arts and trades school, and twenty other schools throughout the district that offered basic instruction, all with a company subsidy.[82] The pastor at Macequece's Our Lady of the Rosary explained the close alignment of the mission's work with the company's commitment to African commercial farming success. The mission's purpose, he wrote, "beyond its own religious and moral function, would be to give greater support to this movement, to build model workshops, teach better farming methods to the natives to realize greater return from their work, spread hygienic practices, which are still very backward . . . organize and animate native agricultural efforts, spread among them the Portuguese language, to prepare what we might call a 'native elite' which could come to be very useful."[83]

## The Perils of Assimilation: "You Couldn't Be Equal to the Whites"

Even before the creation of the explicitly liminal category of *assimilado,* in Mozambique people of Portuguese, African, or Asian descent (and sometimes all three) assimilated new cultural traits to elevate their status and exercise their influence more widely.[84] The Portuguese colonial establishment had long muddied the conceptual waters surrounding racial identity by claiming as a "Portuguese native of Goa" figures such as Manuel António de Sousa, a man with African, Asian, and European ancestors, and a powerful force in nineteenth-century Zambezi politics. His family tree traced the sea voyages that linked Portugal to Zambezia and South Asia. With the same breath Portuguese colonial officials referred to Joaquím Carlos Paiva de Andrada, the company's founder, as "another Portuguese," creating a fuzziness suited to the aims of Portuguese imperial scramblers of the late nineteenth century, when the racial landscape did not yet bear the sharp lines of division it would soon acquire.[85] The juxtaposition, either intentional or unwitting, of categories such as Portuguese, native, European, *mestiço* (of mixed ancestry), and white blurred the boundaries of what were often already overlapping categories—some of the most capable explorers and diplomats were individuals of mixed ancestry and hybrid cultural affinities.[86] Eager to claim African territory, Portugal embraced them all as its nationals.

A heightened sense of racial exclusivity took root in the twentieth century, especially among the growing number of Portuguese settlers, to whom racial boundaries were lines to be policed, defended, and, if necessary, fortified.[87] In urban settings, such as Lourenço Marques, elite African and *mestiço* residents fought against the increasingly rigid social organization of race, mobilizing their ancestry, their wealth, and their erudition to press their claims to a status free from the intense exploitation and petty humiliations of the colonial order, even as working-class whites in Lourenço Marques and Beira feared competition in the labor market or for control of lower-end retail commerce.[88]

A tension at the core of colonial rule in Mozambique and elsewhere was the clash between white privilege created and maintained at the expense of indigenous peoples, on the one hand, and the imperial pretension to saving, improving, or uplifting the colonized, on the other. The path to legal assimilation, narrow and full of pitfalls, kept the number of *assimilados* small to the point of insignificance and protected white colonists' position of advantage. Assimilated status was not won merely by Africans achieving economic, educational, and social status; they were also required to provide proof of the adoption of European customs and practices. Those who chose to submit to the process had to apply for recognition. The bureaucratic procedure brought its own costs, in fees and official documents costly to procure. Applicants encountered white clerks and officials who, in some instances, resented and feared African economic success, and who might seize the opportunity to wield their power to protect or punish. So, too, seeking assimilated status extracted personal resources less easily assessed, such as the self-inflicted damage to the sense of self that came with a decision to efface one's own identity and personal history. Individual isolation and social constriction could result from the consequent rending of social ties, since assimilated status depended on avoiding close association with a "native" environment.

The difference between urban and rural settings was significant to those who might assimilate, because Africans in Beira or the territory's smaller towns had greater access to schooling, the sine qua non for assimilation, and also more opportunities for higher-paying employment and easier entry into commerce or other recognized professions as a teacher, a clerk, or a tailor. Rural dwellers could aim for "farmer" status and the freedom it provided from forced labor, but the benefits of assimilation were still several steps farther away. Company statistics reflected the gap: in 1930, the listing of Africans exempt from paying the hut tax included twenty-one individuals who instead paid a real estate tax levied only on permanent, European-style construction, indicating that they owned buildings, most likely their own homes. All were in Beira, the territory's capital.[89]

Unlike their urban counterparts, Manica's African rural elite made no claims to past European alliances, either marital or strategic. They represented an analogous economic threat to the area's white settler farmers, especially after the Depression exposed the settlers' incapacity.[90] Working the same soil with the same methods and with far less support from the company, African farmers survived and thrived during the Depression, as white farmers failed and were driven out of business. White settler envy of African success, combined with a sense of shame from colonists' unrealized assertion of white racial superiority, nurtured a dangerous racial antagonism.

Only a fortunate African few, therefore, attained "farmer" status and its exemption from forced labor. And even for those few, the last decade of the company's rule remained one of peril, because drought or other environmental shocks could wipe out their harvests, eliminating the basis of their exemption. Locust invasions in 1933 and 1934 left many unable to feed themselves, let alone meet the quota set for the "farmer" designation.[91] And, beyond such risks, even the legal exemption from forced labor did not provide much peace of mind because, as one former farmer remembered, enforcement "was very complicated."[92] Most young men avoided travel on Manica's roads, sticking instead to bush path short-cuts, lest a chance encounter with the police or a white settler lead to being seized for forced labor no matter what one's legal status.[93]

Neither the law on assimilation nor the regulation on "farmer" status ensured positive attitudes of the district's white population toward Africans who achieved that status, making it fragile. Some longtime residents in Manica, when I inquired in 1997 about the presence of white settlers in the district, recalled that "they did not want to see a [black] person going about clean. If they saw someone in rags, or some such, shorts of some sort—there was no problem, one would be left alone. But when they saw someone clean, perhaps with a coat, or trousers, shoes, tie, that—they might not even take you there, to the administration." Instead, they would "force you to some muddy spot" and give you some task there, "whatever odd job so that you should get filthy and end up covered in mud. You could not be equal to the whites, it could not be. Going about clean . . . you couldn't. You had to go about dirty."[94] One man explained how "troublesome" such treatment had been: "When they saw someone there who was clean, they would grab them, beat them, toss them in mud, dirty them up, and leave them like that."[95]

The unpredictability of senseless humiliations, visited upon them by a settler population "seized by the monomania of wealth," was of a piece with that suffered by Africans in southern Mozambique who sang work songs of the "crazy little whitemen" who came from Portugal to Africa.[96] Even the educated aspirants to middle-class life among the urban African population of the capital, Lourenço Marques, "walked in fear."[97] Though they might be literate in Portuguese and possess neater handwriting than their white employers, a claim to such skills, however truthful, was a challenge to settlers' faith in their racial superiority. Racial privilege was robust, and a mere accusation of misdeeds could put "assimilated" Africans at risk for deportation and a sentence of correctional labor in São Tomé.[98]

Humiliation was inflicted on Africans up and down the social ladder. People in Manica complained that, when seized for forced labor, they received feed sacks to wear while they worked in the fields. People in southern Mozambique bitterly mocked Manuel Mendes, a farmer who dressed his workers, "Oh Manuel Mendes, dresses us in pig sacks. Ah Mendes, old boy, you enjoy doing it, don't you Mendes."[99] They resented the pointless hardships visited upon them, as when maize farmers forbade them to sit in the shade while eating. The labor law might require a break from work while taking a midday meal, but it did not specify where they might eat it; one older man recalled the nastiness, with some bitterness, of such practices when speaking with me in 1998: "You must eat there, in the sun, in no matter what time of heat, you must stay in the sun while eating."[100]

For *assimilados* or formally designated "farmers," elite status and the protection it provided from depredations at employers' or officials' hands remained tenuous. Offering little better than lip service to the rhetoric of civilization and improvement, the regulations on assimilation and farmer status nonetheless opened narrow spaces in which the fortunate and ambitious could operate with somewhat greater freedom.

# Conclusion

## Forced Labor's Legacy

THE LAST OF PORTUGAL'S ROYAL COMPANIES, THE Mozambique Company, had outlasted, by more than a decade, its chartered siblings elsewhere in Africa—of Portugal's creation or otherwise—none of which had survived the 1920s. Company rule in Mozambique came to an end on 18 July 1942, with the end of its charter. Its central Mozambican concession reverted to direct administration by Portugal's colonial ministry, a post previously held by Portugal's dictator, António Salazar, who aimed to reduce and curb all autonomy in the colonies. The company's territory became two provinces, Manica and Sofala, in the colony of Mozambique. The era of forced labor itself would, however, continue for another two decades.

As part of the territory's incorporation into state administration, Portugal had decreed that company officials be integrated into the state bureaucracy and "given similar charges to the ones they are holding or given others according to their capabilities."[1] The seamlessness of the transition is clear in the archives' evidence of continuity of administration and in statements by individual employees and by company management. Several years earlier the company's director of native affairs had reflected on the importance of the colonies to Portugal, quoting the minister for the colonies, Armindo Monteiro: The "true Portuguese ideal lies overseas. . . . [The colonies] can give us everything—from collective pride, which makes the people great, to the certainty of work, the glory of accomplishments, wealth, to well-being, strength."[2] Similarly, on the day in July when the company's charter expired, its board of directors wired the governor its gratitude to all company employees, "from the highest ranking to the most humble"; "all had contributed so that the old aspirations for the growth of the Territory might be transformed into a undeniable truth.... The colonization of land in Africa is a result of unshakeable faith, of constant sacrifices, of persistent efforts. The development of Manica and Sofala is proof that the Portuguese of today have preserved whole the qualities they inherited from the ancients."[3]

When, three months later, Governor-General Bettencourt issued a circular of uniform guidelines for labor policy throughout the colony (from the Maputo River on the southern border with South Africa to the Rovuma River separating Mozambique from British-ruled Tanganyika), there had been no change in Africans' obligation to work. The guidelines cited "an axiom of the civilized world that all human beings have the obligation to win the right to life through fatal submission to the general law of work." If anything, the obligation would be even more rigorously enforced. Rejecting any "assault on these truths," the guidelines warned of "a wave of humanitarian idealism that might seek to redress certain excesses, creating for the native African a special situation."[4] Another circular blamed a growing shortage of labor on certain administrators' "laxity" in permitting "natives to live in complete idleness provided they paid their taxes," and signaled an end to Mozambique's brief "flirtation with *laissez-faire* labor policy."[5] Bettencourt set the new direction in his circular: The "conduct of work in Africa cannot continue to depend on the whim of the black." African labor "must be ruled by the general needs of the country to which he belongs."[6]

*"Aquí é Portugal"* (This is Portugal) was spelled out in black and white stones in sidewalks in Mozambique's capital, Lourenço Marques. For Portugal's colonial faithful, the Africans of Mozambique, Angola, Guinea-Bissau, or São Tomé e Principe did not "belong" to those countries as such but to the greater Portuguese empire. Africans who attended school memorized the names of Portugal's monarchs from the thirteenth century; they did not study the history of Gungunhana and the Nguni empires that had ruled the region.[7] From the time António Salazar consolidated his control, in the early 1930s, he had ruled with an authoritarian nationalism that drew on Portugal's past imperial grandeur. The centrality of its African empire to the nation, expressed in the slogan, *"Portugal não é um pais pequeno!"* (Portugal is not a small country!), was taught to schoolchildren and illustrated by a map in which a "greater" Portugal, colonies included, was superimposed over the continent of Europe (see illustration 19).[8]

Portugal's needs, not Africans' interests, were to govern African labor. Portugal would use its colonies to lift the country from the depths of the lingering Depression. In the intervening two decades from the late 1930s onward, forced cotton cultivation blanketed much of Mozambique, with fixed low prices that led African growers to declare, "Cotton is the mother of poverty."[9] Under Salazar,

Portugal determined to pursue a radical mercantilist policy toward its colonies at a time when expanding global wartime needs generated growing demand for tropical agricultural products. African labor would produce cotton, sugar, and rice to export to Portugal and, before long, would support growing waves of Portuguese colonists emigrating to Africa, nearly 150,000 to Mozambique alone in the decades after World War II, many of them the country's poorest. Mozambique's African labor policy, for the coming two decades, so Governor-General Bettencourt proclaimed, would be informed by the "hard lesson of colonial life in the last ten years [that] has remade the rules of work for all people who manage and make use of the value of black labor." To Bettencourt, Africans were "by temperament and natural environment prone to the minimum effort."[10] The lesson of the Depression for Portuguese colonial administrators, then, was not that black farmers competed with, and bested, whites in tough market conditions (though that was just what had happened in much of the company's territory), but that white colonists' success depended on coercive state intervention to supply African labor: the state's heavy hand must replace the market's invisible hand.

The governing rules for conditions under which Africans would labor, particularly in agriculture, were provision of "the food which will rejuvenate his physical being, the lodging which offers him suitable rest, the clothing which shields him from the elements, the salary which allows him to elevate his quality of life." The new labor policy reestablished the requirement for Africans to work six months annually, either for the state or for private employers; or, if they farmed for themselves, to cultivate specified minimum areas, often of cotton or rice, and prove that their labor provided, "with sufficient largesse, the sustenance and clothing of the family and the satisfaction of all tax burdens."[11]

These measures remained in place until 1961, when combined pressure from the International Labour Organization and decolonization elsewhere in Africa made it difficult for Portugal to maintain legally sanctioned forced labor.[12] Forced labor recruitment for the state administration and private employers thus persisted in Mozambique (as in the rest of Portugal's African empire) into the era of African nationalism and independent African states. Even after Portugal abolished forced labor in its colonies in 1962, the practices of forced labor of generations ceased only slowly during the remaining dozen years of colonial rule and up until 1975, when Mozambique became an independent state. The impoverishment of rural African communities through the prolonged theft of their labor power would take far longer to reverse.

In large part because Portugal retained control over its colonies a full decade longer than other imperial powers did, many have regarded its colonial rule as fundamentally different—more akin to the holdout white minority regimes in Southern Rhodesia (becoming independent Zimbabwe only in 1980) and South

Africa (where black majority rule took effect in 1994)—from what Perry Anderson has called "the normal imperial pattern."[13] Prior to its final relinquishment of empire, Portugal had welcomed the exceptional label, though not the accompanying criticism of its rule, if only because it offered a rationale for continuing colonial rule in a decolonizing continent. Though studies of Portugal's African empire and colonial rule have evolved considerably since 1966, when Richard Hammond wrote of Portugal as "the sick man of western Europe," the sidelining of Portuguese colonial rule as an outlier that might be ignored has continued even as the focus of such studies has shifted from Portugal to Africa.[14]

More recently, however, the scholarly focus has been less on Portugal's exceptionalist rule as a weak colonial power than as an extraordinarily brutal one, the two seemingly inconsistent judgments tied together by the claim that Portugal, lacking the resources to construct and maintain effective state institutions, governed through terror—"weak but brutal."[15] Even though Portugal's forced labor regime was more prevalent and lasted far longer than elsewhere in Africa, the history of colonial rule does not support a conclusion that institutionalized violence to extract African labor was a peculiarly Portuguese approach. The Belgian Congo's early years as the personal fiefdom of King Leopold II from 1885 to 1908 had set a high bar for colonial terror and avarice, and forced labor there backed up with state violence continued long after the Belgian state assumed control from the king, and did not end until after World War II. French concessionary companies, too, relied on systemic coercion and violence throughout central Africa, as did the French colonial administration in West Africa. France did not abolish forced labor in its African colonies until 1946, and then only under intense pressure from African politicians. Nor did British practices differ from this norm: up through World War II, forced labor, both sanctioned by law and otherwise, was widespread throughout Kenya, the Rhodesias, Ghana, Malawi, and South Africa. Yet there is no question that parts of Portuguese-ruled Africa fell at the far end of a spectrum of brutality of labor practices.

Portugal was truly exceptional, however, in the longevity of its empire.[16] In this, it is Portugal itself, rather than its colonies, that provides the exception. Among all the colonial powers, only Portugal was a dictatorship; Salazar's unyielding grip had consequences for Portuguese policy and practice in Africa. In London and in Paris, critics of government policy and, eventually, of colonial rule itself could voice their doubts and advocate change, sometimes with consequential outcomes. In Lisbon, such voices, few and faint, could scarcely be heard, in a context of arrest, torture, and secret imprisonment. Dissent was confined to the courageous, the foolhardy, or those with little to lose.[17] The dictatorship's uncompromising commitment to power meant that challenge to its own control and to its empire, when it came, was also uncompromising and violent. The change was unexpected and tumultuous: for Lisbon, an army coup; for Mozambique, a "People's Revolution"; and for Angola, the beginning of a three-decade civil war.

Just as Portugal's abolition of legalized forced labor in 1962 failed to bring an immediate end to practices that had long existed outside the law, so, too, Mozambique's independence, thirteen years later, was a less than complete revolution, despite the new government's embrace of the term and the concept. Independence in 1975, after a dozen years of guerrilla struggle and an army coup in Lisbon against the dictatorship, brought far greater freedom in political and social life. Mozambique's new government, led by Frelimo, a self-described socialist vanguard party, made important investments, in health and education, in particular. Workers enjoyed much improved conditions and terms of service, many as state employees in nationalized industry. Gone was the system of governance designed to protect white privilege, and, with its disappearance, tens of thousands of Portuguese settlers fled, most of them back to Portugal, others to the white haven of South African apartheid. But external intervention, first from Southern Rhodesia and then from South Africa, together with internal opposition, helped to create a devastating conflict in Mozambique that, through the 1980s, brought the country to the verge of collapse before a negotiated settlement, political reform, and an end to neighboring white rule completed the transformation.[18] The Frelimo government abandoned socialism, won elections, and remained in power, embracing economic prescriptions of the International Monetary Fund and World Bank. The country since then has experienced steady, though geographically lopsided, economic growth. Yet for many laborers, especially rural Mozambicans, there has been continuity alongside change. In May 2005, when workers on a sisal plantation in the northern Mozambican province of Nampula were mistreated, they protested and reported to investigators, "There is no respect for human rights here. They beat us as if we were slaves and we are fired without cause. When one of us is injured while cutting sisal, the bosses don't provide medical attention or treatment, the salaries are low, and so we have asked Mr. Minister to help us get out of this situation."[19] They asked the Mozambican minister of labor to intervene. Giving up employment, terrible though it was, seemed less feasible to them than asking a senior minister in the national government to interest himself in their plight. The unnamed workers' success in gaining the attention of a national politician and newspaper is the unusual part of this story; the conditions under which they worked, atrocious as they were, were, apparently, entirely ordinary.

Two years later a similar case connected to a national politician drew attention, but for different reasons. A horticultural firm, Golden Fields, intending to

cultivate roses for export, hired about 100 workers from central Mozambique for
its operations in the southern part of the country. On their arrival in the south,
workers found their housing was only of tents made of sacking. Worse still, the
makeshift accommodations lacked sanitation facilities—running water and
plumbing—and the only water provided was untreated and drawn straight from
the Incomati River.[20] Workers protested at the local district administration offices, and the resultant press attention triggered an inspection from the ministry
of labor, whereupon the protesting workers were dismissed without pay and
barred from the property, and with no means to return to their distant homes.[21]
After the labor ministry's inspection attracted the attention of the Mozambican
Human Rights League, the league's representative argued, in November 2007,
that the conditions faced by workers at Golden Fields constituted "enslavement
in the true sense of the term. Those people are treated like things and not like
humans."[22] The ministry of labor ordered the firm shut down, and, in the ensuing public clamor, the prime minister, Luisa Diogo, expressed the government's
"disgust at the labor relations found at this company," perhaps especially because
the firm was owned by a former minister of foreign affairs and a member of the
ruling party. The Mozambican Human Rights League representative suggested
that the situation was "not a new case and not the only one . . . there exist many
identical cases."[23]

The case of the Golden Fields workers, like that of those on the sisal plantation, is remarkable less in itself than for the publicity it attracted.[24] Workers in
Mozambique who face similar conditions or worse seldom garner much public
attention or support from those in power. Quite the contrary: touring the country early in 2007, Mozambique's president, Armando Guebuza, spoke in a way
reminiscent of past attitudes of his countrymen's "lack of a habit of hard work
[which perpetuates] hunger and poverty. We have to work more and harder."
Lest his comments be misinterpreted, he expanded to blame a "massive apathy
toward work. . . . There are many lazybones in Mozambique."[25] Guebuza's focus
on a culturally rooted laziness sounds strangely unchanged from what a colonial
officer might have written. What is different is the broader institutional environment: nothing remotely like the Mozambique Human Rights League did or could
have existed in the colonial era. Nor do ideas about African laziness carry the
same weight as they once did, though despite the Mozambican Human Rights
League acting as a gadfly, those in power can and do ignore its criticisms. The gap
between law and practice has narrowed, but it still remains.

The history of the Mozambique Company's rule, for all of its particularities,
underscores deep and enduring processes common to Africa's colonial legacy.

There was a many-layered conversation among actors in the drama over slavery and forced labor during the interwar years, a drama enacted on a broad stage. The voices from the periphery, coming from isolated rural districts, as well as from the centers of power, were still those of European administrators, but their conversations were powerfully shaped by what Africans, by their actions, had demonstrated to be possible and effective. These lessons were more readily absorbed in parts of Africa that were ruled by powers with domestic political systems more open than Portugal's. As a consequence, the end of both forced labor and colonial rule itself came sooner elsewhere than in Mozambique and Portugal's other African colonies.

This history points to how wide a gap often exists between law and practice. Although such a gap was part of the normal process of colonial rule, in central Mozambique, this distance was so great that it took on the status, however formally illegal, of an institution. That status, and how the company helped craft it, is worth remembering, especially in the light of the degree of continuity often existing between colonial and postcolonial institutions. The sovereignty of the state in independent Africa provides some protection from criticism when the state fails to enforce its own laws, shielding it from criticism in a way that colonial governments were, at least near the end of the colonial era, less able to avoid. For ordinary Africans, however, the effect is much the same; in consequence they have often received far less than full protection from the legal institutions that govern their lives.

# Notes

## Abbreviations

| | |
|---|---|
| AHM | Arquivo Histórico de Moçambique |
| AHU | Arquivo Histórico Ultramarino |
| ATI | Associação do Trabalho Indígena |
| ATICE | Associação do Trabalho Indígena Correspondência Expedida |
| ATID | Associação do Trabalho Indígena Dossiés |
| ATIR | Associação do Trabalho Indígena Relatórios |
| *BAGC* | *Boletím da Agência Geral das Colonias* |
| *BCM* | *Boletím da Companhia de Moçambique* |
| Cx. | Caixa |
| D.A. | District Administrator |
| D.G. | Director General |
| FCM | Fundo da Companhia de Moçambique |
| FM | Fundo de Moçambique |
| NIP | Negócios Indígenas Processos |
| NLD | Native Labor Department |
| OT | Oral Testimony |
| *RMS* | *Revista de Manica e Sofala* |
| S.G. | Secretary General |
| SGC | Secretaria Geral Correspondência |
| SGCE | Secretaria Geral Correspondência Expedida |
| SGP | Secretaria Geral Processos |
| SGPC | Secretaria Geral Processos Confidencias |
| SGR | Secretaria Geral Relatórios |

## Preface

1. Costa, "Inventário do Fundo," 48–49.

2. Ibid.

3. Ibid., 49.

4. Neil-Tomlinson, "Mozambique Chartered Company," 331. In Lisbon, the AHU holds some Mozambique Company material, but those holdings are, for the most part, duplicative of or digested from original company correspondence and reports held in Maputo. One exception is material related to the metropolitan end of the company's activity: boardroom politics and relations between the company and Portuguese governments. Neil-Tomlinson used this material, and his dissertation is, accordingly, quite strong on the company's high-level financial maneuvers and wranglings. Besides the AHU material, there were for a time unverified rumors of additional company documents in Lisbon, information now confirmed since 2001, when the company's commercial successor, Entreposto, donated company documents to the National Archives (the Torre de Tombo) in Lisbon. These holdings come from the company's Lisbon-based administration, with a correspondingly heavier emphasis on the European side of its operations.

5. Cruz, "História da formação."

6. In "Complicit Critic," Rosemary Galli examines the service of another company employee, Gustavo de Bivar Pinto Lopes, exploring his role in governance and considering his sometimes critical stance on colonial policy.

7. OT, Machipanda (Bairro Chiqueia), 14 May 1997.

## Introduction

1. Europeans' first slave purchases came much earlier, beginning with the Portuguese in the fifteenth century, but a large volume of slave exports from Africa into the Atlantic world came only two centuries later.

2. Chattel slavery was not itself entirely uniform, either, but did share the principle of the slave as transferable property.

3. Ross, *Cape of Torments;* Elphick and Giliomee, *Shaping of South African Society;* Shell, *Children of Bondage;* Keegan, *Colonial South Africa;* Isaacman, *Mozambique;* Newitt, *Portuguese Settlement.*

4. Historical scholarship on slavery and the slave trade in Africa is vast. Paul Lovejoy and John Thornton have written masterful overviews: *Transformations in Slavery,* and *Africa and Africans in the Making of the Atlantic World, 1400–1800,* respectively. More detailed studies on early Afro-European interactions include Isaacman, *Mozambique;* Newitt, *Portuguese Settlement;* Miller, *Way of Death;* Worden, *Slavery in Dutch South Africa;* Thornton, *Kongolese Saint Anthony;* Newton-King, *Masters and Servants.*

5. Diffie and Winius, *Foundations of the Portuguese Empire,* 53. Or nearly so: Macao, the last slender fragment of the empire, reverted to Chinese sovereignty only in 1999.

6. Elkiss, *Quest for an African Eldorado;* Reis, *Empresa da Conquista;* Ellert, *Rivers of Gold.*

7. For more on Andrada's early exploits and on the terms of the charter, see Nowell, *Rose-Colored Map;* Neil-Tomlinson, "Mozambique Chartered Company"; Costa, "No Centenário"; Beach, "Origins of Moçambique and Zimbabwe." The charter as issued in 1892 was for only twenty-five years; it was extended to fifty through a revision in 1897.

8. The fourteen-month transition saw periods of instability, which Margaret Hall and

Tom Young dub "the confused interregnum," and included a brief and unsuccessful white-led revolt against the handover of power to Frelimo. See Hall and Young, *Confronting Leviathan*, 36–60; Power, "Aqui Lourenço Marques!!" 605–6.

9. Denmark had led the way in outlawing the slave trade in 1803, but, lacking the power Britain wielded with its powerful navy, the Danish move was less influential.

10. Portugal still held bits of territory in Asia—Macao, Goa, and East Timor—and though I recognize the significance of continued Portuguese rule of these possessions well into the twentieth century, they did not figure significantly in the last century of Portugal's empire.

11. The law was passed by decree on 9 November 1899. Cunha, *Trabalho indígena*, 147, 149.

12. AHM/FCM/SGP/Cx. 71: D.A. Mossurize to Governor, no. 216, 22 November 1910.

13. OT, Penhalonga, 19 May 1997.

14. OT, Messika (25 de Setembro), 31 May 1997.

15. See, for example, AHM/FCM/SGP/Cx. 71: D.A. Gorongosa to D.A. Manica, 10 May 1911.

16. Enes, *Moçambique*, 75.

17. Ibid.

18. Ibid., 70–71.

19. Morel, *Red Rubber*; Hochschild, *King Leopold's Ghost*.

20. Grant, *Civilised Savagery*; Duffy, *Question of Slavery*.

21. Nevinson, *Modern Slavery*, 37.

22. League of Nations, Slavery Convention 1926, Article 1, Article 5. The league had taken on the question in its 1922 sessions.

23. Miers, *Slavery in the Twentieth Century*, 100–151.

24. Ibid., 152–73.

25. Harris, *Africa*.

26. Henrique Galvão, a Portuguese colonial official who in the late 1940s made public a report critical of Portuguese colonial policy, is a notable exception. His ability to do so without suffering more serious reprisals (a two-year prison sentence—though for suspicion of involvement in an attempted coup, not for his outspokenness) from the Salazar government has yet to be satisfactorily explained. Wheeler, "Galvão Forced Labor Report."

27. Killingray, "Labour Mobilisation in British Africa." Forced labor was prevalent in wartime Europe as well, primarily in areas under German and Soviet control; some forced labor in Europe continued past the war's end. Parts of Moscow State University were built by German prisoners of war in the latter half of the 1940s.

28. The phrase comes from British prime minister Harold Macmillan's 1960 speech, delivered in Ghana and South Africa in January and February, respectively.

29. Péclard, "Religion and Politics," 166–67; Cruz e Silva, "Identity and Political Consciousness," 226.

30. International Labour Office, *Portugal in Africa*; Vail and White, *Capitalism and Colonialism*, 382–83.

31. I owe the phrasing here to Kennedy, *Islands of White*. Southern Rhodesia made its Unilateral Declaration of Independence, by which it exited the British Commonwealth, that year, while South Africa had declared its republic in 1961.

32. For those pursuing historical scholarship on colonial Mozambique, a valuable early starting point is Pélissier's two-volume *Naissance du Mozambique*. Its sixty-page bibliography, found in Volume 2, contains an exhaustive listing of published material, including many key

contemporary sources. It is a remarkable unintentional finding aid for researchers in their early stages. For work on the Mozambique Company, Vail's 1976 *Journal of African History* article, "Mozambique's Chartered Companies," raises some of the questions addressed here, and Neil-Tomlinson's unpublished 1987 doctoral dissertation, "The Mozambique Chartered Company," provides important guideposts. Although Neil-Tomlinson did not have access to the company archives in Mozambique, he made good use of sources in the AHU in Lisbon. His footnotes offer a rough and partial guide to the vast, and famously unorganized, AHU archives, and his own source note attempts to compensate for the absence of a finding aid or index to the material there. However, his notes are based on research conducted in the late 1970s and early 1980s, and, as he remarks, the room numbers on which his references are based "have been known to change." Additionally, as he also notes, multiple boxes or files of documents may share the same reference number, with no way to distinguish among them. Suffice it to say that research on Mozambique's colonial period in the AHU requires both patience and a good deal of time in Lisbon.

Those who hope to conduct research on the history of Mozambique should consult several books of breadth. For the most up-to-date overview in English, embracing the entire country since the sixteenth century, Newitt's *History of Mozambique* is a vital starting point. The three-volume *História de Moçambique* similarly covers the entire country and, under the direction of scholars in the Department of History at Eduardo Mondlane University, reflects a more local viewpoint, together with deft integration of primary sources. Pélissier's *Naissance du Mozambique* has remarkable coverage, if of a briefer period. On the history of the Portuguese empire more broadly, key contributions include Clarence-Smith, "Myth of Uneconomic Imperialism" and *Third Portuguese Empire*; Newitt, *History of Portuguese Overseas Expansion*; Duffy, *Portuguese Africa*; and Pírio's important but never published 1982 doctoral dissertation, "Commerce, Industry and Empire."

For the earlier history of Portuguese activity in central Mozambique, the authoritative works are Isaacman, *Mozambique*; and Newitt, *Portuguese Settlement*. Pre-nineteenth-century historical scholarship on the rest of the country is relatively thin; Beach's scholarship on precolonial Shona history, though focused farther west, still has relevance for the west-central regions of Mozambique. The nine volumes of *Documents on the Portuguese in Mozambique and Central Africa* make accessible in Portuguese and English translation rich sources for the period up to 1615. In *Mulheres Invisíveis*, Zimba offers a rare and valuable account of gender and the politics of trade in southern Mozambique from the early eighteenth to the early nineteenth centuries. Smith's never-published 1970 Ph.D. dissertation, "The Struggle for Control of Southern Mozambique," remains an important study. Liesegang has published a number of shorter studies on the Gaza empire, chief among them "Notes on the Internal Structure of the Gaza Kingdom." Alpers's work, *Ivory and Slaves*, documents the history of the area north of the Zambezi Valley and its growing involvement in international commerce from the seventeenth century onward.

For the vital center, there is no single more important book than Vail and White's *Capitalism and Colonialism in Mozambique: A Study of Quelimane District*. Misleadingly subtitled, it is much more than a district study, embracing broad questions of political and economic change that bound the wider lower Zambezi Valley to areas far afield and across the full range of colonial society. Other work on the center includes Isaacman and Isaacman, *Slavery and Beyond*; MacGonagle, *Crafting Identity*; and Neves, "Economy, Society and Labour Migration."

Northern Mozambique remains a relative desert for colonial history; Neil-Tomlinson's "Niassa Chartered Company"; Medeiros's *História de Cabo Delgado e do Niassa;* and Chilundo's *Os Camponeses e os Caminhos* are among the few published works. Hafkin's unpublished 1973 doctoral dissertation, "Trade, Society, and Politics in Northern Mozambique," is still one of the only other works on the north that crosses into the twentieth century. In contrast, the literature on southern Mozambique is well developed, and the most consulted works include Harries, *Work, Culture, and Identity;* Penvenne, *African Workers and Colonial Racism;* Covane, *Trabalho Migratório;* and Cruz e Silva, *Igrejas Protestantes.* Gengenbach's *Binding Memories* is not yet a classic, but has already begun to exert a strong influence on research in gender history in Mozambique and farther afield.

Many areas remain underresearched; colonial Mozambique's religious history is mostly unexamined, though Morier-Genoud's "Catholic Church, Religious Orders and the Making of Politics in Colonial Mozambique" has set a research agenda for others who might follow him. Other than Alexander Keese's *Living with Ambiguity,* there is little historical scholarship on Mozambique (or Portuguese Africa more generally) that offers comparative analysis with other colonial territories. Scholarship on Beira, until recently the country's second-largest city, is thin, aside from a special issue of *Arquivo* (1989) and parts of Sheldon's *Pounders of Grain.* There is little work that examines in much depth the history of non-African communities, whether the white population, which numbered 200,000 by the early 1970s, or South Asian or *mestiço* Mozambicans. Similarly, scholarship on colonial education in Mozambique is limited, though it offers exciting possibilities for future research in cultural and political history.

33. See, for example, Miller, *Way of Death;* Barry, *La Sénégambie du XVe au XIXe Siècle;* Thornton, *Africa and Africans;* Lovejoy, *Transformations in Slavery.*

34. Cooper, "Problem of Slavery," 104, 105, 106.

35. Clark remarks on this problem in "Ties That Bind."

36. Miers, "Slavery and the Slave Trade"; Hogendorn and Lovejoy, *Slow Death for Slavery;* for similar questions in India, see Chatterjee, "Abolition by Denial."

37. League of Nations, "Temporary Slavery Commission, Minutes of the Second Session," 102 (Annex I: Note on Forced Labour).

38. Ibid., 8, 10.

39. Quoted in Miers, *Slavery in the Twentieth Century,* 146.

40. Berlin, *Generations of Captivity.* Frederick Cooper makes this point as well. Cooper, "Problem of Slavery," 107.

41. Willis develops this explanation in "Men on the Spot." Willis attributes the phrase to Mungeam, *British Rule in Kenya.*

42. Cooper, Holt, and Scott, *Beyond Slavery,* 131.

43. Ag Chief Secretary to Department Public Works, 23 July 1912, quoted in Willis, "Men on the Spot," 37.

44. Cooper, *Decolonization and African Society,* 34.

45. Brown, *"We Were All Slaves."*

46. Coquery-Vidrovitch, *Le Congo;* Thomas, "Forced Labour"; Echenberg and Filipovich, "African Military Labour"; Vickery, "Second World War Revival of Forced Labor"; Johnson, "Settler Farmers"; Fall, *Le Travail Forcé;* Willis, "Men on the Spot"; Akurang-Parry, "Loads Are Heavier Than Usual"; Sunseri, *Vilimani;* Ball, "Colossal Lie." Pitcher suggests this longevity made Portugal "unique." Pitcher, *Politics in the Portuguese Empire,* 65.

47. Echenberg and Filipovich, "African Military Labour"; Fall, *Le Travail Forcé.*

48. Coquery-Vidrovitch, *Le Congo.*

49. Thomas, "Forced Labour"; Willis, "Men on the Spot"; Vickery, "Second World War Revival of Forced Labor"; Bradford, "Getting Away with Murder," 99–102.

50. This view is especially prevalent in studies of colonial Mozambique.

51. AHM/FCM/SGP/Cx. 71: Indígenas para Manica, Governor to Managing Director, no. 1441 of 1910, 3 November 1910.

52. Ross, *Report on the Employment of Native Labor,* 20.

53. Oshinsky, *"Worse than Slavery."*

54. This characterization of slavery draws closely on Bales, "Expendable People."

55. Patterson develops this paradigm-defining approach in *Slavery and Social Death.*

56. Cooper, "Problem of Slavery," 106.

57. Aptheker, "Maroons"; Price, *Maroon Societies;* Franklin and Schweninger, *Runaway Slaves;* Asiwaju, "Migrations as Revolt"; Isaacman, "Peasants and Rural Social Protest."

58. Beckles, "Economic Life of Their Own"; Marshall, "Provision Ground and Plantation Labour"; McDonald, "Independent Economic Production by Slaves."

59. Eaton, "Slave-Hiring in the Upper South"; Wade, *Slavery in the Cities;* Bolland, "Proto-Proletarians?"; Lamounier, "Between Slavery and Free Labour."

60. This is a vast literature; for a recent analysis of many of the relevant questions, see Johnson, "On Agency." James C. Scott develops a conceptual model for such hidden resistance in *Weapons of the Weak* and *Domination and the Arts of Resistance.* In "Conflict and Connection," Cooper nicely presents how the literature on colonial Africa fits into a broader scholarly landscape, including subaltern studies.

61. I previously made tentative suggestions along these lines in Allina-Pisano, "Resistance and the Social History of Africa."

62. My phrasing here has been influenced here in part by Scott, *Degrees of Freedom.*

63. My phrasing and my thinking here have been shaped by the character of Henry in Edward P. Jones, *The Known World,* in particular his mother's hope that "the bigger he could make the world he lived in, the freer he would be." Jones, *Known World,* 113.

## 1. Ending Slavery and Creating Empire in Africa

1. The Indian Ocean region has in recent years seen increasing attention as an integrated system; see Bose, *Hundred Horizons;* Pearson, *Port Cities and Intruders;* Nurse and Spear, *Swahili;* Risso, *Merchants and Faith.*

2. For these earlier efforts, led by Francisco Barreto, see "Narrative (Copy) by Father Francisco de Monclaro, of the Society of Jesus, of the Expedition to Monomotapa, led by Francisco Barreto," in *Documents on the Portuguese in Mozambique and Central Africa,* 8: 325–429.

3. Dos Santos, *Ethiopia Oriental,* 1:229. I have written more about the Zimba and how dos Santos may have come to believe they were cannibals in "The Zimba, the Portuguese, and Other Cannibals."

4. Newitt covers many of Portugal's difficulties during this period in *History of Mozambique,* chapters 3–11.

5. Isaacman and Isaacman, "Prazeros as Transfrontiermen." For the early history of the Afrikaners, see, among others, the essays in Elphick and Giliomee, *Shaping of South African Society.*

6. Decree of 10 December 1836, published in *Documentos Officiaes Relativos à Negocia-ção*, 76.

7. Report of the Overseas Council, 3 February 1855, in *Documentos relativos ao apresamento*, Document 3-A, 5.

8. Minister of the Navy to French Ambassador, 5 May 1857, in *Documentos relativos ao apresamento*, Document 15-D, 22.

9. Report of the Overseas Council, 3 February 1855, in *Documentos relativos ao apresamento*, Document 3-A, 6.

10. Duffy, *Portuguese Africa*, 148; Marques, *Sounds of Silence*, 183.

11. Marques, *Sounds of Silence*, 183–84. Portugal and Britain were commercial allies since their 1661 treaty.

12. For the history of Portugal's movement toward abolition, see Capela, *Escravatura*; Marques, *Sounds of Silence*.

13. Serpa Pinto, *Como eu atravessei a África*.

14. The history of this contestation is covered comprehensively in Axelson, *Portugal and the Scramble for Africa*.

15. For a broad overview, see Northrup, *Indentured Labor*.

16. Coelho, *Dezoito Annos em África*, 379.

17. Alpers, *Ivory and Slaves*, chapter 7; Harries, "Slavery"; Isaacman and Isaacman, *Slavery and Beyond*, especially 233–52.

18. Livingstone, *Missionary Travels*, 703.

19. Livingstone and Livingstone, *Narrative of an Expedition*, 637.

20. Preamble to the General Act of the Conference of Berlin, in Hertslet, *Map of Africa by Treaty*, 468.

21. General Act of the Conference of Berlin, Chapter 1, Article 6, in Hertslet, *Map of Africa by Treaty*, 473.

22. Scottish Presbyterians stationed on the shores of Lake Niassa were witness to the ongoing export of slaves from the interior to Africa's Indian Ocean coast.

23. General Act of the Brussels Conference Relative to the Africa Slave Trade, in Hertslet, *Map of Africa by Treaty*, 488.

24. Ibid., 490.

25. Alpers, *Ivory and Slaves*, especially 229–53; Isaacman and Rosenthal, "Slaves, Soldiers, and Police"; Northrup, "Ending of Slavery," 465–67.

26. Quoted in Pakenham, *Scramble for Africa*, 217.

27. Scholarship on the *mfecane* and its causes is extensive; for a good analytical overview of the history and the surrounding debates, see Eldredge, "Sources of Conflict."

28. Here, as elsewhere in parts of conquest-era Africa, treaty-making was a temporary pause before eventual betrayal of African allies. See Liesegang, *Vassalagem ou Tratado de Amizade?*

29. AHU/FCM/Cx. 899: F. Cortes to Director Geral do Ultramar, 3 April 1888.

30. My phrasing is inspired by Winks, *British Imperialism*.

31. Andrada founded his first company, the Société des Fondateurs de la Compagnie Générale du Zambèze, in 1878, but this early company had little more than a paper existence, attracting virtually no investment in Europe and achieving little in Africa.

32. The map was based on data provided by the Portuguese Colonial Office, but printed in Paris. Nowell, *Rose-Colored Map*, 136.

33. Pírio provides a painstaking explanation of the financial and political context in which the chartered companies were established. Pírio, "Commerce, Industry and Empire," chapter 3.

34. Vail, "Mozambique's Chartered Companies," 390.

35. Quoted in Nowell, *Rose-Colored Map*, 145.

36. Neil-Tomlinson, "Mozambique Chartered Company," 27–28.

37. Duffy, *Portuguese Africa*, 222; Smith, "António Salazar," 655.

38. Pírio, "Commerce, Industry and Empire," 15.

39. Smith, "Idea of Mozambique," 498, citing FO 179/390, Report on the Portuguese Colonial Possessions in Africa by Mr. Peel, enclosed in MacDonell to Lansdowne, 11 January 1904; see also Newitt, *History of Mozambique*, 333.

40. Beach suggests that this helped lead to Andrada's downfall at the hands of his English rival, Rhodes; had Andrada kept Lisbon better informed, the Portuguese government might have been in a better position to defend his land claims for Portugal. Beach, "Origins of Moçambique and Zimbabwe."

41. Smith, "Idea of Mozambique," gives an excellent treatment of the strategic differences and rivalries of the two factions. Pírio's analysis is even more detailed, though also weighted down with an unwieldy materialist framework. Pírio, "Commerce, Industry and Empire," chapter 3.

42. Associação Commercial de Lisboa, Annual Report 1889, 109, cited in Pírio, "Commerce, Industry and Empire," 45. The backdrop to elite maneuvers was popular nationalist interest in empire, and though politics was largely an affair of the elite, government was subject to being buffeted by popular sentiment, especially in the unsettled economic environment of the era.

43. *As Actas das Sessões da Sociedade da Geografia de Lisboa*, Vol. 10 (1890), 38, cited in Pírio, "Commerce, Industry and Empire," 86.

44. Neil-Tomlinson, "Mozambique Chartered Company," 22.

45. Pírio, "Commerce, Industry and Empire," 42–43.

46. Ibid., 49–50.

47. Ibid., 98–99. The decree applied only to concessions over 1,000 hectares.

48. The patchwork is to some extent reflected in the historical scholarship on the colony overall. The southern region, particularly the social and economic effects of its links to South Africa, is especially well covered. The history of northern Mozambique is nearly unknown for the colonial era, and the areas of the Zambezi Valley under the control of the colonial state have also received only scant attention, while those controlled by the plantation companies are considerably better documented.

49. For a sense of this fiscal anarchy, see *O Guia do Museu: Museu Nacional da Moeda* [*Guide to the Museum: National Currency Museum*], especially 20–26.

50. Vail, "Mozambique's Chartered Companies"; Neil-Tomlinson, "Niassa Chartered Company"; Medeiros, *História de Cabo Delgado e do Niassa*.

51. *Correio da Beira* 56 (22 April 1894), 122.

52. *Correio da Beira* 50 (11 March 1894), 73.

53. Barahona e Costa, *Passado, Presente e Futuro dos Territórios de Manica e Sofala*, 34.

54. Martins, *História das Colónias Portuguesas*, 294, quoted in Wheeler, "Gungunyane the Negotiator," 587.

55. Beach, "Origins of Moçambique and Zimbabwe," 14. Beach suggests that Andrade's

nickname came from his frenetic activity, and it may well have. But one of the company's steam launches, used to travel from the coast up the navigable portions of the Pungué and Buzi, was also named the *Mafambice,* and so it seems possible that Andrade, traveling on the launch, became associated with it.

56. "Como se estabeleceu em África a primeira Companhia de Moçambique," *RMS,* Series 1, no. 7 (September 1904), 83.

57. "Como se estabeleceu," *RMS,* Series 1, no. 1 (March 1904), 82; Series 1, no. 8 (October 1904), 94; Series 1, no. 9 (November 1904), 106; Series 1, no. 11 (January 1905), 133; Series 1, no. 12 (February 1905), 146.

58. "Como se estabeleceu," *RMS,* Series 2, no. 13 (March 1905), 7.

59. "Como se estabeleceu," *RMS,* Series 2, no. 22 (December 1905), 118.

60. "Como se estabeleceu," *RMS,* Series 3, no. 25 (March 1906), 8.

61. "Como se estabeleceu," *RMS,* Series 1, no. 11 (January 1905), 132; Series 2, no. 23 (January 1906), 129; Series 3, no. 25 (March 1906), 8.

62. OT, Penhalonga, 19 May 1997; Beach, "Origins of Moçambique and Zimbabwe," 37–39.

63. Beach, "Origins of Moçambique and Zimbabwe," 38–39, 42.

64. "Como se estabeleceu," *RMS,* Series 2, no. 16 (June 1905), 43–44.

65. "Como se estabeleceu," *RMS,* Series 3, no. 32 (October 1906), 94.

66. "Como se estabeleceu," *RMS,* Series 3, no. 34 (December 1906), 115.

67. Martins, *Portugal em Africa,* 217.

68. Beach covers this episode comprehensively in "Origins of Moçambique and Zimbabwe"; see also Axelson, *Portugal and the Scramble for Africa;* and Nowell, *Rose-Colored Map.*

69. Nowell provides a detailed account in "Portugal and the Partition of Africa," 16–17.

70. This paragraph summarizes Wheeler, "Gungunyane the Negotiator," 597–600.

71. Companhia de Moçambique, *Handbook,* ix.

72. Neil-Tomlinson, "Mozambique Chartered Company," 27.

73. Companhia de Moçambique, *Handbook,* 16–17.

74. Ibid., xii.

75. Galbraith, *Crown and Charter,* 122. The Mozambique Company charter gave the company the right to print its own currency, though it used the same currency units as the rest of Mozambique. Up until 1910, the unit was the *reis,* with 1000 *reis* equal to one *milreis,* written as 1$000. When the Portuguese Republic replaced the monarchy in 1910, a new currency unit, the *escudo,* comprised of 100 *centavos,* came into use (one *centavo,* $01; one *escudo,* 1$00). The new system came into use gradually, with the *centavo* and *escudo* entering into common usage only by the mid to late 1910s.

76. Enes, "Colonização europeia de Moçambique," 14, 19.

77. AHM/FCM/SGR/Cx. 236: Manica District Annual Report, SGR/5045/01, 8; AHM/FCM/SGCE/Cx. 178: Circular 2, 2 January 1920.

78. *Correio da Beira* 44 (28 January 1894), 28; AHM/FCM/SGR/Cx. 223: Manica District Report, SGR/4889/01, 8 March 1897, 11.

79. Vail, "Mozambique's Chartered Companies," 397.

80. Companhia de Moçambique, *Handbook,* v.

81. Ibid., 16–17.

82. AHM/FCM/SGR/Cx. 223: Manica Annual Report 1897, SGR/4889/01, 11–12.

83. Ibid., 11.

84. Ibid., 13.

85. Enes, *Moçambique,* 70–71.

86. Ibid., 75.

87. Ibid., 70.

88. "Regulamentação do Trabalho dos Indígenas," in ibid., 495.

89. Ibid., 75.

90. Enes et al., "Trabalho dos indígenas," 27.

91. General Act of the Conference of Berlin, Chapter 1, Article 6, "Preservation and Improvement of Native Tribes; Slavery, and the Slave Trade," in Hertslet, *Map of Africa by Treaty,* 473.

92. Enes, *Moçambique,* 69; General Act of the Conference of Berlin, Chapter 1, Article 6, in Hertslet, *Map of Africa,* 473.

93. Binger, *Esclavage, Islamisme et Christianisme* (Paris: Société des Editions scientifiques, 1891), 92; *District and Consular Reports on Pemba* (London: Foreign Office, 1900), 12; both quoted in Cooper, "Conditions Analogous to Slavery," 115, 121.

94. Enes et al., "Trabalho dos indígenas," 27.

95. Ibid.

96. "Regulamentação do Trabalho dos Indígenas," in Enes, *Moçambique,* 495.

97. For the history of the *prazos* and of early Portuguese activity in the Zambezi Valley, the authoritative works are Isaacman, *Mozambique;* and Newitt, *Portuguese Settlement.* Vail and White detail the transition to plantation company rule in the lower Zambezi *prazos* in *Capitalism and Colonialism,* chapters 2–3.

98. Harries, *Work, Culture, and Identity,* 140. For the early formative years of the mine owners' efforts to organize a collective recruitment system, see Jeeves, *Migrant Labour,* 40–48.

99. Van Onselen describes this process (and the various reorganizations of the RNLB) in *Chibaro,* especially chapter 3. Elizabeth Schmidt explains how these developments had an especially strong impact on rural African women in *Peasants, Traders, and Wives,* chapter 2.

100. AHM/FCM/SGP/Cx. 183: Chamber of Mines Secretary to Inspector General of Exploitation, 21 March 1900; Oceana Consolidated Company, Ltd., to Colonel Alfred J. Arnold, 16 May 1900.

101. AHM/FCM/SGP/Cx. 182: Witwatersrand Native Labor Association to Governor, 14 November 1902.

102. AHM/FCM/SGP/Cx. 104: A. Lawley to Governor Beira, 23 December 1899.

103. AHM/FCM/SGP/Cx. 104: Governor to the British South Africa Company, 29 August 1901.

104. AHM/FCM/SGP/Cx. 104: A. Lawley to Governor Beira, 23 December 1899; Governor to A. Lawley, 24 January 1900.

105. *BCM* 174 (16 November 1900), "Regulamento do trabalho do indígena," Article 18.

106. AHM/FCM/SGR/Cx. 3: Governor Annual Report 1907, SGR/007/01, 5–6.

107. AHM/FCM/SGP/Cx. 182: "Regulamento dos Serviços Indígenas em Manica," Chapter 2, Article 12.

108. AHM/FCM/SGR/Cx. 5: Governor Annual Report 1911, SGR/011/01, 7.

109. AHM/FCM/SGR/Cx. 231: Manica District Report September 1908, SGR/4987/01; Manica District Report October 1908, SGR/4988/01, 14.

110. AHM/FCM/SGR/Cx. 224: Manica District Annual Report 1903, SGR/4928/01, attached report from Chimoio, 4.

111. AHM/FCM/SGR/Cx. 256: Moribane District Report March 1902, SGR/5484/01, 16.

112. AHM/FCM/SGR/Cx. 114: Native Affairs Annual Report 1927, SGR/2269/01, 12.

113. AHM/FCM/SGR/Cx. 236: Manica District Census Report 1914, SGR/5040/01, 6.

114. League of Nations, Note of the Secretary General, 27 September 1924, Enclosing "The Question of Slavery," J. Chagas to League of Nations Secretary General, 23 September 1924, 23.

115. Ibid., 21.

116. Ibid., 51.

117. AHM/FCM/NIP/Cx. 23: Director Native Affairs to Governor, no. 19, 29 December 1939, Confidential; Enes, *Moçambique*, 24.

118. Vasse, "Mozambique Company's Territory," 264.

119. AHM/FCM/SGR/Cx. 223: Manica District Report, 8 March 1897, SGR/4889/01, 7.

120. Machado, *Moçambique*, 7.

121. Martins, *História das Colónias Portuguesas*, 607.

122. Neil-Tomlinson, "Mozambique Chartered Company," 119–20, 222, 242, 262.

123. AHU/FM/Cx. 888: Managing Director Delegado to Commissário Régio, 21/6/1900.

124. AHM/FCM/SGR/Cx. 224: Manica District Annual Report 1902, 8. Such characterizations are familiar in the context of Portugal's colonial history; see Bender, *Angola Under the Portuguese*, especially chapters 3–4.

125. AHM/FCM/SGR/Cx. 223: Manica District Annual Report 1897, SGR/4889/01, 12; Cx. 234: Manica District Annual Report 1911, SGR/5025/01, 163.

126. Enes et al., "Trabalho dos indígenas," 27; AHM/FCM/SGR/Cx. 236: Manica District Annual Report 1914, SGR/5045/01, 163.

127. AHM/FCM/SGR/Cx. 235: Manica District Annual Report 1912, SGR/5032/01, 141.

128. AHM/FCM/SGR/Cx. 223: Manica District Report November 1898, SGR/4897/01, 10.

129. *Correio da Beira* 44 (28 January 1894), 28.

130. *RMS*, Series 6a, no. 70 (December 1908), 109.

131. AHM/FCM/SGR/Cx. 5: Governor Annual Report 1911, SGR/011/01, 6; *BCM* 13 (12 July 1915), Order 3583; *BCM* 15 (2 August 1915), Circular 22/1698, 26 July 1915; *BCM* 24 (17 December 1917), Order 3814; AHM/FCM/SGC/Cx. 177: Circulars, Circular 61, 23 October 1918.

132. AHM/FCM/SGC/Cx. 15: Governor to Managing Director, no. 357, 30 March 1910.

133. AHM/FCM/SGC/Cx. 15: Governor to Managing Director, no. 357, 30 March 1910.

134. AHM/FCM/SGR/Cx. 69: Department of Mines Report September 1910, SGR/1382/01, attached letter from Governor to Managing Director, 1365, 20 October 1910.

135. AHM/FCM/SGP/Cx. 72: D.A. Manica to Governor, 413-A/1964, 20 July 1910; Cx. 71: Director of Mines to Governor, no. 184 of [n.d.], 1910; Paul Pacotte (Director of Mozambique Mines) to Director of Mines, 26 October 1910.

136. *Beira Post* (16 November 1910), supplement. The juxtaposition of African "boys" with European "men" underscores the commonplace denial of African adult status, a theme Penvenne explores in *African Workers and Colonial Racism*.

137. *BCM* 14 (14 July 1910), Order 3803; AHM/FCM/SGC/Cx. 15: Correspondência Expedida no 4° Trimestre 1910, Interim Governor to Managing Director, no. 1513, 17 November 1910.

138. Neil-Tomlinson, "Mozambique Chartered Company," 312. In light of the monarchy's fall in the face of an armed insurrection only a month earlier, Pinto Basto's concern was not unreasonable, given that the company's authority was based on a royal charter.

139. AHM/FCM/SGR/Cx. 233: Manica District Report November 1910, SGR/5015/01, "No. 36 Occorrências Extraordinárias."

140. AHM/FCM/SGP/Cx. 71: Governor to D.A. Gorongosa, telegram 430/3114, 17 No-

vember 1910; Cx. 70: Governor to D.A. Sena, telegram, 16 November 1910; Cx. 72: S.G. to D.A. Govuro, 17 November 1910.

141. AHM/FCM/SGC/Cx. 15: Correspondência Expedida no 4° Trimestre 1910, Governor to Managing Director, no. 1608, 15 December 1910.

142. AHM/FCM/SGR/Cx. 234: Manica District Annual Report 1911, SGR/5025/01, 165.

143. AHM/FCM/SGP/Cx. 69: D.A. Manica to Governor, 27 July 1914.

144. AHU/FM/Cx. 913: Actas da Sessão do Conselho de Administração, 24 January 1911.

145. AHM/FCM/SGP/Cx. 69: Inspector of Finance and Exploration to Governor, no. 374/1924, 28 August 1924.

146. AHM/FCM/SGP/Cx. 74: Governor to Managing Director, no. 1465/1910, 10 November 1910.

147. AHM/FCM/SGR/Cx. 234: Manica District Annual Report 1911, SGR/5025/01, 161. I have taken some small license in translating *fulano* as "Farmer So-and-So." In Portuguese, the phrasing for the last is *"sol na eira e chuva no nabal."*

148. Ibid., 161.

149. AHM/FCM/SGR/Cx. 236: Manica District Annual Report 1914, SGR/5045/01, 163.

150. AHM/FCM/SGR/Cx. 48: Inspector General of Exploration Report October 1914, SGR/1024/01, 5.

151. AHU/FM/Cx. 913: letter 1655, 22 December 1910, contained in Actas da Sessão do Conselho de Administração, 28 March 1911.

152. AHM/FCM/SGR/Cx. 64: Mines Department Annual Report 1899, SGR/1305/01, 247; Cx. 230: Manica District Report October 1907, SGR/4976/01, 4.

153. Duffy, *Portuguese Africa*, 147; Martin, *Comores;* Monnier, *Esclaves de la Canne à Sucre.*

154. Douglas Wheeler notes that the idiom is, in part, the product of Portugal's long history of alliance with a much more powerful English partner; during the period from 1650 to 1945, Portugal was dependent, to varying degrees, on England, and when faced with requests (or demands) that Lisbon could not or preferred not to meet, a superficial response to London sometimes followed. Wheeler, *Historical Dictionary of Portugal,* 38.

155. AHM/FCM/SGP/Cx. 73: D.A. Chiloane to D.A. Sofala, no. 23, 9 July 1913.

156. OT, Machipanda (Bairro Chiqueia), 14 May 1997; OT, Chiteve, 15 May 1997; OT, Messika (25 de Setembro), 31 May 1997; OT, Chazuca, 29 July 1997. On *chibaro* more generally, see, for example, Van Onselen, *Chibaro.*

157. AHM/FCM/SGC/Cx. 15: Governor to Managing Director, no. 357, 30 March 1910.

158. AHM/FCM/ATI/CE/Cx. 5: D.G. to Director Buzi Company, 11 May 1928.

159. This system was very similar to, and perhaps modeled on, the system that governed the earnings of southern Mozambicans recruited by the Witwatersrand Native Labor Association to work in the South African mines. There, the system guaranteed that half of the very substantial accumulated earnings of scores of thousands of Mozambicans would be repatriated to Mozambique, where returned migrants would use the money to pay taxes and otherwise float the colonial economy.

160. *BCM* 14 (17 July 1911), Order 3216, "Regulamento provisório para o recrutamento e fornecimento da mão d'obra indigena pela Companhia de Moçambique," Articles 49–50. The company tinkered with the finer details of this payment regime, sometimes changing the percentages to 60–40 and, for workers from some districts, temporarily paying them nothing at work, reserving the entire balance of their salaries for payment on return to their home district. Such temporary and one-off arrangements offered further opportunity for an un-

scrupulous employer or administrator to steal a worker's wages and claim that the worker was "confused" over how much he was due, and where, and when.

161. AHM/FCM/SGP/Cx. 73: D.A. Lacerdonia to D.A. Sena, no. 102, 8 July 1913.

162. Royal Charter of 11 February 1891, Article 21, no. 6, as amended by Royal Decree of 30 July 1891, reproduced in Companhia de Moçambique, *Handbook;* Pírio, "Commerce, Industry and Empire," chapter 2.

163. AHM/FCM/SGR/Cx. 229: Manica District Annual Report 1906, SGR/4965/01, 94, Instructions for the Supply of Native Workers in Manica District, Article 13; Cx. 236: Manica District Hut Tax Collection Report 1914, SGR/5039/01, 2; Cx. 237: Manica District Hut Tax Collection Report 1915, SGR/ 5046/01; AHM/FCM/SGP/Cx. 69: Inspector of Finance and Exploration to Governor, no. 374, 28 August 1924.

164. AHM/FCM/SGC/Cx. 176: Circular 45 from S.G. to D.A. Chimoio, 18 June 1899; AHM/FCM/SGC/177: Circular 7/554, 7 March 1916; AHM/FCM/SGR/Cx. 10: Governor Annual Report 1923, Vol. 1, SGR/021/01, 53.

165. AHM/FCM/SGC/Cx. 180: Circular 30, 20 May 1931; AHM/FCM/NIP/Cx. 23: Director Native Affairs to Governor, no. 39, 13 May 1932, Confidential.

166. *BCM* 174 (16 November 1900), Regulations on Native Labor, Article 19, no. 5, paragraph 1; *BCM* 10 (16 May 1907), General Regulations on the Supply of Natives to Employers in the Territory, Article 8; *BCM* 18 (16 September 1907), General Regulations on Native Labor in the Territory of the Mozambique Company, Article 19; *BCM* 14 (17 July 1911), Provisional Regulations on the Recruitment and Supply of Native Labor by the Mozambique Company, Article 41, no. 2, 3, 10 [final approval on 22 December 1914, *BCM* 4, 16 February 1915]; Suplemento ao *BCM* 20 (23 October 1930), Regulations on Native Labor in the Colony of Mozambique, Article 204.

167. AHM/FCM/SGR/Cx. 226: Manica District Report June 1904, SGR/4935/01, Native Affairs Section, 3.

168. AHM/FCM/SGP/Cx. 67: Indígenas fugidos, "Auto da Queixa," n.d. [1910].

169. AHM/FCM/NIP/Cx. 15: Inspector of Native Affairs to D.A. Neves Ferreira, 4 July 1929.

170. AHM/FCM/SGR/Cx. 230: Manica District Annual Report, SGR/4978/01, 268–69.

171. AHM/FCM/SGR/Cx. 111: NLD Annual Report 1912, SGR/2212/01, 4, 103; AHM/ FCM/ATI/CE/Cx. 8: General Director to Director Native Affairs, no. 295, 14 March 1930; AHM/FCM/ATI/CE/Cx. 9: General Director Agent Macequece, no. 668, 19 June 1930.

172. AHM/FCM/SGR/Cx. 111: NLD Annual Report 1912, SGR/2212/01, 103.

173. AHM/FCM/SGR/Cx. 235: Manica District Annual Report 1912, SGR/5032/01, 141.

174. AHM/FCM/SGP/Cx. 321: Manica District Hut Tax Collection, D.A. Manica to Governor, no. 200 A, 12 June 1913.

175. AHM/FCM/SGR/Cx. 236: Manica District Annual Report 1914, SGR/5045/01, 8.

## 2. From Law to Practice

1. AHM/FCM/ATI/CE/Cx. 13: Agent Neves Ferreira to D.A. Neves Ferreira, 27 May 1929.

2. AHM/FCM/ATI/CE/Cx. 13: Agent Neves Ferreira to D.G., 15 May 1929.

3. AHM/FCM/ATI/CE/Cx. 13: Agent Neves Ferreira to George Diakuo, Monte Chiluvios, 13 January 1929.

4. Suplemento ao *BCM* 6 (19 March 1929), Decreto 16:199, "Codigo do trabalho dos indígenas nas colónias portuguesas de Africa," 145–85.

5. Livingstone and Livingstone, *Narrative of an Expedition*, 175, quoted in Vail and White, *Capitalism and Colonialism*, 7.

6. AHM/FCM/SGP/Cx. 182: "Regulamento dos Serviços Indígenas em Manica," Article 8, SGP/0290/01.

7. OT, Machipanda (Bairro Chiqueia), 14 May 1997; OT, Chiteve, 15 May 1997.

8. AHM/FCM/SGR/Cx. 234: Manica District Annual Report 1911, SGR/5025/01, 155.

9. Those tally lists can be found in the district-level annual census reports. District administrators described the recruitment process: AHM/FCM/SGP/Cx. 74: D.A. Neves Ferreira to Governor, letter 498, 25 June 1913; D.A. Gorongosa to Governor, letter 26/99, 28 June 1913; D.A. Chiloane to D.A. Sofala, note 23, 9 July 1913; D.A. Sanca to D.A. Sena, letter 135, 9 July 1913; D.A. Sofala to Governor, letter 84, 12 July 1913; D.A. Cheringoma to D.A. Beira, letter 84, 16 July 1913; D.A. Tambara to D.A. Sena, letter 133, 22 July 1913; D.A. Chimoio to Governor, 15 September 1913. Interviewees described the process as well. OT, Chazuca, 30 May 1997; OT, Chinhambudzi, 28 May 1997.

10. OT, Chinhambudzi, 28 May 1997; OT, Chazuca, 30 May 1997.

11. AHM/FCM/SGP/Cx. 73: D.A. Sanca to D.A. Sena, no. 129, 9 July 1913.

12. AHM/FCM/SGP/Cx. 70: D.A. Moribane to D.A. Manica, no. 153, 10 July 1919; AHM/FCM/SGR/Cx. 239: Manica District Report First Semester 1920, SGR/5069/01, attached report from Moribane.

13. AHM/FCM/SGP/Cx. 73: D.A. Gorongosa to Governor, 28 June 1913.

14. AHM/FCM/SGP/Cx. 73: D.A. Govuro to Governor, 30 August 1913.

15. AHM/FCM/SGR/Cx. 64: Mines Department Annual Report 1899, SGR/1308/01.

16. *BCM* 176 (17 December 1900), Circular 83, 4 December 1900. The percentage paid was reduced quite substantially to 3 percent in 1927. AHM/FCM/SGC/Cx. 179: Circular 98, 30 September 1927.

17. AHM/FCM/NIP/Cx. 27: D.A. Manica to Governor, 12 November 1902.

18. AHM/FCM/SGR/Cx. 64: Mines Department Annual Report 1899, SGR/1305/01, 248ff.

19. *BCM* 14 (17 July 1911), "Regulamento provisório para o recrutamento e fornecimento da mão d'obra indígena pela Companhia de Moçambique," Article 47.

20. AHM/FCM/SGR/Cx. 229: Manica District Annual Report 1906, SGR/4965/01, Native Affairs Report December 1906, 4.

21. AHM/FCM/SGR/Cx. 230: Manica District Annual Report 1907, SGR/4978/01, 253–254.

22. AHM/FCM/SGR/Cx. 228: Manica District Report October 1906, SGR/4963/01, 5–6.

23. AHM/FCM/SGP/Cx. 73: D.A. Chiloane to D.A. Sofala, no. 23, 9 July 1913.

24. AHM/FCM/SGP/Cx. 73: D.A. Tambara to D.A. Sena, no. 133, 22 July 1913.

25. AHM/FCM/SGP/Cx. 71: D.A. Gorongosa to Governor, no. 67/1910, 26 February 1910.

26. AHM/FCM/SGP/Cx. 74: D.A. Mossurize to Governor, no. 20/1910, 18 January 1910.

27. AHM/FCM/SGP/Cx. 71: D.A. Gorongosa to Governor, no. 298/1909, 30 September 1909; Cx. 72: D.A. Mocoque to D.A. Govuro, 27 November 1909.

28. *BCM* 18 (16 September 1907), "Regulamento geral do trabalho dos Indígenas no Território da Companhia de Moçambique," [General regulations of Native labor in the Territory of the Mozambique Company]. Similar regulations had been in place in Manica District since the previous year. See AHM/FCM/SGR/Cx. 229: Manica District Annual Report for 1906, SGR/4965/01, 94, laying out regulations in accordance with Circular 33, 26 June 1906. For violations of work hours, see AHM/FCM/SGR/Cx. 230: Manica District Report for October 1908, SGR/4988/01, D.A. Sena to D.A. Manica, no. 207, 1 October 1908; AHM/FCM/SGP/Cx.

74: Processo 199, "Fuga de Indígenas para o território inglez," D.A. Sena to Governor, no. 345/3146 of 1910, 8 November 1910.

29. *BCM* 18 (16 September 1907), "Regulamento geral do trabalho dos Indígenas no Território da Companhia de Moçambique"; AHM/FCM/SGR/Cx. 230: Manica District Report for October 1908, SGR/4988/01, D.A. Sena to D.A. Manica, no. 207, 1 October 1908; AHM/FCM/SGP/Cx. 74: Processo 199, "Fuga de Indígenas para o território inglez," D.A. Sena to Governor, no. 345/3146 of 1910, 8 November 1910.

30. AHM/FCM/SGP/Cx. 71: "Indígenas para Manica/Diversas," Governor to Managing Director, no. 1441 of 1910, 3 November 1910; AHM/FCM/SGR/Cx. 234: Manica District Annual Report 1911, SGR/5025/01, 170.

31. AHM/FCM/ATI/CE/Cx. 1: Director ATI to D. Adelaide Faria, 21 February 1927.

32. AHM/FCM/SGC/Cx. 15: Governor to Managing Director, no. 1637, 15 December 1910, attached note from Inspector General; *BCM* 14 (17 July 1911), "Regulamento provisório para o recrutamento e fornecimento da mão d'obra indigena pela Companhia de Moçambique," Article 41, no. 1, but see also the suggestion for even greater specificity by the director of the NLD, AHM/FCM/SGR/Cx. 111: NLD Annual Report 1912, SGR/2212/01, 102; the governor offered the comment about the "whiff": AHM/FCM/SGP/Cx. 71: Governor to Managing Director Delegado, no. 1441, 3 November 1910.

33. AHM/FCM/SGP/Cx. 74: Director NLD to Governor, letter 57/1348, 19 June 1918; Cx. 69: Processo 199, Mão de Obra Indígena, Inspecção de Finanças e Exploração to Governor, no. 374, 28 August 1924.

34. This paragraph draws on AHM/FCM/ATI/CE/Cx. 13: Agent Neves Ferreira to D.A. Neves Ferreira, 13 October 1928.

35. AHM/FCM/ATI/CE/Cx. 13: Agent Neves Ferreira to D.A. Neves Ferreira, 13 October 1928, 2.

36. AHM/FCM/ATI/CE/Cx. 13: D.G. to D.A. Neves Ferreira, 5 March 1928.

37. AHM/FCM/SGP/Cx. 72: Processo 199—Regulamento de fornecimento de Indígenas a particulares, Circular 16/392, 21 February 1908.

38. AHM/FCM/SGR/Cx. 235: Manica District Annual Report 1912, SGR/5032/01, 146; AHM/FCM/SGP/Cx. 70: Commission to D.A. Manica, 31 December 1919.

39. AHM/FCM/SGP/Cx. 70: D.A. Manica to Governor, 302/2304, 31 December 1919, SGP/0130/39; Commission report to D.A. Manica, 31 December 1919, SGP/0130/39 [attached to letter 302/2304, D.A. Manica to Governor].

40. AHM/FCM/SGR/Cx. 236: Manica District Annual Report 1914, SGR/5045/01, 8.

41. OT, Chiteve, 15 May 1997. Nearly every person I interviewed in 1997 and 1998 responded to my question about what happened when the company arrived with a description of *machila* carrier service; this description of the work draws on those conversations.

42. Andrada, *Manica*, 47.

43. AHM/FCM/SGR/Cx. 256: Moribane District Report for October 1898, 2.

44. AHM/FCM/SGR/Cx. 64: Serviço de Minas, "Relatório do Sr. Bourbon, Primeira Parte (Cópia textual)," SGR/1304/01, 36; "Relatório Anual 1899," SGR/1305/01, 247; Cx. 66: Mines Department Annual Report 1906, SGR/1336/01, 29; AHM/FCM/SGP/Cx. 73: "Salários na Rhodesia e no Transvaal a indígenas empregados na Agricultura" [1919].

45. AHM/FCM/SGR/Cx. 73: Mines Department Annual Report 1915, SGR/1451/01, 24.

46. Ibid.

47. Accident reports were few, though operators surely reported accidents only when a report was unavoidable. In 1907, Africans died at a rate of 9.7 per 1,000, which, while high,

compared quite favorably with the rate of 42 per 1,000 in Southern Rhodesia. AHM/FCM/ SGR/Cx. 68: Mines Department, Annual Report 1908, SGR/1350/01, 42.

48. Coplan, *In the Time of Cannibals*, 130. I am indebted to Coplan—or more precisely, to the men who recited oral poetry (*lifela*) for him—for this attempt to capture the texture of deep-level mine work; see ibid., chapter 5. Jeff Guy and Motlatsi Thabane describe a very different perspective in their analysis of the strong association of Basotho mine workers with the shaft-sinking process in South African gold mines. Guy and Thabane, "Technology, Ethnicity, and Ideology."

49. Phimister, "Pre-Colonial Gold Mining."

50. AHM/FCM/SGR/Cx. 64: Serviço de Minas "Relatório Anual 1899," SGR/1305/01, 274.

51. Ibid., 248; AHM/FCM/SGR/Cx. 64: "Relatório do Snr. Bourbon, Primeira Parte (Cópia textual);" 37.

52. AHM/FCM/SGP/Cx. 71: S.G. to D.A. Manica, 27 October 1910; D.A. Mossurize to Governor, no. 216, 22 November 1910; D.A. Mossurize to Governor, no. 272, 27 December 1910.

53. The development of agricultural methods, or lack thereof, is described in a number of reports. AHM/FCM/SGR/Cx. 48: Inspector General of Exploration, Report September 1910, SGR/1014/01, 4; Cx. 235: Manica District Annual Report 1914, SGR/5045/01, 129–130, 152–154.

54. Duffy, *Portuguese Africa*, 155.

55. AHM/FCM/SGR/Cx. 234: Manica District Annual Report 1911, SGR/5025/01, 165.

56. AHM/FCM/SGR/Cx. 235: Manica District Annual Report 1912, SGR/5032/01, 140.

57. AHM/FCM/SGP/Cx. 69: Inspecção de Finanças e Exploração to Governor, letter 378, 28 August 1924, 5; OT, Chitunga 12 August 1998.

58. AHM/FCM/SGR/Cx. 74: D.A. Sena to Governor, letter 345/3146 of 1910, 8 November 1910; AHM/FCM/SGR/Cx. 231: Manica District Report October 1908, SGR/4988/01, D.A. Sena to S.G., telegram no. 516, 3 October 1908.

59. AHM/FCM/SGP/Cx. 67: Indígenas fugidos, "Cópia-Auto de Queixa"; AHM/FCM/ SGR/Cx. 230: Manica District Report October 1908, SGR/4988/01, D.A. Sena to D.A. Manica, no. 203, 29 September 1908.

60. AHM/FCM/SGR/Cx. 66: Mines Department Report August 1905, SGR/1323/01/08, "Report of an Inspection of the 'Edmundian' Copper Mine," 8.

61. AHM/FCM/SGP/Cx. 71: D.A. Sena to Governor, 277/2867 of 1910, 19 October 1909.

62. AHM/FCM/SGP/Cx. 69: Inspecção de Finanças e Exploração to Governor, letter 374, 28 August 1924, 5; D.A. Manica to Governor, 27 July 1914.

63. AHM/FCM/SGP/Cx. 69: Inspecção de Finanças e Exploração to Governor, letter 374, 28 August 1924, 5; Cx. 71: Indígenas para Manica, Governor to Managing Director, letter 1441 of 1910, 3 November 1910.

64. The first phrase comes from the authors of the Portuguese colonial labor code of 1899, in *Antologia Colonial Portuguesa*, 1:27; the second uttered by Jules Carde, governor-general of French West-Africa, quoted in Cooper, *Decolonization and African Society*, 35.

65. OT, Chitunga, 12 August 1998.

66. AHM/FCM/SGR/Cx. 236: Manica District Annual Report 1914, SGR/5045/01, 130.

67. For company administrators' assessments of the recruits' capacity for the tasks they faced, see AHM/FCM/SGR/Cx. 235: Manica District Annual Report 1912, SGR/5032/01, 154; Cx. 236: Manica District Annual Report 1914, SGR/5045/01, 130; AHM/FCM/SGP/Cx. 69: Letter from D.A. Manica to Governor, 27 July 1914.

68. AHM/FCM/SGC/Cx. 15: Governor to Managing Director, no. 357, 30 March 1910; AHM/FCM/SGP/Cx.74: Agricultores Vila Pery to Governor, 22 April 1918, SGP/0130/39.

69. "Fit for labor" was the term used in district-level census reports to record the number of men and adolescent boys who might be conscripted.

70. AHM/FCM/ATIR/Cx. 127: Letter from Subagent, Vila Machado to Director ATI [incomplete, n.d.].

71. AHM/FCM/SGR/Cx. 111: NLD Annual Report 1912, SGR/2212/01, 63.

72. AHM/FCM/SGR/Cx. 111–113: NLD Reports, 1911–1926.

73. AHM/FCM/SGR/Cx. 48: Inspector General of Exploration, Annual Report 1914, SGR/1025/01, 21.

74. AHM/FCM/SGR/Cx. 235: Manica District Fourth Trimester Report 1912, SGR/5031/01, "Serviço de Vigilância."

75. AHM/FCM/SGR/Cx. 111: NLD Annual Report 1913, SGR/2216/01, 82.

76. AHM/FCM/SGR/Cx. 111: NLD Annual Report 1912, SGR/2212/01, 106.

77. AHM/FCM/SGP/Cx. 70: Director NLD to Governor, letter 100/2829, 6 December 1919.

78. AHM/FCM/ATIR/Cx. 127: Letter from Subagent Vila Machado to Director ATI [incomplete, n.d.].

79. OT, Bandula, 10 August 1998.

80. AHM/FCM/ATID/Cx. 27: Correspondência Confidencial 1927–1929, Agent Vila Pery to D.G., 10 June 1927.

81. AHM/FCM/SGP/Cx. 73: D.A. Sanca to D.A. Sena, letter 135, 9 July 1913, SGP/0130/39; AHM/FCM/SGR/Cx. 111: NLD Annual Report 1913, SGR/2216/01, 82.

82. AHM/FCM/ATICE/Cx. 2: Director ATI to Director Companhia Colonial de Buzi, CL/542, 17 May 1927; AHM/FCM/NIP/Cx. 23: Confidenciais, Diversos Assuntos 1927–1932, Director of Native Affairs to Governor, letter 10/203, 6 February 1930.

83. AHM/FCM/SGR/Cx. 111: NLD Third Trimester Report 1912, SGR/2211/01, Manica Delegation Report, 3.

84. The mortality rate for NLD recruits in Manica averaged 2.9 percent in the last quarter of 1912 and the first quarter of 1913. During 1911 and the first three quarters of 1912, the rate had averaged just 0.5 percent. AHM/FCM/SGR/Cx. 234: Manica District Annual Report 1911, Manica Delegation Report 1911, SGR/5025/01, 9; Cx. 111: NLD Second Trimester Report 1912, SGR/2209/01, 27; NLD Third Trimester Report 1912, SGR/2211/01, 3 of annexed Manica Delegation Report; NLD Annual Report 1912, SGR/2212/01, 73; NLD First Trimester Report 1913, SGR/2213/01, 33. Data on the total number of recruits in Manica during these years comes from AHM/FCM/SGR/Cx. 236: Manica District Annual Report 1914, SGR/5045/01, 132.

85. Data on the *evadidos* comes from AHM/FCM/SGR/Cx. 111: NLD Third Trimester Report 1912, SGR/2211/01, 27; NLD Annual Report 1912, SGR/2212/01, 71; Cx. 235: Manica District Third Trimester Report 1912, SGR/5030/01, n.p.; Manica District First Trimester Report 1913, SGR/5035/01, n.p.

86. AHM/FCM/SGR/Cx. 111: NLD Annual Report 1912, SGR/2212/01, 73; NLD First Trimester Report 1913, SGR/2213/01, 33.

87. *BCM* 14 (17 July 1911), Order 3216, 12 July 1911.

88. Ibid., Article 58.

89. Ibid., Article 55. For the total number of recruit deaths, see AHM/FCM/SGR/Cx. 234: Manica District Annual Report 1912, NLD Delegation Report, SGR/5025/01, 9; Cx. 111: NLD Annual Report 1912, SGR/2212/01, 73; NLD Annual Report 1913, SGR/2216/01, 88; NLD Annual Report 1914, SGR/2220/01, 66. For the one death that was compensated, see Cx. 111: NLD

Annual Report 1914, SGR/2220/01, 69. The one compensation case involved a fatal mining accident.

90. AHM/FCM/SGR/Cx. 111: NLD Annual Report 1915, SGR/2221/01, 88–89.

91. Ibid., 4, 74, 88–89.

92. AHM/FCM/SGP/Cx. 71: D.A. Sena to Governor, 19 October 1909.

93. AHM/FCM/SGR/Cx. 111: NLD Annual Report 1911, SGR/2212/01, 65.

94. *BCM* 174 (16 November 1900), "Regulamento do trabalho dos indígenas," Order 1741, Article 1; Neil-Tomlinson, "Mozambique Chartered Company," 285–89.

95. AHM/FCM/SGP/Cx. 71: D.A. Gorongosa to Governor, nos. 67 and 68, 26 February 1910.

96. AHM/FCM/SGR/Cx. 3: Governor Annual Report 1909, SGR/009/01, 427.

97. AHM/FCM/SGP/Cx. 74: Governor to Managing Director, no. 67, 13 January 1910.

98. AHM/FCM/SGP/Cx. 74: Managing Director to Governor, no. A-324, 5 April 1910.

99. *BCM* 14 (17 July 1911), Order 3216, 12 July 1911.

100. Ibid.

101. Ibid.

102. AHM/FCM/SGP/Cx. 73: D.A. Chiloane to D.A. Sofala, no. 23, 9 July 1913.

103. *BCM* 14 (17 July 1911), Order 3216, Article 15, paragraph 2; AHM/FCM/SGC/Cx. 178: Circular 2, 2 February 1920. The company had first attempted to impose a yearlong contract in 1917, but suspended its implementation when the Makombe uprising broke out early that year. AHM/FCM/SGP/Cx. 70: Circular 46/2739, 9 December 1916; AHM/FCM/SGC/Cx. 177: Circular 7, 30 January 1918.

104. AHM/FCM/SGR/Cx. 111: NLD Annual Report 1912, SGR/2212/01, 3; Cx. 112: NLD Annual Report 1920, SGR/2244/01, 124.

105. AHM/FCM/SGR/Cx. 112: NLD Annual Report 1920, SGR/2248/01, 9.

106. *BCM* 16 (16 August 1926), Order 5087, 3 August 1926.

107. Ibid.

108. *BCM* 18 (16 September 1926), 312.

109. These areas were the Zambezi Valley districts, particularly Chemba; the southern districts of Mossurize, Sofala, and Govuro; and Beira's northern hinterland of Chiloane and Gorongosa.

110. AHM/FCM/ATICE/Cx. 1: D.G. to Director of Native Affairs, 27 December 1926.

111. AHM/FCM/SGR/Cx. 114: Native Affairs Administration Annual Report 1927, SGR/2269/01, 5.

112. AHM/FCM/ATICE/Cx. 1: D.G. to Director Native Affairs, 27 December 1926; AHM/FCM/ATID/Cx. 36: Subagent Macequece to D.G., 8 July 1927; AHM/FCM/SGR/Cx. 113: NLD Annual Report 1925 SGR/2264/01, 115.

113. AHM/FCM/ATIR/Cx. 127: ATI Annual Report 1926, 1; Cx. 128: ATI Annual Report 1928, SGR/7152/01; AHM/FCM/SGR/Cx. 113: NLD Annual Report 1925, SGR/2264/01, 20.

114. AHM/FCM/ATID/Cx. 27: Agent Moribane to Agent Vila Pery, 12 October 1927.

115. AHM/FCM/ATID/Cx. 27: Correspondência Confidential, Agent Chimoio to D.G., no. 299, 13 October 1927.

116. AHM/FCM/ATICE/Cx. 1: D.G. to Director Native Affairs, 27 December 1926.

117. AHM/FCM/ATID/Cx. 27: Agent Chimoio to D.G., 13 October 1927.

118. AHM/FCM/ATICE/Cx. 3: D.G. to Director of Native Affairs Department, no. 1034, 6 October 1927, Confidential.

119. AHM/FCM/SGR/Cx. 114: Native Affairs Department Annual Report 1927, SGR/

2269/01, 5–6. Two years later, the company moved to give administrators a financial incentive, allowing them to receive per capita payments for "supervising" labor contracts. AHM/FCM/ATICE/Cx. 7: Circular 1050, 7 October 1929.

120. AHM/FCM/SGCE/Cx. 179: Circular 118, 3 November 1927, 2.

121. AHM/FCM/SGCE/Cx. 179: Circular Note 9, 16 September 1926, 3.

122. AHM/FCM/SGP/Cx. 68: S.G. to Warehouse Director, 9 March 1926; AHM/FCM/SGC/Cx. 179: Circular 104, 10 November 1926; *BCM* 24 (16 December 1927), Order 5613, 14 December 1927; AHM/FCM/SGP/Cx. 68: Circular 134, 29 December 1926. The total male population, including boys of any age, was just over 150,000 in 1927, while those judged "fit for labor" totaled 72,639. AHM/FCM/SGR/Cx. 114: Native Affairs Department Annual Report 1927, SGR/2269/01, 44. In previous years, only those conscripted by the company's labor department had been required to carry a pass.

123. AHM/FCM/SGR/Cx. 114: Native Affairs Department Annual Report 1928, SGR/2269/01, 11.

124. OT, Messika (25 de Setembro), 31 May 1997.

125. AHM/FCM/SGP/Cx. 68: Circular 134, 29 December 1926.

126. AHM/FCM/SGR/Cx. 114: Native Affairs Department Annual Report 1927, SGR/2269/01, 34; AHM/FCM/SGCE/Cx. 179: Circular 72, 8 August 1927.

127. AHM/FCM/SGP/Cx. 68: Director Native Affairs to District Administrators, Circular Note no. 9/641, 24 August 1927; AHM/FCM/SGR/Cx. 114: Native Affairs Department Annual Report 1927, SGR/2269/01, 8–10.

128. AHM/FCM/ATID/Cx. 27: Agent Chimoio to D.G., 13 October 1927; AHM/FCM/SGR/Cx. 114: Native Affairs Department Annual Report 1927, SGR/2269/01, 8–10.

129. AHM/FCM/SGR/Cx. 114: Native Affairs Department Annual Report 1927, SGR/2269/01, 6.

130. AHM/FCM/ATICE/Cx. 5: D.G. to Luiz Ribas, Telegram 1 September 1928.

131. AHM/FCM/ATID/Cx. 27: Agent Vila Pery to D.G., no. 7, 30 September 1927, Confidential.

132. AHM/FCM/ATICE/Cx. 3: D.G. to Agent Vila Machado, no. 1144, 4 October 1927, Confidential; D.G. to Agent Gorongosa, no. 1147, 4 November 1927, Confidential.

133. AHM/FCM/SGP/Cx. 73: D.A. Govuro to Governor, no. 81/596, 30 August 1913; Cx. 68: Circular Note no. 9/641, 24 August 1927; AHM/FCM/ATICE/Cx. 5: D.G. to Agricultural Company of Beira, no. 619, 1 June 1928.

134. AHM/FCM/NIP/Cx. 18: Native Affairs Administration Annual Report 1928, 6.

135. AHM/FCM/SGP/Cx. 68: S.G. to Governor, 1 November 1927. His suggestion was adopted for the final version, which was issued as Circular 118, 3 November 1927.

136. AHU/FCM/Cx. 900: Managing Director to D.G. of the Ultramarino, 21 July 1896; Managing Director to Royal Commissioner, no. 177, 15 October 1896.

137. Neil-Tomlinson, "Mozambique Chartered Company," 61.

138. AHM/FCM/SGP/Cx. 71: D.A. Sanca to D.A. Sena, no. 110, 30 September 1909.

139. AHM/FCM/SGR/Cx. 240: Manica District Third Trimester Report 1922, SGR/5083/01, "No. 12—Native Agriculture and Livestock"; attached report from Moribane.

140. AHU/FCM/Cx. 900: Managing Director to Royal Commissioner, no. 84, 28 May 1896.

141. AHM/FCM/SGR/Cx. 256: Moribane District Report March 1902, SGR/5484/01, 16. Joseph Conrad created a character—the company agent Kurtz—whose Congo headquarters was ringed with human skulls mounted on posts.

142. AHM/FCM/SGP/Cx. 183: Manica Report May 1902; OT, Machipanda, 14 May 1997.

143. This paraphrases the description offered by an English observer, quoted in Vail and White, *Power and the Praise Poem*, 202.

144. AHM/FCM/SGP/Cx. 183: Manica Report May 1902.

145. AHM/FCM/SGP/Cx. 74: Fuga de Indígenas para o Território inglez; Inspector General of Exploration to Governor, no. 411 of 1901, 22 November 1901, Confidential.

146. AHM/FCM/SGR/Cx. 256: Moribane District Report March 1902, SGR/5484/01.

147. OT, Davide Franque, 18 August 1998; Hanna, *Standard Shona Dictionary*, 189.

148. AHM/FCM/SGR/Cx. 256: Moribane District Report March 1902, SGR/5484/01, 16.

149. Ibid. A *tostão* was a silver coin with a face value of $100 *reis*. The mock calculation of 225 *tostões* was equal to £5.

150. AHM/FCM/SGR/Cx. 64: Mines Department Annual Report 1899, SGR/1305/01, 272.

151. AHM/FCM/NIP/Cx. 15: Department of Native Affairs Inspector to D.A. Neves Ferreira, 4 July 1929.

152. OT, Machipanda (Bairro Chiqueia), 14 May 1997.

153. AHM/FCM/SGR/Cx. 231: Manica District Report October 1908, "No. 26 Mão d'Obra Indígena," SGR/4988/01, Telegram no. 203, 29 September 1908 from D.A. Sena to D.A. Manica.

154. AHM/FCM/SGP/Cx. 105: P. Bindé to D.A. Moribane, 17 July 1900.

155. AHM/FCM/NIP/Cx. 23: Native Hospital Director (Beira) to Director of Native Affairs, 9 March 1932.

156. Nevinson, *Modern Slavery*.

157. AHM/FCM/SGR/Cx. 256: Moribane District Report March 1902, SGR/5484/01, 16.

### 3. The Critiques and Defenses of Modern Slavery

1. Livingstone and Livingstone, *Narrative of an Expedition*, 486, 636.

2. Paul Lovejoy discusses the dynamics of nineteenth-century slave exports in *Transformations in Slavery*, 140–64. The landmark study of this phenomenon is Hogendorn and Lovejoy, *Slow Death for Slavery;* for parts of French-ruled Africa, see Klein, "Slavery and French Rule."

3. Nevinson, *Modern Slavery*, 207–8.

4. Ibid., 58, 167.

5. Ibid., 37.

6. For the history of the arrangement between South Africa and Portugal governing African labor migration to South Africa, see Katzenellenbogen, *South Africa and Southern Mozambique*.

7. I have written somewhat more extensively on Nevinson and the society in Allina, "Fallacious Mirrors," 12–13.

8. Cited in *Anti-Slavery Reporter* 27, no. 3 (June–July 1907): 79.

9. See especially Grant, *Civilised Savagery*, chapter 4.

10. *BCM* 10 (15 May 1907), "Regulamento Geral para o fornecimento de indígenas a particulares no Território."

11. *RMS*, Series 3, no. 25 (March 1906), 2.

12. Vasse, "Mozambique Company's Territory, II," 388.

13. AHM/FCM/SGR/Cx. 3: Governor Annual Report 1907, SGR/007/01, Circular 33, 26 June 1906, 30.

14. AHM/FCM/SGR/Cx. 48: Inspector General Report October, November, December 1907, SGR/0989/01, 10.

15. AHM/FCM/SGR/Cx. 3: Governor Annual Report 1907, SGR/007/01, 3.

16. See Grant, *Civilised Savagery*, chapter 2. Alice Harris was an early pioneer in the use of photography to document atrocities. Ibid., 39–40. The hymn appears in Louis and Stenger eds., *E. D. Morel's History of the Congo Reform Movement*, 210, quoted in Grant, *Civilised Savagery*, 67–68.

17. Harris, *Portuguese Slavery*, 10. The book was published under John Harris's name, but it seems possible that Alice Harris (née Seeley) may have been at least a coauthor. She had considerably more formal education than he, having attended King's College, London, and at least one other book he authored was based on material she had originally written. Grant, *Civilised Savagery*, 31, 147.

18. Andrade, *Rapport Présenté au Ministre des Colonies*, 3, 5, 6.

19. CO445/44/24800, Lugard to S/S, dispatch no. 39, 8 April 1918; encl. no. 1, Culiffe to Lugard, March 3, 1918, enclosing report on Nigerian overseas contingent by Dr. T. M. R. Leonard, 28 March 1918, quoted in Killingray and Matthews, "Beasts of Burden," 18.

20. Pélissier, *Naissance du Mozambique*, 684.

21. The devastation in northern Mozambique was widespread; see Neil-Tomlinson, "Nyassa Chartered Company," 120–21; Pélissier, *Naissance du Mozambique*, 681–722; Medeiros, *História de Cabo Delgado e do Niassa*, 148–49.

22. Ross, *Report on Employment of Native Labor.*

23. Edward A. Ross Papers Microform, Reel 15, Correspondence 1922–25, E. A. Ross to A. L. Warnshuis, 17 March 1925 (Madison: State Historical Society of Wisconsin, 1985). Ross was cagey about who had recruited him for the mission, referring in his autobiography, published eleven years later, only to "some Americans who care about the fate" of the African population. Ross, *Seventy Years of It*, 190. His initial discretion, at least, was motivated by concern for his missionary interlocutors in Angola and Mozambique, who rightly feared retaliation by local authorities for having assisted Ross. See, for example, correspondence to Ross from Rev. William C. Bell, representative of the American Board of Commissioners for Foreign Missions at Bailundo, Angola, 10 September 1924, Edward A. Ross Papers Microform, Reel 15, Correspondence 1922–25.

24. Edward A. Ross Papers Microform, Reel 15, Correspondence 1922–25, E. A. Ross to A. L. Warnshuis, 23 May 1925.

25. Ross, *Seventy Years of It*, 190.

26. Ibid., 195. Although Ross was accompanied during part of the trip by R. Melville Cramer, a New York–based physician, Ross wrote the report, which, under a tight deadline with the typesetter, went to press without Cramer's cosignature. Neither Cramer nor Ross later chose to share the credit. Edward A. Ross Papers Microform, Reel 15, Correspondence 1922–25, E. A. Ross to A. L. Warnshuis, 21 May 1925, and A. L. Warnshuis to E. A. Ross, 26 May 1925. Excerpts also appeared in the *Nation* 121, no. 3136 (12 August 1925), 195–96.

27. Ross, *Report on Employment of Native Labor*, 60.

28. Ibid., 6.

29. Ibid., 12.

30. Ibid., 20.

31. Ibid., passim and 53.

32. Ibid., 60.

33. Ibid., i.

34. Miers, *Slavery in the Twentieth Century*, 100–101. Miers writes that the British Foreign Office distrusted nongovernmental organizations, such as the Anti-Slavery Society, to provide wholly accurate information, and none of the other colonial powers was any more eager to give critics a voice. As Miers puts it, "The colonial powers wanted it [the Temporary Slavery Commission] to be pliant, short-lived, and without the power to conduct investigations." Ibid., 102.

35. *New York Times*, 14 July 1925.

36. *New York Times*, 15 July 1925.

37. *New York Times*, 22 February 1925.

38. "Algumas Observações ao Relatório do Professor Ross," *BAGC*, 151.

39. Edward A. Ross Papers Microform, Reel 15, Correspondence 1922–25, A. L. Warnshuis to E. A. Ross, 16 July 1925.

40. "Algumas Observações," 156.

41. Vasconcelos, "Os Portugueses Não São Incapazes Colonizadores," *BAGC*, 3–5. Vasconcelos was at that time a member of the government commission charged with planning Portugal's exhibit for the 1931 International Colonial Exhibition in Paris.

42. Ibid.

43. League of Nations, Note of the Secretary General, 27 September 1924, enclosing "The Question of Slavery" J. Chagas to League of Nations Secretary General, 23 September 1924, 11.

44. Ibid., 51, 16.

45. Ibid., 22–23.

46. League of Nations, "Report Presented to the Sixth Assembly by the Sixth Committee," 3; League of Nations, Slavery Convention 1926, Article 5.

47. For this point, see Miers, *Slavery in the Twentieth Century*, 114.

48. League of Nations, "Temporary Slavery Commission, Minutes of the Second Session," 78.

49. Ibid., 77.

50. See Miers's discussion of these negotiations among committee members in *Slavery in the Twentieth Century*, 100–114.

51. Miers, *Slavery in the Twentieth Century*, 110.

52. League of Nations, "Temporary Slavery Commission, Letter from the Chairman of the Commission to the President of the Council and Report of the Commission," 13.

53. League of Nations, "Temporary Slavery Commission, Letter from the Chairman of the Commission to the President of the Council and Report of the Commission," 25 July 1925, 13.

54. League of Nations, "Draft Convention on Slavery, Replies from Governments," Reply of the Portuguese Government [translation], 2.

55. Vail and White, *Capitalism and Colonialism*, 206–9, 222.

56. League of Nations, "Draft Convention on Slavery, Replies from Governments," Reply of the Portuguese Government [translation], 2.

57. Ibid., 2–3.

58. Ibid., 3.

59. AHM/FCM/SGR/Cx. 114: Native Affairs Administration, Annual Report 1927, SGR/2269/01, 3.

60. Miers, *Slavery in the Twentieth Century*, 141.

61. International Labour Organisation, Forced Labour Convention of 1930, Article 1, paragraph 1.

62. Miers, *Slavery in the Twentieth Century,* 148.

63. Suplemento ao *BCM* 6 (19 March 1929), Colonial Ministry Decree 16:199, 6 December 1928, 146, 147.

64. Suplemento ao *BCM* 20 (23 October 1930), Order 1:180, 4 September 1930, 366, "Regulamento do Trabalho dos Indígenas na Colónia de Moçambique," Article 300.

65. Ibid., 367, "Regulamento do Trabalho dos Indígenas na Colónia de Moçambique," Article 302.

66. AHM/FCM/SGP/Cx. 72: D.A. Mocoque to D.A. Govuro, EXTRA, 27 November 1909; AHM/FCM/SGR/Cx. 235: Manica District Annual Report 1912, SGR/5032/01, 140.

67. AHM/FCM/ATICE/Cx. 1: ATI Director to D. Adelaide Faria, 21 February 1927.

68. AHM/FCM/SGP/Cx. 71: D.A. Gorongosa to Governor, 30 September 1909.

69. AHM/FCM/SGP/Cx. 69: Inspecção de Finanças e Exploração to Governor, no. 378, 28 August 1924, 5.

70. AHM/FCM/SGP/Cx. 71: Governor to Managing Director, no. 1441, 3 November 1910.

71. AHM/FCM/SGR/Cx. 226: Manica District Report June 1904, "Secção de Negócios Indígenas," SGR/4935/01, 9.

72. AHM/FCM/SGR/Cx. 223: Manica Report for March, April, and May 1900, SGR/4911/01, 10.

73. Ibid.

74. AHM/FCM/SGP/Cx. 74: Fuga de Indígenas para o Território Ingéz, D.A. Manica to Governor, no. 73 of 1901, 18 December 1901, 5.

75. AHM/FCM/SGR/Cx. 223: Manica Report for March, April, and May 1900, SGR/4911/01, 10.

76. AHM/FCM/SGR/Cx. 256: Moribane District Report March 1902, SGR/5484/01, 16.

77. Ibid.

78. Ibid.

79. AHM/FCM/SGR/Cx. 111: NLD Annual Report 1912, SGR/2212/01, 4.

80. AHM/FCM/SGP/Cx. 183: Report, Macequece, 1 May 1902. The Shona *gunda* means to cut with an ax; *m'pungo* is a corruption of the Shona *gumbo,* or leg.

81. AHM/FCM/SGR/Cx. 257: Moribane District Census Report 1915, SGR/5530/01 [n.p.].

82. AHM/FCM/SGP/Cx. 70: D.A. Moribane to D.A. Manica, no. 116 of 1916, 28 December 1916.

83. AHM/FCM/SGP/Cx. 70: D.A. Mossurize to Governor, no. 187 of 1919, 12 June 1919; D.A. Mocoque to D.A. Govuro, no. 319, 9 September 1919.

84. AHM/FCM/SGP/Cx. 70: D.A. Moribane to D.A. Manica, no. 153 of 1919, 10 July 1919.

85. Quoted in Duffy, *Portuguese Africa,* 238.

86. AHM/FCM/SGP/Cx. 70: D.A. Moribane to D.A. Manica, no. 153 of 1919, 10 July 1919.

87. AHM/FCM/SGR/Cx. 257: Moribane District Annual Report 1924, SGR/5559/01, "Mão d'Obra"; Cx. 258: Moribane District Second Trimester Report 1925, SGR/5561/01, "Mão de Obra."

88. AHM/FCM/SGR/Cx. 239: Manica District First Semester Report 1920, SGR/5069/01, attached report from Moribane.

89. AHM/FCM/SGR/Cx. 258: Moribane District Third Trimester Report 1925, SGR/5562/01, 8.

90. AHM/FCM/SGR/Cx. 258: Moribane District Annual Report 1926, SGR/5568/01, 33; Moribane District Third Trimester Report 1925, SGR/5562/01, 8.

91. AHM/FCM/SGR/Cx. 258: Moribane District Annual Report 1926, SGR/5568/01, 33.

92. AHM/FCM/SGR/Cx. 224: Manica District Annual Report 1902, 38; Manica District Report October 1903, SGR/4926/01, 3.

93. AHM/FCM/SGP/Cx. 71: D.A. Sanca to D.A. Sena, no. 110, 30 September 1909, SGP/0130/39.

94. *BCM* 18 (16 September 1907), Regulamento geral do trabalho dos Indígenas no Território da Companhia de Moçambique, Article 19; OT, Munzongo, 14 May 1997.

95. For one case, see AHM/FCM/SGR/Cx. 231: Manica District Report October 1908, SGR/4988/01, "No. 26 Mão d'Obra Indígena," transcribing telegram 203, 29 September 1908, from D.A. Sena to D.A. Manica.

96. AHM/FCM/SGR/Cx. 230: Manica District Annual Report 1908, SGR/4978/01, 250.

97. AHM/FCM/SGR/Cx. 231: Manica District Report October 1908, SGR/4988/01, "No. 26 Mão d'Obra Indígena," transcribing telegram no. 202-A/1099, 17 October 1908, D.A. Manica to Governor.

98. AHM/FCM/ATIR/Cx. 127: Agent Vila Machado to Director ATI, n.d., 3.

99. AHM/FCM/SGP/Cx. 71: D.A. Mossurize to Governor, no. 215 15 September 1909, 2.

100. AHM/FCM/SGR/Cx. 239: Manica District Report First Semester 1920, SGR/5069/01, attached report from Moribane, "Native Labor."

101. AHM/FCM/SGP/Cx. 69: Director Native Labor to Governor, no. 34, 6 May 1924.

102. AHM/FCM/SGPC/Cx. 12: D.A. Chemba to Director NLD, 26 December 1923.

103. AHM/FCM/SGPC/Cx. 12: D.A. Manica to Governor, 22 January 1924.

104. AHM/FCM/SGPC/Cx. 12: Circular [Manica District], 4 January 1924; Manica Farmers to Governor, 9 February 1924. The farmers' letter is so suggestive of bad blood between them and the district administrator that one wonders whether his investigation was intended more to settle a score than to defend Africans' rights.

105. AHM/FCM/SGPC/Cx. 12: Governor to Managing Director, 22 February 1924.

106. AHM/FCM/ATID/Cx. 36: Macequece, 1928; Subagent Macequece to D.A. Manica, no. 214 11 July 1928.

107. AHM/FCM/ATICE/Cx. 3: D.G. to Director Native Affairs, no. 1227, 23 November 1927.

108. AHM/FCM/ATID/Cx. 27: Confidential Correspondence, 1927–1929, Agent Moribane to Agência Chimoio, no. 7, 10 November 1927.

109. Suplemento ao *BCM* 20 (23 October 1930), Order 1:180, 4 September 1930, 367, "Regulamento do Trabalho dos Indígenas na Colónia de Moçambique," Article 302.

## 4. Mobility and Tactical Flight

1. Liesegang, "Notes," 178; Harries, "Slavery."

2. This paragraph and the next draw on oral testimony I collected in 1997 and 1998: OT, Machipanda (Bairro Chiqueia), 14 May 1997; OT, Munzongo, 14 May 1997; OT, Penhalonga, 19 May 1997; OT, Penhalonga, 8 August 1998; OT, Bandula, 10 August 1998; OT, Chitunga, 12 August 1998; OT, Guindingue, 26 August 1998.

3. This account draws in particular on OT, Munzongo, 14 May 1997. Informants also made reference to this history in OT, Penhalonga, 19 May 1997, and OT Chitunga, 12 August 1998. H. K. K. Bhila describes a similar incident in which Mutasa staged an ambush of Gaza soldiers during a beer-drinking party. Bhila, *Trade and Politics*, 185.

4. AHM/FCM/SGR/Cx. 229: Manica District Annual Report 1906, SGR/4965/01, 91.

5. AHM/FCM/SGR/Cx. 223: Manica District, Report for June and July 1898, SGR/4393/01, 3.

6. Ibid., 8.

7. Ibid., 3.

8. Ibid., 6.

9. AHM/FCM/SGR/Cx. 223: Manica District Annual Report 1896, SGR/4889/02, 11; AHM/FCM/SGP/Cx. 321: "Cobrança do Imposto de Palhota Manica," 1899. In theory, the imbalance could have been due to polygamy rather than men in hiding, but its incidence was nowhere near that high.

10. AHM/FCM/SGP/Cx. 71: D.A. Gorongosa to Governor, no. 298, 30 September 1909.

11. AHM/FCM/SGR/Cx. 223: Manica District Report for March, April, and May 1900, SGR/4911/01, 25; Manica District Report, Native Affairs, 31 December 1902, SGR/4918/01, 7; Cx. 224: Manica District Report 1902.

12. AHM/FCM/SGR/Cx. 223: Manica District Report for March, April, and May 1900, SGR/4911/01, 25.

13. AHM/FCM/NIP/Cx. 27: D.A. Chimoio to D.A. Manica, 27 September 1902.

14. AHM/FCM/SGR/Cx. 256: Moribane Subdistrict Report March 1902, SGR/5484/01, 18.

15. AHM/FCM/SGP/Cx. 183: Manica District Report May 1902, 2.

16. AHM/FCM/SGR/Cx. 227: Manica District Report June 1905, SGR/4946/01 Native Affairs Section, 2.

17. OT, Machipanda (Bairro Chiqueia), 14 May 1997; OT, Gomoramatede, 18 May 1997; OT, Penhalonga, 19 May 1997.

18. AHM/FCM/SGR/Cx. 224: Manica District Report 30 September 1903, SGR/4925/01, attached report from Moribane.

19. AHM/FCM/SGR/Cx. 64: Mines Department Annual Report 1899, SGR/1308/01.

20. AHM/FCM/SGP/Cx. 67: D.A. Mossurize to Governor, 13 September 1909. Asiwaju, "Migrations as Revolt," long ago recognized the political content of some migratory movement, a theme also explored by Neves, "Tete e o Trabalho Migratório" and "Início da emigração de mão-de-obra moçambicana"; Hughes, *From Enslavement to Environmentalism;* Tornimbeni and Newitt, "Transnational Networks and Internal Divisions."

21. AHM/FCM/SGP/Cx. 72: D.A. Manica to Governor, no. 702-A/3155, 2 December 1910.

22. AHM/FCM/SGP/Cx. 74: D.A. Moribane to D.A. Manica, no. 202, 5 November 1901; AHM/FCM/SGR/Cx. 256: Moribane District Report March 1902, SGR/5484/01, 4.

23. AHM/FCM/SGP/Cx. 67: D.A. Mossurize to Governor, 13 September 1909.

24. AHM/FCM/SGP/Cx. 74: D.A. Mossurize to Governor, 18 January 1910.

25. AHM/FCM/SGP/Cx. 71: D.A. Gorongosa to Governor, 30 September 1909.

26. AHM/FCM/SGP/Cx. 71: S.G. to D.A. Manica, 617-A/2870, 3 November 1910; AHM/FCM/SGR/Cx. 48: Inspector General Annual Report 1914, SGR/1025/01, 21.

27. AHM/FCM/SGC/Cx. 15: Governor to Managing Director, no. 357, 30 March 1910.

28. AHM/FCM/SGR/Cx. 188: Gorongosa District Annual Report 1909, SGR/4100/01, 11.

29. AHU/FM/Cx. 888: "Repatriação dos Chinezes de São Tomé [1900]"; Nascimento, *Desterro e Contrato.*

30. *BCM* 2 (16 January 1909), Order 2966.

31. AHM/FCM/SGP/Cx. 448: "Indígenas vadios e incorrigiveis" [Lazy and incorrigible natives], D.A. Manica to Governor, no. 349, 21 November 1906.

32. AHM/FCM/SGP/Cx. 448: D.A. Manica to Governor, 21 November 1906.

33. *BCM* 23 (2 December 1907), Order 2870, 23 November 1907.

34. AHM/FCM/SGR/Cx. 224: Manica District Annual Report 1902; Manica District October Report 1903, SGR/4926/01.

35. AHM/FCM/SGR/Cx. 230: Manica District Annual Report 1908, SGR/4978/01, 241–42; Cx. 231: Manica District August Report 1908, SGR/4986/01; Cx. 235: Manica District Annual Report 1912, SGR/5032/01, 130; Cx. 236: Manica District Annual Report 1914, SGR/5045/01, 117; *BCM* 2 (16 January 1909), Order 2966, 13 January 1909.

36. AHM/FCM/SGP/Cx. 104: Mines Director to Governor, no. 100, 2 August 1901.

37. AHM/FCM/SGR/Cx. 235: Manica District Annual Report 1912, SGR/5032, 131.

38. AHM/FCM/SGP/Cx. 69: Director NLD to Manica delegation, 11 July 1914. For Sena recruits, see AHM/FCM/SGR/Cx. 111: NLD Annual Report 1912, SGR/2212/01, 38; NLD Annual Report 1913, SGR/2216/01, 58; NLD Annual Report 1914, SGR/2210/01, 34.

39. AHM/FCM/SGP/Cx. 69: Inspector of Finance and Exploration to Governor, 28 August 1924.

40. AHM/FCM/SGP/Cx. 74: D.A. Mossurize to Governor, 18 January 1910.

41. AHM/FCM/SGP/Cx. 73: D.A. Govuro to Governor, 30 August 1913.

42. Data on worker flight for 1911 can be found in AHM/FCM/SGR/Cx. 234: Manica District, Annual Report for 1911 from the Delegation of the Department of Native Labor, SGR/5025, 8; for 1912–1926, see the reports from the Department of Native Labor, AHM/FCM/SGR/Cx. 111–113. The "fiery sun" comment can be found in AHM/FCM/SGR/Cx. 236: Manica District Fourth Trimester Report 1914, SG/5044/01, "Mão d'Obra Indígena."

43. AHM/FCM/SGR/Cx. 234: Manica District Fourth Trimester Report 1911, SGR/5024/01, "Serviço de Vigilância."

44. AHM/FCM/SGP/Cx. 74: D.A. Manica to Governor, no. 116, 8 June 1921.

45. AHM/FCM/SGP/Cx. 72: D.A. Mocoque to D.A. Govuro, 27 November 1909.

46. AHM/FCM/SGP/Cx. 71: D.A. Gorongosa to Governor, no. 256, 22 November 1906.

47. AHM/FCM/SGP/Cx. 71: D.A. Inharuca to D.A. Sena, 16 June 1910.

48. AHM/FCM/SGR/Cx. 238: Manica District Report on Hut Tax Collection for 1918, SGR/5058/01, 2; OT, Chazuca, 29 July 1997; OT, Bandula, 10 August 1998.

49. *BCM* 20 (16 October 1918), Order 3887, 15 October 1918; *BCM* 21 (1 November 1918), Order 3892, 23 October 1918, Order 3893, 26 October 1918.

50. AHM/FCM/SGR/Cx. 75: Mines Department Annual Report 1918, SGR/1492/01, 15.

51. AHM/FCM/SGR/Cx. 112: NLD Annual Report 1918, SGR/2236/01, 3.

52. AHM/FCM/SGR/Cx. 75: Mines Department Annual Report 1918, SGR/1492/01, 15.

53. AHM/FCM/SGR/Cx. 239: Manica District Second Trimester Report 1919, SGR/5070/01, attached report for Moribane, "Mão de Obra Indígena."

54. AHM/FCM/SGR/Cx. 112: NLD Annual Report 1919, SGR/2240/01, 1, 3.

55. AHM/FCM/SGP/Cx. 71: D.A. Neves Ferreira to Governor, no. 213, 21 August 1909; D.A. Mambone to D.A. Govuro, no. 182, 25 August 1909; D.A. Mossurize to Governor, no. 215, 15 September 1909, 1.

56. AHM/FCM/SGP/Cx. 70: D.A. Mocoque to D.A. Govuro, no. 319, 9 September 1919; D.A. Mossurize to Governor, no. 187, 12 June 1919.

57. AHM/FCM/SGR/Cx. 234: Manica District Second Trimester Report 1911, SGR/5022/01, "Serviço de Vigilância." Keletso E. Atkins explores African notions of labor time among Zulu workers, and its importance for their engagement in wage labor activity, in nineteenth-century Natal. Atkins, *Moon Is Dead!*

58. AHM/FCM/SGC/Cx. 178: Circular 2, 2 February 1920.

59. AHM/FCM/SGR/Cx. 112: NLD Annual Report 1920, SGR/2244/01, 9, 66, 67, 68, 111.

60. AHM/FCM/SGR/Cx. 112: NLD Annual Report 1922, SGR/2252/01, 114.

61. AHM/FCM/SGR/Cx. 239: Manica District Annual Report 1921, SGR/5078/01, 68–69.

62. AHM/FCM/SGP/Cx. 74: D.A. Manica to Governor, no. 116/803, 8 June 1921; Director NLD to Governor, no. 107/2359, 24 October 1921; AHM/FCM/SGR/Cx. 112: NLD Annual Report 1921, SGR/2248/01, 3.

63. AHM/FCM/SGR/Cx. 256: Moribane Subdistrict Report March 1902, SGR/5484/01, 18.

64. AHM/FCM/SGP/Cx. 70: D.A. Chemba to D.A. Sena, no. 190, 13 November 1910.

65. AHM/FCM/SGR/Cx. 231: Manica District Report September 1908, SGR/4987/01.

66. This paragraph and the three that follow are based on AHM/FCM/SGR/Cx. 230: Manica District Annual Report 1908, SGR/4978/01, 329–33.

67. For Pery de Lind as the champion of employers' interests in Manica, see Neil-Tomlinson, "Mozambique Chartered Company," 312.

68. The disease had a very limited impact on the district's cattle population. Herds belonging to the district administration and whites both increased over the previous year, while African holdings—small to begin with—decreased by just 10 percent. Moreover, when the district secretary conducted the census in October, he encountered no cases among African-held cattle, which he declared to have "splendid appearance." AHM/FCM/SGR/Cx. 231: Manica District Report October 1908, Arrolamento de palhotas e recenseamento da população Indígena e gado no ano de 1908, SGR/4988/01, 17. For the earlier epidemic, see Van Onselen, "Reactions to Rinderpest"; Ballard, "Repercussions of Rinderpest"; Phoofolo, "Epidemics and Revolutions."

69. AHM/FCM/SGR/Cx. 231: Manica District Report September 1908, SGR/4987/01, transcribed letter from D.A. Manica to Governor, 23 September 1908.

70. See Vail and White, *Capitalism and Colonialism*, especially chapters 4–7; AHM/FCM/SGR/Cx. 231: Manica District October Report, SGR/4988/01, transcribed letter from D.A. Sena to D.A. Manica, 1 October 1908.

71. AHM/FCM/SGR/Cx. 231: Manica District October Report, SGR/4988/01, transcribed letter from D.A. Sena to D.A. Manica, 1 October 1908.

72. AHM/FCM/SGR/Cx. 231: Manica District October Report, SGR/4988/01, transcribed letter from D.A. Sena to D.A. Manica, 29 September 1908.

73. Ibid.

74. AHM/FCM/SGR/Cx. 230: Manica District Annual Report 1908, SGR/4978/01, 333.

75. AHM/FCM/SGR/Cx. 231: Manica District Report October 1908, SGR/4988/01, "Mão de Obra," Order 172, 14 October 1908.

76. AHM/FCM/SGR/Cx. 231: Manica District Report October 1908, SGR/4988/01, "Mão de Obra," Circular 230–0/1119, 15 October 1908.

77. AHM/FCM/SGR/Cx. 233: Manica District Report December 1910, SGR/5016/01, "Supervision service," 3.

78. AHM/FCM/ATID/Cx. 36: Agent Macequece to D.G., 19 May 1927.

79. AHM/FCM/SGPC/Cx. 12: D.A. Chemba to Director NLD, 26 December 1923.

80. AHM/FCM/ATID/Cx. 36: Agent Macequece to D.G., 19 May 1927.

81. AHM/FCM/ATID/Cx. 27: Confidential Correspondence, D.G. to Agent Vila Pery, 29 March 1927.

82. Ibid.; AHM/FCM/ATICE/Cx. 1: D.G. to Agent Nova Sofala, 16 April 1927.

83. AHM/FCM/ATID/Cx. 37: Native Affairs Department Circular Note 10/566, 15 April 1930, 2.

84. Nascimento, *Desterro e contrato*.

## 5. Targeting Chiefs

1. This account is based on interviews I conducted in Manica: OT, Munzongo, 14 May 1997; OT, Penhalonga, 19 May 1997; OT, Chitunga, 12 August 1998; and on a document titled "Cobrança do imposto de palhota em Morivane" [Hut tax collection in Morivane], 30 November 1895, AHM/FCM/SGR/Cx. 223. "Morivane" is a variant of "Moribane." Additional information comes from Beach, "Zimbabwe Plateau," 268, 271; Liesegang, "Notes," 197; Bhila, "Manyika's Relationship with the Portuguese and the Gaza-Nguni," 33.

2. AHM/FCM/SGR/Cx. 256: Moribane District Report March 1902, SGR/5484/01, 16.

3. AHM/FCM/SGR/Cx. 223: "Cobrança do imposto de palhota em Morivane."

4. Ibid.

5. AHM/FCM/SGCE/Cx. 114: Director to D.A. Manica, 2 December 1895, enclosing telegram from Governor to D.A. Manica.

6. J. J. Machado to J. d'Almeida, 9 December 1895, in Coelho, *Dezoito Annos em África*, 534.

7. AHU/FCM/Cx. 900, Managing Director to Royal Commission, no. 84, 28 May 1896; Neil-Tomlinson, "Mozambique Chartered Company," 62; Cruz, "História da formação," 112.

8. AHM/FCM/SGR/Cx. 223: "Cobrança do imposto de palhota em Morivane" [Hut tax collection in Morivane], 30 November 1895.

9. A widespread practice throughout colonial Africa often designated at the time as indirect rule; Kiwanuka, "Colonial Policies," argues it was more widely shared among colonial powers than sometimes acknowledged. Berry, "Hegemony on a Shoestring," calls the practice "hegemony on a shoestring"; Mamdani, *Citizen and Subject,* dubs it "decentralized despotism."

10. Beach, "Zimbabwe Plateau," 247–48; see also AHM/FCM/SGR/Cx. 225: Manica District Annual Report 1904, SGR/4929/01, 64; AHM/FCM/SGP/Cx. 445: "Usos e Costumes dos Indígenas da Circumscripção de Manica" [Customs and practices of the natives of Manica District], SGP/0721/01, 22. The author of this report, written in 1907, was Cezare Augusto Cardotte.

11. See the introductory essay in Kopytoff, *African Frontier.*

12. AHM/FCM/SGR/Cx. 1: Governor Annual Report 1901, SGR/0002/01, 19. For the nature of precolonial chiefly authority, see Isaacman, *Mozambique,* 25–26; Beach, "Zimbabwe Plateau," 247–48; MacGonagle, *Crafting Identity,* 43–46, 87–89.

13. OT, Messika (25 de Setembro), 31 May 1997.

14. OT, Gomorematede, 23 May 1997; OT, Chazuca, 30 May 1997.

15. AHM/FCM/SGP/Cx. 183: Report, Macequece, 1 May 1902.

16. OT, Machipanda (Bairro Chiqueia), 14 May 1997.

17. See the district administrator's descriptions of tax collection difficulties in the Manica District reports for the 1890s and early 1900s, AHM/FCM/SGR/Cxs. 223–224.

18. AHM/FCM/SGR/Cx. 236: Manica District Annual Report 1914, SGR/5045/01, 8.

19. AHM/FCM/NIP/Cx. 27: D.A. Chimoio to D.A. Manica, no. 178, 27 September 1902.

20. AHM/FCM/SGR/Cx. 231: Manica District Report October 1908, SGR/4988/01, Hut Tax Collection, 1.

21. AHM/FCM/SGR/Cx. 232: Manica District Report December 1909, SGR/5002/01, attached census report for Moribane.

22. See especially Willis, "Men on the Spot."

23. AHM/FCM/SGR/Cx. 1: Governor Annual Report 1901, SGR/002/01, 19.

24. AHM/FCM/SGR/Cx. 256: Moribane District Report June 1898.

25. AHM/FCM/SGR/Cx. 256: Moribane District Report March 1902, SGR/5484/01, 16.

26. AHM/FCM/SGR/Cx. 224: Manica District Report September 1903, SGR/4925/01 [n.p.].

27. AHM/FCM/SGR/Cx. 1: Governor Annual Report 1901, SGR/002/01, 19.

28. *RMS*, Series 1, no. 11 (January 195), 136.

29. AHM/FCM/SGR/Cx. 2: Governor Annual Report 1905, SGR/006/01, 46.

30. AHM/FCM/SGR/Cx. 5: Governor Annual Report 1911, SGR/011/01, 20.

31. AHM/FCM/SGP/Cx. 73: D.A. Tambara to D.A. Sena, no. 133, 22 July 1913.

32. On confiscation of advances: AHM/FCM/SGP/Cx. 73: Director NLD to Governor, 15 September 1913; on chiefs as guarantors: *BCM* 14 (17 July 1911), "Provisional Regulations on the Recruitment and Supply of Native Labor by the Mozambique Company," Article 50, paragraph 2; AHM/FCM/SGP/Cx. 73: D.A. Lacerdonia to D.A. Sena, 8 July 1913.

33. AHM/FCM/SGP/Cx. 73: Director NLD to Governor, 13 July 1916.

34. AHM/FCM/SGP/Cx. 74: Circular 29/2010, 1 September 1916.

35. AHM/FCM/SGP/Cx. 73: Director NLD to Governor, 13 July 1916.

36. AHM/FCM/SGP/Cx. 73: Managing Director to Governor, 7 February 1919; AHM/FCM/SGP/Cx. 74: D.A. Sofala to Director Native Affairs, 15 January 1918.

37. AHM/FCM/SGC/Cx. 178: Circular 179, 29 December 1921.

38. AHM/FCM/SGR/Cx. 113: NLD Annual Report 1926, SGR/2268/01, 18, 20–161.

39. AHM/FCM/SGR/Cx. 241: Manica District Tax Collection Report 1933, SGR/5118/01, 4.

40. This account is based on the October 1903 report of the Manica District native affairs section. AHM/FCM/SGR/Cx. 224: Manica District Report October 1903, SGR/4026/01.

41. Amaral used the word *"filho,"* or son, but M'vumbi may well have been a more distant junior male relative. Mutasa's rule is described in Bhila, *Trade and Politics*. For an account of Mutasa's maneuvering with the Portuguese and the British and the eventual partition, see Beach, "Origins of Moçambique and Zimbabwe."

42. Van Onselen, *Chibaro*, 94–95.

43. Ibid., 94.

44. *BCM* 176 (17 December 1900), Circular 83, 4 December 1900.

45. AHM/FCM/SGR/Cx. 224: Manica District Report October 1903, SGR/4926/01.

46. *BCM* 176 (17 December 1900) Circular 83, 4 December 1900; AHM/FCM/SGR/Cx. 227: Manica District Report June 1905, SGR/4946/01, 7.

47. AHM/FCM/SGR/Cx. 2: Governor Annual Report 1905, SGR/006/01, 46.

48. AHM/FCM/SGR/Cx. 227: Manica District Report June 1905, SGR/4946/01, 7.

49. Ibid.

50. This interesting history has received less attention than one might expect; see Isaacman and Isaacman, *Tradition of Resistance*; Pélissier, *Naissance du Mozambique*, Vol. 2.

51. AHM/FCM/SGR/Cx. 226: Manica District Report, Finance Section, June 1904, SGR/4935/01, 12.

52. AHM/FCM/SGR/Cx. 3: Governor Annual Report 1909, SGR/009/01, 427.

53. This paragraph and the next are based on AHM/FCM/SGR/Cx. 228: Manica District Report March 1906, SGR/4956/01, 9.

54. AHM/FCM/SGR/Cx. 228: Manica District Report May 1906, SGR/4958/01, Native Affairs Section.

55. AHM/FCM/SGR/Cx. 228: Manica District Report August 1906, SGR/4961/01, 6; Cx.

229: Manica District Annual Report 1906, SGR/4965/01, Native Affairs Section Report December 1906, 2.

56. AHM/FCM/SGR/Cx. 228: Manica District Report May 1906, SGR/4958/01, Native Affairs Section.

57. AHM/FCM/SGR/Cx. 230: Manica District Report February 1907, SGR/4968/01, 5.

58. AHM/FCM/SGR/Cx. 229: Manica District Annual Report 1907, SGR/4966/01, 166; AHM/FCM/SGP/Cx. 320: Manica District Native Population Census 1907, SGP/0438/22.

59. AHM/FCM/SGR/Cx. 228: Manica District Report May 1906, SGR/4958/01, Native Affairs Section.

60. AHM/FCM/SGR/Cx. 229: Manica District Annual Report 1907, SGR/4966/01, 126. Jardím's death is mentioned in the June 1907 report, located in Cx. 230.

61. The phrasing "virtue out of failure" comes from Frederick Cooper, who uses it to characterize Britain's accommodation to African elite slaveholding in early-twentieth-century northern Nigeria, as well as Frederick Lugard's "genius" to label as formal policy Britain's reliance on African political hierarchies. Cooper, Holt, and Scott, *Beyond Slavery*, 124, 125.

62. AHM/FCM/SGR/Cx. 229: Manica District Annual Report 1907, SGR/4966/01, 126

63. AHM/FCM/SGR/Cx. 231: Manica District Report September 1908, SGR/4987/01, "Communicações;" *RMS*, Series 6a, no. 68 (October 1909), 87.

64. AHM/FCM/SGR/Cx. 231: Manica District Report September 1908, SGR/4987/01, "Communicações."

65. Ibid.

66. AHM/FCM/SGR/Cx. 231: Manica District Report October 1908, SGR/4988/01, 14.

67. AHM/FCM/SGR/Cx. 231: Manica District Report September 1908, SGR/4987/01, no. 26 Mão d'Obra Indígena.

68. AHM/FCM/SGR/Cx. 231: Manica District Report October 1908, SGR/4988/01, 14.

69. AHM/FCM/SGR/Cx. 229: Manica District Annual Report 1906, SGR/4965/01, Native Affairs Section December 1906 Report, 2.

70. AHM/FCM/SGR/Cx. 229: Manica District Annual Report 1906, SGR/4965/01, Native Affairs Section December 1906 Report, 2.

71. Ibid., 3.

72. *"Saguate"* is in common usage in Lusophone Asia and East Africa, and the Portuguese almost certainly borrowed it from Konkani, a language spoken in coastal Goa, one of the earliest Portuguese settlements in Asia. See Dalgado, *Glosário Luso-Asiático*, 2:271. I am grateful to K. David Jackson for this reference.

73. Mudenge, *Political History of Munhumutapa*, 258–59, 349–50; Zimba, *Mulheres Invisíveis*, 126–29.

74. Harries, *Work, Culture, and Identity*, 81, 95–96.

75. AHM/FCM/SGR/Cx. 228: Manica District Report June 1906, SGR/4959/01.

76. AHM/FCM/SGR/Cx. 229: Manica District Annual Report 1907, SGR/4966/01, 126.

77. The distribution of administrators' cut of the hut tax was established in the *BCM* 176 (17 December 1900), Secretary-General Circular 83, and revised in *BCM* 1 (2 January 1928) in accordance with Decree 14:582 of the Colonial Ministry.

78. AHM/FCM/SGR/Cx. 235: Manica District Census Report 1913, SGR/5034/01, 9.

79. AHM/FCM/SGR/Cx. 236: Manica District Census Report 1914, SGR/5040/01, 5. Britain's and Portugal's alliance dated to their 1661 treaty, in which Britain pledged to defend Portugal's colonial possessions. The alliance began to unravel in important ways early in the

nineteenth century, when British interests began to covet Portugal's east African settlements. Haight, *European Powers*, 151–57.

80. See, for example, AHM/FCM/SGR/Cx. 235: Manica District Tax Collection Report 1913, SGR/5033/01, attached "Acta da Banja Geral," 2. Several chiefs received £8 or £9, while Chirara, ruler of by far the district's most populous chiefdom, received more than £18.

81. AHM/FCM/SGR/Cx. 236: Manica District Tax Collection Report 1914, SGR/5039/01, attached "Acta da Banja Geral," 2, 4.

82. AHM/FCM/SGR/Cx. 235: Manica District Tax Collection Report 1913, SGR/5033/01, attached "Acta da Banja Geral," 3.

83. OT, Machipanda (Bairro Chiqueia), 14 May 1997.

84. These were some of the activities Gaivão noted; AHM/FCM/SGR/Cx. 236: Manica District Third Trimester Report 1914, SGR/5043/01.

85. AHM/FCM/SGR/Cx. 241: Manica District Census Report 1928, SGR/5104/01, 11; this 1928 report summarizes past years, with reference in this instance to 1918.

86. AHM/FCM/SGR/Cx. 237: Manica District Second Trimester Report 1915, SGR/5049/01, "Transport and Communications."

87. AHM/FCM/SGR/Cx. 231: Manica District Report October 1908, SGR/4988/01, attached Census Report, 14.

88. AHM/FCM/SGR/Cx. 236: Manica District Census Report 1914, SGR/5040/01, 5.

89. AHM/FCM/SGR/Cx. 223: Manica District Report June/July 1898, SGR/4893/01, 8.

90. Isaacman and Isaacman, *Tradition of Resistance*.

91. Ibid., 164.

92. Ibid., 166–69.

93. Ibid., 169–71.

94. Details on Buzi's labor force from AHM/FCM/SGR/Cx. 112: NLD First Trimester Report 1918, SGR/2235/01, 3.

95. This paragraph draws on AHM/FCM/SGP/Cx. 74: D.A. Buzi to Governor, no. 69/50 of 1918, [n.d.].

96. AHM/FCM/SGP/Cx. 74: D.A. Buzi to Governor, no. 69/50 of 1918 [n.d.].

97. Isaacman and Isaacman, *Tradition of Resistance*, 97.

98. AHM/FCM/SGP/Cx. 70: D.A. Gorongosa to Governor, no. 249, 7 July 1919.

99. Ibid.; AHM/FCM/SGR/Cx. 238: Manica District Census Report 1918, SGR/5059/01, 3–4.

100. AHM/FCM/SGR/Cx. 188: Gorongosa District Census Report 1919, SGR/4149/01, 11.

101. AHM/FCM/SGP/Cx. 70: D.A. Gorongosa to Governor, no. 249, 7 July 1919.

102. AHM/FCM/SGR/Cx. 188: Gorongosa District Census Report 1919, SGR/4149/01, 4–5.

103. Ibid., 5, 4.

104. Ibid., 3–4.

105. Ibid., 1–2, 3, 5.

106. Ibid., 6–8.

107. Ibid., 5–6.

108. AHM/FCM/SGR/Cx. 238: Manica District Census Report 1918, SGR/5059/01, 4.

109. AHM/FCM/SGR/Cx. 188: Gorongosa District Census Report 1919, SGR/4149/01, 1; Cx. 112: NLD Annual Report 1919, SGR/2240/01, 105.

110. AHM/FCM/SGP/Cx. 70: D.A. Neves Ferreira to Governor, no. 201, 10 April 1919.

111. AHM/FCM/SGR/Cx. 8: Governor Annual Report 1917, SGR/017/01, 16; Governor Annual Report 1918, SGR/018/01, 4.

112. AHM/FCM/SGR/Cx. 238: Manica District Census Report 1918, SGR/5059/01, 3.

113. AHM/FCM/SGR/Cx. 237: Manica District Census Report 1916, SGR/5052/01, Table 1; Cx. 238: Manica District Census Report 1918, SGR/5059/01. The Census Report for 1917 was missing from the archives; given the tumult caused by the uprising, it seems likely that no census was conducted.

114. AHM/FCM/SGP/Cx. 320: Manica District Census Report 1926 [transcribed copy].

115. AHM/FCM/SGP/Cx. 321: D.A. Manica to Governor, no. 30/176, 26 February 1926; AHM/FCM/SGR/Cx. 240: Manica District First Trimester Report 1925, SGR/5095/01, 6; Manica District Annual Report 1925, SGR/5098/01, 60.

116. AHM/FCM/SGP/Cx. 320: Manica District Census Report 1926 [transcribed copy].

117. AHM/FCM/SGP/Cx. 320: Manica District Census Report 1926.

118. Ibid.

119. AHM/FCM/SGR/Cx. 83: Mines Department Annual Report 1935, SGR/1707/01, 50.

120. AHM/FCM/SGR/Cx. 84: Mines Department Annual Report 1938, SGR/1746/01, 39.

## 6. Seniority and Subordination

1. Recent literature on this phenomenon is extensive; see Mamdani, *Citizen and Subject;* Schmidt, *Peasants, Traders, and Wives;* Chanock, *Law, Custom, and Social Order;* Byfield, "Marriage, Divorce and the Emerging Colonial State."

2. AHM/FCM/SGP/Cx. 445: Gorongosa District, "Usos e costumes indígenas da circumscripção," SGP/0721/01 [1907]; Manica District, "Usos e costumes indígenas da circumscripção," SGP/0721/01 [1907]; McKittrick, *To Dwell Secure;* Carton, *Blood from Your Children;* Jeater, *Marriage, Perversion, and Power;* McClendon, *Genders and Generations Apart.*

3. AHM/FCMSGP/Cx. 67: Circular 48, 15 January 1901, Processo 199, SGP/0130/49.

4. AHM/FCM/NIP/Cx. 27: S.G. to D.A. Govuro, 18 September 1901.

5. AHM/FCM/SGR/Cx. 224: Manica District Annual Report 1902.

6. AHM/FCM/SGR/Cx. 230: Manica District Annual Report 1908, SGR/4978/001, 249.

7. AHM/FCM/SGP/Cx. 71: D.A. Manica to Governor, 11 September 1909.

8. AHM/FCM/SGP/Cx. 71: D.A. Manica to Governor, 16 April 1910.

9. AHM/FCM/SGP/Cx. 71: D.A. Govuro to Governor, 3 December 1909.

10. AHM/FCM/SGR/Cx. 227: Manica District Report June 1907, Native Affairs Report, 7.

11. AHM/FCM/SGP/Cx. 72: D.A. Mambone to D.A. Govuro, 14 March 1910.

12. AHM/FCM/SGR/Cx. 230: Manica District Annual Report 1908, SGR/4978/01, 248–49; *BCM* 14 (17 July 1911), Article 47, paragraph 1. This differential remained in place until 1930, when the new labor code for the colonies specified that boys between the ages of fourteen and eighteen would earn half what adults did. Suplemento ao *BCM* 20 (23 October 1930), "Regulamento do Trabalho dos Indígenas na Colónia de Moçambique," Article 180.

13. AHM/FCM/SGR/Cx. 111: NLD Annual Report 1913, SGR/2216/01, 1; Cx. 236: Manica District Annual Report 1914, SGR/5045/01, 130.

14. There was one such complaint in 1915 and another in 1928; the second is likely evidence of the administrative disarray that followed the abolition of company conscription. AHM/FCM/SGR/Cx. 236: Manica District Annual Report 1914, SGR/5045/01, 130; AHM/FCM/ATID/Cx. 36: Agent Macequece to D.G., 31 July 1928.

15. For earlier pawning practices, see Isaacman and Isaacman, "Slavery and Social Stratification."

16. *BCM* 14 (17 July 1911), "Regulamento provisório para o recrutamento e fornecimento da mão d'obra indígena pela Companhia de Moçambique," Article 50. The article in question states that the advance "may be paid," raising the question of how often conscripts actually received such advance payments.

17. Isaacman and Isaacman, "Slavery and Social Stratification"; see also the more general discussion offered by Falola and Lovejoy, "Pawnship in Historical Perspective."

18. AHM/FCM/SGC/Cx. 177: Circular Note 4-A/243, 27 January 1915.

19. AHM/FCM/SGC/Cx. 179: Circular 87, 19 December 1924.

20. AHM/FCM/ATID/Cx. 36: Subagent Macequece to Agent Mossurize, 23 February 1928.

21. My phrasing here evokes McKittrick's *To Dwell Secure,* which is greatly concerned with generational tensions, though in the political context of missionary activity under colonial rule.

22. Carton, *Blood from Your Children.*

23. My thinking here has been very fruitfully guided by the work of Carton, Jeater, Schmidt, and McClendon.

24. Harries and Moodie demonstrate this dynamic for Mozambique in the southern African context: Harries, *Work, Culture, and Identity;* Moodie, *Going for Gold.* The tendency describes a far wider field; Berry, *Fathers Work for Their Sons.*

25. This paragraph draws on the argument Carton makes in *Blood from Your Children.* The classic study of the 1906 rebellion is Marks, *Reluctant Rebellion.*

26. Quoted in McClendon, *Genders and Generations Apart,* 58.

27. Ibid., 57.

28. Quoted in ibid., 48.

29. McClendon discusses the Native Service Contract Act in ibid., 90–98.

30. Carton, *Blood from Your Children.*

31. AHM/FCM/SGP/Cx. 73: D.A. Sanca to D.A. Sena, 9 July 1913.

32. AHM/FCM/SGR/Cx. 223: Manica District Report August 1900, SGR/4915/01, attached Moribane report, 5.

33. AHM/FCM/SGP/Cx. 183: Report, Macequece, 1 May 1902, 3.

34. Ibid. The practice continued for decades, evolving at times, so that wives might be jailed until men—absent on labor contracts—made outstanding hut tax payments. AHM/FCM/ATICE/Cx. 5: D.G. to Director Native Affairs, letter 1096, 18 October 1928; Cx. 6: D.G. to Director Native Affairs, letter 1191, 15 November 1928.

35. AHM/FCM/SGP/Cx. 73: D.A. Tambara to D.A. Sena, no. 133, 22 July 1913.

36. AHM/FCM/SGP/Cx. 70: D.A. Sena to Governor, 24 January 1911.

37. AHM/FCM/SGP/Cx. 183: Report, Macequece, 1 May 1902, 4.

38. AHM/FCM/SGPC/Cx. 28: D.A. Chiloane to Governor, 7 March 1931. While detained, women faced a high risk of sexual assault at the hands of police. This vulnerability for African women in Mozambique is documented in Vail and White, *Power and the Praise Poem,* chapter 6; Isaacman, *Cotton Is the Mother of Poverty,* chapter 3.

39. AHM/FCM/SGPC/Cx. 28: D.A. Govuro to Governor, 10 March 1931.

40. AHM/FCM/SGC/Cx. 177: Circular Note 14-A/1911, 1 August 1911.

41. OT, Chazuca, 30 May and 29 July 1997.

42. OT, Jéqua, 20 May 1997.

43. OT, Chazuca, 30 May 1997. Michael Gelfand specifies that the provision of water for morning washing lasts only during a wife's first week of residence with her husband; his pres-

entist approach, however, in which he describes practices he observes as if they have continuously existed in their current manifestation, leads me to treat such details in his work with some caution. Gelfand, *Genuine Shona*, 32–33. Elizabeth Schmidt provides a more exhaustive account of women's labor responsibilities in *Peasants, Traders, and Wives*, 44–52, 82–86.

44. Thus, even though women sometimes contributed the greater part of labor to African agricultural production, white settler farmers tended to hire men only, at least for ongoing wage work, while taking on women laborers only for poorly paid causal work at harvest time.

45. Schmidt, *Peasants, Traders, and Wives*, is especially strong on this point.

46. For example, Southern Rhodesia's Native Marriages Ordinance of 1901, amended in 1912 and 1917, and the Natives Adultery Punishment Ordinance of 1916. Schmidt discusses the effects thereof in "Negotiated Spaces"; see also Hay and Wright, *African Women and the Law*.

47. AHM/FCM/SGP/Cx. 74: D.A. Sena to Governor, 2 October 1916.

48. AHM/FCM/SGP/Cx. 71: D.A. Inharuca to D.A. Sena, 16 June 1910; Cx. 72: S.G. to D.A. Manica, 22 December 1911; AHM/FCM/SGR/Cx. 111: NLD Annual Report 1913, SGR/2216/01, 83; Cx. 236: Manica District Third Trimester Report 1914, SGR/5043/01, [n.p.]; AHM/FCM/SGP/Cx. 320: Manica District Census Report 1926 [transcription].

49. AHM/FCM/SGP/Cx. 71: D.A. Gorongosa to Governor, 7 November 1907.

50. AHM/FCM/SGC/Cx. 15: Correspondence Fourth Trimester 1910, Governor to Managing Director, 15 December 1910.

51. AHM/FCM/SGP/Cx. 74: D.A. Sofala to Director of NLD, 15 January 1918.

52. OT, Penhalonga, 8 August 1998; OT, Chitunga, 12 August 1998.

53. Such labor exchanges were (and still are) widely practiced throughout east and southern Africa; see Schmidt, *Peasants, Traders, and Wives*, 45–47; Davison, *Gender, Lineage, and Ethnicity*, 117, 122; Willis, *Potent Brews*, 17–18; Beach, "Zimbabwe Plateau," 248.

54. OT, Jécua, 20 May 1997; OT, Bandula, 10 August 1998; OT, Chitunga, 12 August 1998; OT, Chazuca, 12 August 1998; OT, Guindíngue, 26 August 1998. Thanks to Davide Franque for a full elucidation of the *madzande*. Women also brewed beer for consumption on other occasions, notably celebratory and spiritual rituals; see MacGonagle, *Crafting Identity*, 82–85.

55. The six words are *"masvetu," "maheu," "mapiswa," "makandirwa," "mahanga,"* and *"madirwa."* See Hannan, *Standard Shona Dictionary*, 769–70.

56. OT, Penhalonga, 8 August 1998. Both Schmidt, *Peasants, Traders, and Wives*, 65, 68, and Willis, *Potent Brews*, 26, also note the labor intensity involved.

57. Jeater, *Marriage, Perversion, and Power*, 114.

58. AHM/FCM/SGP/Cx. 71: D.A. Tambara to D.A. Sena, no. 21, 21 September 1909.

59. AHM/FCM/SGP/Cx. 73: D.A. Chiloane to D.A. Sofala, no. 23, 9 July 1913.

60. Ibid.

61. AHM/FCM/SGP/Cx. 74: D.A. Neves Ferreira to Governor, 22 September 1921.

62. OT, Bandula, 10 August 1998.

63. Jeater, *Marriage, Perversion, and Power*, 114. Leroy Vail and Landeg White explore some such concerns as expressed in song and musical performance. Vail and White, *Power and the Praise Poem*, chapter 4.

64. Jeater, *Marriage, Perversion, and Power*, 111–12.

65. AHM/FCM/NIP/Cx. 23: Confidential Diverse Subjects, Dispatch to Cabinet, 7 July 1937.

66. Jeater, *Marriage, Perversion, and Power*, 114.

67. AHM/FCM/NIP/Cx. 23: Manica Confidential, M. Correia 7 July 1937.

68. AHM/FCM/SGR/Cx. 241: Manica District Census Report 1932, SGR/5115/01, Native Affairs chart 13; Manica District Tax Collection Report 1932, SGR/5116/01, Native Affairs chart 21. Prior to the Depression years, district administrators routinely reported achieving 100 percent collection rates before year's end.

69. AHM/FCM/NIP/Cx. 25: Director Native Affairs to Inspector of Finances and Exploration, 30 June 1932, 6.

70. *BCM* 19 (1 October 1933), Order 6683, 27 September 1933; AHM/FCM/NIP/Cx. 23: D.A. Manica to Director Native Affairs, 12 August 1933; AHM/FM/NIP/Cx. 23: Director Native Affairs to Governor, 13 May 1932, 3.

71. AHM/FCM/SGR/Cx. 241: Manica District Census Report 1933, SGR/5118/01, 20.

72. AHM/FCM/NIP/Cx. 23: D.A. Manica to Director Native Affairs, 12 August 1933.

73. AHM/FCM/NIP/Cx. 23: Director Native Affairs to Governor, 16 August 1933; Director Native Affairs to D.A. Manica, 17 August 1933.

74. AHM/FCM/SGR/Cx. 242: Manica District Inspection Report May 1938, SGR/5127/01, 2.

75. AHM/FCM/SGR/Cx. 239: Manica District Annual Report 1921, SGR/5078/01, 69.

## 7. An "Absolute Freedom" Circumscribed and Circumvented

1. *BCM* 174 (16 November 1900), "Regulamento do trabalho dos indígenas."

2. Suplemento ao *BCM* 6 (19 March 1929), Decreto 16:199, "Código do trabalho dos indígenas nas colónias portuguesas de África," chapter 1, article 3.

3. Ibid., introduction.

4. AHM/FCM/SGR/Cx. 223: Manica District Native Affairs Report December 1902, SGR/4918/01, 5.

5. AHM/FCM/SGR/Cx. 239: Manica District Annual Report 1921, SGR/5078/01, 71.

6. Ibid.

7. AHM/FCM/SGR/Cx. 258: Moribane District Annual Report 1926, SGR/5568/01, 33.

8. AHM/FCM/SGR/Cx. 239: Manica District First Trimester Report 1920, SGR/5069/01, attached report from Moribane.

9. AHM/FCM/SGR/Cx. 237: Manica District Tax Collection Report 1916, SGR/5053/01, 1.

10. AHM/FCM/SGR/Cx. 234: Manica District Annual Report 1911, SGR/5025/01, 156; AHM/FCM/SGP/Cx. 321: D.A. Manica to Governor, no. 200-A/934, 12 June 1913.

11. AHM/FCM/SGR/Cx. 237: Manica District Census Report 1916, SGR/5052/01, 2–3.

12. AHM/FCM/SGR/Cx. 237: Manica District Census Report 1915, SGR/5047/01, 3–4.

13. AHM/FCM/SGP/Cx. 69: S.G. to Governor, n.d.

14. AHM/FCM/SGR/Cx. 237: Manica District Census Report 1916, SGR/5052/01, 5.

15. AHM/FCM/SGR/Cx. 238: Manica District Census Report 1918, SGR/5059/01, 9; OT, Messika (25 de Setembro), 31 May 1997.

16. AHM/FCM/SGP/Cx. 71: Director NLD to Governor, 30 March 1914.

17. AHM/FCM/SGR/Cx. 113: NLD Annual Report 1925, SGR/2264/01, 91.

18. AHM/FCM/SGP/Cx. 69: Inspector General to Governor, no. 374, 28 August 1924.

19. Harries, *Work, Culture, and Identity,* chapter 2.

20. Covane, *Trabalho Migratório,* 101–12; Penvenne, *African Workers and Colonial Racism,* 24–27. The literature on southern Mozambique, mine labor, and its historical impact is vast; the subject is better researched than any other in Mozambican history, with perhaps the exception of the Zambezi Valley *prazos.* The following citations suggest a starting point

for further research rather than exhaustive coverage: Moodie, *Going for Gold;* First et al., *Mineiro Moçambicano;* Harries, *Work, Culture, and Identity.* For a comprehensive bibliography, see Souto, *Guia Bibliográfico.*

21. For more on the agreement between South Africa and Portugal, see Katzenellenbogen, *South Africa and Southern Mozambique.*

22. See, for example, AHM/FCM/SGP/Cx. 104: A. Lawley, BSAC Administrator to Governor, 23 December 1899; Governor to A. Lawley, 24 January 1900; Cx. 182: Witwatersrand Native Labour Association to Governor, 14 November 1902.

23. South Africa guaranteed Portugal that a certain percentage of South African imports would pass through Lourenço Marques, generating import revenue for the Mozambican economy.

24. Harries, *Work, Culture, and Identity,* 140. The figure rarely dropped below 70,000, though the proportion of Mozambicans in the total mine workforce fell to between a quarter and a third. See First et al., *Mineiro Moçambicano,* 204.

25. AHM/FCM/SGR/Cx. 3: Governor Annual Report 1908, SGR/008/01, 230.

26. AHM/FCM/SGR/Cx. 228: Manica District Report October 1908, SGR/4963/01, 5–6.

27. AHM/FCM/ATIC/Cx. 1: D.G. to Director Native Affairs Department, 27 December 1926.

28. AHM/FCM/SGR/Cx. 85: Mines Department Report April 1938, SGR/1737/01, attached letter from Mines Director to S.G., 23 November 1938.

29. AHM/FCM/SGP/Cx. 71: D.A. Govuro to Governor, 12 August 1901.

30. AHM/FCM/SGP/Cx. 67: D.A. Mossurize to Governor, 4 November 1909.

31. AHM/FCM/NIP/Cx. 23: D.A. Moribane to Director Native Affairs Department, 7 June 1930, Confidential.

32. AHM/FCM/ATID/Cx. 27: Correspondência Confidencial, Agent Mossurize to Agent Vila Pery, 30 May 1927.

33. AHM/FCM/SGP/Cx. 70: D.A. Moribane to D.A. Manica, no. 153, 10 July 1919.

34. Quoted in Breckenridge, "Allure of Violence," 671.

35. Patrick Harries describes these dangers quite poignantly in *Work, Culture, and Identity,* 28–32; see also Bradford, "Getting Away with Murder," 99–102. By the time some migrants arrived at the mines, they were in no shape to engage in manual labor. See Packard, *White Plague, Black Labor,* 70.

36. Bradford, "Getting Away with Murder," 106–10; Murray, "Factories in the Fields," 79–81, 85–88.

37. AHM/FCM/SGP/Cx. 71: Inspector General to Governor, 13 January 1909. Emphasis added.

38. AHM/FCM/SGR/Cx. 6: Governor Annual Report 1913, SGR/013/01, 202.

39. AHM/FCM/SGP/Cx. 69: Inspector of Finance and Exploration to Governor, 28 August 1924, 5.

40. AHM/FCM/NIP/Cx. 23: D.A. Moribane to Director Native Affairs Department, 7 June 1930, Confidential.

41. AHM/FCM/SGP/Cx. 67: D.A. Mossurize to Governor, 4 November 1909.

42. AHM/FCM/SGR/Cx. 236: Manica District Annual Report 1914, SGR/5045/01, 8; AHM/FCM/NIP/Cx. 11: D.A. Moribane to Governor, 27 March 1927; Cx. 23: Presidente da Associacao de Classe dos Agricultores de Manica e Sofala [President of the Farmers' Association of Manica and Sofala], to Governor, 25 March 1930; D.A. Mossurize to Governor, 11 April 1930.

43. AHM/FCM/NIP/Cx. 23: President Farmers' Association of Manica and Sofala to Governor, 25 March 1930; D.A. Mossurize to Governor, 11 April 1930.

44. AHM/FCM/SGP/Cx. 50: D.A. Mossurize to Governor, 22 July 1938.

45. Randall Packard has written extensively on the impact of the mine environment on worker health. See Packard, *White Plague, Black Labor;* Packard, "Invention."

46. AHM/FCM/SGR/Cx. 237: Manica District Annual Report 1920, SGR/5072/01, attached report from Moribane. The association of mine work, and even specific underground skills, with particular ethnic groups was not exclusively a European belief; see Guy and Thabane, "Technology, Ethnicity, and Ideology."

47. The statutes of the association, published in *BCM* 18 (16 September 1926), 312, include a list of its members.

48. AHM/FCM/ATICE/Cx. 1: Director ATI to Director Native Affairs, 27 December 1926.

49. AHM/FCM/SGR/Cx. 113: NLD Annual Report 1926, SGR/2268/01, 269.

50. AHM/FCM/ATICE/Cx. 1: Director to D.A. Chemba, 23 December 1926.

51. AHM/FCM/ATICE/Cx. 1: D.G. to Director Native Affairs, 27 December 1926.

52. AHM/FCM/ATICE/Cx. 1: D.G. to Agent Vila Pery, 6 January 1927.

53. AHM/FCM/ATID/Cx. 27: Correspondência Confidencial, Director to Agent Vila Pery, 29 March 1927.

54. AHM/FCM/ATICE/Cx. 1: D.G. to Agent Chemba, 8 February 1927.

55. AHM/FCM/ATICE/Cx. 2: D.G. to Director Native Affairs, 23 August 1927; AHM/FCM/SGR/Cx. 114: Native Affairs Department Annual Report 1927, SGR/2269/01, 23.

56. AHM/FCM/ATICE/Cx. 1: D.G. to D.A. Chemba, 2 April 1927.

57. Forte held a 0.5 percent stake in the association's capital. *BCM* 18 (16 September 1926), 312.

58. AHM/FCM/ATID/Cx. 36: Andrada Mines to Subagent Macequece, 18 August 1927 [copy].

59. AHM/FCM/ATICE/Cx. 1: D.G. to D.A. Chemba, 2 April 1927.

60. AHM/FCM/ATID/Cx. 27: Correspondência Confidencial, Agent Chimoio to D.G., 12 April 1927.

61. AHM/FCM/ATICE/Cx. 1: D.G. to D.A. Chemba, 16 April 1927.

62. AHM/FCM/ATICE/Cx. 1: D.A. Chemba to D.G., n.d [telegram].

63. AHM/FCM/ATICE/Cx. 1: D.G. to Director Native Affairs, 18 April 1927.

64. AHM/FCM/ATICE/Cx. 2: D.G. to D.A. Chemba, 17 June 1927.

65. AHM/FCM/ATID/Cx. 27: Correspondência Confidencial, Agent Vila Pery to D.G., 25 May 1927.

66. AHM/FCM/ATICE/Cx. 1: D.G. to Director Native Affairs, 18 April 1927.

67. AHM/FCM/ATID/Cx. 27: Correspondência Confidencial, Agent Vila Pery to D.G., 25 May 1927.

68. AHM/FCM/ATID/Cx. 36: Subagent Macequece to D.G., 13 June 1927.

69. AHM/FCM/ATICE/Cx. 1: D.G. to D.A. Chemba, 23 April 1927; Cx. 2: D.G. to Director Native Affairs, 18 July 1927.

70. AHM/FCM/NIP/Cx. 19: Director Native Affairs to Governor, 29 July 1929.

71. AHM/FCM/ATIR/Cx. 127: ATI Annual Report 1926, 2.

72. Ibid.; AHM/FCM/ATICE/Cx. 2: D.G. to Director Native Affairs, 23 August 1927.

73. AHM/FCM/NIP/Cx. 19: Director Native Affairs to Governor, 29 July 1929.

74. AHM/FCM/SGR/Cx. 80: Mines Department Annual Report 1929, SGR/1635/01, 1.

75. AHM/FCM/ATICE/Cx. 12: Agent Vila Pery to D.G., 10 August 1930; Cx. 6: D.G. to Director Native Affairs, 6 May 1929.

76. AHM/FCM/NIP/Cx. 11: Circular Note 17, 14 September 1931.

77. AHM/FCM/ATICE/Cx. 10: D.G. to D.A. Chemba, 9 October 1931, transcribing the letter from the Buzi Company.

78. AHM/FCM/SGR/Cx. 241: Manica District Census Report, SGR/5118/01, 20.

79. AHM/FCM/ATICE/Cx. 8: D.G. to Director Buzi Colonial Company, 14 March 1930, citing the association agent in Chemba; AHM/FCM/SGR/Cx. 242: Manica District Census Report 1934, SGR/5120/01, 14.

80. AHM/FCM/SGR/Cx. 241: Manica District Census Report 1931, SGR/5111/01, "Palhotas."

81. AHM/FCM/NIP/Cx. 19: Curador of Native Affairs to Governor, 8 September 1931, Confidential; Cx. 25: Director Native Affairs to Inspector of Finance and Exploration, 30 June 1932.

82. AHM/FCM/NIP/Cx. 19: Director Native Affairs to General Manager of the Agricultural Credit Board, 29 November 1932.

83. AHM/FCM/SGR/Cx. 242: Manica District Tax Collection Report, SGR/5119/01, Report from Mavita Post, 2.

84. AHM/FCM/NIP/Cx. 25: Director Native Affairs to Inspector of Finances and Exploration, 30 June 1932, 1.

85. AHM/FCM/NIP/Cx. 18: Curador dos Indígenas Report 1936, 2.

86. AHM/FCM/NIP/Cx. 23: Director Native Affairs to Governor, 13 May 1932, 6. For the tax rate north of the Zambezi, see AHM/FCM/SGR/Cx. 114: Native Affairs Department Annual Report 1927, SGR/2269/01, 37.

87. AHM/FCM/NIP/Cx. 23: Director Native Affairs to Governor, 13 May 1932, 6.

88. AHM/FCM/SGR/Cx. 242: Manica District Tax Report 1934, SGR/5119/01, 3; AHM/FCM/NIP/Cx. 25: Director Native Affairs to Inspector of Finances and Exploration, 30 June 1932, 11.

89. These data calculated based on information in the hut tax and census reports for Manica from 1928 to 1938, AHM/FCM/SGR/Cx. 241–242.

90. AHM/FCM/SGR/Cx. 241: Manica District Census Report 1931, SGR/5111/01, "Palhotas."

91. AHM/FCM/SGR/Cx. 84: Mines Department Report March 1937, SGR/1723/01; Mines Department Annual Report 1937, SGR/1733/01, 66; Mines Department Report May 1937, SGR/1725/01, attached letter from Governor to Managing Director, 17 July 1937.

92. AHM/FCM/SGR/Cx. 84: Mines Department Annual Report 1938, SGR/1746/01 37. The original Portuguese better captures the administrator's attempt at humor, since his play on words ("*mineiros, pantomineiros*") rhymes more nicely.

93. AHM/FCM/SGR/Cx. 84: Mines Department Annual Report 1937, SGR/1733/01, 66.

94. AHM/FCM/SGR/Cx. 84: Mines Department Report March 1937, SGR/1723/01; Mines Department Annual Report 1937, SGR/1733/01, 66; Mines Department Report May 1937, SGR/1725/01, attached letter from Governor to Managing Director, 17 July 1937.

95. AHM/FCM/NIP/Cx. 26: Report, 29 July 1936, 2, 7, 5, 6.

96. AHM/FCM/NIP/Cx. 39: Director Native Affairs to D.A. Gorongosa, 19 July 1937.

97. AHM/FCM/NIP/Cx. 39: "Information" attached to Director Native Affairs to D.A. Gorongosa, 29 September 1937.

98. Ibid.

99. Ibid.

100. AHM/FCM/NIP/Cx. 26: Native Affairs Circular Note 1, 4 March 1938; Circular note 1, 24 January 1939.

101. AHM/FCM/NIP/Cx. 26: Native Affairs Circular Note 2, 12 October 1938.

102. AHM/FCM/NIP/Cx. 26: Director Native Affairs to Governor, 18 August 1939.

103. AHM/FCM/NIP/Cx. 32: Report of Observations on Native Labor, July 1942, 7.

104. AHM/FCM/NIP/Cx. 26: Native Affairs Circular Note 3, 15 November 1939.

105. AHM/FCM/NIP/Cx. 26: Native Affairs Circular Note 4, 18 November 1939, 4.

106. AHM/FCM/NIP/Cx. 23: Director Native Affairs to Governor, 29 December 1939, 4, 5, Confidential.

107. AHM/FCM/NIP/Cx. 26: Native Affairs Circular note 1, 24 January 1940.

108. Ibid.

109. The endeavor is the subject of Isaacman's magisterial work, *Cotton Is the Mother of Poverty*, as well as an important study in the history of Portugal's imperial economic policy by Pitcher, *Politics in the Portuguese Empire*. Portugal was not alone in developing forced cotton schemes, which were prevalent throughout Africa. See the essays in Isaacman and Roberts, *Cotton, Colonialism and Social History*.

110. Isaacman and Mandala, "Rural Communities Under Siege," 307–12.

111. AHM/FCM/NIP/Cx. 7: Post Administrator Dombe to D.A. Manica, 21 January 1942.

112. AHM/FCM/NIP/Cx. 32: Report of Observations on Native Labor, July 1942, 2.

113. Ibid., 7.

114. Ibid., 14.

115. Vickery, "Second World War Revival"; Johnson, "Settler Farmers."

116. AHM/FCM/NIP/Cx. 32: Report of Observations on Native Labor, July 1942, 12.

## 8. Upward Mobility

1. Portugal, Colonial Act of 1930, Article 2.

2. Portaria E-No. 113, 18 February 1928, in Colónia de Moçambique, *Moçambique na Exposição Colonial*, 93.

3. Colónia de Moçambique, *Moçambique na Exposição Colonial*, 5.

4. Companhia de Moçambique, *Histoire*, 13.

5. Ibid.

6. AHM/FCM/NIP/Cx. 18: Apontamentos para a Monografia do Indigenato, 9.

7. Ibid., 5.

8. I summarize the criteria from Errante, "White Skin, Many Masks," 20; AHM/FCM/NIP/Cx. 18: Apontamentos para a Monografia do Indigenato, 5.

9. AHM/FCM/NIP/Cx. 18: Apontamentos para a Monografia do Indigenato, 5.

10. AHM/FCM/NIP/Cx. 18: Managing Director to Governor, 14 November 1928, enclosed in Report on Social Assistance to the Native, 1929.

11. AHM/FCM/NIP/Cx. 18: Report on Social Assistance to the Native, 1929, 1–2.

12. Ibid., 2–3.

13. Ibid., 3.

14. See Newitt, *History of Mozambique*, 56–57; Reis, *Empresa da Conquista*.

15. Morier-Genoud, "Catholic Church," chapters 1–2.

16. AHM/FCM/NIP/Cx. 18: Report on Social Assistance to the Native, 1929, 3–4.

17. For the challenges faced by Protestant missionaries, see Neves, "American Board Mission."

18. AHM/FCM/NIP/Cx. 18: Report on Social Assistance to the Native, 1929, 4.

19. Ibid., 6.

20. Ibid., 7, 11.

21. Ibid., 18,

22. AHM/FCM/SGR/Cx. 242: Manica District Census Report 1934, 4.

23. AHM/FCM/SGR/Cx. 224: Manica District Annual Report 1903, SGR/4928/01, attached report from Chimoio District, 39.

24. AHM/FCM/SGR/Cx. 235: Manica District Annual Report 1912, SGR/5032/01, vi.

25. AHM/FCM/SGR/Cx. 224: Manica District Annual Report 1903, SGR/4928/01, attached report from Chimoio District, 39–40. "Machamba," a word of Bantu origin that has entered the Luso-African lexicon, refers to cultivated land, and, depending on context, may designate anything from a garden plot to a multihectare field.

26. AHM/FCM/SGR/Cx. 231: Manica District Report March 1908, SGR/4981/01, [n.p.].

27. AHM/FCM/SGR/Cx. 234: Manica District Census Report 1911, SGR/5019/01, 7.

28. AHM/FCM/SGP/Cx. 321: D.A. Manica to Governor, 12 June 1913; AHM/FCM/SGR/Cx. 230: Manica District Report April 1907, SGR/4970/01, 3.

29. AHM/FCM/SGR/Cx. 234: Manica District Census Report 1911, SGR/5019/01, 8; OT, Penhalonga, 8 August 1998; OT, Guindingue (Zonue Ponte), 26 August 1998.

30. AHM/FCM/SGR/Cx. 237: Manica District Census Report 1916, SGR/5052/01, 8; Manica District Tax Collection Report 1916, SGR/5053/01, 2.

31. AHM/FCM/SGR/Cx. 234: Manica District Census Report 1911, SGR/5019/01, 8; OT, Penhalonga, 8 August 1998; OT, Guindingue (Zonue Ponte), 26 August 1998.

32. AHM/FCM/SGR/Cx. 5: Governor Annual Report 1911, SGR/011/01, 5; BCM 13 (12 July 1915), Order 3583; BCM 24 (17 December 1917), Order 3814; AHM/FCM/SGC/Cx. 177: Circular 61, 23 October 1918.

33. AHM/FCM/SGR/Cx. 234: Manica District Census Report 1911, SGR/5019/01, 8.

34. AHM/FCM/SGP/Cx. 73: D.A. Tambara to D.A. Sena, 22 July 1913.

35. AHM/FCM/SGR/Cx. 234: Manica District Census Report 1911, SGR/5019/01, 7–8; Cx. 235: Manica District Fourth Trimester Report 1913, SGR/5038/01, [n.p.].

36. AHM/FCM/SGR/Cx. 239: Manica District Census Report 1920, SGR/5067/01, 7; Manica District Annual Report 1920, attached report from Moribane.

37. AHM/FCM/SGR/Cx. 9: Governor Annual Report 1921, SGR/020/01, 283, 285. Scholarship on Africans' often enthusiastic adoption of market-oriented production includes Bundy, "Emergence and Decline of a South African Peasantry"; Vail and White, *Capitalism and Colonialism;* Anderson and Throup, "Agrarian Economy of Central Province"; Mandala, *Work and Control;* Schmidt, *Peasants, Traders, and Wives.*

38. AHM/FCM/SGR/Cx. 241: Manica District Census Report 1926, SGR/5099/01, 5.

39. AHM/FCM/SGR/Cx. 114: Department of Native Affairs Annual Report 1927, SGR/2269/01, 3, 30.

40. Ibid.

41. AHM/FCM/SGR/Cx. 241: Manica District Second Trimester Report 1931, SGR/5113/01.

42. AHM/FCM/SGR/Cx. 241: Manica District Census Report 1931 SGR/5111/01, [n.p.].

43. Ibid.

44. AHM/FCM/SGR/Cx. 241: Manica District Second Trimester Report 1931, SGR/5113/

01; AHM/FCM/NIP/Cx. 20: D.A. Manica to Governor, 22 October 1931, Confidential. On African cultivators' disappointment with poor prices in 1921, see AHM/FCM/SGR/Cx. 239: Manica District Second Trimester Report 1921, SGR/5076/01, no. 12.

45. AHM/FCM/SGR/Cx. 241: Manica District Census Report 1931, SGR/5111/01, "Population."

46. AHM/FCM/SGR/Cx. 242: Manica District Tax Collection Report 1934, SGR/5119/01, 2.

47. AHM/FCM/SGR/Cx. 241: Manica District Tax Report 1933, 22.

48. AHM/FCM/SGR/Cx. 241: Manica District Census Report 1931, SGR/5111/01; Cx. 242: Manica District Census Report 1937, SGR/5125/01, 9; AHM/FCM/NIP/Cx. 18: Native Affairs Department Report for 1931, "Professiões dos Indígenas."

49. AHM/FCM/SGR/Cx. 242: Manica District Inspection Report May 1938, SGR/5127/01, 2.

50. For cattle holdings in Manica and the territory overall, see AHM/FCM/SGR/Cx. 114: Native Affairs Department Annual Report 1927, SGR/2269/01, 48; AHM/FCM/NIP/Cx. 18: Native Affairs Department Annual Report 1928; Native Affairs Department, Statistical Report for the Indigenato 1929, chart 16; Native Affairs Department, Statistical Report for 1930; Native Affairs Department, Report for 1931. For population figures, see AHM/FCM/SGR/Cx. 114: Native Affairs Department Annual Report 1927, SGR/2269/01, 44; AHM/FCM/NIP/Cx. 18: Native Affairs Department Annual Report 1928; Native Affairs Department, Statistical Report for the *Indigenato* 1929, chart 1; Native Affairs Department, Statistical Report for 1930; Native Affairs Department, Report for 1931. One caveat is necessary: the prevalence of tsetse fly—a vector for trypanosomiasis, deadly to cattle—in the southern districts of the territory may have limited cattle-keeping possibilities at this time. If so, then comparison with Manica would not be quite so striking. The extent of fly infestation changed with time, and unfortunately no detailed livestock census data are available for this time. I am grateful to Jessica Schafer for clarifying this specific point for me.

51. AHM/FCM/SGR/Cx. 241: Manica District Tax Collection Report 1933, SGR/5118/01, 22.

52. OT, Machipanda (Bairro Chiqueia), 14 May 1997.

53. AHM/FCM/SGR/Cx. 3: Governor Annual Report 1907, SGR/007/01, 26; Circular 23, 28 March 1906.

54. AHM/FCM/SGR/Cx. 235: Manica District Census Report 1913, SGR/5034/01, 5; Cx. 237: Manica District Tax Collection Report 1915, SGR/5046/01; Manica District Census Report 1915, SGR/5047/01, 7; Manica District Census Report 1916, SGR/5052/01; AHM/FCM/SGP/Cx. 73: D.A. Manica to Governor, 7 August 1913.

55. Companhia de Moçambique, *Handbook*, Royal Charter of 11 February 1891, 22, Article 8.

56. This description of the board's activities draws on "Reports of Missions in Africa," Exhibit A, 3. This typescript includes letters and reports produced between 1918 and 1923 and is held at the Day Mission Library, Yale University. Parts of the typescript were produced by Fred Robert Bunker, an American and longtime Congregationalist missionary with the American Board of Commissioners for Foreign Missions. Evidence from English-speaking Protestant missionaries needs to be handled carefully, because sectarian and national identities tended to skew their judgment, as Bunker's commentary occasionally showed: "*We may not forget* that Portugal, dragged down as she has been for centuries by the bonds of Rome, has been reaping a bountiful harvest of atheists, who through their opposition to the idea

of a living God violently oppose all teaching of Christianity." From "Reports of Missions in Africa," Exhibit B, 9.

57. *BCM* 6 (16 March 1921), Colonial Ministry Decree no. 7151, Article 1.

58. *BCM* 24 (17 December 1928), 382, Colonial Legislative Diploma 36, 12 November 1927.

59. AHM/FCM/SGR/Cx. 114: Native Affairs Department Annual Report 1927, SGR/2269/01, 28.

60. Ibid.

61. Ibid., 29.

62. *Proceedings of the Royal Colonial Institute*, 30 (1898–1899), 53. The statement came from Sidney Shippard, an associate of Cecil Rhodes and former resident commissioner in Britain's Bechuanaland Protectorate.

63. The "hewers of wood" statement is more infamously associated with Hendrik Verwoerd, the South African prime minister (1958–1966), who used it in a speech on apartheid education policy; Verwoerd made the "greener pastures" comment when, as minister of native affairs, he rolled out the apartheid policy of Bantu Education.

64. AHM/FCM/NIP/Cx. 18: Native Affairs Department, Notes for a Monograph of the *Indigenato* 1929, 25.

65. AHM/FCM/SGR/Cx. 241: Manica District Census Report 1931, SGR/5111/01; Manica District Census Report 1932, SGR/5115/01, 18; Manica District Census Report 1933, SGR/5118/01, 18; AHM/FCM/NIP/Cx. 18: Native Affairs Department Annual Report 1931.

66. *BCM* 24 (17 December 1928), 382, Colonial Legislative Diploma 36, 12 November 1927.

67. AHM/FCM/SGR/Cx. 241: Manica District Tax Report 1933, SGR/5118/01, 4

68. AHM/FCM/SGR/Cx. 242: D.A. Manica to Governor, 30 January 1936, 3, filed with Manica District Tax Report 1934, SGR/5119/01.

69. AHM/FCM/NIP/Cx. 26: Report 29 July 1936, 4.

70. AHM/FCM/NIP/Cx. 26: D.A. Manica to Director Native Affairs, 12 April 1937.

71. Ibid.

72. Ibid.

73. AHM/FCM/SGR/Cx. 241: Manica District Census Report 1926, SGR/5099/01, 5.

74. AHM/FCM/SGR/Cx. 242: Manica District Inspection Report May 1938, SGR/5127/01, 20.

75. AHM/FCM/SGR/Cx. 241: Manica District Tax Report 1933, SGR/5118/01, 22; 3.

76. AHM/FCM/SGR/Cx. 234: Manica District Third Trimester Report 1911, SGR/5023/01, [n.p.]; Cx. 235: Manica District Annual Report 1912, SGR/5032/01, 131.

77. AHM/FCM/SGR/Cx. 237: Manica District Hut Tax Collection 1915, SGR/5046/01. Irregular rainfall notwithstanding, the year's harvest was, in the end, "very abundant." Manica District Third Trimester Report 1916, SGR/5056/01.

78. AHM/FCM/SGR/Cx. 236: Manica District Hut Tax Collection 1914, SGR/5039/01, 2.

79. AHM/FCM/SGR/Cx. 241: Manica District Census Report 1928, SGR/5104/01, 20.

80. AHM/FCM/SGR/Cx. 241: Manica District Census Report 1929, SGR/5107/01, [n.p.].

81. For women's commercial activity as beer brewers, see Bradford, "We Are Now the Men"; Bonner, "Desirable or Undesirable Basotho Women?"; Schmidt, *Peasants, Traders, and Wives*, 59–60, 94. Bloke Modisane's autobiography movingly sketches the dangers that came with illegal brewing in South Africa. Modisane, *Blame Me on History*, 35–40.

82. AHM/FCM/SGR/Cx. 242: Manica District Inspection Report 1938, 19.

83. Ibid., 20–21.

84. Newitt, *Portuguese Settlement;* Isaacman, *Mozambique;* Isaacman and Isaacman, "Prazeros as Transfrontiersmen"; Peter Mark, in *"Portuguese" Style and Luso-African Identity,* and George Brooks, in *Landlords and Strangers,* have written of similar processes in west Africa.

85. Companhia de Moçambique, *Histoire,* 12.

86. Penvenne, "We Are All Portuguese!" especially 263–64.

87. Penvenne, *African Workers and Colonial Racism,* especially chapter 7. Although Portugal's hold on Mozambique came under threat from South African interests in the early 1920s, the decisive role then came from a combination of disinterest, inertia, and dissent within the Britain's Colonial and Foreign offices, rather than from local players. Vail and White, *Capitalism and Colonialism,* 208–10.

88. Penvenne, "We Are All Portuguese!" 267–68. There were some settings, such as more rural and isolated areas, where the racial boundaries were not as rigidly drawn, at least for some encounters. See, for example, Gengenbach, "What My Heart Wanted."

89. AHM/FCM/NIP/Cx. 18: Native Affairs Department Statistics Report 1930, chart 3.

90. The struggles of João dos Santos Albasini, an *assimilado* of Lourenço Marques who could claim just these sorts of alliances, in addition to being an erudite member of Mozambique's African intelligentsia, were emblematic of the trap in which *assimilados* were caught. See Penvenne, "João dos Santos Albasini."

91. AHM/FCM/SGR/Cx. 241: Manica District Census Report 1933, SGR/5118/01, 20, 25; Cx. 242: Manica District Census Report 1934, SGR/5120/01, 14. Allen Isaacman discusses an analogous category of African farmers, though within the cotton regime that prevailed mostly after World War II, in *Cotton Is the Mother of Poverty,* chapters 6 and 8.

92. OT, Chiteve, 15 May 1997.

93. OT, Munzongo, 14 May 1997.

94. OT, Chiteve, 15 May 1997.

95. OT, Gomorematede, 18 May 1997.

96. AHM/FCM/SGR/Cx. 236: Manica District Annual Report 1914, SGR/5045/01, 163; Penvenne, *African Workers and Colonial Racism,* 212.

97. Penvenne, "Here Everyone Walked in Fear"; Penvenne, *African Workers and Colonial Racism,* 113.

98. Penvenne, *African Workers and Colonial Racism,* 111–12.

99. OT, Chitunga, 12 August 1998; Penvenne, *African Workers and Colonial Racism,* 2.

100. OT, Chitunga, 12 August 1998.

## Conclusion

1. "Portuguese East Africa," 239.

2. AHM/FCM/SGR/Cx. 242: Director Native Affairs to S.G., 2 May 1938, attached to Report of an Inspection to Manica District, May 1938, SGR/5127/01.

3. Suplemento ao *BCM* 14 (18 July 1942), Telegram from Board of Directors to Governor, 18 July 1942.

4. AHM/FCM/NIP/Cx. 26: Governo Geral da Colónia de Moçambique, Circular 818/D-7, 7 October 1942.

5. Bettencourt, *Relatório do Governador-Geral de Moçambique,* 2:78–79, quoted in Vail and White, *Capitalism and Colonialism,* 280–82.

6. AHM/FCM/NIP/Cx. 26: Governo Geral da Colónia de Moçambique, Circular 818/D-7, 7 October 1942.

7. See Errante, "Education and National Personae"; Mendy, "Portugal's Civilizing Mission."

8. Pitcher emphasizes how this centrality was a major driver of imperial economic policy under Salazar. Pitcher, *Politics in the Portuguese Empire*, 12, 71, 141.

9. From thence came the title of Allen Isaacman's magisterial study of Mozambique's cotton regime, *Cotton Is the Mother of Poverty*.

10. AHM/FCM/NIP/Cx. 26: Governo Geral da Colónia de Moçambique, Circular 818/D-7, 7 October 1942.

11. Ibid., 2.

12. Vail and White, *Capitalism and Colonialism*, 382–83.

13. Anderson, "Portugal and the End of Ultracolonialism," 113.

14. Hammond, *Portugal and Africa*. The phrase comes from Hammond's first chapter title, "The Sick Man of Western Europe."

15. Isaacman, *Cotton Is the Mother of Poverty*; Newitt, "Late Colonial State in Portuguese Africa." This line of argument relies on an orthodoxy in the social sciences, that weak states must rely on violence while strong states rule through the cultivation and imposition of hegemonic discourse.

16. Macao, the remnant of its East Asian outposts, did not revert to Chinese sovereignty until 1999.

17. One such individual, Henrique Galvão, falls into the category of the foolhardy; a colonial official who served in Angola, he presented a report to Parliament in 1947 highly critical of colonial policy, especially labor practices. For more on Galvão and his 1947 report, see Wheeler, "Galvão Forced Labor Report."

18. Cahen, *Mozambique*; Penvenne, "Mozambique"; Hall and Young, *Confronting Leviathan*, chapters 5–8.

19. "Governo investiga espancamento de trabalhadores em Nampula" [Government investigates beating of workers in Nampula], *Notícias*, 30 May 2005.

20. Agência de Informação de Moçambique, "Labour Ministry Shuts Down Roses Company," 2 November 2007; "Simão Protests at Labour Ministry Demands," 7 November 2007.

21. Agência de Informação de Moçambique, "Golden Fields Defies Labour Ministry," 8 November 2007.

22. "Escravatura ainda é una realidade" [Slavery is still a reality], *Notícias*, 7 November 2007.

23. Ibid.

24. Catherine Dolan has published important work on some of the ethical questions raised by luxury vegetable and flower production in similar contexts. Dolan, "On Farm and Packhouse."

25. "Falta de hábito ao trabalho perpetua fome no país" [Lack of a work ethic perpetuates hunger in the country] *Notícias*, 19 April 2007.

# Bibliography

*Note on Sources:* The material on the Mozambique Company at Mozambique's Historical Archives in Maputo is not cataloged with the rest of Mozambique's archives. The company archives are chronologically organized and divided into categories, such as reports and correspondence, but as yet have no fully detailed inventory other than indications of the range of years covered or geographic or administrative focus (for example, "Secretary General" and "Native Affairs"). A set of finding aids guides researchers to the appropriate *caixa*, or box, but they are not perfectly accurate, sometimes listing material that is not, in fact, held at the archives, nor do the aids provide more than rough guides to the chronology or subject of the material held in a particular container. The aids are, however, a reliable road map to holdings on general geographic areas within Manica and Sofala provinces, and on overall spheres of Mozambique Company administrative activity. Still, a researcher will need some time to gain familiarity with the organization of the archives—for example, to learn that "Native Affairs" was nearly synonymous with matters related to African labor, or that a good deal of material related to worker flight is to be found in files labeled "Lazy and Incorrigible Natives."

In addition to long stints of work in the AHM, I consulted material in the municipal archives in the city of Manica. At the time I used this facility in 1997, it resembled a storeroom and was wholly unorganized; the holdings relate primarily to the post–Mozambique Company period, with significant overlap with the *Official Bulletin* of the colony. Researchers focusing on more recent history may nonetheless find it useful. Finally, one remaining visible legacy of the Mozambique Company's activities in Manica is a small museum that highlights the history of mining in the south-central African region. The Manica District office of the Ministry of Mineral and Natural Resources also holds documentation on the local mining industry, though this consists primarily of published, rather than archival, sources.

## Archival Sources

*Arquivo Histórico de Moçambique [Mozambique Historical Archives]. Maputo.*
Fundo da Companhia de Moçambique [Mozambique Company collection].

*Arquivo Histórico Ultramarino (Overseas Historical Archives). Lisbon.*
Fundo de Moçambique and Fundo da Companhia de Moçambique [Collections on Mozambique and on the Mozambique Company].

## Oral Sources

Interviews conducted with more than 100 individuals in Manica, Chimoio, and Sussendenga districts in 1997 and 1998; see preface for more on the interviewees.

## Journals and Periodicals

*Agência de Informação de Moçambique*
*Anti-Slavery Reporter*
*Boletím da Companhia de Moçambique*
*Correio da Beira/Beira Post*
*New York Times*
*Notícias*
*Proceedings of the Royal Colonial Institute* 30 (1898–1899)
*Revista de Manica e Sofala*

## Other Sources

Agência de Informação de Moçambique. News Reports.

Akurang-Parry, Kwabena Opare. "'The Loads Are Heavier Than Usual': Forced Labor by Women and Children in the Central Province, Gold Coast (Colonial Ghana), ca. 1900–1940. *African Economic History* 30 (2002): 31–51.

Allina, Eric. "'Fallacious Mirrors': Colonial Anxiety and Images of African Labor in Mozambique, ca. 1929." *History in Africa* 24 (1997): 9–52.

———. "The Zimba, the Portuguese, and Other Cannibals in Late Sixteenth-Century Southeast Africa." *Journal of Southern African Studies* 37, no. 2 (2011): 211–27.

Allina-Pisano, Eric. "Resistance and the Social History of Africa." *Journal of Social History* 37, no. 1 (2003): 187–98.

Alpers, Edward A. *Ivory and Slaves: Changing Patterns of International Trade in East Central Africa to the Later Nineteenth Century.* Berkeley: University of California Press, 1975.

Anderson, David, and David Throup. "The Agrarian Economy of Central Province, Kenya, 1919 to 1939." In *The Economics of Africa and Asia in the Inter-War Depression,* edited by Ian Brown, 8–28. London: Routledge, 1989.

Anderson, Perry. "Portugal and the End of Ultracolonialism. Part II." *New Left Review* 16 (1962): 88–123.

Andrada, Joaquím Carlos Paiva de. *Manica: Being a Report Addressed to the Minister of the Marine and the Colonies of Portugal.* London: George Philip & Son, 1891.

Andrade, Alfredo Augusto Freire de. *Rapport présenté au Ministre des Colonies, à propos du livre Portuguese Slavery, du missionnaire John Harris.* Lisbon: Imprimerie Nationale, 1914.

Anon. "Algumas Observações ao Relatório do Professor Ross." *Boletím da Agência Geral das Colónias* 2, no. 7 (January 1926): 149–62.

*Antologia Colonial Portuguesa.* Vol. 1, *Política e Administração.* Lisbon: Agência Geral das Colónias, 1946.

Aptheker, Herbert. "Maroons within the Present Limits of the United States." *Journal of Negro History* 24, no. 2 (1939): 167–84.

Asiwaju, A. I. "Migrations as Revolt: The Example of the Ivory Coast and the Upper Volta before 1945." *Journal of African History* 17, no. 4 (1976): 544–94.

Atkins, Keletso E. *The Moon Is Dead! Give Us Our Money! The Cultural Origins of an African Work Ethic, Natal, South Africa, 1843–1900.* Portsmouth, N.H.: Heinemann, 1993.

Axelson, Eric. *Portugal and the Scramble for Africa, 1875–1891.* Johannesburg: Witwatersrand University Press, 1967.

Bales, Kevin. "Expendable People: Slavery in the Age of Globalization." *Journal of International Affairs* 53, no. 2 (2000): 461–84.

Ball, Jeremy. "'The Colossal Lie': The Sociedade Agrícola de Cassequel and Portuguese Labor Policy in Angola, 1899–1975." Ph.D. diss., University of California, Los Angeles, 2003.

Ballard, Charles. "The Repercussions of Rinderpest: Cattle Plague and Peasant Decline in Colonial Natal." *International Journal of African Historical Studies* 19, no. 3 (1986): 421–50.

Barahona e Costa, Henrique Cesar da Silva. *Passado, presente e futuro dos territórios de Manica e Sofala.* Lisbon: Typographia do Commercio, 1901.

Barry, Boubacar. *La Sénégambie du XVe au XIXe Siècle: Traite négrière, Islam et conquête coloniale.* Paris: L'Harmattan, 1988.

Beach, David N. "The Origins of Moçambique and Zimbabwe: Paiva de Andrada, the Companhia de Moçambique, and African Diplomacy, 1881–1891." Working Paper no. 89, University of Zimbabwe Department of History, 1992.

———. "The Zimbabwe Plateau and Its Peoples." In *History of Central Africa*, Vol. 1, edited by David Birmingham and Phyllis M. Martin, 245–77. London: Longmans, 1983.

Beckles, Hilary. "An Economic Life of Their Own: Slaves as Commodity Producers and Distributors in Barbados." In *The Slaves' Economy: Independent Production by Slaves in the Americas*, edited by Ira Berlin and Philip D. Morgan, 31–47. London: Frank Cass, 1991.

Bender, Gerald J. *Angola Under the Portuguese: The Myth and the Reality.* Berkeley: University of California Press, 1978.

Berlin, Ira. *Generations of Captivity: A History of African-American Slaves.* Cambridge, Mass.: Harvard University Press, 2003.

Berry, Sara. *Fathers Work for Their Sons: Accumulation, Mobility and Class Formation in an Extended Yoruba Community.* Berkeley: University of California Press, 1985.

———. "Hegemony on a Shoestring: Indirect Rule and Access to Agricultural Land." *Africa* 62, no. 3 (1992): 329–55.

Bhila, H. K. K. "Manyika's Relationship with the Portuguese and the Gaza-Nguni from 1832 to 1890." *Rhodesian History* 7 (1976): 31–37.

———. *Trade and Politics in a Shona Kingdom: The Manyika and Their African and Portuguese Neighbors, 1575–1902.* Essex: Longman, 1982.

Bolland, Nigel. "Proto-Proletarians? Slave Wages in the Americas: Between Slave Labour and Free Labour." In *From Chattel Slaves to Wage Slaves: The Dynamics of Labour Bargaining in the Americas*, edited by Mary Turner, 123–47. Bloomington: Indiana University Press, 1993.

Bonner, Phil. "'Desirable or Undesirable Basotho Women?' Liquor, Prostitution, and the Migration of Basotho Women to the Rand, 1920–1945." In *Women and Gender in Southern Africa to 1945*, edited by Cherryl Walker, 221–50. Cape Town: David Philip, 1990.

Bose, Sugata. *A Hundred Horizons: The Indian Ocean in the Age of Global Empire*. Cambridge, Mass.: Harvard University Press, 2006.

Bradford, Helen. "Getting Away with Murder: 'Mealie Kings,' the State and Foreigners in the Eastern Transvaa, c. 1918–1950." In *Apartheid's Genesis, 1935–1962*, edited by Philip Bonner, Peter Delius, and Deborah Posel, 96–125. Braamfontein: Ravan Press, 1993.

———. "'We Are Now the Men': Women's Beer Protests in the Natal Countryside." In *Class, Community, and Conflict: South African Perspectives*, edited by Belinda Bozzoli, 292–322. Johannesburg: Ravan Press, 1987.

Breckenridge, Keith. "The Allure of Violence: Men, Race and Masculinity on the South African Goldmines, 1900–1950." *Journal of Southern African Studies* 24, no. 4 (1998): 669–93.

Brooks, George. *Landlords and Strangers: Ecology, Society, and Trade in Western Africa, 1000–1630*. Boulder, Colo.: Westview Press, 1993.

Brown, Carolyn A. *"We Were All Slaves": African Miners, Culture, and Resistance at the Enugu Government Colliery*. Portsmouth, N.H.: Heinemann, 2003.

Bundy, Colin. "The Emergence and Decline of a South African Peasantry." *African Affairs* 71, no. 285 (172): 369–88.

Bunker, Fred Robert. "Reports of Missions in Africa." N.p.: n.p., 1918. Held in the Day Mission Library, Yale University.

Byfield, Judith. "Marriage, Divorce and the Emerging Colonial State in Abeokuta (Nigeria), 1892–1904." *Canadian Journal of African Studies* 30, no. 1 (1996): 32–51.

Cahen, Michel. *Mozambique La Révolution Implosée: Études sur 12 ans d'indépendance (1975–1987)*. Paris: L'Harmattan, 1987.

Capela, José. *Escravatura: A empresa do saque. O abolicionismo, 1810–1875*. Porto: Afrontamento, 1974.

Carton, Benedict. *Blood from Your Children: The Colonial Origins of Generational Conflict in South Africa*. Charlottesville: University Press of Virginia, 2000.

Chanock, Martin. *Law, Custom, and Social Order: The Colonial Experience in Malawi and Zambia*. Cambridge: Cambridge University Press, 1985.

Chatterjee, Indrani. "Abolition by Denial: The South Asian Example." In *Abolition and Its Aftermath in the Indian Ocean and Africa*, edited by Gwynn Campbell, 150–68. New York: Routledge, 2005.

Chilundo, Arlindo Gonçalo. *Os Camponeses e os Caminhos de Ferro e Estradas em Nampula (1900–1961)*. Maputo: Promédia, 2001.

Clarence-Smith, William Gervase. "The Myth of Uneconomic Imperialism: The Portuguese in Angola, 1836–1926." *Journal of Southern African Studies* 5 (1979): 165–80.

———. *The Third Portuguese Empire: A Study in Economic Imperialism*. Manchester: Manchester University Press, 1985.

Clark, Andrew. "'The Ties That Bind': Servility and Dependency among the Fulbe of Bundu (Senegambia), c. 1930s to 1980s." *Slavery and Abolition* 19, no. 2 (1998): 91–108.

Coelho, Trindade. *Dezoito annos em África: Notas e documentos para a biografia do conselheiro José d'Almeida*. Lisbon: Typografia de Adolpho de Mendonça, 1898.

Colónia de Moçambique. *Moçambique na Exposição Colonial Internacional de Paris: Relatório do delegado da colónia, 1930–1931*. Lourenço Marques: Imprensa Nacional, 1932.

Companhia de Moçambique. *Handbook of the Mozambique Company*. London: William Clowes & Sons, 1893.

———. *Histoire: La Conquête et l'occupation*. Lisbon: Sociedade Nacional de Tipografia, 1931.

Cooper, Frederick. "Conflict and Connection: Rethinking Colonial African History." *American Historical Review* 99, no. 5 (1994): 1516–45.

———. *Decolonization and African Society: The Labor Question in French and British Africa.* Cambridge: Cambridge University Press, 1996.

———. "The Problem of Slavery in African Studies. *Journal of African History* 20, no. 1 (1979): 103–25.

Cooper, Frederick, Thomas C. Holt, and Rebecca J. Scott. *Beyond Slavery: Explorations of Race, Labor and Citizenship in Postemancipation Societies.* Chapel Hill: University of North Carolina Press, 2000.

Coplan, David B. *In the Time of Cannibals: The Word Music of South Africa's Basotho Migrants.* Chicago: University of Chicago Press, 1994.

Coquery-Vidrovitch, Catherine. *Le Congo au temps des grandes compagnies concessionnaires, 1898–1930.* 2 vols. Paris: Mouton, 1972.

Costa, Maria Inês Nogueira da. "Inventário do fundo da Companhia de Moçambique, 1892–1942: Uma abordagem funcional da descrição dos arquivos permanentes." Ph.D. diss., Eduardo Mondlane University, 1993.

———. "No Centenário da Companhia de Moçambique, 1888–1988." *Arquivo* 6 (1989): 65–76.

Covane, Luís António. *O Trabalho Migratório e a Agricultura no Sul de Moçambique (1920–1992).* Maputo: Promédia, 2001.

Cruz, Miguel da. "História da formação da classe trabalhadora em Manica e Sofala ao sul do Pungue, 1892–1926." Licenciatura thesis, Eduardo Mondlane University, 1982.

Cunha, Joaquím Moreira da Silva. *O Trabalho indígena: Estudo de direito colonial.* 2nd ed. Lisbon: Agência Geral do Ultramar, 1955.

Dalgado, Sebastião. *Glosário Luso-Asiático.* Vol. 2. Hamburg: Buske, 1982.

Davison, Jean. *Gender, Lineage, and Ethnicity in Southern Africa.* Boulder, Colo.: Westview Press, 1997.

Departamento da História, Universidade Eduardo Mondlane. *História de Moçambique.* 3 vols. Maputo: Cadernos Tempo, 1982–1993.

Diffie, Bailey W., and George D. Winius. *Foundations of the Portuguese Empire, 1415–1580.* Minneapolis: University of Minnesota Press, 1977.

*Documentos Officiaes Relativos à Negociação do Tractado entre Portugal e a Gran Bretanha para a Suppressão do Tráfico da Escravatura.* Lisbon: Imprensa Nacional, 1839.

*Documentos relativos ao apresamento, julgamento e entrega da barca franceza Charles e Georges: E em geral ao engajamento de negros, debaixo da denominação de trabalhadores livres nas possessões da coroa de Portugal no costa oriental e occidental de Africa para as colonias francezas: Apresentados ás cortes na sessão legislativa de 1858.* Lisbon: Imprensa Nacional, 1858.

*Documentos sobre os Portugueses em Moçambique e na África Central, 1497–1840.* 9 vols. Lisbon: National Archives of Rhodesia and Centro de Estudos Históricos Ultramarinos da Junta de Investigações Cienfíficas do Ultramar, 1962–1989.

Dolan, Catherine. "On Farm and Packhouse: Employment at the Bottom of a Global Value Chain." *Rural Sociology* 69, no. 1 (2004): 99–126.

Duffy, James. *Portuguese Africa.* Cambridge, Mass.: Harvard University Press, 1959.

———. *A Question of Slavery.* Cambridge, Mass.: Harvard University Press, 1967.

Eaton, Clement. "Slave-Hiring in the Upper South: A Step toward Freedom." *Mississippi Valley Historical Review* 46, no. 4 (1960): 663–78.

Echenberg, Myron, and Jean Filipovich. "African Military Labour and the Building of the *Office du Niger* Installations, 1925–1950." *Journal of African History* 27, no. 3 (1986): 533–51.

Edward A. Ross Papers Microform. Reel 15. Madison: State Historical Society of Wisconsin, 1985.

Eldredge, Elizabeth A. "Sources of Conflict in Southern Africa c. 1800–1830: The 'Mfecane' Reconsidered." *Journal of African History* 33, no. 1 (1992): 1–35.

Elkiss, Terry H. *The Quest for an African Eldorado: Sofala, Southern Zambezia, and the Portuguese, 1500–1865*. Waltham, Mass.: Crossroads Press, 1981.

Ellert, H. *Rivers of Gold*. Gweru: Mambo Press, 1994.

Elphick, Richard, and Hermann Giliomee, eds. *The Shaping of South African Society, 1652–1840*. 2nd ed. Middletown, Conn.: Wesleyan University Press, 1989.

Enes, António. "A colonização europeia de Moçambique." In *Antologia Colonial Portuguesa*, Vol. 1, *Política e Administração*, 7–21. Lisbon: Agência Geral das Colónias, 1946.

———. *Moçambique: Relatório Apresentado ao Governo*. Lisbon: Imprensa Nacional, 1971 [1893].

Enes, António, et al. "O trabalho dos indígenas e o crédito agrícola." In *Antologia Colonial Portuguesa*, Vol. 1, *Política e Administração*, 23–64. Lisbon: Agência Geral das Colónias, 1946.

Errante, Antoinette. "Education and National Personae in Portugal's Colonial and Postcolonial Transition." *Comparative Education Review* 43, no. 3 (1998): 267–308.

———. "White Skin, Many Masks: Colonial Schooling, Race, and National Consciousness among White Settler Children in Mozambique, 1934–1974." *International Journal of African Historical Studies* 36, no. 1 (2003): 7–33.

Fall, Babacar. *Le Travail forcé en Afrique Occidentale française*. Paris: Karthala, 1993.

Falola, Toyin, and Paul E. Lovejoy. "Pawnship in Historical Perspective." In *Pawnship, Slavery, and Colonialism in Africa*, edited by Toyin Falola and Paul E. Lovejoy, 1–26. Trenton, N.J.: Africa World Press, 2003.

First, Ruth, et al. *O Mineiro Moçambicano: Um estudo da exportação de mão de obra em Inhambane*. Maputo: Center for African Studies, 1998 [1979].

Franklin, John Hope, and Loren Schweninger. *Runaway Slaves: Rebels on the Plantation*. New York: Oxford University Press, 1999.

Galbraith, John S. *Crown and Charter: The Early Years of the British South Africa Company*. Berkeley: University of California Press, 1973.

Galli, Rosemary E. "Complicit Critic: Mozambique Company Misrule through the Eyes of Gustavo de Bivar Pinto Lopes." *Portuguese Studies Review* 19, nos. 1–2 (in press).

Gelfand, Michael. *The Genuine Shona: Survival Values of an African Culture*. Gweru: Mambo Press, 1973.

Gengenbach, Heidi. *Binding Memories: Women as Makers and Tellers of History in Magude, Mozambique*. New York: Columbia University Press, 2006.

———. "'What My Heart Wanted': Gendered Stories of Early Colonial Encounters in Southern Mozambique." In *Women in African Colonial Histories*, edited by Jean Allman, Susan Geiger, and Nakanyike Musisi, 19–47. Bloomington: Indiana University Press, 2002.

Grant, Kevin. *A Civilised Savagery: Britain and the New Slaveries in Africa, 1884–1926*. New York: Routledge, 2005.

Guy, Jeff, and Motlatsi Thabane. "Technology, Ethnicity, and Ideology: Basotho Miners and Shaft-Sinking on the South African Gold Mines." *Journal of Southern African Studies* 14, no. 2 (1988): 257–78.

Haight, Mabel V. Jackson. *European Powers and South-East Africa: A Study of International Relations on the South-East Coast of Africa.* New York: Praeger, 1967.

Hall, Margaret, and Tom Young. *Confronting Leviathan: Mozambique since Independence.* Athens: Ohio University Press, 1997.

Hammond, Richard J. *Portugal and Africa 1815–1910: A Study in Uneconomic Imperialism.* Stanford, Calif.: Stanford University Press, 1966.

Hanna, S. J. *Standard Shona Dictionary.* Rev. ed. Harare: College Press, 1987.

Harries, Patrick. "Slavery, Social Incorporation, and Surplus Extraction: The Nature of Free and Unfree Labour in South-East Africa." *Journal of African History* 22, no. 3 (1981): 309–30.

———. *Work, Culture, and Identity: Migrant Laborers in Mozambique and South Africa, c. 1860–1910.* Portsmouth, N.H.: Heinemann, 1994.

Harris, John. *Africa: Slave or Free.* London: Student Christian Movement, 1919.

———. *Portuguese Slavery: Britain's Dilemma.* London: Methuen, 1913.

Hay, Margaret Jean, and Marcia Wright, eds. *African Women and the Law: Historical Perspectives.* Boston: Boston University African Studies Center, 1982.

Hertslet, Edward. *The Map of Africa by Treaty.* Vol. 2. London: Frank Cass, 1967.

Hochschild, Adam. *King Leopold's Ghost: A Story of Greed, Terror, and Heroism in Colonial Africa.* New York: Houghton Mifflin, 1998.

Hogendorn, Jan S., and Paul E. Lovejoy. *Slow Death for Slavery: The Course of Abolition in Northern Nigeria, 1897–1936.* Cambridge: Cambridge University Press, 1993.

Hughes, David. *From Enslavement to Environmentalism: Politics on a Southern African Frontier.* Seattle: University of Washington Press, 2006.

International Labour Office. *Portugal in Africa: Report of the I.L.O. Commission on the Observance by Portugal of the Abolition of Forced Labour Convention, 1957 (no. 105).* London: Portuguese Embassy, 1962.

International Labour Organisation. Forced Labour Convention of 1930.

Isaacman, Allen. *Cotton Is the Mother of Poverty: Peasants, Work, and Rural Struggle in Colonial Mozambique, 1938–1961.* Portsmouth, N.H.: Heinemann, 1996.

———. *Mozambique: The Africanization of a European Institution; the Zambesi Prazos 1750–1902.* Madison: University of Wisconsin Press, 1972.

———. "Peasants and Rural Social Protest in Africa." *African Studies Review* 33, no. 2 (1990): 1–120.

Isaacman, Allen F., and Barbara Isaacman. "The Prazeros as Transfrontiermen: A Study in Social and Cultural Change." *International Journal of African Historical Studies* 8, no. 1 (1975): 1–39.

———. *Slavery and Beyond: The Making of Men and Chikunda Ethnic Identities in the Unstable World of South-Central Africa, 1750–1920.* Portsmouth, N.H.: Heinemann, 2004.

———. *The Tradition of Resistance in Mozambique: Anti-colonial Activity in the Zambesi Valley, 1850–1921.* London: Heinemann, 1976.

Isaacman, Allen, and Elias Mandala. "Rural Communities Under Siege: Cotton, Work, and Food Insecurity in Colonial Malawi and Mozambique, 1907–1960." In *Paths Toward the Past: African Historical Essays in Honor of Jan Vansina,* edited by Robert W. Harms, Joseph C. Miller, David S. Newbury, and Michele D. Wagner, 293–324. Atlanta: African Studies Association Press, 1994.

Isaacman, Allen, and Richard Roberts, eds. *Cotton, Colonialism and Social History in Sub-Saharan Africa.* Portsmouth, N.H.: Heinemann, 1995.

Isaacman, Allen, and Anton Rosenthal. "Slaves, Soldiers, and Police: Power and Dependency among the Chikunda of Mozambique, ca. 1825–1920." In *The End of Slavery in Africa*, edited by Suzanne Miers and Richard Roberts, 220–53. Madison: University of Wisconsin Press, 1988.

Isaacman, Barbara, and Allen Isaacman. "Slavery and Social Stratification among the Sena of Mozambique: A Study of the Kaporo System." In *Slavery in Africa: Historical and Anthropological Perspectives*, edited by Suzanne Miers and Igor Kopyoff, 105–20. Madison: University of Wisconsin Press, 1977.

Jeater, Diana. *Marriage, Perversion, and Power: The Construction of Moral Discourse in Southern Rhodesia (Zimbabwe) 1894–1930*. Oxford: Clarendon Press, 1993.

Jeeves, Alan H. *Migrant Labour in South Africa's Mining Economy: The Struggle for the Gold Mines' Labour Supply 1890–1920*. Montreal: McGill-Queen's University Press, 1985.

Johnson, David. "Settler Farmers and Coerced African Labour in Southern Rhodesia, 1936–46." *Journal of African History* 33, no. 1 (1992): 111–28.

Johnson, Walter. "On Agency," *Journal of Social History* 37, no. 1 (2003): 113–24.

Jones, Edward P. *The Known World*. New York: Amistad, 2006.

Katzenellenbogen, Simon E. *South Africa and Southern Mozambique: Labour, Railways, and Trade in the Making of a Relationship*. Manchester: Manchester University Press, 1982.

Keegan, Timothy J. *Colonial South Africa and the Origins of the Racial Order*. Charlottesville: University Press of Virginia, 1996.

Keese, Alexander. *Living with Ambiguity: Integrating an African Elite in French and Portuguese Africa, 1930–61*. Stuttgart: Franz Steiner, 2007.

Kennedy, Dane. *Islands of White: Settler Society and Culture in Kenya and Southern Rhodesia, 1890–1939*. Durham, N.C.: Duke University Press, 1987.

Killingray, David. "Labour Mobilisation in British Africa for the War Effort, 1939–1946." In *Africa and the Second World War*, ed. David Killingray and Richard Rathbone, 68–91. Basingstroke: Macmillan, 1986.

Killingray, David, and James Matthews. "Beasts of Burden: British West African Carriers in the First World War." *Canadian Journal of African Studies* 13, nos. 1–2 (1979): 5, 7–23.

Kiwanuka, M. Semakula. "Colonial Policies and Administrations in Africa: The Myths of the Contrasts. *African Historical Studies* 3, no. 2 (1970): 295–315.

Klein, Martin A. "Slavery and French Rule in the Sahara." In *Slavery and Colonial Rule in Africa*, edited by Suzanne Miers and Martin A. Klein, 73–90. London: Routledge, 1999.

Kopytoff, Igor, ed. *The African Frontier: The Reproduction of Traditional African Societies*. Bloomington: Indiana University Press, 1987.

Lamounier, Lucia. "Between Slavery and Free Labour. Early Experiments with Free Labour and Patterns of Slave Emancipation in Brazil and Cuba." In *From Chattel Slaves to Wage Slaves: The Dynamics of Labour Bargaining in the Americas*, edited by Mary Turner, 185–200. Bloomington: Indiana University Press, 1993.

League of Nations. "Draft Convention on Slavery, Replies from Governments." A.10(B).1926. VI. Reply of the Portuguese Government [translation], 26 August 1926. Geneva: League of Nations, 1926.

———. Note of the Secretary General, 27 September 1924. C.532.M.186.VI. Enclosing "The Question of Slavery, Letter from the Head of the Portuguese Delegation and Memorandum from the Portuguese Government Concerning the Question of Slavery," J. Chagas to League of Nations Secretary General, 23 September 1924, 11. Geneva: League of Nations, 1924.

———. "Question of Slavery, Report Presented to the Sixth Assembly by the Sixth Committee." 26 September 1925. A.130.1925.VI. Geneva: League of Nations, 1925

———. Slavery Convention 1926. Geneva: League of Nations, 1926.

———. "Temporary Slavery Commission, Letter from the Chairman of the Commission to the President of the Council and Report of the Commission." 25 July 1925. A.19.1925.VI. Geneva: League of Nations, 1925,

———. "Temporary Slavery Commission, Minutes of the Second Session." 13–25 July 1925. C.426.M.157.1925.VI. Geneva: League of Nations, 1925.

Liesegang, Gerhard. "Notes on the Internal Structure of the Gaza Kingdom of Southern Mozambique, 1840–1895." In *Before and After Shaka: Papers in Nguni History,* edited by Jeff B. Peires, 178–229. Grahamstown: Rhodes University, 1981.

———. *Vassalagem ou tratado de amizade? História do acto de vassalagem de Ngungunyane nas relações externas de Gaza.* Maputo: Arquivo Histórico Nacional, 1986.

Livingstone, David. *Missionary Travels and Researches in South Africa; Including a Sketch of Sixteen Years' Residence in the Interior of Africa.* New York: Harper & Brothers, 1858.

Livingstone, David, and Charles Livingstone. *Narrative of an Expedition to the Zambesi and Its Tributaries; and of the Discovery of the Lakes Shirwa and Nyassa. 1858–64.* New York: Harper & Bros., 1866.

Lovejoy, Paul E. *Transformations in Slavery: A History of Slavery in Africa.* 2nd ed. Cambridge: Cambridge University Press, 2003.

MacDonald, Roderick A. "Independent Economic Production by Slaves on Antebellum Louisiana Sugar Plantations. In *The Slaves' Economy: Independent Production by Slaves in the Americas,* edited by Ira Berlin and Philip D. Morgan, 182–208. London: Frank Cass, 1991.

MacGonagle, Elizabeth. *Crafting Identity in Zimbabwe and Mozambique.* Rochester, N.Y.: University of Rochester Press, 2007.

Machado, Joaquím José. *Moçambique: Communicação à Sociedade de Geografia de Lisboa nas sessões de 6, 13 e 22 de Dezembro de 1880.* Lisbon: Casa da Sociedade de Geografia, 1881.

Mamdani, Mahmood. *Citizen and Subject: Contemporary Africa and the Legacy of Late Colonialism.* Princeton, N.J.: Princeton University Press, 1996.

Mandala, Elias C. *Work and Control in a Peasant Economy: A History of the Lower Tchiri Valley in Malawi, 1859–1960.* Madison: University of Wisconsin Press, 1990.

Mark, Peter. *"Portuguese" Style and Luso-African Identity: Precolonial Senegambia, Sixteenth–Nineteenth Centuries.* Bloomington: Indiana University Press, 2002.

Marks, Shula. *Reluctant Rebellion: The 1906–08 Disturbances in Natal.* Oxford: Clarendon Press, 1980.

Marques, João Pedro. *The Sounds of Silence: Nineteenth-Century Portugal and the Abolition of the Slave Trade.* [English translation of *Os sons do silêncio: O Portugal de Oitocentos e a abolição do tráfico de escravos.*] Trans. Richard Wall. New York: Berghahn Books, 2006.

Marshall, Woodville K. "Provision Ground and Plantation Labour in Four Windward Islands: Competition for Resources during Slavery." In *The Slaves' Economy: Independent Production by Slaves in the Americas,* edited by Ira Berlin and Philip D. Morgan, 48–67. London: Frank Cass, 1991.

Martin, Jean. *Comores: Quatre îles entre pirates et planteurs.* Vol. 1. Paris: Harmattan, 1983.

Martins, J. P. Oliveira. *Portugal em Africa: A questão colonial—o conflito anglo-portuguez.* Porto: Lugan & Genelioux, 1891.

Martins, Rocha. *História das colónias portuguesas.* Lisbon: Empresa Nacional da Publicidade, 1933.

McClendon, Thomas. *Genders and Generations Apart: Labor Tenants and Customary Law in Segregation-Era South Africa, 1920s to 1940s.* Portsmouth, N.H.: Heinemann, 2002.

McKittrick, Meredith. *To Dwell Secure: Generation, Christianity, and Colonialism in Ovamboland.* Portsmouth, N.H.: Heinemann, 2002.

Medeiros, Eduardo da Conceição. *História de Cabo Delgado e do Niassa (c. 1836–1929).* Maputo: Central Impressora, 1997.

Mendy, Peter Karibe. "Portugal's Civilizing Mission in Colonial Guinea-Bissau: Rhetoric and Reality." *International Journal of African Historical Studies* 36, no. 1 (2003): 35–58.

Miers, Suzanne. "Slavery and the Slave Trade as International Issues, 1890–1939." *Slavery and Abolition* 19, no. 2 (1998): 16–37.

———. *Slavery in the Twentieth Century: The Evolution of a Global Pattern.* Walnut Creek, Calif.: Alta Mira Press, 2003.

Miller, Joseph C. *Way of Death: Merchant Capitalism and the Angolan Slave Trade, 1730–1830.* Madison: University of Wisconsin Press, 1988.

Modisane, Bloke. *Blame Me on History.* New York: Simon and Schuster, 1990.

Monclaro, Father Francisco de. "Narrative (Copy) by Father Francisco de Monclaro, of the Society of Jesus, of the Expedition to Monomotapa, led by Francisco Barreto." In *Documents on the Portuguese in Mozambique and Central Africa,* 8:325–429. Lisbon: National Archives of Rhodesia and Centro de Estudos Históricos Ultramarinos da Junta de Investigações Científicas do Ultramar, 1975.

Monnier, Jehanne-Emmanuelle. *Esclaves de la canne à sucre: Engagés et planteurs à Nossi-Bé, Madagascar 1850–1880.* Paris: L'Harmattan, 2006.

Moodie, T. Dunbar, with Vivian Ndatshe. *Going for Gold: Men, Mines, and Migration.* Berkeley: University of California Press, 1994.

Morel, E. D. *Red Rubber: The Story of the Rubber Trade Flourishing on the Congo in the Year of Grace 1907.* London: T. F. Unwin, 1907.

Morier-Genoud, Eric. "The Catholic Church, Religious Orders and the Making of Politics in Colonial Mozambique: The Case of the Diocese of Beira, 1940–1974." Ph.D. diss., SUNY Binghamton, 2005.

Mudenge, S. I. G. *A Political History of Munhumutapa c. 1400–1902.* Harare: Zimbabwe Publishing House, 1988.

Mungeam, Gordon Hudson. *British Rule in Kenya, 1895–1912: The Establishment of Administration in the East Africa Protectorate.* Oxford: Oxford University Press, 1966.

Murray, Martin J. "Factories in the Fields: Capitalist Farming in the Bethal District, c. 1910–1950." In *White Farms, Black Labor: The State and Agrarian Change in Southern Africa, 1910–1950,* edited by Alan H. Jeeves and Jonathan Crush, 75–93. Portsmouth, N.H.: Heinemann, 1997.

Museu Nacional da Moeda. *O Guia do museu: Museu nacional da moeda.* Maputo: Eduardo Mondlane University, 1983.

Nascimento, Augusto. *Desterro e contrato: Moçambicanos a caminho de S. Tomé e Principe (anos 1940 à 1960).* Maputo: Arquivo Histórico de Moçambique, 2002.

Neil-Tomlinson, Barry. "The Mozambique Chartered Company, 1892–1910." Ph.D. diss., University of London, 1987.

———. "The Niassa Chartered Company, 1891–1929." *Journal of African History* 18, no. 1 (1977): 109–28.

Neves, Joel das. "A American Board Mission e os desafios do protestantismo em Manica e Sofala (Moçambique), ca. 1900–1950." *Lusotopie* (1998): 335–43.

———. "Economy, Society and Labour Migration in Central Mozambique, 1930–c.1965: A Case Study of Manica Province." Ph.D. diss., University of London, 1998.

———. "O Início da emigração de mão-de-obra moçambicana para a Rodésia do Sul (1890–1913)." In *Moçambique—16 anos de historiagrafia: Focos, problemas metodologias: Desafios para a década de 90*, edited by Alexandrino José and Paula Maria G. Meneses, 281–94. Maputo: CEGRAF, 1991.

———. "Tete e o trabalho migratório para a Rodésia do Sul, 1890–1913." *Arquivo* 10 (1991): 83–101.

Nevinson, Henry R. *A Modern Slavery*. New York: Harper & Brothers, 1906.

Newitt, Malyn. *A History of Mozambique*. Bloomington: Indiana University Press, 1995.

———. *A History of Portuguese Overseas Expansion, 1400–1668*. New York: Routledge, 1995.

———. "The Late Colonial State in Portuguese Africa." *Itinerário* 3/4 (1999): 110–22.

———. *Portuguese Settlement on the Zambesi: Exploration, Land Tenure and Colonial Rule in East Africa*. New York: Africana Publishing, 1973.

Newitt, Malyn, and Corrado Tornimbeni. "Transnational Networks and Internal Divisions in Central Mozambique: An Historical Perspective from the Colonial Period." *Cahiers d'études africaines* 4, no. 192 (2008): 707–40.

Newton-King, Susan. *Masters and Servants on the Eastern Cape Frontier, 1760–1803*. Cambridge: Cambridge University Press, 1999.

Northrup, David. "The Ending of Slavery in the Eastern Belgian Congo." In *The End of Slavery in Africa*, edited by Suzanne Miers and Richard Roberts, 462–82. Madison: University of Wisconsin Press, 1988.

———. *Indentured Labor in the Age of Imperialism, 1834–1922*. Cambridge: Cambridge University Press, 1995.

Nowell, Charles E. "Portugal and the Partition of Africa." *Journal of Modern History* 19, no. 1 (1947): 1–17.

———. *The Rose-Colored Map: Portugal's Attempt to Build an African Empire from the Atlantic to the Indian Ocean*. Lisbon: Junta de Investigações Científicas do Ultramar, 1982.

Nurse, Derek, and Thomas Spear. *The Swahili: Reconstructing the History and Language of an African Society, 800–1500*. Philadelphia: University of Pennsylvania Press, 1985.

Oshinsky, David. *"Worse than Slavery": Parchman Farm and the Ordeal of Jim Crow Justice*. New York: Free Press, 1996.

Packard, Randall. "The Invention of the 'Tropical Worker': Medical Research and the Quest for Central African Labor on the South African Gold Mines, 1903–36." *Journal of African History* 34, no. 2 (1993): 271–92.

———. *White Plague, Black Labor: Tuberculosis and the Political Economy of Health and Disease in South Africa*. Berkeley: University of California Press, 1989.

Pakenham, Thomas. *The Scramble for Africa: The White Man's Conquest of the Dark Continent from 1876 to 1912*. New York: Random House, 1991.

Patterson, Orlando. *Slavery and Social Death: A Comparative Study*. Cambridge, Mass.: Harvard University Press, 1982.

Pearson, Michael N. *Port Cities and Intruders: The Swahili Coast, India, and Portugal in the Early Modern Era*. Baltimore: Johns Hopkins University Press, 1998.

Péclard, Didier. "Religion and Politics in Angola: The Church, the Colonial State and the Emergence of Angolan Nationalism, 1940–1961." *Journal of Religion in Africa* 28, no. 2 (1998): 160–86.

Pélissier, René. *Naissance du Mozambique: Résistance et révoltes anticoloniales, 1854–1918.* 2 vols. Orgeval: Pélissier, 1984.

Penvenne, Jeanne Marie. *African Workers and Colonial Racism: Mozambican Strategies and Struggles in Lourenço Marques, 1877–1962.* Portsmouth, N.H.: Heinemann, 1995.

——. "'Here Everyone Walked in Fear': The Mozambican Labor System and the Workers of Lourenço Marques, 1945–1962." In *Struggle for the City: Migrant Labor, Capital, and the State,* edited by Frederick Cooper, 131–66. Berkeley, Calif.: Sage, 1983.

——. "João dos Santos Albasini (1876–1922): The Contradictions of Politics and Identity in Colonial Mozambique." *Journal of African History* 37, no. 3 (1996): 419–64.

——. "Mozambique: A Tapestry of Conflict." In *History of Africa: The Contemporary Years since 1960,* edited by David Birmingham and Phyllis M. Martin, 231–66. New York: Longman, 1998.

——. "'We Are All Portuguese!' Challenging the Political Economy of Assimilation, Lourenço Marques, 1870–1933." In *The Invention of Tribalism in Southern Africa,* edited by Leroy Vail, 255–88. Berkeley: University of California Press, 1989.

Phimister, Ian R. "Pre-Colonial Gold Mining in Southern Zambezia: A Reassessment." *African Social Research* 21 (1976): 1–30.

Phoofolo, Pule. "Epidemics and Revolutions: The Rinderpest Epidemic in Late Nineteenth-Century Southern Africa." *Past and Present* 138 (1993): 112–43.

Pírio, Gregory. "Commerce, Industry and Empire: The Making of Modern Portuguese Colonialism in Angola and Mozambique, 1890–1914." Ph. D. diss., University of California, Los Angeles, 1982.

Pitcher, M. Anne. *Politics in the Portuguese Empire: The State, Industry, and Cotton, 1926–1974.* Oxford: Clarendon Press, 1993.

"Portuguese East Africa: The Reincorporation of the Territories of the Mozambique Company into Direct State Administration." *Journal of the Royal African Society* 41, no. 165 (1942): 238–39.

Power, Marcus. "Aqui Lourenço Marques!! Radio Colonization and Cultural Identity in Colonial Mozambique, 1932–1974." *Journal of Historical Geography* 26, no. 4 (2000): 605–28.

Price, Richard, ed. *Maroon Societies: Rebel Slave Communities in the Americas.* Baltimore: Johns Hopkins University Press, 1996.

Reis, João C. *A Empresa da conquista do senhorio do Monomotapa.* Lisbon: Heuris, 1984.

Risso, Patricia. *Merchants and Faith: Muslim Commerce and Culture in the Indian Ocean.* Boulder, Colo.: Westview Press, 1995.

Ross, Edward Alsworth. *Report on the Employment of Native Labor in Portuguese Africa.* New York: Abbott Press, 1925.

——. *Seventy Years of It: An Autobiography.* New York: Arno Press, 1977 [1936].

Ross, Robert. *Cape of Torments: Slavery and Resistance in South Africa.* London: Routledge, 1983.

Santos, João dos. *Ethiopia Oriental.* 2 vols. Lisbon: Biblioteca de Classicos Portuguezes, 1891 [1609].

Schmidt, Elizabeth. "Negotiated Spaces and Contested Terrain: Men, Women, and the Law in Colonial Zimbabwe, 1890–1939." *Journal of Southern African Studies* 16, no. 4 (1990): 622–48.

——. *Peasants, Traders, and Wives: Shona Women in the History of Zimbabwe: 1870–1939.* Portsmouth, N.H.: Heinemann, 1995.

Scott, James C. *Domination and the Arts of Resistance: Hidden Transcripts*. New Haven, Conn.: Yale University Press, 1990.

——. *Weapons of the Weak: Everyday Forms of Peasant Resistance*. New Haven, Conn.: Yale University Press, 1985.

Scott, Rebecca J. *Degrees of Freedom: Louisiana and Cuba after Slavery*. Cambridge, Mass.: Harvard University Press, 2005.

Serpa Pinto, Alexandre Alberto da Rocha de. *Como eu atravessei a África; do Atlántico ao mar Índico, viagem de Benguella à contra-costa, através regiões desconhecidas; determinações geográficas e estudos etnográficos*. 2 vols. London: S. Low, Marston, Searle, and Rivington, 1881.

Sheldon, Kathleen E. *Pounders of Grain: A History of Women, Work, and Politics in Mozambique*. Portsmouth, N.H.: Heinemann, 2002.

Shell, Robert Carl-Heinz. *Children of Bondage: A Social History of Slave Society at the Cape of Good Hope*. Hanover, N.H.: Wesleyan University Press, 1994.

Silva, Teresa Cruz e. "Identity and Political Consciousness in Southern Mozambique, 1930–1974: Two Presbyterian Biographies Contextualised." *Journal of Southern African Studies* 24, no. 2 (1998): 223–36.

——. *Igrejas protestantes e consciência política no sul de Moçambique: O caso da Missão Suiça (1930–1974)*. Maputo: Promédia, 2001.

Smith, Alan K. "António Salazar and the Reversal of Portuguese Colonial Policy." *Journal of African History* 15, no. 4 (1974): 653–67.

——. "The Idea of Mozambique and Its Enemies, c. 1890–1939." *Journal of Southern African Studies* 17, no. 3 (1991): 496–524.

——. "The Struggle for Control of Southern Moçambique, 1720–1835." Ph.D. diss., University of California, Los Angeles, 1971.

Souto, Amélia Neves de. *Guia bibliográfico para o estudante de história de Moçambique*. Maputo: Centro de Estudos Africanos, 1996.

Sunseri, Thaddeus. *Vilimani: Labor Migration and Rural Change in Early Colonial Tanzania*. Portsmouth, N.H.: Heinemann, 2002.

Thomas, Roger G. "Forced Labour in British West Africa: The Case of the Northern Territories of the Gold Coast 1906–1927." *Journal of African History* 14, no. 1 (1973): 79–103.

Thornton, John. *Africa and Africans in the Making of the Atlantic World, 1400–1800*. 2nd ed. Cambridge: Cambridge University Press, 1998.

——. *The Kongolese Saint Anthony: Dona Beatriz Kimpa Vita and the Antonian Movement, 1684–1706*. New York: Cambridge University Press, 1999.

Vail, Leroy. "Mozambique's Chartered Companies: The Rule of the Feeble." *Journal of African History* 17, no. 3 (1976): 389–416.

Vail, Leroy, and Landeg White. *Capitalism and Colonialism in Mozambique: A Study of Quelimane District*. Minneapolis: University of Minnesota Press, 1980.

——. *Power and the Praise Poem: Southern African Voices in History*. Charlottesville: University Press of Virginia, 1991.

Van Onselen, Charles. *Chibaro: African Mine Labour in Southern Rhodesia 1900–1933*. London: Pluto Press, 1977.

——. "Reactions to Rinderpest in Southern Africa 1896–97." *Journal of African History* 13, no. 3 (1972): 473–88.

Vasconcelos, Ernesto. "Os Portugueses Não São Incapazes Colonizadores." *Boletím da Agência Geral das Colónias* 2, no. 7 (January 1926): 3–5.

Vasse, Guillaume. "The Mozambique Company's Territory." *Journal of the Royal African Society* 6, no. 23 (1907): 259–68.

———. "The Mozambique Company's Territory, II." *Journal of the Royal African Society* 6, no. 24 (1907): 385–89.

Vickery, Kenneth P. "The Second World War Revival of Forced Labor in the Rhodesias." *International Journal of African Historical Studies* 22, no. 3 (1989): 423–37.

Wade, Richard C. *Slavery in the Cities: The South, 1820–1860*. New York: Oxford University Press, 1964.

Wheeler, Douglas. "The Galvão Forced Labor Report, 1947: A Re-examination in Historical Context." Paper delivered at the African Studies Association meeting, San Francisco, 2006.

———. "Gungunyane the Negotiator: A Study in African Diplomacy." *Journal of African History* 9, no. 4 (1968): 585–602.

———. *Historical Dictionary of Portugal*. Metuchen, N.J.: Scarecrow Press, 1993.

Willis, Justin. "'Men on the Spot', Labor, and the Colonial State in East Africa: The Mombasa Water Supply, 1911–1917." *International Journal of African Historical Studies* 28, no. 1 (1995): 25–48.

———. *Potent Brews: A Social History of Alcohol in East Africa 1850–1999*. Athens: Ohio University Press, 2002.

Winks, Robin. *British Imperialism: Gold, God, Glory*. New York: Holt, Rinehart, and Winston, 1973.

Worden, Nigel. *Slavery in Dutch South Africa*. Cambridge: Cambridge University Press, 1985.

Zimba, Benigna. *Mulheres invisíveis: O género e as políticas comerciais no Sul de Moçambique, 1720–1830*. Maputo: Promédia, 2003.

# Index

# Reconsiderations in Southern African History

CPSIA information can be obtained
at www.ICGtesting.com
Printed in the USA
BVHW031305210222
629684BV00011B/58